STORMIE OMARTIAN

The Power of
PRAYING®

3 in 1
COLLECTION

The Power of a
PRAYING®
WIFE

The Power of a
PRAYING®
PARENT

The Power of a
PRAYING®
WOMAN

HARVEST HOUSE PUBLISHERS

EUGENE, OREGON

THE POWER OF PRAYING®
Copyright © 2006 by Stormie Omartian
Published by Harvest House Publishers
Eugene, Oregon 97402
www.harvesthousepublishers.com

ISBN-13 978-0-7369-1974-6

Cover design by Koechel Peterson & Associates, Minneapolis, Minnesota

Compilation of:

The Power of a Praying® Wife
Copyright © 1997 by Stormie Omartian
ISBN-13 978-1-56507-572-6
ISBN-10 1-56507-572-2

The Power of a Praying® Parent
Copyright © 1995 by Stormie Omartian
ISBN-13 978-0-7369-1598-4
ISBN-10 0-7369-1598-2

The Power of a Praying® Woman
Copyright © 2002 by Stormie Omartian
ISBN-13 978-0-7369-0855-9
ISBN-10 0-7369-0855-2

Printed in China

THE POWER OF A

Praying Wife

STORMIE OMARTIAN

HARVEST HOUSE PUBLISHERS

EUGENE, OREGON

Cover Design by Koechel Peterson & Associates, Minneapolis, Minnesota

THE POWER OF A PRAYING is a registered trademark of The Hawkins Children's LLC. Harvest House Publishers, Inc., is the exclusive licensee of the federally registered trademark THE POWER OF A PRAYING.

THE POWER OF A PRAYING® WIFE

Copyright © 1997 by Stormie Omartian
Eugene, Oregon 97402
www.harvesthousepublishers.com

Library of Congress Cataloging-in-Publication Data

Omartian, Stormie.
  The power of a praying wife / Stormie Omartian.
     p.   cm.
  ISBN 1-56507-572-2 (Trade Edition)
  ISBN 0-7369-0600-2 (Deluxe Edition)
  1. Wives—Religious life.   2. Intercessory prayer—Christianity.
  I. Title.
  BV4527.043   1997   97-7436
  248.8'435—dc21   CIP

Tosin Thomas

Have a testimony
filled 2019 and beyond

This book is dedicated with love to my husband,
Michael, who has consistently given me more
than I ever wanted to pray about. You and I both
know that prayer works.

Jamie

Contents

Acknowledgments

With special thanks:

❧ To my secretary, Susan Martinez, for bearing the load of another book deadline. Your love as a sister, faithfulness as a friend, and richness as a prayer partner can only be equaled by your efficiency and dedication as my highly treasured and irreplaceable assistant.

❧ To my prayer partners and fellow praying wives, Sally Anderson, Susan Martinez, Donna Summer, Katie Stewart, Roz Thompson, and Jan Williamson, who have experienced along with me what gut-level, crying-out-to-God intercession for our husbands really means. Without your deep and faithful commitment to God and to prayer, this book might never have been written. You are eternal treasures in my heart.

❧ To my daughter, Mandy, and my son, Chris, for loving your dad and me, even through the times we didn't model for you the best way to run a marriage. I regret any time we argued in front of you, before we learned that prayer is more powerful than contention. I pray that you will carry all the good we have learned into your own marriages.

❧ To my new son, John David Kendrick, for letting me be your mom on earth now that your dad is in heaven with your mom. You are what our family has been missing all these years and we didn't know it until you came to be with us.

❧ To Pastor Jack and Anna Hayford, and Pastor Dale and Joan Evrist for teaching me how to pray and showing me the way a good marriage works.

❧ To my Harvest House family, Bob Hawkins Sr., Bob Hawkins Jr., Bill Jensen, Julie McKinney, Teresa Evenson, Betty Fletcher, and LaRae Weikert for your enthusiasm about the book and your consistently positive input. You are all a delight. And to Editorial Director Carolyn McCready for being such a joy. Thank you for your encouragement.

❧ To my editor, Holly Halverson, for your good eye and sharp mind.

❧ To Tom and Patti Brussat, Michael and Terry Harriton, Jan and Dave Williamson, and Dave and Priscilla Navarro for sharing your lives and experiences in order to give me good examples of the power of a praying wife.

Foreword

There is a joke in our household when I refer to the number of years Stormie and I have been married. I always say, "It's been twenty-five wonderful years for me and twenty-five miserable years for her." After twenty-five years of marriage to Stormie, there aren't any phases of my complex personality left for her to discover. She has seen me triumph, fail, struggle, be fearful and depressed, and doubt my competency as a husband, father, and musician. She has seen me angry at God because He wouldn't jump when I asked Him to. She has witnessed miracles, as God redeemed something from the ashes to gold. Every step of the way has been accompanied by her prayers and this book was written from her experience over the years. I cannot imagine what my life would be without her praying for me. It gives me comfort and security, and also fulfills the mission the Lord has for us to pray for each other and bear one another's burdens. I can think of no better way to truly love your husband than by lifting him up in prayer on a consistent basis. It is a priceless gift that helps him experience God's blessings and grace.

Stormie, I love you.

Your covered-in-prayer husband,
Michael

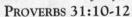

Who can find a virtuous wife? For her worth is far above rubies. The heart of her husband safely trusts her; so he will have no lack of gain. She does him good and not evil all the days of her life.

PROVERBS 31:10-12

The Power

irst of all, let me make it perfectly clear that the power of a praying wife is not a means of gaining control over your husband, so don't get your hopes up! In fact, it is quite the opposite. It's laying down all claim to power in and of yourself, and relying on *God's* power to transform you, your husband, your circumstances, and your marriage. This power is not given to wield like a weapon in order to beat back an unruly beast. It's a gentle tool of restoration appropriated through the prayers of a wife who longs to *do* right more than *be* right, and to *give life* more than *get even*. It's a way to invite God's power into your husband's life for his greatest blessing, which is ultimately yours, too.

When my husband, Michael, and I were first married and differences arose between us, praying was definitely not my first thought. In fact, it was closer to a last resort. I tried other methods first such as arguing, pleading, ignoring, avoiding, confronting, debating, and of course the ever-popular silent treatment, all with far less than satisfying results. It took some time to realize that by praying *first*, these unpleasant methods of operation could be avoided.

By the time you read this book, Michael and I will have been married over a quarter of a century. This is nothing less than miraculous. It's certainly not a testimony to our greatness, but to God's faithfulness to answer prayer. I confess that even after all these years, I am still learning about this and it doesn't come easy. While I may not have as much practice doing it right as I have had doing it wrong, I can say without reservation that *prayer works*.

Unfortunately, I didn't learn how to *really* pray for my husband until I started praying for my children. As I saw profound answers to prayer for them, I decided to try being just as detailed and fervent in praying for him. But I found that praying for children is far easier. From the first moment we lay eyes on them, we want the best for their lives—unconditionally, wholeheartedly, without question. But with a husband, it's often not that simple—especially for someone who's been married awhile. A husband can hurt your feelings, be inconsiderate, uncaring, abusive, irritating, or negligent. He can say or do things that pierce your heart like a sliver. And every time you start to pray for him, you find the sliver festering. It's obvious you can't give yourself to praying the way God wants you to until you are rid of it.

Praying for your husband is not the same as praying for a child (even though it may seem similar), because you are not your husband's mother. We have authority over our children that is given to us by the Lord. We *don't* have authority over our husbands. However, we have been given authority "over all the power of the enemy" (Luke 10:19) and can do great damage to the enemy's plans when we pray. Many difficult things that happen in a marriage relationship are actually part of the enemy's plan set up for its demise. But we can say, "I will not allow anything to destroy my marriage."

"I will not stand by and watch my husband be wearied, beaten down, or destroyed."

"I will not sit idle while an invisible wall goes up between us."

"I will not allow confusion, miscommunication, wrong attitudes, and bad choices to erode what we are trying to build together."

"I will not tolerate hurt and unforgiveness leading us to divorce." We can take a stand against any negative influences in our marriage relationship and know that God has given us authority in His name to back it up.

You have the means to establish a hedge of protection around your marriage because Jesus said, "Whatever you bind on earth will be bound in heaven, and whatever you loose on earth will be loosed in heaven" (Matthew 18:18). You have authority in the name of Jesus to *stop evil* and *permit good*. You can submit to God in prayer whatever controls your husband—alcoholism, workaholism, laziness, depression, infirmity, abusiveness, anxiety, fear, or failure— and pray for him to be released from it.

Wait! Before You Write Off the Marriage . . . . .

I confess right now that there was a time when I considered separation or divorce. This is an embarrassing disclosure because I don't believe either of those options is the best answer to a troubled marriage. I believe in God's position on divorce. He says it's not right and it grieves Him. The last thing I want to do is grieve God. But I know what it's like to feel the kind of despair that paralyzes good decision making. I've experienced the degree of hopelessness that causes a person to give up on trying to do what's right. I understand the torture of loneliness that leaves you longing for anyone who will look into your soul and see *you*.

I've felt pain so bad that the fear of dying from it propelled me to seek out the only immediately foreseeable means of survival: escape from the source of agony. I know what it's like to contemplate acts of desperation because you see no future. I've experienced such a buildup of negative emotions day after day that separation and divorce seemed like nothing more than the promise of pleasant relief.

The biggest problem I faced in our marriage was my husband's temper. The only ones who were ever the object of his anger were me and the children. He used words like weapons that left me crippled or paralyzed. I'm not saying that I was without fault—quite the contrary. I was sure I was as much to blame as he, but I didn't know what to do about it. I pleaded with God on a regular basis to make my husband more sensitive, less angry, more pleasant, less irritable. But I saw few changes. Was God not listening? Or did He favor the husband over the wife, as I suspected?

After a number of years, with little change, I cried out to the Lord one day in despair, saying, "God, I can't live this way anymore. I know what You've said about divorce, but I can't live in the same house with him. Help me, Lord." I sat on the bed holding my Bible for hours as I struggled with the strongest desire to take the children and leave. I believe that because I came to God in total honesty about what I felt, He allowed me to thoroughly and clearly envision what life would be like if I left: Where I would live, how I would support myself and care for the children, who would still be my friends, and worst of all, how a heritage of divorce would affect my son and daughter. It was the most horrible and unspeakably sad picture. If I left I would find some relief, but at the price of everything dear to me. I knew it wasn't God's plan for us.

As I sat there, God also impressed upon my heart that if I would deliberately lay down my life before His throne, die to the desire to leave, and give my needs to Him, He would teach me how to lay down my life in prayer for Michael. He would show me how to really intercede for him as a son of God, and in the process He would revive my marriage and pour His blessings out on both of us. We would be better together, if we could get past this, than we could ever be separated and alone. He showed me that Michael was caught in a web from his past that rendered him incapable of being different from what he was at that moment, but God would use me as an instrument of His deliverance if I would consent to it. It hurt to say yes to this and I cried a lot. But when I did, I felt hopeful for the first time in years.

I began to pray every day for Michael, like I had never prayed before. Each time, though, I had to confess my own hardness of heart. I saw how deeply hurt and unforgiving of him I was. *I don't want to pray for him. I don't want to ask God to bless him. I only want God to strike his heart with lightning and convict him of how cruel he has been*, I thought. I had to say over and over, "God, I confess my unforgiveness toward my husband. Deliver me from all of it."

Little by little, I began to see changes occur in both of us. When Michael became angry, instead of reacting negatively, I prayed for him. I asked God to give me insight into what was causing his rage. He did. I asked Him what I could do to make things better. He showed me. My husband's anger became less frequent and more quickly soothed. Every day, prayer built something positive. We're still not perfected, but we've come a long way. It hasn't been easy, yet I'm convinced that God's way is worth the effort it takes to walk in it. It's the only way to save a marriage.

A wife's prayers for her husband have a far greater effect on him than anyone else's, even his mother's. (Sorry, Mom.) A mother's prayers for her child are certainly fervent. But when a man marries, he leaves his father and mother and becomes one with his wife (Matthew 19:5). They are a team, one unit, unified in spirit. The strength of a man and wife joined together in God's sight is *far* greater than the sum of the strengths of each of the two individuals. That's because the Holy Spirit unites them and gives added power to their prayers.

That's also why there is so much at stake if we *don't* pray. Can you imagine praying for the right side of your body and not the left? If the right side is not sustained and protected and it falls, it's going to bring down the left side with it. The same is true of you and your husband. If you pray for yourself and not him, you will never find the blessings and fulfillment you want. What happens to him happens to you and you can't get around it.

This oneness gives us a power that the enemy doesn't like. That's why he devises ways to weaken it. He gives us whatever we will fall for, whether it be low self-esteem, pride, the need to be right, miscommunication, or the bowing to our own selfish desires. He will tell you lies like, "Nothing will ever change." "Your failures are irreparable." "There's no hope for reconciliation." "You'd be happier with someone else." He'll tell you whatever you will believe, because he knows if he can get you to believe it, there is no future for your marriage. If you believe enough lies, your heart will eventually be hardened against God's truth.

In every broken marriage, there is at least one person whose heart is hard against God. When a heart becomes hard, there is no vision from God's perspective. When we're miserable in a marriage, we feel that anything will be an improvement over what we're experiencing. But we don't see the whole picture. We only see the way it is, not the way God wants it to become. When we pray, however, our hearts become *soft* toward God and we get a vision. We see there is hope. We have faith that He will restore all that has been devoured, destroyed, and eaten away from the marriage. "I will restore to you the years that the swarming locust has eaten" (Joel 2:25). We can trust Him to take away the pain, hopelessness, hardness, and unforgiveness. We are able to envision His ability to resurrect love and life from the deadest of places.

Imagine Mary Magdalene's joy when she went to Jesus' tomb the third day after He had been crucified and found that He was not dead after all, but had been raised up by the power of God. The joy of seeing something hopelessly dead brought to life is the greatest joy we can know. The power that resurrected Jesus is the very same power that will resurrect the dead places of your marriage and put life back into it. "God both raised up the Lord and will also raise us up by His power" (1 Corinthians 6:14). It's the only power that can. But it doesn't happen without a heart for God that is willing to gut it out in prayer, grow through tough times, and wait for love to be resurrected. We have to go through the pain to get to the joy.

You have to decide if you want your marriage to work, and if you want it badly enough to do whatever is necessary, within healthy parameters, to see it happen. *You* have to believe the part of your relationship that has been eaten away by pain, indifference, and selfishness can be restored. *You* have to trust that what has swarmed over you, such as abuse, death of a child, infidelity, poverty, loss, catastrophic illness, or accident, can be relieved of its death grip. *You* have to determine that everything consuming you and your husband, such as workaholism, alcoholism, drug abuse, or depression, can be destroyed. *You* have to know that whatever has crept into your relationship so silently and stealthily as to not even be perceived as a threat until it is clearly present— such as making idols of your career, your dreams, your kids, or your selfish desires—can be removed. *You* have to trust that God is big enough to accomplish all this and more.

If you wake up one morning with a stranger in your bed and it's your husband, if you experience a silent withdrawal from one another's lives that severs all emotional connection, if you sense a relentless draining away of love and hope, if your relationship is in so bottomless a pit of hurt and anger that every day sends you deeper into despair, if every word spoken drives a wedge further between you until it becomes an impenetrable barrier keeping you miles apart, be assured that none of the above is God's will for your marriage. God's will is to break down all these barriers and lift you out of that pit. He can heal the wounds and put love back in your heart. Nothing and no one else can.

But you have to rise up and say, "Lord, I pray for an end to this conflict and a breaking of the hold strife has on us. Take away the hurt and the armor we've put up to protect ourselves. Lift us out of the pit of unforgiveness. Speak through us so that our words reflect Your love, peace, and reconciliation. Tear down this wall between us and teach us how to walk through it. Enable us to rise up from this paralysis and move into the healing and wholeness You have for us."

Don't write off the marriage. Ask God to give you a new husband. He is able to take the one you have and make him a new creation in Christ. Husbands and wives are not destined to fight, emotionally disconnect, live in marital deadness, be miserable, or divorce. We have God's power on our side. We don't have to leave our marriages to chance. We can fight for them in prayer and not give up, because as long as we are praying, there is hope. With God, nothing is ever as dead as it seems. Not even your own feelings.

It's natural to enter int... the prayer venture wondering if your husband will ever be praying for you the same way you're praying for him. While that would certainly be great, don't count on it. Praying for your husband will be an act of unselfish, unconditional love and sacrifice on your part. You must be willing to make this commitment knowing it is quite possible—even highly probable—that he will never pray for you in the same way. In some cases, he may not pray for you at all. You can ask him to, and you can pray for him to pray for you, but you can't demand it of him. Regardless, whether he does or doesn't is not your concern, it's God's. So release him from that obligation. If he doesn't pray for you, it's *his* loss more than yours anyway. Your happiness and fulfillment will not ride on whether he prays, it will depend on your own relationship with the Lord. Yes, wives need prayer, too. But I'm convinced we should not depend on our husbands to be the sole providers of it. In fact, looking to your husband to be your dedicated prayer partner could be a setup for failure and disappointment for both of you.

I learned that the best thing for our marriage was for me to have women prayer partners with whom I prayed every week. I now believe this is vital for any marriage. If you can find two or more strong, faith-filled women whom you thoroughly trust, and with whom you can share the longings of your heart, set up a weekly prayer time. It will change your life. This doesn't mean you have to tell your prayer partners everything about your husband or expose the private details of his life. The purpose is to ask God to make *your* heart right, show *you* how to be a good wife, share the burdens of *your* soul, and seek God's blessing on your husband.

...there is an issue with serious consequences, ...an trust your prayer partners with the confidential ...ture of your request, by all means share it. I've seen many marriages end in separation or divorce because people were too prideful or afraid to share their problems with someone who could pray for them. They go along putting up a good front and suddenly one day the marriage is over. Be sure to stress the confidential nature of what you're sharing with your prayer partners, but don't throw away the marriage because you're hesitant to pray about it with others. If you have a prayer partner who can't keep a confidence, find someone else with more wisdom, sensitivity, and spiritual maturity.

Even without prayer partners or a praying husband, when you pray fervently you'll see things happen. *Before* your prayers are answered there will be blessings from God that will come to you simply because you are praying. That's because you will have spent time in the presence of God, where all lasting transformation begins.

One Prayer at a Time

Don't be overwhelmed by the many ways there are to pray for your husband. It's not necessary to do it all in one day, one week, or even a month. Let the suggestions in this book be a guide and then pray as the Holy Spirit leads you. Where there are tough issues and you need a dynamic breakthrough, fasting will make your prayers more effective. Also, praying Scripture over your husband is powerful. That's what I have done in the prayers at the end of each chapter, wherever you see a Scripture reference.

Above all, don't give place to impatience. Seeing answers to your prayers can take time, especially if your marriage is deeply wounded or strained. Be patient to persevere and wait for God to heal. Keep in mind that you are both imperfect people. Only the Lord is perfect. Look to God as the source of all you want to see happen in your marriage, and don't worry about *how* it will happen. It's your responsibility to pray. It's God's job to answer. Leave it in *His* hands.

CHAPTER ONE

His Wife

The hard part about being a praying wife, other than the sacrifice of time, is maintaining a pure heart. It must be clean before God in order for you to see good results. That's why praying for a husband must begin with praying for his wife. If you have resentment, anger, unforgiveness, or an ungodly attitude, even if there's good reason for it, you'll have a difficult time seeing answers to your prayers. But if you can release those feelings to God in total honesty and then move into prayer, there is nothing that can change a marriage more dramatically. Sometimes wives sabotage their own prayers because they don't pray them from a right heart. It took me awhile to figure that out.

My Favorite Three-Word Prayer

I wish I could say that I've been regularly praying for my husband from the beginning of our marriage until now. I haven't. At least not like I'm suggesting in this book. Oh, I prayed. The prayers were short: "Protect him, Lord." They were to the point: "Save our marriage." But most commonly they were my favorite three-word prayer: "Change him, Lord."

When we were first married, I was a new believer coming out of a life of great bondage and error and had much to learn about the delivering and restoring power of God. I thought I had married a man who was close to perfect, and what wasn't perfect was cute. As time went on, cute became irritating and perfect became driving perfectionism. I decided that what irritated me most about him had to be changed and then everything would be fine.

It took a number of years for me to realize my husband was never going to conform to my image. It took a few years beyond that to understand I couldn't make him change in *any* way. In fact, it wasn't until I started going to God with what bothered me that I began to see any difference at all. And then it didn't happen the way I thought it would. *I* was the one God worked on first. *I* was the one who began to change. My heart had to be softened, humbled, pummeled, molded, and reconstructed before He even started working on my husband. *I* had to learn to see things according to the way God saw them—not how I thought they should be.

Gradually I realized it's impossible to truly give yourself in prayer for your husband without first examining your own heart. I couldn't go to God and expect answers to prayer if I harbored unforgiveness, bitterness, or resentment. I couldn't pray *my* favorite three-word prayer without knowing in the deepest recesses of my soul that I had to first pray *God's* favorite three-word prayer: "Change me, Lord."

Who, Me? . . . Change?

Don't say I didn't warn you. When you pray for your husband, especially in the hopes of changing him, you can surely expect some changes. But the first changes won't be in *him*. They'll be in *you*. If this makes you as mad as it made me, you'll say, "Wait a minute! I'm not the one that needs changing here!" But God sees things we don't. He knows where we have room for improvement. He doesn't have to search long to uncover attitudes and habits that are outside His perfect will for us. He requires us to not sin in our hearts because sin separates us from Him and we don't get our prayers answered. "If I regard iniquity in my heart, the Lord will not hear" (Psalm 66:18). God wants our hearts to be right so the answers to our prayers are not compromised.

This whole requirement is especially hard when you feel your husband has sinned against you with unkindness, lack of respect, indifference, irresponsibility, infidelity, abandonment, cruelty, or abuse. But God considers the sins of unforgiveness, anger, hatred, self-pity, lovelessness, and revenge to be just as bad as any others. Confess them and ask God to set you free from anything that is not of Him. One of the greatest gifts you can give your husband is your own wholeness. The most effective tool in transforming him may be your own transformation.

Don't worry, I struggled with all this, too. In fact, every time my husband and I came to an impasse, God and I had a conversation that went something like this:

"Do you see the way he is, Lord?"

"Do you see the way *you* are?"

"Lord, are You saying there are things you want to change in me?"

"Many things. Are you ready to hear them?"

"Well, I guess so."

"Tell me when you're really ready."

"Why me, God? *He's* the one that needs to change."

"The point is not who *needs* to change. The point is who is *willing* to change."

"But God, this isn't fair."

"I never said life is fair, I said *I* am fair."

"But I . . ."

"Someone has to be willing to start."

"But. . . ."

"How important is preserving your marriage?"

"Very important. The other options are unacceptable."

"I rest my case. Let's get on with changing you."

"Help me to have a good attitude about this, Lord."

"That's up to you."

"Do I have to pray for my husband even if he's not praying for me?"

"Precisely."

"But that's not . . . okay, okay, I remember. Life's not fair. *You're* fair!"

(Silent nodding from heaven)

"I give up. Go ahead. Oh, this is going to be painful! Cha . . . change. . . . I can't believe I'm saying this."

(Deep breath) "Change me, Lord."

Painful? Yes! Dying to yourself is always painful. Especially when you are convinced that the other person needs more changing than you. But this kind of pain leads to *life*. The other alternative is just as painful and its ultimate end is the death of a dream, a relationship, a marriage, and a family.

God can resurrect the deadest of marriages, but it takes humbling ourselves before Him and desiring to live His way— forgiveness, kindness, and love. It means letting go of the past and all hurt associated with it and being willing to lose the argument in order to win the battle. I'm not saying you have to become a person void of personality, feelings, or thoughts of your own, or be the whipping post for a husband's whim. God doesn't require that of you. (In fact, if you are in any kind of physical or emotional danger, remove yourself immediately from the situation to a place of safety and get help. You can pray from there while your husband receives the counseling he needs.) Submission is something you give from your heart, not something demanded of you. Jesus said, "He who loses his life for My sake will find it" (Matthew 10:39). But laying down your life is something you willingly do, *not* something that is forcefully taken from you. What I'm saying is that your attitude must be, "Whatever You want, Lord. Show me and I'll do it." It means being willing to die to yourself and say, "Change me, Lord."

The Ultimate Love Language

Something amazing happens to our hearts when we pray for another person. The hardness melts. We become able to get beyond the hurts, and forgive. We even end up loving the person we are praying for. It's miraculous! It happens because when we pray we enter into the presence of God and He fills us with His Spirit of love. When you pray for your husband, the love of God will grow in your heart for him. Not only that, you'll find love growing in *his* heart for *you*, without him even knowing you are praying. That's because prayer is the ultimate love language. It communicates in ways we can't. I've seen women with no feelings of love for their husbands find that as they prayed, over time, those feelings came. Sometimes they felt differently even after the first heartfelt prayer.

Talking to God about your husband is an act of love. Prayer gives rise to love, love begets more prayer, which in turn gives rise to more love. Even if your praying is not born out of completely selfless motives, your motives will become more unselfish as prayer continues. You'll find yourself more loving in your responses. You'll notice that issues which formerly caused strife between you will no longer do that. You'll be able to come to mutual agreements without a fight. This unity is vital.

When we are not united, everything falls apart. Jesus said, "Every kingdom divided against itself is brought to desolation, and every city or house divided against itself will not stand" (Matthew 12:25). Prayer brings unity even if you aren't praying together. I've seen great tension relieved between my husband and me simply by praying for him. Also, asking him, "How can I pray for you?" brings an aspect of love and care into the situation. My husband will usually stop and answer that question in great detail when he might otherwise not say anything. I know of even nonbelieving husbands who respond positively to that question from their wives.

The point in all this is that as husband and wife we don't want to be taking separate roads. We want to be on the same path together. We want to be deeply compatible, lifelong companions, and have the love that lasts a lifetime. Prayer, as the ultimate love language, can make that happen.

I Don't Even Like Him—How Can I Pray for Him?

Have you ever been so mad at your husband that the last thing you wanted to do was pray for him? So have I. It's hard to pray for someone when you're angry or he's hurt you. But that's exactly what God wants us to do. If He asks us to pray for our *enemies*, how much more should we be praying for the person with whom we have become one and are supposed to love? But how do we get past the unforgiveness and critical attitude?

The first thing to do is be completely honest with God. In order to break down the walls in our hearts and smash the barriers that stop communication, we have to be totally up front with the Lord about our feelings. We don't have to "pretty it up" for Him. He already knows the truth. He just wants to see if we're willing to admit it and confess it as disobedience to His ways. If so, He then has a heart with which He can work.

If you are angry at your husband, tell God. Don't let it become a cancer that grows with each passing day. Don't say, "I'm going to live my life and let him live his." There's a price to pay when we act entirely independently of one another. "Neither is man independent of woman, nor woman independent of man, in the Lord" (1 Corinthians 11:11).

Instead say, "Lord, nothing in me wants to pray for this man. I confess my anger, hurt, unforgiveness, disappointment, resentment, and hardness of heart toward him. Forgive me and create in me a clean heart and right spirit before You. Give me a new, positive, joyful, loving, forgiving attitude toward him. Where he has erred, reveal it to him and convict his heart about it. Lead him through the paths of repentance and deliverance. Help me not to hold myself apart from him emotionally, mentally, or physically because of unforgiveness. Where either of us needs to ask forgiveness of the other, help us to do so. If there is something I'm not seeing that is adding to this problem, reveal it to me and help me to understand it. Remove any wedge of confusion that has created misunderstanding or miscommunication. Where there is behavior that needs to change in either of us, I pray You would enable that change to happen. As much as I want to hang on to my anger toward him because I feel it is justified, I want to do what *You* want. I release all those feelings to You. Give me a renewed sense of love for him and words to heal this situation."

If you feel you are able, try this little experiment and see what happens. Pray for your husband every day for a month using each one of the thirty areas of prayer focus I have included in this book. Pray a chapter a day. Ask God to pour out His blessings on him and fill you both with His love. See if your heart doesn't soften toward him. Notice if his attitude toward you doesn't change as well. Observe whether your relationship isn't running more smoothly. If you have trouble making that kind of prayer commitment, think of it from the Lord's perspective. Seeing your husband through God's eyes—not just as your husband, but as God's child, a son whom the Lord loves—can be a great revelation. If someone called and asked you to pray for his or her son, you would do it, wouldn't you? Well, God is asking.

"Shut Up and Pray"

There is a time for everything, it says in the Bible. And it is never more true than in a marriage, especially when it comes to the words we say. There is a time to speak and a time *not* to speak, and happy is the man whose wife can discern between the two. Anyone who has been married for any length of time realizes that there are things that are better left unsaid. A wife has the ability to hurt her husband more deeply than anyone else can, and he can do the same to her. No matter how much apology, the words can not be erased. They can only be forgiven and that is not always easy. Sometimes anything we say will only hinder the flow of what God wants to do, so it's best to, well, shut up and pray.

When Michael and I were first married, I didn't say much if I felt something was wrong. I stuffed my feelings inside. After our first child was born, I became increasingly vocal. But the more I voiced my objections and opinions, the more he resisted and the more we would argue. Whatever I said not only accomplished nothing in the area I wanted it to, it had the opposite effect. It took me a number of years to learn what millions of women have learned over the centuries. *Nagging doesn't work!* Criticizing doesn't work. Sometimes, just plain talking doesn't accomplish anything either. I've found that prayer is the only thing that *always* works. The safeguard you have with prayer is that you have to go through God to do it. This means you can't get away with a bad attitude, wrong thinking, or incorrect motives. When you pray, God reveals anything in your personality that is resistant to His order of things.

My husband will not do something he doesn't want to do. And if he ends up doing something he doesn't want to do, his immediate family members will pay for it. If there is anything I really want him to do, I've learned to pray about it until I have God's peace in my heart *before* I ask. Sometimes God changes my heart about it, or shows me a different way so I don't have to say anything. If I do need to say something, I try not to just blurt it out. I pray first for God's leading.

It took me a long time to figure this out, however. It happened one day when I came across the Proverb, "Better to dwell in the wilderness, than with a contentious and angry woman" (Proverbs 21:19). For *some reason* it struck a nerve.

"But, Lord," I questioned, "what about 'Open rebuke is better than love carefully concealed' [Proverbs 27:5]? Don't we wives have to tell our husbands when something is wrong?"

He replied, "There is . . . a time for every purpose under heaven . . . a time to keep silence and a time to speak" (Ecclesiastes 3:1,7). "The problem is you don't know when to do either. And you don't know how to do it in love."

"Okay, Lord," I said. "Show me when to speak and when to just keep quiet and pray."

The first opportunity for this came right away. I had started a new weekly women's prayer group in my home, and it was so life-changing I suggested to my husband that he start a similar group for men. But he wouldn't hear of it.

"I don't have time," was his not-too-pleased-at-the-idea answer.

The more I talked about it, the more irritated Michael became. After getting my "Be quiet and pray" directions from God, I decided to try that approach. I stopped talking about it and started praying. I also asked my prayer group to pray along with me. It was more than two years after I stopped mentioning it to him and started praying that Michael abruptly announced one day he was organizing a weekly men's prayer group. It has been going ever since, and he still doesn't know I prayed. Even though it took longer than I would have liked, it did happen. And there was peace in the waiting, which I wouldn't have had if I had not kept quiet.

Queen Esther in the Bible prayed, fasted, and sought God's timing before she approached her husband, the king, about a very important matter. There was a lot at stake and she knew it. She didn't run in and scream, "Your hoodlum friends are going to ruin our lives!" Rather she prayed first and then ministered to him in love, while God prepared his heart. The Lord will always give us words to say, and show us when to say them if we ask Him. Timing is everything.

I've known people who use the excuse of "just being honest" to devastate others with their words. The Bible says, "A fool vents all his feelings, but a wise man holds them back" (Proverbs 29:11). In other words, it's foolish to share every feeling and thought. Being honest doesn't mean you have to be completely frank in your every comment. That hurts people. While honesty is a requirement for a successful marriage, telling your husband everything that is wrong with him is not only ill-advised, it probably doesn't reveal the complete truth. The total truth is from God's perspective and He, undoubtedly, doesn't have the same problem with some of your husband's actions as you do. Our goal must not be to get our husbands to do what *we* want, but rather to release them to God so He can get them to do what *He* wants.

Distinguish carefully between what is truly right and wrong. If it doesn't fall clearly into either of those categories, keep your personal opinions to yourself. Or pray about them and then, as the Lord leads, reveal them for calm discussion. The Bible says, "Do not be rash with your mouth, and let not your heart utter anything hastily before God. For God is in heaven, and you on earth; therefore let your words be few" (Ecclesiastes 5:2). There are times when we are just to listen and not offer advice, to support and not offer constructive criticism.

I'm not for a moment suggesting that you become a timid doormat who doesn't ever confront your husband with the truth—especially when it's for his greater good. By all means you must clearly communicate your thoughts and feelings. But once he has heard them, don't continue to press him until it becomes a point of contention and strife.

If you *do* have to say words that are hard to hear, ask God to help you discern when your husband would be most open to hearing them. Pray for the right words and for his heart to be totally receptive. I know that's difficult to do if you have a few choice words you're dying to let loose. But hard as it may seem, it's best to let God hear them first so He can temper them with His Spirit. This is especially true when talking has ceased altogether and every word only brings more pain. I wish I had learned earlier to pray before I spoke. My words too often set up a defensive reaction in my husband that produced harsh words we both regret. He received my suggestions as pressure to do or be something, even though I always had his best interests at heart. It had to come to him from God.

When we live by the power of God rather than our flesh, we don't have to strive for power with our words. "For the kingdom of God is not in word but in power" (1 Corinthians 4:20). It's not the words we speak that make a difference, it is the power of God accompanying them. You'll be amazed at how much power your words have when you pray before you speak them. You'll be even more amazed at what can happen when you shut up and let God work.

Believer or Not

If your husband is not a believer, you probably already know how much good it does to keep talking to him about the Lord if he didn't respond the first number of times. It's not that you can't ever say anything to him, but if what you say is always met with indifference or irritation, the next step is to keep silent and pray. The Bible says a wife can win over her husband without saying anything, because what he *observes* in his wife speaks more loudly than what she tells him. "They, without a word, may be won by the conduct of their wives" (1 Peter 3:1,2).

God says He speaks of things that are not as though they were. You can do that, too. You can say, "I'm not going to pretend, but I'm going to speak of things that are *not* part of my husband's life as though they *were* a part of it. Even though he doesn't have faith, I'm going to pray for him as if he does." Of course you can't force him to do something he doesn't want to do, but you can access God's power through praying for His voice to penetrate your husband's soul. No matter how long you have to pray for your husband to come to know the Lord, even if it takes his whole life, the time will not be wasted. In the meantime, whether your husband is a believer or not, you can still pray all the prayers in this book for him and expect to see significant answers to them.

Creating a Home

I don't care how liberated you are, when you are married there will always be two areas that will ultimately be your responsibility: home and children. Even if you are the only one working and your husband stays home to keep the house and tend the kids, you will still be expected to see that the heart of your home is a peaceful sanctuary—a source of contentment, acceptance, rejuvenation, nurturing, rest, and love for your family. On top of this, you will also be expected to be sexually appealing, a good cook, a great mother, and physically, emotionally, and spiritually fit. It's overwhelming to most women, but the good news is that you don't have to do it all on your own. You can seek God's help.

Ask the Lord to show you how to make your home a safe haven that builds up your family—a place where creativity flows and communication is ongoing. Ask God to help you keep the house clean, the laundry done, the kitchen in order, the pantry and the refrigerator full, and the beds made. These are basic things a man may not compliment his wife on every day (or ever), but he will notice if they are *not* done. My husband may not look in the cupboard for a light bulb or a battery for months. But when he does, he wants it to be there. Nor does he want to come home late from work one night and find that there is no bread for a sandwich. I do my best to make sure it is there. I ask God to help me maintain a house that my husband is pleased to come home to and bring his friends. It's not necessary to have expensive furniture or a decorator in order to do all that. My first home was small and had second-hand furniture I bought from yard sales. I painted the entire place myself (with the help of a girlfriend) and made it look attractive. It just takes some thought and a little care.

Part of making a house a home is allowing your husband to be the head so you can be the heart. Trying to be both is too much. God placed the husband as the head over the family, whether he deserves it or not and whether he rises up to take his position or not. It's God's order of things. This doesn't mean that one position is more important than the other. They work together. If your husband is to be the head of the house, you must allow him that headship. If you are to be the heart of the home, you still must take the steps necessary to do so, even if you are a major contributor to the financial support. Trying to reverse that keeps a constant struggle going.

This doesn't mean that the wife can't work and the husband can't care for the home; it's the attitudes of the heart and head that makes the difference. There were weeks of time during the finishing of each book I've written when my husband took care of the house and the children so I could meet the deadline. It never minimized his headship or caused me to usurp his position. It was something he did for me. There were times he needed me to work so he could rest. It's what I did for him. It's a delicate balance for most people, so it's best to pray that the integrity of the two positions in the home—head and heart—are not compromised.

Keeping order in the home doesn't mean it has to be perfect, but it shouldn't be out of control. If you are working as hard as he is to bring home a paycheck, the responsibilities should be shared in the home. If he doesn't want to share them, spending a certain amount of money for someone to help you a few hours a week is a lot cheaper than a divorce, a chiropractor, a therapist, a medical doctor, or a funeral. Ask God to show you about that.

Everything I've said about the home goes for your body, soul, and spirit as well. Some effort must be put into maintaining them. I once heard a radio talk show where a woman called in to complain to a popular psychologist that her husband told her he no longer found her attractive. The host said, "What are you doing to make yourself attractive?" The caller had no answer. The point is, being attractive doesn't just happen. Even the most gorgeous women in the world do much to maintain their attractiveness. Queen Esther was one of the most beautiful women in her country and she still spent a year beautifying herself before she met the king.

We have to ask ourselves the same question. "What am I doing to make myself attractive to my husband?" Do I keep myself clean and smelling good? Do I see that my internal self is cleansed and rejuvenated with regular exercise? Do I preserve my strength and vitality with a healthful diet? Do I dress attractively? And most important: Do I spend time alone with God every day? I guarantee that the more time you spend with the Lord, the more radiant you will become. "Charm is deceitful and beauty is passing, but a woman who fears the LORD, she shall be praised" (Proverbs 31:30).

You can't afford not to make this investment in yourself, your health, and your future. It's not selfish to do it. It's selfish *not* to do it. Pray for God to show you what steps to take and then enable you to take them. Invite the Holy Spirit to dwell in you *and* your home.

Letting Go of Expectations

Shortly after we were married, my husband called from work and said he wanted me to prepare a certain chicken dish for dinner. I went to the store, got the food, prepared the dish, and when he came home, he walked in the door and said bluntly, "I don't feel like chicken tonight, I want lamb chops." I needn't tell you the thoughts that went through my mind because I'm sure you already know them. This was not an isolated incident. Similar ones happened far too frequently. I can't count the number of times Michael promised to be home for dinner and called ten minutes *after* dinner was ready to say he was going to work late and would eat out with his coworkers. I finally learned that it did no good to be angry, hurt, or resentful. That only made matters worse. It made him defensive because he thought I didn't understand his situation. I realized it was healthier for both of us if I rearranged my expectations. From then on, I prepared meals as if only I and the children would be eating them. If Michael was able to join us, it was a pleasant surprise. If he didn't, I could live with it.

I've learned that when disappointing things happen, it's best to remind myself of my husband's good qualities. I recount how he sometimes helps with the household chores and the cooking. He is faithful and does not give me reason to doubt it. He is a believer who goes to church, reads his Bible, prays, and has high moral standards. He loves me and our children. He uses his talents for God's glory. He is a good and generous provider. Things could be a lot worse, so I won't complain about whether he's home for dinner or not.

I think if I could help a new wife in any area, it would be to discourage her from coming into her marriage with a big list of expectations and then being upset when her husband doesn't live up to them. Of course there are some basics that should be agreed upon before the wedding date, such as fidelity, financial support, honesty, kindness, basic decency, high moral standards, physical and emotional love, and protection. When you don't get those things, you can ask for them. When you still don't get them, you can pray.

But when it comes to specifics, you can't require one person to meet all of your needs. The pressure to do that and fulfill your dreams at the same time can be overwhelming to a man. Instead, take your needs to God in prayer and look to *Him* for the answers. If we try to control our husbands by having a big list for them to live up to and then are angry and disappointed when they can't, *we* are the ones in error. The biggest problems in my marriage occurred when my expectations of what I thought Michael should be or do didn't coincide with the reality of who he was.

Let go of as many expectations as possible. The changes you try to make happen in your husband, or that your husband tries to make in himself to please you, are doomed to failure and will bring disappointment for you both. Instead, ask God to make any necessary changes. He will do a far better job because "whatever God does, it shall be forever. Nothing can be added to it, and nothing taken from it" (Ecclesiastes 3:14). Accept your husband the way he is and pray for him to grow. Then when change happens, it will be because God has worked it in him and it will be lasting. "My soul, wait silently for God alone, for my expectation is from Him" (Psalm 62:5). Your greatest expectations must be from God, not your husband.

With All Due Respect

It's interesting that God requires the husband to *love* his wife, but the wife is required to have *respect* for her husband. "Let each one of you in particular so love his own wife as himself, and let the wife see that she respects her husband" (Ephesians 5:33). I assume no woman would marry a man she didn't love, but too often a wife loses respect for her husband after they've been married awhile. Loss of respect seems to precede loss of love and is more hurtful to a man than we realize.

The consequences of losing respect for your husband can be very serious. King David's wife, Michal, watched her husband dancing for joy before the Lord in front of the people, without his kingly clothing and in his undergarments, as the ark of the covenant was being brought into the city. Michal not only didn't share his joy, she had contempt for him (2 Samuel 6:16). She was critical instead of trying to understand the situation from God's perspective. She paid a dear price for her lack of respect; God's judgment caused her to be unable to ever bear children. I believe we not only bring defeat into our marriages and our husbands when we don't have respect for them, but it shuts the door to new life in us as well.

In another example, Queen Vashti refused to go to the king at his command. The king was giving a feast for his friends, he was in a party mood, and he wanted to show off his beautiful wife. All he asked of her was that she put on her royal clothes, don her royal crown, and make a royal appearance to the people he was entertaining. She declined, knowing full well it would be humiliating for him. "Queen Vashti refused to come at the king's command brought by his eunuchs; therefore the king was furious, and his anger burned within him" (Esther 1:12). The result was that Vashti lost her position as queen. She not only wronged her husband, the king, but the people as well. Unless a wife wants to lose her position as queen of her husband's heart, and hurt her family and friends besides, she mustn't humiliate her husband no matter how much she thinks he deserves it. The price is too high.

If this has already happened to you, and you know you've shown disrespect for your husband, confess it to God right now. Say, "Lord, I confess I do not esteem my husband the way Your Word says to. There is a wall in my heart that I know was erected as a protection against being hurt. But I am ready to let it come down so that my heart can heal. I confess the times I have shown a lack of respect for him. I confess my disrespectful attitude and words as sin against You. Show me how to dismantle this barrier over my emotions that keeps me from having the unconditional love You want me to have. Tear down the wall of hardness around my heart and show me how to respect my husband the way You want me to. Give me *Your* heart for him, Lord, and help me to see him the way You see him."

Praying like this will free you to see your man's potential for greatness, as opposed to his flaws. It will enable you to say something positive that will encourage, build up, give life, and make the marriage better. Love is diminished if we dwell on the negatives. Love grows if we focus on the positive. When you have God's heart for your husband, you will be able to see through new eyes. There are times when you can't understand where your husband is coming from, what he is feeling, and why he is doing the things he does, unless you have the discernment of God. Ask God to give it to you.

When you are praying for yourself—his wife—remember this model of a good wife from the Bible. It says she takes care of her home and runs it well. She knows how to buy and sell and make wise investments. She keeps herself healthy and strong and dresses attractively. She works diligently and has skills which are marketable. She is giving and conscientiously prepares for the future. She contributes to her husband's good reputation. She is strong, solid, honorable, and not afraid of growing older. She speaks wisely and kindly. She doesn't sit around doing nothing, but carefully watches what goes on in her home. Her children and her husband praise her. She doesn't rely on charm and beauty but knows that the fear of the Lord is what is most attractive. She supports her husband and still has a fruitful life of her own which speaks loudly for itself (Proverbs 31).

This is an amazing woman, the kind of woman we can become only through God's enablement and our own surrendering. The bottom line is that she is a woman whose husband trusts her because "she does him good and not evil all the days of her life." I believe the most important "good" a wife can do for her husband is pray. Shall we?

Prayer

Lord, Help me to be a good wife. I fully realize that I don't have what it takes to be one without Your help. Take my selfishness, impatience, and irritability and turn them into kindness, long-suffering, and the willingness to bear all things. Take my old emotional habits, mindsets, automatic reactions, rude assumptions, and self-protective stance, and make me patient, kind, good, faithful, gentle, and self-controlled. Take the hardness of my heart and break down the walls with Your battering ram of revelation. Give me a new heart and work in me Your love, peace, and joy (Galatians 5:22,23). I am not able to rise above who I am at this moment. Only You can transform me.

Show me where there is sin in my heart, especially with regard to my husband. I confess the times I've been unloving, critical, angry, resentful, disrespectful, or unforgiving toward him. Help me to put aside any hurt, anger, or disappointment I feel and forgive him the way You do—totally and completely, no looking back. Make me a tool of reconciliation, peace, and healing in this marriage. Enable us to communicate well and rescue us from the threshold of separation where the realities of divorce begin.

Make me my husband's helpmate, companion, champion, friend, and support. Help me to create a peaceful, restful, safe place for him to come home to. Teach me how to take care of myself and stay attractive to him. Grow me into a creative and confident woman who is rich in mind, soul, and spirit. Make me the kind of woman he can be proud to say is his wife.

I lay all my expectations at Your cross. I release my husband from the burden of fulfilling me in areas where I should be looking to You. Help me to accept him the way he is and not try to change him. I realize that in some ways he may never change, but at the same time, I release him to change in ways I never thought he could. I leave any changing that needs to be done in Your hands, fully accepting that neither of us is perfect and never will be. Only You, Lord, are perfect and I look to You to perfect us.

Teach me how to pray for my husband and make my prayers a true language of love. Where love has died, create new love between us. Show me what unconditional love really is and how to communicate it in a way he can clearly perceive. Bring unity between us so that we can be in agreement about everything (Amos 3:3). May the God of patience and comfort grant us to be like-minded toward one another, according to Christ Jesus (Romans 15:5). Make us a team, not pursuing separate, competitive, or independent lives, but working together, overlooking each other's faults and weaknesses for the greater good of the marriage. Help us to pursue the things which make for peace and the things by which one may edify another (Romans 14:19). May we be "perfectly joined together in the same mind and in the same judgment" (1 Corinthians 1:10).

I pray that our commitment to You and to one another will grow stronger and more passionate every day. Enable him to be the head of the home as You made him to be, and show me how to support and respect him as he rises to that place of leadership. Help me to understand his dreams and see things from his perspective. Reveal to me what he wants and needs and show me potential problems before they arise. Breathe Your life into this marriage.

Make me a new person, Lord. Give me a fresh perspective, a positive outlook, and a renewed relationship with the man You've given me. Help me see him with new eyes, new appreciation, new love, new compassion, and new acceptance. Give my husband a new wife, and let it be me.

POWER TOOLS

Whatever things you ask when you pray, believe
that you receive them, and you will have them. And
whenever you stand praying, if you have anything
against anyone, forgive him, that your Father in
heaven may also forgive you your trespasses.
MARK 11:24,25

Be kind to one another, tenderhearted, forgiving
one another, even as God in Christ forgave you.
EPHESIANS 4:32

Ask, and it will be given to you; seek, and you will
find; knock, and it will be opened to you. For
everyone who asks receives, and he who seeks finds,
and to him who knocks it will be opened.
MATTHEW 7:7,8

Through wisdom a house is built, and by
understanding it is established; by knowledge
the rooms are filled with all precious
and pleasant riches.
PROVERBS 24:3,4

Let us not grow weary while doing good, for in due
season we shall reap if we do not lose heart.
GALATIANS 6:9

CHAPTER TWO

His Work

Bill seldom works. He's willing to let his wife, Kim, support the family while he pursues his dream. The problem is that Kim is not content to bear the entire burden of supporting the family on her shoulders indefinitely, and Bill has been pursuing his dream for seventeen years with nothing to show for it. I believe the root of Bill's inactivity is fear. He's afraid that if he doesn't get the job of his dreams, he will end up in a job he hates and be stuck there forever.

Steven is working himself to death. He can never rest and enjoy the success of his labor. He seldom spends time with his family, and his teenagers are fast approaching adulthood. He doesn't work that hard because he has to, but because he is afraid. He fears that if he ever stops, he will be worth nothing in everyone's eyes, including his own.

These are extreme examples of how a man can relate to his work. On the one hand is laziness—avoiding work out of selfishness, fear, lack of confidence, depression, or apprehension about the future. Of the lazy, God says, "As a door turns on its hinges, so does the lazy man on his bed" (Proverbs 26:14). "Drowsiness will clothe a man with rags" (Proverbs 23:21). "The way of the lazy man is like a hedge of thorns" (Proverbs 15:19). "The desire of the lazy man kills him, for his hands refuse to labor" (Proverbs 21:25). In other words, a lazy man will never get anywhere, he will never have anything, he will have a rough road ahead, and it will ultimately destroy him.

The opposite extreme is workaholism—obsessing over work to the exclusion of all else and losing one's life in the process. Of the workaholic, God says, "So are the ways of everyone who is greedy for gain; it takes away the life of its owners" (Proverbs 1:19). "I looked on all the works that my hands had done and on the labor in which I had toiled; and indeed all was vanity and grasping for the wind. There was no profit under the sun" (Ecclesiastes 2:11). In other words, workaholism is draining and pointless.

Neither extreme promotes happiness and fulfillment. Only a perfect balance between the two, which God can help a man find, will ever bring that quality of life.

What causes a man to go to either extreme can be, oddly enough, the same reason: fear. That's because a man's identity is often very tied up in his work. He needs to be appreciated and he needs to win, and his work is often a means of seeing both happen. It frightens him to think he may never experience either. If he is doing work that is demeaning to him, he feels devalued as a person. If his work is not successful, he feels like a loser.

God recognizes that a man's work is a source of fulfillment to him. He says there is nothing better than for a man to "enjoy the good of all his labor—it is the gift of God" (Ecclesiastes 3:13). The fact that many men are not fulfilled in their work has less to do with what their work is than with whether or not they have a sense of purpose. A man who doesn't have that can eventually come to a place where he has worked hard and long for so little reward that he no longer sees a future for himself—at least not one worth living. If there's also the specter of age creeping up on him, he may hear words in his head like, "You're not valuable to anyone." "You're replaceable." "You can't do what you used to." "You're too old to learn new things." "You don't have it." "You have no purpose." This is a dangerous place for a man to be.

Gary, his father, and his grandfather all had difficulty making a living. In fact, it was very late in each of their lives before they were even able to discern what they were supposed to be doing. They went from job to job without any clear leading. They struggled financially. None of them had parents who prayed for them to have their gifts and talents revealed, to know the calling of God on their lives, to have doors opened to them, and to become all they were created to be. History tends to repeat itself without the intervention of God.

I've observed that people who have had actively praying parents seem to find their life's work early. Their careers may not take off immediately, but they have a sense of purpose and destiny that propels them in the right direction. They don't live with the frustration and aimlessness that the others do. While many parents have an agenda for their children, not enough of them seek out God's plan for their lives. When a child's life is left to chance that way, a kind of vocational wandering can result. There is needless floundering, disappointment, doubt, and despair as he tries to carve out a place for himself. If your husband had that kind of start, your prayers can change his life.

If your husband didn't have praying parents, you can step in the gap. You can pray for his eyes to be opened to see what God wants him to do, and where God is leading. Your prayers can help him feel appreciated and encouraged enough to recognize he has worth no matter what he does. You can assure him that God has uniquely gifted him with ability and talent and has something good ahead for him. Then pray for God to reveal it and open a door of opportunity which no man can shut. Your prayers can pave a path for him.

Even if your husband already has a successful career, it's still good to pray that he is where God wants him to be and that everything will continue to go smoothly. My husband, who is a songwriter and record producer, said he felt my prayers have prevented him from working with the wrong clients. He has never worked with anyone who is difficult, weird, evil, or unsuitable, which is nothing less than a miracle in his business. He knew I always prayed that God would lead him to the right people and remove from his path those who would be trouble. While our prayers cannot ensure a trouble-free road for our husbands, they can certainly steer them clear of many problems.

If your husband is a hard worker, make sure he has times of rest and enjoyment—to do things that entertain him and give him a reprieve from the weight of a lifetime of supporting a family. Men need periods of refreshing. If they don't have them, they are prone to burnout and temptation of all kinds. Your prayers can help your husband understand that the true meaning of life doesn't come from work, it comes from following God. Let's pray for our husbands to find that perfect balance.

Prayer

Lord, I pray that You would bless the work of my husband's hands. May his labor bring not only favor, success, and prosperity, but great fulfillment as well. If the work he is doing is not in line with Your perfect will for his life, reveal it to him. Show him what he should do differently and guide him down the right path. Give him strength, faith, and a vision for the future so he can rise above any propensity for laziness. May he never run from work out of fear, selfishness, or a desire to avoid responsibility. On the other hand, help him to see that he doesn't have to work himself to death for man's approval, or grasp for gain beyond what is a gift from You. Give him the ability to enjoy his success without striving for more. Help him to excel, but free him from the pressure to do so.

I pray that You will be Lord over his work, and may he bring You into every aspect of it. Give him enough confidence in the gifts You've placed in him to be able to seek, find, and do good work. Open up doors of opportunity for him that no man can close. Develop his skills so that they grow more valuable with each passing year. Show me what I can do to encourage him.

I pray that his work will be established, secure, successful, satisfying, and financially rewarding. May he not be "lagging in diligence, [but] fervent in spirit, serving the Lord" (Romans 12:11). Let him be like a tree planted by the stream of Your living water, which brings forth fruit in due season. May he never wither under pressure, but grow strong and prosper (Psalm 1:3).

POWER TOOLS

Do you see a man who excels in his work?
He will stand before kings; he will not stand
before unknown men.
PROVERBS 22:29

Do not overwork to be rich; because of your own
understanding, cease! Will you set your eyes on that
which is not? For riches certainly make themselves
wings; they fly away like an eagle toward heaven.
PROVERBS 23:4,5

For what profit is it to a man if he gains the whole
world, and loses his own soul? Or what will a man
give in exchange for his soul?
MATTHEW 16:26

Because of laziness the building decays, and through
idleness of hands the house leaks.
ECCLESIASTES 10:18

Let the beauty of the LORD our God be upon us, and
establish the work of our hands for us; yes, establish
the work of our hands.
PSALM 90:17

～ CHAPTER THREE ～

His Finances

Much of who your husband is and what he experiences in life is wrapped up in how he relates to his finances. Is he giving or miserly? Is he thankful or envious of others? Is money a blessing or a curse? Is he wise or reckless with what he has? Is he in agreement with you as to how it is to be spent, or does your marriage exhibit financial strife? Nothing puts more pressure on a marriage than financial irresponsibility, lack of money, and huge debt. Only when we recognize that all we have comes from God and seek to make Him Lord over it can we avoid the pitfalls that money, or the lack of it, brings.

Although my husband has always made a good living, the nature of his business is "feast or famine" with regard to when and how much money comes in. One year there was a recession in the music business and everybody felt it. Even the companies who owed us money withheld payment because of their own lack of cash flow. It was a frightening time, but it would have been much worse if we hadn't had faith in the Lord and committed our finances to Him. Our comfort came in knowing that we had obeyed God in tithing our money to the church. "Bring all the tithes into the storehouse" and see if He "will not open for you the windows of heaven and pour out for you such blessing that there will not be room enough to receive it" (Malachi 3:10). We had also been faithful to give to the poor and those in need. "Blessed is he who considers the poor; the LORD will deliver him in time of trouble. The LORD will preserve him and keep him alive, and he will be blessed on the earth" (Psalm 41:1,2). We also knew the Bible promises that "those who seek the LORD shall not lack any good thing" (Psalm 34:10). We certainly were seeking the Lord. We believed that by looking to God as our source and living in obedience to His ways, He would provide for us and we would have everything we need. He did and we do.

So many money problems can be solved by putting all finances under God's covering and doing what He says to do with them. That means giving when He says to give. When you do, God promises to deliver you, protect you, bless you, heal you, and keep you alive. When you don't, you will experience the same desolation the poor do. "Whoever shuts his ears to the cry of the poor will also cry himself and not be heard" (Proverbs 21:13). Not giving cuts off your own ability to enjoy what you have and leads to lifelong difficulties.

To be sure, there are wealthy people who do not give. But if you were to check closely into their lives, you'd find that they are missing many of the Lord's blessings. The blessings of wholeness, protection, love, peace, health, and fulfillment continually elude them and they don't know why. They gain wealth but lose the ability to enjoy it, all because they don't know that the key to life is knowing the Lord and living His way. This means giving time, energy, love, talent, and finances according to His direction.

Pray that your husband gets hold of this key to life and understands God's will for his finances. Pray that he becomes a giving person who is content to live within his means and not always strive for more. I'm not saying he should never try to increase his earnings—quite the contrary. A man deserves to earn what his work is worth and his wife should pray he does. Backbreaking drudgery that leads to gut-wrenching poverty and with it bitterness, anguish, sickness, and envy should not be accepted as a way of life. By all means pray that the storehouses of blessing will be opened upon him, but pray that it all comes from the hand of God. "The blessing of the LORD makes one rich, and He adds no sorrow with it" (Proverbs 10:22).

It may not be possible to use prayer to avoid every financial problem because God sometimes uses finances to get our attention and teach us things. But your prayers will certainly help protect your husband from unnecessary struggle and loss. God's desire is to bless those who have obedient, grateful, and giving hearts, whose true treasure is in the Lord. "Where your treasure is, there your heart will be also" (Matthew 6:21). God wants your husband to find his treasure in Him, not in his finances.

Prayer

Lord, I commit our finances to You. Be in charge of them and use them for Your purposes. May we both be good stewards of all that You give us, and walk in total agreement as to how it is to be dispersed. I pray that we will learn to live free of burdensome debt. Where we have not been wise, bring restoration and give us guidance. Show me how I can help increase our finances and not decrease them unwisely. Help us to remember that all we have belongs to You, and to be grateful for it.

I pray that (husband's name) will find it easy to give to You and to others as You have instructed in Your Word. Give him wisdom to handle money wisely. Help him make good decisions as to how he spends. Show him how to plan for the future. I pray that he will find the perfect balance between spending needlessly and being miserly. May he always be paid well for the work he does, and may his money not be stolen, lost, devoured, destroyed, or wasted. Multiply it so that what he makes will go a long way. I pray that he will not be anxious about finances, but will seek Your kingdom first, knowing that as he does, we will have all we need (Luke 12:31).

POWER TOOLS

Do not seek what you should eat or what you
should drink, nor have an anxious mind. For all
these things the nations of the world seek after,
and your Father knows that you need these things.
But seek the kingdom of God, and all these
things shall be added to you.
LUKE 12:29-31

As for every man to whom God has given riches and
wealth, and given him power to eat of it, to
receive his heritage and rejoice in his labor;
this is the gift of God.
ECCLESIASTES 5:19

He who gives to the poor will not lack, but he
who hides his eyes will have many curses.
PROVERBS 28:27

I have been young, and now am old; yet I have not
seen the righteous forsaken, nor his descendants
begging bread.
PSALM 37:25

My God shall supply all your need according to
His riches in glory by Christ Jesus.
PHILIPPIANS 4:19

CHAPTER FOUR

His Sexuality

We're hitting the top priorities in a man's life right away in this book. I feel if we can contribute to our husbands' happiness in these areas most dear to their hearts, we will have greater success making inroads in other areas that are crucial to their wellbeing.

After twenty years of praying with women about their failing, struggling, unfulfilling, or dead marriages, I've observed that frequently the sexual relationship is a low priority in their minds. It isn't that the wife cares nothing about that part of her life. It's that there are so many other things screaming for her attention, such as raising children, work, finances, managing a home, emotional stress, exhaustion, sickness, and marital strife. In the wife's juggling of priorities, sex can end up on the bottom of her list. Some women allow week after week, month after month, six months, a year, or even more to go by without having sexual relations with their husbands for one reason or another. When disaster hits, they are surprised. Even though the wife may have felt fine about this arrangement, her husband was being neglected in an important part of his being.

For a wife, sex comes out of affection. She doesn't want to be affectionate with a man who makes her feel angry, hurt, lonely, disappointed, overworked, unsupported, uncared for, or abandoned. But for a husband, sex is pure need. His eyes, ears, brain, and emotions get clouded if he doesn't have that release. He has trouble hearing anything his wife says or seeing what she needs when that area of his being is neglected. Wives sometimes have it backwards. They think, *We can have sex after we get these other issues settled.* But actually there is a far greater chance of settling the other issues if sex comes first.

That's why it's important to make sex a matter of priority in your marriage. Whether all conditions are perfect or whether you feel like it or not isn't the point. The point is meeting the needs of your husband and keeping communication lines open. A man can easily be made to feel insignificant, beaten down, discouraged, destroyed, or tempted in this area of his being. There is probably no more important means of fulfillment for a man, and no area where he is more vulnerable.

Sexual problems are quite common because many women don't have a clear grasp of what God's view is on the subject. But the Bible is crystal clear. "The wife does not have authority over her own body but the husband does. And likewise the husband does not have authority over his own body but the wife does. Do not deprive one another except with consent for a time, that you may give yourselves to fasting and prayer; and come together again so that Satan does not tempt you because of your lack of self-control" (1 Corinthians 7:4,5). Sex between a husband and wife is God's idea. Unless we're fasting and praying for weeks at a time, or are experiencing physical infirmity or separation, there is no excuse not to engage in it regularly.

When we're married, our bodies are not our own. We *owe* each other physical attention and we're not to deprive one another. The frequency of sex depends on the *other person's* need, not ours alone. If your attitude about having sex comes down to only what *you* need or what *you* don't want, then you don't have God's perspective. He says our body is to be used to comfort and complete the *other* person. Something is built up in the man and the marriage when this need is met by his wife. Something is diminished when it is not. You leave yourselves open for temptation, and far more destruction than you can imagine, when this area of intimate communication is neglected. It can happen to anyone, and that's why the sexual aspect of your marriage and your husband's sexuality need to be covered in prayer. And it's best to start praying about it *before* you have to.

If your husband desires sex more frequently and you are the one keeping it from happening, pray for God to help you change your ways. I've found that the most difficult time to deal with the issue of sex is when the children are small and can't do much for themselves. By the time you get them in bed, you are exhausted and ready to drop. You're thinking about getting to sleep as soon as possible, while your husband has been making other plans for you. Your options are to totally shut him down and say, "Forget about it. I'm tired," or communicate how exhausted you are and hope *he'll* say, "No problem. You get some rest," or proceed with a bad attitude and make him feel guilty or angry. But I've found a fourth option which works much better. Try this and see if it doesn't work for you.

When your husband communicates to you what he has in mind, as only a husband can do, don't roll your eyes and sigh deeply. Instead, say, "Okay, give me fifteen minutes." (Or ten or twenty, or whatever you need.) During that time, do something to make yourself feel attractive. For example, take a shower or a relaxing bath. Put on scented body lotion or his favorite perfume. (Have perfume you wear only for these times alone with him.) Comb your hair. Wash your face and prepare it with products that make your skin look dewy and fresh. Put on lip gloss and blush. Slip into lingerie you know he finds irresistible. Don't worry about your imperfections; he's not thinking about them. If you feel self-conscious, wear a beautiful nightgown that covers areas that bother you. While you're doing this, pray for God to give you renewed energy, strength, vitality, and a good attitude. Hopefully, when you're ready, your husband will find you were worth the wait. You'll be surprised at how much better a sex partner you are when you feel good about yourself. He'll be happier and you'll both sleep better. This is a small investment of time to see great rewards in your marriage.

Sometimes there is the opposite situation, where the wife is sexually neglected by her husband. His lack of interest can happen for many reasons—physical, mental, or emotional. But if he is content to go month after month without sex, then something is wrong. If there is no physical problem hindering him, maybe he's having deep feelings of failure, disappointment, depression, or hopelessness that need to be addressed. Prayer can help reveal what the problem is and how to solve it. Get professional help if you need to. It's cheaper than a divorce or the physical, emotional, and mental ravages of a dead marriage. Don't let negative emotions like resentment, bitterness, self-pity, and unforgiveness build up in you. Keep yourself healthy and attractive. If you don't think highly enough of yourself to take care of your body, do it as an act of kindness for *him*. Have special lingerie that *he* likes and put it on when you're with him. Get a new hairstyle. Surprise him with a new attitude. Keep your mind refreshed and growing. Basically, *don't do nothing*.

Bad things develop when the sexual part of a marriage is neglected. Don't let that happen to you. Keep an eye on the calendar and refuse to allow much time to go by without coming together physically. If it has been too long, ask God to show you why and help you remedy the situation. And remember, it's never too late to pray for sexual purity, no matter what has occurred in either of your pasts. Sometimes sexual problems in a marriage happen as a result of sexual experiences before the marriage. Pray to be set free and healed of those memories. Purity happens the moment it takes root in the heart. Prayer is where it starts. Don't jeopardize or forfeit what God has for your marriage by neglecting to pray for this vital area of your life.

Prayer

Lord, bless my husband's sexuality and make it an area of great fulfillment for him. Restore what needs to be restored, balance what needs to be balanced. Protect us from apathy, disappointment, criticism, busyness, unforgiveness, deadness, or disinterest. I pray that we make time for one another, communicate our true feelings openly, and remain sensitive to what each other needs.

Keep us sexually pure in mind and body, and close the door to anything lustful or illicit that seeks to encroach upon us. Deliver us from the bondage of past mistakes. Remove from our midst the effects of any sexual experience—in thought or deed—that happened outside of our relationship. Take away anyone or anything from our lives that would inspire temptation to infidelity. Help us to "abstain from sexual immorality" so that each of us will know "how to possess his own vessel in sanctification and honor" (1 Thessalonians 4:3-5). I pray that we will desire each other and no one else. Show me how to make myself attractive and desirable to him and be the kind of partner he needs. I pray that neither of us will ever be tempted to think about seeking fulfillment elsewhere.

I realize that an important part of my ministry to my husband is sexual. Help me to never use it as a weapon or a means of manipulation by giving and withholding it for selfish reasons. I commit this area of our lives to You, Lord. May it be continually new and alive. Make it all that You created it to be.

POWER TOOLS

Flee sexual immorality. Every sin that a man does is outside the body, but he who commits sexual immorality sins against his own body. Or do you not know that your body is the temple of the Holy Spirit who is in you, whom you have from God, and you are not your own? For you were bought at a price; therefore glorify God in your body and in your spirit, which are God's.

1 CORINTHIANS 6:18-20

The body is not for sexual immorality but for the
Lord, and the Lord for the body.
1 CORINTHIANS 6:13

Drink water from your own cistern, and running
water from your own well. Should your fountains be
dispersed abroad, streams of water in the streets? Let
them be only your own, and not for strangers with
you. Let your fountain be blessed, and rejoice with
the wife of your youth. As a loving deer and a
graceful doe, let her breasts satisfy you at all times;
and always be enraptured with her love.
PROVERBS 5:15-19

CHAPTER FIVE

His Affection

T om and Patti had been married a number of years before she actually had a serious talk with him about his lack of affection. Tom was a wonderful husband in every other way and their sexual relationship was good, but apart from the sexual act there was no affection. It wasn't because Tom didn't love Patti—he adored her. It was because affection was something he grew up without as a child. Patti felt guilty about the way she was feeling and didn't want to criticize or hurt Tom, but she had not known affection as a child, either, and that's why she needed it so in her marriage. Each time Patti confronted Tom about this problem he would try to change, but soon things were back to the way they had been. This led to great frustration and hurt in both of them. Eventually Patti became hopeless and felt like she was dying inside. She didn't see how she could live the rest of her life without affection, but she saw no hope of Tom's ever being any different.

Finally, Patti's misery forced her to take the problem to her prayer partners. They diligently covered it in prayer every week and as they prayed, God worked on Patti. He spoke to her about obeying Him in the area of eating right and getting proper exercise—an area where she had always been in rebellion. When she totally submitted to God regarding this and started doing the things He had been telling her to do, she began to feel better about herself and realized that she *deserved* to be treated affectionately by her husband. She didn't have to feel guilty about wanting affection because the Lord wanted that for her, too. Soon she felt the leading of God to confront Tom about it again. This time it would be different because she was now led by the Holy Spirit, and she and her prayer partners had been praying for a miraculous transformation in Tom.

"It took courage for me to even speak of this again," she told me. "I was afraid it could lead to divorce because we were both so hurt and saw no hope in each other. But God gave me the ability to speak in love the words that needed to be said, and this time the conversation brought immediate breakthrough."

"The turning point came," Tom recalled, "when Patti said to me, 'Honey, how can someone as wonderful as you, with all your attributes, someone I love and trust so much, not be able to be affectionate?'"

"Because I said words that affirmed him," Patti explained further, "it gave him hope that it was worth trying again."

Tom proceeded differently this time. He took the problem to his own prayer group of men, who instantly rallied around him. They decided not only to support him daily in prayer, but also to keep him accountable to show some form of affection to Patti each day.

"This was something I welcomed, because I wanted to change," Tom said. "I love Patti and hated that I was hurting her. I wanted to be different and I knew that true transformation can only happen by the power of the Holy Spirit."

Every day for a number of weeks, one of the men from the group called Tom and said, "What have you done to show affection to Patti today?" They also suggested *ways* to show affection and affirm her. They told Tom to check in regularly with Patti and say, "How am I doing?" For someone whose heart had not been prepared by the Holy Spirit, this could have been extremely annoying. But because Tom welcomed the Lord's working in him, it brought no burden.

"Now the first thing he does when he comes home is give me a hug and a kiss," Patti said with a radiant smile. "I felt like a new person after five hugs."

Tom and Patti's situation is not a rare one. Many people, even godly men and women, live in marriages that are dead because there is no affection. And women endure it because their husbands are good in other ways, or they don't feel worthy enough to ask for affection. But this is not the way God designed the marital relationship. "Let the husband render to his wife the affection due her, and likewise also the wife to her husband" (1 Corinthians 7:3). There is "a time to embrace," the Bible says (Ecclesiastes 3:5). When you're married, it's definitely the time. Affection isn't at the top of a man's priority list because men often see sex and affection as being the same. A woman's greatest need is for affection. If you are in a marriage that lacks it, pray for the Holy Spirit's transformation.

Prayer

Lord, I pray for open physical affection between my husband and me. Enable each of us to lay aside self-consciousness or apathy and be effusive in our display of love. Help us to demonstrate how much we care for and value each other. Remind us throughout each day to affectionately touch one another in some way. Help us to not be cold, undemonstrative, uninterested, or remote. Enable us to be warm, tender, compassionate, loving, and adoring. Break through any hardheadedness on our part that refuses to change and grow. If one of us is less affectionate to the other's detriment, bring us into balance.

Where any lack of affection has planted a negative view of marriage in our children, or taught them an incorrect way of relating to a marriage partner, help us to model the right way so that they can observe it. Show us how to openly confess our errors to them and demonstrate our commitment to live differently.

Change our habits of indifference or busyness. May we not so take each other for granted that we don't make the effort to reach out and touch one another with affection. Help us not to weaken the marriage through neglect of this vital means of communication. I pray that we always "greet one another with a kiss of love" (1 Peter 5:14). I know that only the transforming power of the Holy Spirit can make changes that last. I trust You to transform us and make us the husband and wife You called us to be.

POWER TOOLS

If there is any consolation in Christ, if any
comfort of love, if any fellowship of the Spirit, if
any affection and mercy, fulfill my joy by being
like-minded, having the same love, being of
one accord, of one mind.
PHILIPPIANS 2:1,2

So husbands ought to love their own wives as their
own bodies; he who loves his wife loves himself. For
no one ever hated his own flesh, but nourishes and
cherishes it, just as the Lord does the church.
EPHESIANS 5:28,29

Let each of you look out not only for his own
interests, but also for the interests of others.
PHILIPPIANS 2:4

His left hand is under my head, and his right
hand embraces me.
SONG OF SOLOMON 2:6

Let no one seek his own, but each one the
other's well-being.
1 CORINTHIANS 10:24

CHAPTER SIX

His Temptations

From the time Michael and I were married, I prayed for God to remove temptation from our lives. I don't know if it has been the result of prayer or the fact that we both guard ourselves against such things, but we've never given each other a single moment of concern. I'm sure it's due more to the hand of God than the strength of human restraint, but both are important.

I know several couples who experienced adultery in their marriages, but because in each case there was a wife who was willing to pray and a husband open to allowing God to change and restore him, the marriages are still intact and successful today. Only prayer, a submitted heart, and the transforming power of the Holy Spirit can work those kinds of miracles.

I have another friend whose husband had numerous affairs before they finally divorced. Each time it was with one of her best friends. I questioned her choice of "friends," but I never questioned her godliness or commitment to pray. She prayed. But a heart that refuses to listen to the promptings of the Holy Spirit will not change, no matter how hard you pray.

Temptation is everywhere today and we're fools if we think we or our husbands can't be lured by it in some form or another. The Bible says, "The eyes of man are never satisfied" (Proverbs 27:20). If that's true, temptation is always a possibility and we must be ever watchful. Certain people are tempted by alcohol and drugs; others have a lust for money and power. Still others find food addictions, pornography, or sexual immorality to be irresistible lures. The enemy of our souls knows where our flesh is the weakest and he will put temptations in our paths at our most vulnerable points. The question is not whether there will be temptations, it's how we will handle them when they arise. I recommend praying through them. While prayer may not be able to stop a man from doing something he is determined to do, it *can* diminish the voices of temptation and strengthen his resolve. It can pave the way for him to make right choices.

The Bible says that God does not tempt us. It is our *desires* that draw us away to what entices us. It is our *desires* that cause us to sin and bring death into our lives. But "blessed is the man who endures temptation; for when he has been approved, he will receive the crown of life which the Lord has promised to those who love Him" (James 1:12). God wants us to get through temptation because He wants to bless us. But He needs to see if we can be trusted to chose His ways over our fleshly desires. He'll always give us a way out if we want it badly enough to seek Him for it.

The best time to start praying about this is *before* anything happens. Jesus instructed His disciples to "pray that you may not enter into temptation" (Luke 22:40). He said to be watchful because "the spirit indeed is willing, but the flesh is weak" (Mark 14:38). If your husband struggles in a certain area, pray that he will want to have godly prayer partners with whom he can share openly, be accountable, and receive prayer. Open confession before God and other believers does more to minimize the power of the tempter than anything else. Unfortunately, many men are reticent to reveal what tempts them most and so they shut off to the very thing that could protect them.

If after all your praying, your husband still falls into the hands of temptation, do not blame yourself. The decision is ultimately his. He has chosen to walk in the flesh and not in the Spirit. "Walk in the Spirit, and you shall not fulfill the lust of the flesh. For the flesh lusts against the Spirit, and the Spirit against the flesh; and these are contrary to one another, so that you do not do the things that you wish" (Galatians 5:16,17). Don't stop praying for him. No matter how hopeless it seems when you see him being tempted again and again, know that God has provided a means of escape and you may be the instrument He will use to help him find it. If there is no temptation problem in your marriage, be thankful and pray that it stays that way.

Prayer

Lord, I pray that You would strengthen my husband to resist any temptation that comes his way. Stamp it out of his mind before it ever reaches his heart or personal experience. Lead him not into temptation, but deliver him from evils such as adultery, pornography, drugs, alcohol, food addiction, gambling, and perversion. Remove temptation especially in the area of <u>(name specific temptation)</u>. Make him strong where he is weak. Help him to rise above anything that erects itself as a stronghold in his life. May he say, "I will set nothing wicked before my eyes; I hate the work of those who fall away; it shall not cling to me" (Psalm 101:3).

Lord, You've said that "Whoever has no rule over his own spirit is like a city broken down, without walls" (Proverbs 25:28). I pray that <u>(husband's name)</u> will not be broken down by the power of evil, but raised up by the power of God. Establish a wall of protection around him. Fill him with Your Spirit and flush out all that is not of You. Help him to take charge over his own spirit and have self-control to resist anything and anyone who becomes a lure. May he "abhor what is evil. Cling to what is good" (Romans 12:9). I pray that he will be repulsed by tempting situations. Give him courage to reject them. Teach him to walk in the Spirit so he will not fulfill the lust of the flesh.

POWER TOOLS

Let no one say when he is tempted, "I am
tempted by God"; for God cannot be tempted
by evil, nor does He Himself tempt anyone.
But each one is tempted when he is drawn
away by his own desires and enticed. Then,
when desire has conceived, it gives birth to
sin; and sin, when it is full-grown,
brings forth death.

JAMES 1:13-15

No temptation has overtaken you except such as is common to man; but God is faithful, who will not allow you to be tempted beyond what you are able, but with the temptation will also make the way of escape, that you may be able to bear it.

1 CORINTHIANS 10:13

Let us walk properly, as in the day, not in revelry and drunkenness, not in lewdness and lust, not in strife and envy. But put on the Lord Jesus Christ, and make no provision for the flesh, to fulfill its lusts.

ROMANS 13:13,14

Those who desire to be rich fall into temptation and a snare, and into many foolish and harmful lusts which drown men in destruction and perdition.

1 TIMOTHY 6:9

The works of the flesh are evident, which are: adultery, fornication, uncleanness, lewdness, idolatry, sorcery, hatred, contentions, jealousies, outbursts of wrath, selfish ambitions, dissensions, heresies, envy, murders, drunkenness, revelries, and the like; of which I tell you beforehand, just as I also told you in time past, that those who practice such things will not inherit the kingdom of God.

GALATIANS 5:19-21

CHAPTER SEVEN

His Mind

I used to attribute my husband's mind struggles to his musical genius. You know the artistic temperament—bright and brilliant on one hand, dark and moody on the other. When he would get down, the words in his mind told him he was going to fail, be worth nothing, that he was incapable of doing what he needed to do. It had no basis in reality because he had those kinds of thoughts even in the midst of his most productive and successful work. I didn't realize for a long time that the mind battles he endured did not have to be written off as "just the way he is." Nor did he have to fight them alone. If he and I were one, then an assault on his mind was an assault on me as well. I could stand with him in the battle by declaring, "This is not *God* speaking into my husband's life, it's the voice of the enemy. I'm not going to stand by and watch deadly games being played with his mind and our lives."

I decided to try my own experiment and "stand against the wiles of the devil" on his behalf (Ephesians 6:11). After all, the Bible talks about "praying always with all prayer and supplication in the Spirit, being watchful to this end with all perseverance and supplication for all the saints" (Ephesians 6:18). Surely "all the saints" is a category, even if it's not a description, which includes my husband. As I persevered in prayer for him over the next few months, I was amazed at the results. Not only did he become better able to control the thoughts in his mind, but eventually I could even see the onslaught coming and attack it in prayer before it gained a foothold. The more he saw my prayers answered, the more he realized where the lies were coming from and the less willing he was to believe them.

As I have traveled the country with my speaking engagements and talked with women from all walks of life, I have been amazed to see how universal this problem is. In fact, it didn't seem to matter what temperaments or backgrounds their husbands had, they experienced the same kind of lies in their mind. I finally realized that all men have an enemy who wants to undermine what God desires to do in their lives. Women have that same enemy, but men seem to be more vulnerable to his attacks in certain areas. Even the strongest man can get exhausted, overwhelmed, burdened, desperate, or caught up in things that keep him away from the presence of God. He doesn't always see the traps of an enemy who wants him to believe that what he faces is insurmountable. His mind fills with words like "hopeless," "no good," "failure," "impossible," "it's over," and "why try?" A wife can pray that her husband will discern the lies and hear instead words like "hope," "prosperity," "possibility," "success," and "new beginning," and know that they're from God.

The two most powerful weapons against the attack of lies upon your husband's mind are the *Word of God* and *praise*. "The Word of God is living and powerful, and sharper than any two-edged sword, piercing even to the division of soul and spirit, and of joints and marrow, and is a *discerner of the thoughts and intents of the heart*" (Hebrews 4:12). By speaking God's Word, you can reveal wrong thinking and it will lose its power. If your husband won't do it for himself, you can speak the Word of God over him, either in his presence or alone in prayer, and see positive results. I've done that for my husband countless times and he will attest to the power of it. I remind him that God has not given him a spirit of fear, but of power and of love and of a *sound mind* (2 Timothy 1:7). I tell him I'm praying for him to lay claim to that sound mind at all times.

Praise is also a powerful tool because God's presence comes to dwell in our midst when we worship Him. In His presence we find healing and transformation for our lives. "Although they knew God, they did not glorify Him as God, nor were thankful, but became futile in their thoughts, and their foolish hearts were darkened" (Romans 1:21). You don't want futile thoughts to darken your husband's heart. Speak praise to God for your husband's sound mind, and he'll be able to think more clearly about what he will and will not allow into it.

Depression, bitterness, anger, fear, rejection, hopelessness, loneliness, rebellion, temptation, evil, and many diseases all begin in the mind. These things can control your life unless you take control of your mind first. That's why God instructs us not to accept as truth everything we think. "I have stretched out My hands all day long to a rebellious people, who walk in a way that is not good, according to their own thoughts" (Isaiah 65:2). He wants us to share *His* thoughts. "We [who believe] have the mind of Christ" (1 Corinthians 2:16). Let's pray for our husbands to receive the mind of Christ and bring every thought captive under God's control. Who doesn't need that?

Prayer

Lord, I pray for Your protection on my husband's mind. Shield him from the lies of the enemy. Help him to clearly discern between Your voice and any other, and show him how to take every thought captive as You have instructed us to do. May he thirst for Your Word and hunger for Your truth so that he can recognize wrong thinking. Give him strength to resist lying thoughts. Remind him that he has the mind of Christ. Where the enemy's lies have already invaded his thoughts, I push them back by inviting the power of the Holy Spirit to cleanse his mind. Lord, You have given me authority "over all the power of the enemy" (Luke 10:19). By that authority given to me in Jesus Christ, I command all lying spirits away from my husband's mind. I proclaim that God has given (husband's name) a sound mind. He will not entertain confusion, but live in clarity. He will not be tormented with impure, evil, negative, or sinful thoughts, but be transformed by the renewing of his mind, that he may prove what is that good and acceptable and perfect will of God (Romans 12:2).

Enable him to "be strong in the Lord and in the power of His might" (Ephesians 6:10). Help him to be anxious for nothing, but in everything by prayer and supplication, with thanksgiving, let his requests be made known to You; and may Your peace, which surpasses all understanding, guard his heart and mind through Christ Jesus (Philippians 4:6,7). And finally, whatever things are true, noble, just, pure, lovely, of good report, having virtue, or anything praiseworthy, let him think on these things (Philippians 4:8).

POWER TOOLS

Though we walk in the flesh, we do not war
according to the flesh. For the weapons of our
warfare are not carnal but mighty in God for pulling
down strongholds, casting down arguments and every
high thing that exalts itself against the knowledge of
God, bringing every thought into captivity to the
obedience of Christ.
2 CORINTHIANS 10:3-5

To be carnally minded is death, but to be
spiritually minded is life and peace.
ROMANS 8:6

I see another law in my members, warring against the
law of my mind, and bringing me into captivity to
the law of sin which is in my members.
ROMANS 7:23

With the mind I myself serve the law of God,
but with the flesh the law of sin.
ROMANS 7:25

You shall love the LORD your God with all your
heart, with all your soul, with all your mind,
and with all your strength.
MARK 12:30

CHAPTER EIGHT

His Fears

There are many things in this world to be afraid of; only a fool would say otherwise. But when fear seizes us, tormenting and ruling our lives, we have become captive to it. Men are often susceptible to that because without even realizing it, they get attacked by the "what if's." "What if I can't make enough money?" "What if something happens to my wife and children?" "What if I get a terrible disease?" "What if my business fails?" "What if I can't be a good father?" "What if I become disabled and can't work to support my family?" "What if I'm overpowered or threatened?" "What if I can't perform sexually?" "What if no one respects me?" "What if I'm in an accident?" "What if I die?" Fear can take hold of a man (Psalm 48:6) and cause his life to be wasted (Psalm 78:33). If he is "seized with great fear" (Luke 8:37), it can keep him from all God has for him.

The second year we were married, Michael and I took a trip to Italy, Greece, and Israel with our pastor, Jack Hayford, and his wife, Anna, and some people from our church. Michael had always been a very anxious traveler, so by the time we arrived in Greece, he was stressed. One night, after an exhausting few days, he said, "This is miserable for me. I can't stay on the tour."

"What exactly are you afraid of?" I questioned him.

"I'm not sure," he answered. "But it feels like everything in my life is going to fall apart if I don't go back home right away."

Even though it was late in the evening, I called Pastor Jack's room to tell him we were leaving in the morning. I'm sure he must have been in bed by that time, but he said, "I'll be right there."

He came to our room immediately and Michael shared with him what he was experiencing. Pastor Jack put a compassionate arm around his shoulder and talked about the love his heavenly Father had toward him.

"God has adopted you as His son," he said. "When you're in the presence of a strong and loving Father, there's no need to be afraid."

Pastor Jack prayed for Michael to clearly perceive the love of his heavenly Father, and he also demonstrated a father's love to him. It was a simple act of Holy Spirit-inspired kindness but a powerful revelation to Michael. Because of it, he was able to rise above his fear and we stayed on the tour until the end. And it was a good thing we did. I became pregnant in Jerusalem and nine months later our son, Christopher, was born on Pastor Jack's birthday. Significant things happen in our lives when we don't allow fear to rule the situation.

There is a difference between a fearful thought that comes to mind as a prompting to pray for a particular thing, and a tormenting spirit of fear that paralyzes. You don't want to undermine the promptings of the Holy Spirit to your husband's heart, but you do want to support him as he battles destructive fear. Jesus said, "I will show you whom you should fear: Fear Him who, after He has killed, has power to cast into hell" (Luke 12:5). The only kind of fear we are supposed to have is the fear of the Lord.

When you have the fear of the Lord, God promises to deliver you from your enemies (2 Kings 17:39), protect you from evil (Proverbs 16:6), keep His eye on you (Psalm 33:18), show you His mercy (Luke 1:50), give you riches and honor (Proverbs 22:4), supply everything you need (Psalm 34:9), reveal all you need to know (Psalm 25:14), bless your children and grandchildren (Psalm 103:17), give you confidence (Proverbs 14:26), a satisfying life (Proverbs 19:23), longevity (Proverbs 10:27), and the desires of your heart (Psalm 145:19). What more could you ask? Pray for the comforting, securing, perfect love of the Lord to surround your husband and deliver him from all his fears.

Prayer

Lord, You've said in Your Word that "there is no fear in love; but perfect love casts out fear, because fear involves torment. But he who fears has not been made perfect in love" (1 John 4:18). I pray You will perfect my husband in Your love so that tormenting fear finds no place in him. I know You have not given him a spirit of fear. You've given him power, love, and a sound mind (2 Timothy 1:7). I pray in the name of Jesus that fear will not rule over my husband. Instead, may Your Word penetrate every fiber of his being, convincing him that Your love for him is far greater than anything he faces and nothing can separate him from it.

I pray that he will acknowledge You as a Father whose love is unfailing, whose strength is without equal, and in whose presence there is nothing to fear. Deliver him this day from fear that destroys and replace it with godly fear (Jeremiah 32:40). Teach him Your way, O Lord. Help him to walk in Your truth. Unite his heart to fear Your name (Psalm 86:11). May he have no fear of men, but rise up and boldly say, "The LORD is my helper; I will not fear. What can man do to me?" (Hebrews 13:6) "How great is Your goodness, which You have laid up for those who fear You" (Psalm 31:19).

I say to you (husband's name), "Be strong, do not fear! Behold, your God will come with vengeance, with the recompense of God; He will come and save you" (Isaiah 35:4). "In righteousness you shall be established; you shall be far from oppression, for you shall not fear" (Isaiah 54:14). "You shall not be afraid of the terror by night, nor of the arrow that flies by day, nor of the pestilence that walks in darkness, nor of the destruction that lays waste at noonday" (Psalm 91:5,6). May the Spirit of the Lord rest upon you, "the Spirit of wisdom and understanding, the Spirit of counsel and might, the Spirit of knowledge and of the fear of the LORD" (Isaiah 11:2).

POWER TOOLS

The angel of the LORD encamps all around those who fear Him, and delivers them.
PSALM 34:7

I sought the LORD, and He heard me, and
delivered me from all my fears.
PSALM 34:4

Yea, though I walk through the valley of the
shadow of death, I will fear no evil; for You
are with me; Your rod and Your staff,
they comfort me.
PSALM 23:4

Fear not, for I am with you; be not dismayed,
for I am your God. I will strengthen you, yes,
I will help you, I will uphold you with
My righteous right hand.
ISAIAH 41:10

The LORD is my light and my salvation;
whom shall I fear? The LORD is the strength
of my life; of whom shall I be afraid?
PSALM 27:1

His Purpose

Everyone has a purpose. It's the reason we exist. It's our life's mission, objective, or plan. Generally, we're here to glorify God and do His will. How that specifically translates in our lives is unique to each of us. Your husband needs to know the reason *he* exists. He needs to be sure his life is not just an accident, but that he's here by design. He must be certain he was created for a great purpose. When he discovers that purpose, and is doing what he was created to do, becoming what he was created to be, he will find fulfillment. This can only contribute to *your* happiness as well.

If I've learned anything being married two and one half decades, it's that a wife can't put pressure on her husband to *be* something, but she can pray for him to become it. She can pray that he be molded according to God's plan and not anyone else's. Then, who he becomes will be determined by whether he hears God's call on his life or not. For God has "called us with a holy calling, not according to our works, but according to His own purpose and grace which was given to us in Christ Jesus before time began" (2 Timothy 1:9). Your husband is "predestined according to the purpose of Him who works all things according to the counsel of His will" (Ephesians 1:11,12). But you still need to pray that he hears God's call, so that who he is and what he does lines up with God's purpose for his life.

You can always tell when a man is not living in the purpose for which God created him. You sense his unrest. You get a feeling something is not quite right, even if you can't put your finger on what it is. When you're around a man who is fulfilling his calling and doing what he was created to do, you're aware of his inner direction, confidence, and deep security. How do you feel about what your husband is doing with his life? Do you lack peace about it because he is on a path that's unfulfilling, beating him down, or going nowhere? If so, then pray, "Lord, take my husband from this place, reveal to him what You've called him to be, and open doors to what he should be doing."

Praying that way doesn't mean your husband will be pulled out of what he's doing and dropped into something else. It *can* happen that way, but often what takes place is a change in the man's perspective. I have a friend named David, who has worked for years in a factory, making airplanes. When he heard the call of God on his life, he knew he was to help troubled teenagers in low-income families. He also knew he wasn't to leave his job to do it. As it turned out, his work provided enough money to support his family while it afforded him exactly the kind of hours he needed to do what he had to do. He has organized food distribution to needy families, free concerts for underprivileged teens, Christian outreaches for the unsaved, and peace talks between rival gangs. He has done as much to bring restoration to his strife-torn city as a man could possibly do. His is by no means an easy job, but it is fulfilling. And he has a sense of purpose that is unmistakable when you're around him. Physically, he is not a large man, but he is a spiritual giant and you know it when you're in his presence. His wife, Priscilla, also hears God's call on his life and she supports it in every way she can.

Whatever God has called your husband to be or do, He has also called you to support it and be a part of it, if in no other way than to pray, encourage, and help in whatever way possible. For some women that means creating a good home, raising the children, being there for him, and offering prayer support. Other women may take an active role by becoming a partner or helper. In either case, God does not ask you to deny your own personhood in the process. God has called *you* to something, too. But it will fit in with whatever your husband's calling is, it will not be in conflict with it. God is not the author of confusion, strife, or unworkable situations. He is a God of perfect timing. There is a time for everything, the Bible says. The timing to do what God has called *each* of you to do will work out perfectly, if it's submitted to God.

If your husband is already moving in the purpose for which God has called him, you can count on the enemy of his soul coming to cast doubt—especially if he hasn't yet seen anything close to the finished picture or realized the success he had envisioned. Your prayers can help cast away discouragement and keep it from taking hold. It can help your husband to hear and cling to God's revelation. It can cause him to live his life on purpose.

— *Prayer* —

Lord, I pray that __(husband's name)__ will clearly hear the call You have on his life. Help him to realize who he is in Christ and give him certainty that he was created for a high purpose. May the eyes of his understanding be enlightened so that he will know what is the hope of Your calling (Ephesians 1:18).

Lord, when You call us, You also enable us. Enable him to walk worthy of his calling and become the man of God You made him to be. Continue to remind him of what You've called him to and don't let him get sidetracked with things that are unessential to Your purpose. Strike down discouragement so that it will not defeat him. Lift his eyes above the circumstances of the moment so he can see the purpose for which You created him. Give him patience to wait for Your perfect timing. I pray that the desires of his heart will not be in conflict with the desires of Yours. May he seek You for direction, and hear when You speak to his soul.

POWER TOOLS

Each one has his own gift from God, one in
this manner and another in that.
1 CORINTHIANS 7:7

As God has distributed to each one, as the Lord
has called each one, so let him walk.
1 CORINTHIANS 7:17

We also pray always for you that our God
would count you worthy of this calling, and fulfill
all the good pleasure of His goodness and the
work of faith with power.
2 THESSALONIANS 1:11

The God of our Lord Jesus Christ, the Father of
glory, . . . give to you the spirit of wisdom and
revelation in the knowledge of Him, the eyes of
your understanding being enlightened; that you
may know what is the hope of His calling, what are
the riches of the glory of His inheritance in the
saints, and what is the exceeding greatness of His
power toward us who believe, according to the
working of His mighty power.
EPHESIANS 1:17-19

May He grant you according to your heart's
desire, and fulfill all your purpose.
PSALM 20:4

CHAPTER TEN

His Choices

There was a business deal my husband entered into that he did not mention to me until it was already in motion. From the moment I learned of it I did not have a good feeling. I thought the idea was great and his vision for it was excellent, but I couldn't escape the distinct lack of peace I had about it. In fact, the more I prayed, the stronger I felt. When I mentioned it to him he said defensively, "You don't trust me to make the right decision." He made clear this was something he wanted and he was not about to hear any opposition.

The only recourse I had was to pray, which I did. Time and again I said to God, "Show me if I'm wrong about this. I would love for it to work out because it's a great idea. But if what I'm sensing is correct, reveal it to him in time to stop the process. Show him the truth and close the door."

At the eleventh hour, just before contracts were to be signed, Michael's eyes were suddenly opened to a number of incidents that called into question the true intentions of the other parties involved. The revelation of God exposed everything to him and the entire deal was called off. As hard as it was for him to accept at the time, he is grateful to have been spared much grief.

Sometime later, while I was writing this book, I asked my husband what has meant the most about my praying for him. One of the things he mentioned was that it helped him to make good choices. "When major decisions came up and I was offered certain things, your prayers opened my eyes and kept me from entering into contractual agreements that would have been bad," he explained.

We have to remember that all men think they are doing the right thing. "Every way of a man is right in his own eyes" (Proverbs 21:2). But God is the only one who can give true discernment. He can give us wisdom when we ask for it. Wisdom brings success (Ecclesiastes 10:10), and it enables us to learn from experience (Proverbs 15:31). We want our husbands to be wise men.

The opposite of a wise man is a fool. The Bible describes a fool as someone who only "trusts in his own heart" (Proverbs 28:26). He despises wisdom (Proverbs 23:9). He only wants to talk and doesn't want to listen (Proverbs 18:2). In other words, you can't tell him anything. He is quarrelsome (Proverbs 20:3), and he rages and is arrogant when you try to reason with him (Proverbs 14:16). A fool is someone who is incapable of weighing thoroughly the consequences of his actions. As a result, he doesn't make wise choices. If you have a husband like that, pray for him to have wisdom.

If your husband is not a full-time fool, so to speak, but he does occasionally engage in foolish behavior, don't try to fix him. God is the only one who can do that. Your job is to love and pray for him. The Bible says, "The fear of the LORD is the beginning of wisdom, and the knowledge of the Holy One is understanding" (Proverbs 9:10). This means you start by praying for the fear of the Lord to overtake him. Then pray for him to have godly counsel: "Blessed is the man who walks not in the counsel of the ungodly" (Psalm 1:1). If you keep praying for your husband to have wisdom and godly counsel, then even if he does make a bad decision, you can enjoy the comfort of knowing you did your part and God will bring good out of it.

So much of our lives is affected by decisions our husbands make. We are wise to pray that they make good ones.

Prayer

Lord, fill my husband with the fear of the Lord and give him wisdom for every decision he makes. May he reverence You and Your ways and seek to know Your truth. Give him discernment to make decisions based on Your revelation. Help him to make godly choices and keep him from doing anything foolish. Take foolishness out of his heart and enable him to quickly recognize error and avoid it. Open his eyes to clearly see the consequences of any anticipated behavior.

I pray that he will listen to godly counselors and not be a man who is unteachable. Give him strength to reject the counsel of the ungodly and hear Your counsel above all others. I declare that although "there are many plans in a man's heart, nevertheless the LORD'S counsel—that will stand" (Proverbs 19:21). Instruct him even as he is sleeping (Psalm 16:7), and in the morning, I pray he will do what's right rather than follow the leading of his own flesh. I know the wisdom of this world is foolishness with You, Lord (1 Corinthians 3:19). May he not buy into it, but keep his eyes on You and have ears to hear Your voice.

POWER TOOLS

A wise man will hear and increase learning, and a
man of understanding will attain wise counsel.
PROVERBS 1:5

Do not be wise in your own eyes; fear the
LORD and depart from evil.
PROVERBS 3:7

The fear of the LORD is the beginning of knowledge,
but fools despise wisdom and instruction.
PROVERBS 1:7

They will call on me, but I will not answer; they will
seek me diligently, but they will not find me. Because
they hated knowledge and did not choose the fear of
the LORD, they would have none of my counsel and
despised my every rebuke.
PROVERBS 1:28-30

A man who wanders from the way of understanding
will rest in the assembly of the dead.
PROVERBS 21:16

❧ CHAPTER ELEVEN ❧

His Health

For years my husband cared little about exercise. I would give lectures and meaningful talks, leave magazine articles in his path, and plead and cry about how I didn't want to be a widow, but it all fell on glazed eyes and deaf ears. Then one day I got the brilliant idea that if praying worked for other parts of his life, it might work for this, too. I decided to employ my "shut up and pray" method and ask God to give him the desire and motivation to exercise regularly. I prayed for a number of months without any results, but then one morning I heard an unfamiliar noise coming from another room. I followed the sound and much to my amazement, it was my husband on the treadmill. I didn't say a word. He has been using the treadmill and lifting weights about three days a week ever since. When he later remarked how much better he was feeling and wished he had started doing it sooner, I exercised admirable restraint and didn't even allow the words "I told you so" to be formed with my mouth. To this day he doesn't know I prayed.

Your husband's health is not something to take for granted, no matter what his age or condition. Pray for him to learn to take proper care of himself, and if he becomes ill, pray for him to be healed. I've seen too many answers to prayers for healing in my life and the lives of others to doubt that the God who healed in the Bible is the same yesterday, today, and tomorrow. I believe that when God said, "I am the LORD who heals You," He meant it (Exodus 15:26). I have the same faith as Jeremiah who prayed, "Heal me, O Lord, and I shall be healed" (Jeremiah 17:14). I trust His Word when it promises "I will restore health to you and heal you of your wounds" (Jeremiah 30:17).

Jesus "took our infirmities and bore our sicknesses" (Matthew 8:17). He gave His disciples power to "heal all kinds of sickness and all kinds of disease" (Matthew 10:1). He said "These signs will follow those who believe. . . . They will lay hands on the sick, and they will recover" (Mark 16:17,18). It seems to me that God is interested in healing, and He didn't put a time limit on it; only a faith limit (Matthew 9:22).

My husband told me that my prayers for his healing had the biggest impact on him in the mid-eighties when he discovered several lumps on his body and the doctor believed they were cancerous. A second doctor also suspected it was cancer, so a biopsy was taken. During those days of waiting to find out the results, Michael was tempted to worry. He said my prayers for his good health and peace sustained him until he found out it wasn't cancer at all. He had the lumps removed and there has never been a problem since.

Remember, however, that even though we pray and have faith, the outcome and timing are God's decisions. He says there is "a time to heal" (Ecclesiastes 3:3). If you pray for healing and nothing happens, don't beat yourself up for it. God sometimes uses a man's physical ailments to get his attention so He can speak to him. Keep praying, but know God's decision is the bottom line.

The same is true when praying that God will save someone's life. We don't have the final say over anyone's hour of death. The Bible says there is "a time to die" (Ecclesiastes 3:2), and we are not the ones who decide that, God does. And we must accept it. We can pray, but *He* determines the outcome. We have to give Him that privilege without resenting, faulting, or getting angry at Him. Pray for your husband's health, but leave it in God's hands.

Prayer

Lord, I pray for Your healing touch on (husband's name). Make every part of his body function the way You designed it to. Wherever there is anything out of balance, set it in perfect working order. Heal him of any disease, illness, injury, infirmity, or weakness. Strengthen his body to successfully endure his workload, and when he sleeps may he wake up completely rested, rejuvenated and refreshed. Give him a strong heart that doesn't fail. I don't want him to have heart failure at any time.

I pray that he will have the desire to take care of his body, to eat the kind of food that brings health, to get regular exercise, and avoid anything that would be harmful to him. Help him to understand that his body is Your temple and he should care for it as such (1 Corinthians 3:16). I pray that he will present it as a living sacrifice, holy and acceptable to You (Romans 12:1).

When he is ill, I pray You will sustain him and heal him. Fill him with your joy to give him strength. Specifically, I pray for (mention any area of concern). Give him faith to say. "'O Lᴏʀᴅ my God, I cried out to You, and You healed me' [Psalm 30:2]. Thank You, Lord, that You are my Healer." I pray that my husband will live a long and healthy life and when death does come, may it be accompanied by peace and not unbearable suffering and agony. Thank You, Lord, that You will be there to welcome him into Your presence, and not a moment before Your appointed hour.

POWER TOOLS

Bless the Lᴏʀᴅ, O my soul, and forget not all His benefits: who forgives all your iniquities, who heals all your diseases.

Psᴀʟᴍ 103:2,3

They cried out to the Lᴏʀᴅ in their trouble, and He saved them out of their distresses. He sent His word and healed them, and delivered them from their destructions.

Psᴀʟᴍ 107:19,20

I have heard your prayer, I have seen your tears; surely I will heal you.

2 Kɪɴɢs 20:5

Your light shall break forth like the morning, your healing shall spring forth speedily, and your righteousness shall go before you; the glory of the Lᴏʀᴅ shall be your rear guard.

Isᴀɪᴀʜ 58:8

I will heal them and reveal to them the abundance of peace and truth.

Jᴇʀᴇᴍɪᴀʜ 33:6

CHAPTER TWELVE

His Protection

How many times have we heard stories about men who were on the battlefield and at the very moment when they were in the greatest danger, they experienced miraculous deliverance, only to learn later that someone back home was praying at that same moment? Our husbands are on the battlefield every day. There are dangers everywhere. Only God knows what traps the enemy has laid to bring accidents, diseases, evil, violence, and destruction into our lives. Few places are completely safe anymore, including your own home. But God has said that even though "the wicked watches the righteous, and seeks to slay him, the LORD will not leave him in his hand" (Psalm 37:32,33). He promises that He will be "a shield to those who put their trust in Him" (Proverbs 30:5). He can even be a shield to someone we pray about because of *our* faith.

I have always prayed for my husband and children to be safe while traveling in cars. But one morning I got a call from Michael shortly after he left the house to take our young son to school.

"We've just had an accident," he said, "but Christopher and I are fine."

I drove immediately to where they were, thanking God all the way for protecting them just as I had prayed for years. When I arrived and saw the condition of the car, I completely fell apart. Michael's little sports car, which I was never thrilled about his driving, had been broadsided by a much larger car and pushed into a concrete barrier at the side of the road. There was so much destruction to the little car that it was later considered a total loss by the insurance company. The only way to explain why neither of them were hurt had to be the protecting hand of God. They did have bruises on their chests and shoulders from the seat belts, but they could have been injured far worse or even killed. I firmly believe that the Lord answered my prayers for protection on my family. (I'm still waiting for Him to answer the ones about my husband not buying any more sports cars.)

My prayer group and I regularly pray for our husbands to be safe in planes, cars, the workplace, or walking down the street. We don't even have to think of all the specific dangers, we just ask the Lord to protect them from harm. God promises to "give His angels charge over you, to keep you in all your ways. In their hands they shall bear you up, lest you dash your foot against a stone" (Psalm 91:11,12). But accidents do happen, even to godly people, and when they do they are sudden and unexpected. That's why prayer for your husband's protection needs to be frequent and ongoing. You never know when it might be needed in the battlefield. And if something happens, you'll have the comfort of knowing you've invited God's presence and power into the midst of it.

Prayer

Lord, I pray that You would protect <u>(husband's name)</u> from any accidents, diseases, dangers, or evil influences. Keep him safe, especially in cars and planes. Hide him from violence and the plans of evil people. Wherever he walks, secure his steps. Keep him on Your path so that his feet don't slip (Psalm 17:5). If his foot does slip, hold him up by Your mercy (Psalm 94:18). Give him the wisdom and discretion that will help him walk safely and not fall into danger (Proverbs 3:21-23). Be his fortress, strength, shield, and stronghold (Psalm 18:2,3). Make him to dwell in the shadow of Your wings (Psalm 91:1-2). Be his rock, salvation, and defense, so that he will not be moved or shaken (Psalm 62:6). I pray that even though bad things may be happening all around him, they will not come near him (Psalm 91:7). Save him from any plans of the enemy that seek to destroy his life (Psalm 103:4). Preserve his going out and his coming in from this time forth and even forevermore (Psalm 121:8).

POWER TOOLS

He who dwells in the secret place of the Most High shall abide under the shadow of the Almighty. I will say of the LORD, "He is my refuge and my fortress; my God, in Him I will trust."
PSALM 91:1-2

In the time of trouble He shall hide me in His pavilion; in the secret place of His tabernacle He shall hide me; He shall set me high upon a rock.
PSALM 27:5

Yea, though I walk through the valley of the shadow
of death, I will fear no evil; for You are with me; Your
rod and Your staff, they comfort me.
PSALM 23:4

The LORD is my rock and my fortress and my
deliverer; my God, my strength, in whom I will trust;
my shield and the horn of my salvation, my stronghold. I will call upon the LORD, who is worthy to be
praised; so shall I be saved from my enemies.
PSALM 18:2,3

Show Your marvelous lovingkindness by Your right
hand, O You who save those who trust in You from
those who rise up against them. Keep me as the apple
of Your eye; hide me under the shadow of Your wings.
PSALM 17:7,8

His Trials

Everyone goes through hard times. It's nothing to be ashamed of. Sometimes our prayers help us to avoid them. Sometimes not. It's the attitude we have when we go through them that matters most. If we are filled with anger and bitterness, or insist on complaining and blaming God, things tend to turn out badly. If we go through them with thankfulness and praise to God, He promises to bring good things despite them. He says to "count it all joy when you fall into various trials, knowing that the testing of your faith produces patience" (James 1:2,3).

A wife's prayers for her husband during these times may not change some of the things he must go through. After all, if we never suffered anything, what kind of shallow, compassionless, impatient people would we be? But prayer can help him maintain a positive outlook of gratitude, hope, patience, and peace in the midst of it, and keep him from reaping the penalty of a wrong response.

My friend, Jan, watched her husband, Dave, hover near death as a result of being bitten by a poisonous spider. It was a terrifying time for both of them and the trial lasted for well over a year as he struggled to rise above each new physical problem that happened as a result. On top of that they had just moved to a new state, away from family, friends, and church, and they suffered financially because of the enormous medical bills. There was every reason to be angry and bitter, but they never allowed themselves to stop praying, praising God, and looking to Him as their source.

Through countless tears and fears of her own, Jan fervently prayed that Dave would not get discouraged in the battle, but be able to stand strong through it. God sustained them, Dave did recover, and they have become two of the richest people in the Lord one could ever hope to meet. Not only that, but their three children are all strong believers who use their enormous talents to glorify God. Dave became a music pastor at a church where he and Jan now have a highly successful ministry. Their lives are a testimony to the goodness of the Lord, and I believe that the manner in which they went through this trial has a lot to do with where they are today.

Whether it feels like it or not, when we serve God, His love attends every moment of our lives—even the toughest, loneliest, most painful, and desperate. He is always there in our midst, working things out for good when we pray and look to Him to do so. "We know that all things work together for good to those who love God, to those who are the called according to His purpose" (Romans 8:28). His purpose for our trials is often to bring us humbly before Him to experience a breaking in our independent self-sufficiency and grow us up into compassionate, patient, spiritually strong, God-glorifying people. He uses these situations to teach us how to trust that He loves and cares for us enough to get us through the tough times.

I can't think of any trial that my husband or I have gone through that didn't grow us deeper in the things of God, even though it was miserable to endure at the time and we had little appreciation of where we were headed. But as we prayed through every rough spot, we found our faith growing and our walk with God deepening. And when our attitudes were right, so did our love for one another.

If your husband is going through a difficult time, carry it in prayer, but don't carry the burden. Even though you may want to, don't try to take away his load and make it yours. That will ultimately leave him feeling weak or like a failure. Besides, God doesn't want you doing *His* job. He doesn't want you trying to be the Holy Spirit to your husband. Even though it hurts to see him struggle and you want to fix it, you can't. You can pray, encourage, and support, but God uses trials for His purpose and you must stay out of His way.

If your husband feels crushed under the weight of such things as financial strain, illness, disability, loss of work, problems with the children, marital strife, catastrophes, disasters in the home, or strained relationships, invite the Holy Spirit to move into his circumstances and transform them. Remind your husband of the bigger picture: our suffering will seem like nothing compared to the glory of God worked in us, if we have the right reactions in the midst of the struggle. "For I consider that the sufferings of this present time are not worthy to be compared with the glory which shall be revealed in us" (Romans 8:18). Encourage him to say, "I can do all things through Christ who strengthens me" (Philippians 4:13).

Pray that your husband will be able to press in closer to God until he knows that nothing can separate him from His love—not what he is going through now and not what will happen in the future. "For I am persuaded that neither death nor life, nor angels nor principalities nor powers, nor things present nor things to come, nor height nor depth, nor any other created thing, shall be able to separate us from the love of God which is in Christ Jesus our Lord" (Romans 8:38,39). If nothing can separate him from the love of God, then no matter how bad it gets, he always has hope.

Trials can be a purifying fire and a cleansing water. You don't want your husband to get burned or drowned; you want him to get refined and renewed. God has promised that "in all these things we are more than conquerors through Him who loved us" (Romans 8:37). "He who endures to the end shall be saved" (Matthew 24:13). It's the determination of your husband to stand strong in faith and wait for God to answer his prayers that will save him from the heat and keep him afloat.

Prayer

Lord, You alone know the depth of the burden my husband carries. I may understand the specifics, but You have measured the weight of it on his shoulders. I've not come to minimize what You are doing in his life, for I know You work great things in the midst of trials. Nor am I trying to protect him from what he must face. I only want to support him so that he will get through this battle as the winner.

God, You are our refuge and strength, a very present help in trouble (Psalm 46:1). You have invited us to "come boldly to the throne of grace, that we may obtain mercy and find grace to help in time of need" (Hebrews 4:16). I come before Your throne and ask for grace for my husband. Strengthen his heart for this battle and give him patience to wait on You (Psalm 27:1-4). Build him up so that no matter what happens he will be able to stand strong through it. Help him to be always "rejoicing in hope, patient in tribulation, continuing steadfastly in prayer" (Romans 12:12). Give him endurance to run the race and not give up, for You have said that "a righteous man may fall seven times and rise again" (Proverbs 24:16). Help him to remember that "the steps of a good man are ordered by the LORD, and He delights in his way. Though he fall, he shall not be utterly cast down; for the LORD upholds him with His hand" (Psalm 37:23,24).

I pray he will look to You to be his "refuge until these calamities have passed by" (Psalm 57:1). May he learn to wait on You because "those who wait on the LORD shall renew their strength; they shall mount up with wings like eagles, they shall run and not be weary, they shall walk and not faint" (Isaiah 40:31). I pray that he will find his strength in You and as he cries out to You, You will hear him and save him out of all his troubles (Psalm 34:6).

POWER TOOLS

You have been grieved by various trials, that the genuineness of your faith, being much more precious than gold that perishes, though it is tested by fire, may be found to praise, honor, and glory at the revelation of Jesus Christ.

1 PETER 1:6,7

Cast your burden on the LORD, and He shall
sustain you; He shall never permit the
righteous to be moved.

PSALM 55:22

As for me, I will call upon God, and the LORD shall
save me. Evening and morning and at noon I will
pray, and cry aloud, and He shall hear my voice. He
has redeemed my soul in peace from the battle
that was against me.

PSALM 55:16-18

You, who have shown me great and severe troubles,
shall revive me again, and bring me up again from
the depths of the earth. You shall increase my greatness, and comfort me on every side.

PSALM 71:20,21

CHAPTER FOURTEEN

His Integrity

Integrity is not what you *appear* to be when all eyes are on you. It's who you *are* when no one is looking. It's a level of morality below which you never fall, no matter what's happening around you. It's a high standard of honesty, truthfulness, decency, and honor that is never breached. It's doing for others the way you would want them to do for you.

A man of integrity says something and means it. He doesn't play verbal games so you never really know where he stands. He knows to let his "Yes" be "Yes" and his "No" be "No." "For whatever is more than these is from the evil one" (Matthew 5:37). He will not play both sides of the fence to please everyone. His goal is to please God and do what is right. A man can be highly esteemed among men but an abomination to God (Luke 16:15).

A man of integrity "swears to his own hurt and does not change" (Psalm 15:4). He will keep his word even if it costs him something to do so. When placed in a possibly compromising situation, he will continue to stand strong in what he believes. Above all, he is a man of truth; you can depend on his solid honesty. A man "who walks with integrity walks securely" (Proverbs 10:9), because his integrity guides him and brings him into the presence of God (Psalm 41:12).

My husband is a man of integrity who has had to take a stand a number of times against things he believed were wrong. It often cost him a great deal. I've always prayed for him to do the right thing, but not because he wouldn't have done it without me. He surely would have. However, my prayers supported him as he faced opposition and helped him to stand strong through it. The Bible says, "The righteous man walks in his integrity; his children are blessed after him" (Proverbs 20:7). Whether my children fully recognize it or not, they will receive a heritage from their father's adherence to the principles of high moral integrity. There are blessings they will enjoy because of the kind of man he is. I pray they will pass those on to *their* children.

Integrity happens in the heart. Therefore, being a man of integrity is something your husband must *choose* to do on his own. But you can prayerfully help him fight the enemy that seeks to snare him, blind him, and keep him from making that decision. Even when he makes the right choice, there will be a negative reaction to it in the realm of evil. Your prayers can help shield him from anything that causes him to doubt and waver, and give him strength to do what's right—even when no one's looking.

Prayer

Lord, I pray that You would make my husband a man of integrity, according to Your standards. Give him strength to say "Yes" when he should say "Yes," and courage to say "No" when he should say "No." Enable him to stand for what he knows is right and not waver under pressure from the world. Don't let him be a man who is "always learning and never able to come to a knowledge of the truth" (2 Timothy 3:7). Give him, instead, a teachable spirit that is willing to listen to the voice of wisdom and grow in Your ways.

Make him a man who lives by truth. Help him to walk with Your Spirit of truth at all times (John 16:13). Be with him to bear witness to the truth so that in times of pressure he will act on it with confidence (1 John 1:8,9). Where he has erred in this and other matters, give him a heart that is quick to confess his mistakes. For You have said in Your Word, "If we say that we have no sin, we deceive ourselves, and the truth is not in us. If we confess our sins, He is faithful and just to forgive us our sins and to cleanse us from all unrighteousness" (1 John 1:8,9). Don't let him be deceived. Don't let him live a lie in any way. Bind mercy and truth around his neck and write them on the tablet of his heart so he will find favor and high esteem in the sight of God and man (Proverbs 3:3,4).

POWER TOOLS

Better is the poor who walks in his integrity than one perverse in his ways, though he be rich.
PROVERBS 28:6

The integrity of the upright will guide them, but the perversity of the unfaithful will destroy them.
PROVERBS 11:3

Judge me, O LORD, according to my righteousness,
and according to my integrity within me.
PSALM 7:8

Vindicate me, O LORD, for I have walked in my
integrity. I have also trusted in the LORD;
I shall not slip.
PSALM 26:1

Let integrity and uprightness preserve me,
for I wait for You.
PSALM 25:21

CHAPTER FIFTEEN

His Reputation

A good reputation is a fragile thing, especially in this day of rapid communication and mass media. Just being in the wrong place at the wrong time can ruin a person's life.

A reputation is not something to be taken lightly. A good name is to be chosen over great riches (Proverbs 22:1) and is better than the "precious ointment" (Ecclesiastes 7:1). It's something to value and protect. A person who doesn't value his reputation may someday desire credibility and not find it. Our reputations can be ruined by wrong things we do, by the people with whom we are associated, or by disparaging words spoken about us. In all three cases, evil is involved. One unfortunate court case, a significant round of gossip, an evil influence, an unflattering newspaper article, or fifteen minutes of notoriety can destroy everything a man has worked for all his life. Prayer is our only defense.

The times my husband was most concerned about his reputation was when he or someone else had been misquoted in a newspaper article as saying something that wasn't true. Because we knew how damaging these kinds of things can be, we always called people we thought would be most affected by any misquotes and told them what the truth was. Of course we couldn't possibly call everyone, so we prayed that those we did call would be enough and that God would put an end to it. As it turned out, what could have been wildfires totally burned themselves out within a day or two. It could easily have gone the other way and consumed us. I am certain it was the power of God in response to prayer that kept us protected.

A virtuous wife, the Bible says, has a husband who is respected. He is "known in the gates, when he sits among the elders of the land" (Proverbs 31:23). Does that just happen? Is every virtuous wife guaranteed a husband with a good reputation? Or does she have something to do with that? It's true that a man gets a certain amount of respect for having a good wife, but I believe one of the good things she does is pray for him and his reputation.

Prayer for your husband's reputation should be an ongoing process. However, keep in mind that he has a free will. If he is not sensitive to the leading of the Holy Spirit, he may still choose to go his own way and get into trouble. If something like that happens or has already happened to tarnish his reputation, pray for God to redeem the situation and bring good out of it. He can do that, too.

Prayer

Lord, I pray that (husband's name) will have a reputation that is untarnished. I know that a man is often valued "by what others say of him" (Proverbs 27:21), so I pray that he will be respected in our town and people will speak highly of him. You've said in Your Word that "a curse without cause shall not alight" (Proverbs 26:2). I pray that there would never be any reason for bad things to be said of him. Keep him out of legal entanglements. Protect us from lawsuits and criminal proceedings. Deliver him from his enemies, O God. Defend him from those who rise up to do him harm (Psalm 59:1). Fight against those who fight against him (Psalm 35:1). In You, O Lord, we put our trust. Let us never be put to shame (Psalm 71:1). If You are for us, who can be against us (Romans 8:31)?

Your Word says that "a good tree cannot bear bad fruit, nor can a bad tree bear good fruit. Every tree that does not bear good fruit is cut down and thrown into the fire" (Matthew 7:18,19). I pray that my husband will bear good fruit out of the goodness that is within him, and that he will be known by the good that he does. May the fruits of honesty, trustworthiness, and humility sweeten all his dealings so that his reputation will never be spoiled.

Preserve his life from the enemy, hide him from the secret counsel of the wicked. Pull him out of any net which has been laid for him (Psalm 31:4). Keep him safe from the evil of gossiping mouths. Where there has been ill spoken of him, touch the lips of those who speak it with Your refining fire. Let the responsibility of those involved be revealed. Let them be ashamed and brought to confusion who seek to destroy his life; let them be driven backward and brought to dishonor who wish him evil (Psalm 40:14). May he trust in You and not be afraid of what man can do to him (Psalm 56:11). For You have said whoever believes in You will not be put to shame (Romans 10:11). Lead him, guide him, and be his mighty fortress and hiding place. May his light so shine before men that they see his good works and glorify You, Lord (Matthew 5:16).

POWER TOOLS

Hide me from the secret plots of the wicked, from the rebellion of the workers of iniquity, who sharpen their tongue like a sword, and bend their bows to shoot their arrows—bitter words.

PSALM 64:2,3

Do not let me be ashamed, O LORD, for I have called upon You; let the wicked be ashamed; let them be silent in the grave. Let the lying lips be put to silence, which speak insolent things proudly and contemptuously against the righteous.

PSALM 31:17,18

Blessed are you when they revile and persecute you, and say all kinds of evil against you falsely for My sake. Rejoice and be exceedingly glad, for great is your reward in heaven, for so they persecuted the prophets who were before you.

MATTHEW 5:11,12

Do not go hastily to court; for what will you do in the end, when your neighbor has put you to shame? Debate your case with your neighbor, and do not disclose the secret to another; lest he who hears it expose your shame, and your reputation be ruined.

PROVERBS 25:8-10

Who shall bring a charge against God's elect? It is
God who justifies. Who is he who condemns?
It is Christ who died, and furthermore is also risen,
who is even at the right hand of God, who also
makes intercession for us.

ROMANS 8:33,34

CHAPTER SIXTEEN

His Priorities

$\mathcal{M}$en have many different ideas about what their priorities should be. But every wife feels she should be at the top of her husband's list—right there under God. I've found, however, that if a wife wants her husband's priorities to be in that kind of order, she has to make sure *hers* are in that order as well. In other words, if you want your husband to place you as a priority over work, children, friends, and activities, you need to do the same for him. If God and spouse aren't clearly top priorities in *your* life, your husband will have less incentive to make them so in his.

I know very well about the struggle to keep a right order of priorities, especially if there are little ones in the picture. Children's needs are immediate and urgent and you're the one to take care of them. A husband, after all, is an adult and hopefully can take care of himself. Even if there are no children, it's possible to be consumed by work, home, friends, projects, interests, and activities. It's hard, in the midst of everything that occupies your time and attention, not to allow your husband to fall down on the list—or at least feel as though he has.

Fortunately, priorities don't always have to do with the total amount of time spent on them, otherwise anyone with a forty-hour work week would be putting God second to their job unless he or she was praying at least eight hours a day. And there is no way a wife can give as much time to her husband as she does to a young child without neglecting the child. When it comes to your husband, it's not so much a matter of how much time you take, but that you *do* take time to make him feel like he is a priority.

Just greeting him first thing in the morning with a smile and a hug can make him feel he's important to you. So is asking him, "Is there anything you want me to do for you today?" (And then when he tells you, remember to do it.) Also, let him know you are praying for him and ask what he specifically wants you to pray about. Even checking in with him periodically in the midst of the many other things you are doing assures him he's still at the top of your list.

Priorities have to do with the position in the heart. Planning times for just the two of you—a date, a night or two away, a dinner alone, time in the home without any children or friends—communicates to him that he is a priority in your heart. If you want your husband to love *you* more, you need to love *him* more. It always works, especially if you're praying about it as well.

If you feel that you just don't have the time and energy to put your husband first and still do all that's expected of you, ask God for a fresh filling of His Holy Spirit. Seek Him first and He will help you get your priorities in order. If your schedule doesn't allow time to be with God and draw on His strength, then rework your priorities and make a new schedule. The old one is not working.

In the business my husband is in, we often see people experience success quickly. The problem with that is a spirit of lust for *more* success, *more* power, and *more* wealth usually comes along with it. When these people don't make a special effort to keep their priorities in order, their pride guides them, and they buy into its lure. They slip into overdrive, leaving God, family, church, and friends in their dust. When these shooting stars come back to earth, the landing is often hard. We don't want that to happen, even on a small scale, to our husbands. Pray for your husband to always put God first, you second, and children third. Then, no matter what else is going on in his life, his priorities will be in order and there will be greater peace and happiness ahead for both of you.

Prayer

God, I proclaim You Lord over my life. Help me to seek You first every day and set my priorities in perfect order. Reveal to me how to properly put my husband before children, work, family, friends, activities, and interests. Show me what I can do right now to demonstrate to him that he has this position in my heart. Mend the times I have caused him to doubt that. Tell me how to prioritize everything so that whatever steals life away, or has no lasting purpose, will not occupy my time.

I pray for my husband's priorities to be in perfect order as well. Be Lord and Ruler over his heart. Help him to choose a simplicity of life that will allow him to have time alone with You, Lord, a place to be quiet in Your presence every day. Speak to him about making Your Word, prayer, and praise a priority. Enable him to place me and our children in greater prominence in his heart than career, friends, and activities. I pray he will seek You first and submit his all to You, for when he does I know the other pieces of his life will fit together perfectly.

POWER TOOLS

Seek first the kingdom of God and His
righteousness, and all these things shall
be added to you.
MATTHEW 6:33

Let each of you look out not only for his own
interests, but also for the interests of others.
PHILIPPIANS 2:4

No one can serve two masters; for either he will hate
the one and love the other, or else he will be loyal to
the one and despise the other.
MATTHEW 6:24

The kingdom of heaven is like a merchant seeking
beautiful pearls, who, when he had found one
pearl of great price, went and sold all that he
had and bought it.
MATTHEW 13:45,46

You shall worship the LORD your God, and Him
only you shall serve.
MATTHEW 4:10

CHAPTER SEVENTEEN

His Relationships

Isolation is not healthy. We all need the influence of good people to keep us on the right path. Every married couple should have at least two strong believing couples with whom they can share encouragement, strength, and the richness of their lives. Being around such people is edifying, enriching, balancing, and fulfilling, and it helps us keep perspective when things seem to grow out of proportion. Having the positive qualities of other people rub off on us is the best thing for a marriage.

I remember one time when Michael and I had an argument just before we were to be at another couple's house for dinner. On the drive there we sat in stiffened silence, and all I could think about was how we could possibly get through the evening gracefully without making the other couple very uncomfortable. When we arrived, the warmth, love, and rich godliness we felt from them infected our thoughts and emotions. Soon we were laughing and talking and having a great time, forgetting about what had transpired previously. What those two people had was not just a "let the good times roll" party spirit. It was the joy of the Lord, and it wore off on us.

We've witnessed the exact same thing happen in reverse. There have been numerous instances when a couple in the midst of marital strife came to our house for dinner and went away with peace in their hearts. One particular couple even called just before they were to arrive—when the dinner was completely ready—to say that they'd just had a bad argument and couldn't possibly be enjoyable guests. I told them we completely understood, having experienced the same thing ourselves, but that we wanted them to come, even if they sat in silence all night. "Besides, you do need to eat," I said. "If necessary you can sit at opposite ends of the table." It took some persuading, but they came and it turned out to be a highly enjoyable evening for all. We even ended up laughing about what transpired earlier and they left hand in hand.

Being good friends with godly people who love the Lord doesn't just happen by chance. We must pray that such people will come into our lives. And then when we find them, we should continue to cover the relationships in prayer. We should also pray the bad influences away. The Bible says we must "not be unequally yoked together with unbelievers" (2 Corinthians 6:14). This doesn't mean we can never be around anyone who isn't a Christian, but our closest, most influential relationships should be with people who know and love the Lord, or there will be consequences. "The righteous should choose his friends carefully, for the way of the wicked leads them astray" (Proverbs 12:26). That's why it's very important to have a church home where it's possible to meet the kind of people you need. Choose to be around the highest quality people you can, the ones whose hearts are aimed toward God.

Pray also for your husband to have godly male friends. And when he finds them, give him time to be with them without criticism. Those friends will refine him. "As iron sharpens iron, so a man sharpens the countenance of his friend" (Proverbs 27:17). They will be a good influence. "Ointment and perfume delight the heart, and the sweetness of a man's friend does so by hearty counsel" (Proverbs 27:9). Of course if it becomes obsessive, pray for balance.

After we had children, Michael worked every day and night during the week and on the weekends he spent all his spare time on the golf course or at baseball and football games with his friends. There were many bitter arguments about that, but no changes happened until I started praying that *God* would convict him and turn his heart toward home. God did a much better job than I ever could have.

Often men have fewer close friends than women because of the way their time is consumed with establishing their careers. They don't take the necessary steps to develop close friendships like we do. That's where prayer can make a difference. Even if your husband is not a believer, you can still pray for him to have godly friends. A close friend of mine has a husband who doesn't know the Lord and we have prayed many times for him to have godly friends and be in contact with believers where he works. God has now brought so many strong Christians into his life that we laugh about how the Lord has him surrounded.

Pray about *all* of your husband's relationships. He needs to have good relationships with his parents, brothers, sisters, aunts, uncles, cousins, coworkers, and neighbors. Pray that none of his relationships be marred by his inability to forgive. A husband who is tortured with unforgiveness is not a pretty sight.

Prayer

Lord, I pray for (husband's name) to have good, godly male friends with whom he can openly share his heart. May they be trustworthy men of wisdom who will speak truth into his life and not just say what he wants to hear (Proverbs 28:23). Give him the discernment to separate himself from anyone who will not be a good influence (1 Corinthians 5:13). Show him the importance of godly friendships and help me encourage him to sustain them. Give us believing married couples with whom we can feel comfortable sharing our lives.

I pray for strong, peaceful relationships with each of his family members, neighbors, acquaintances, and coworkers. Today I specifically pray for his relationship with (name of person). Inspire open communication and mutual acceptance between them. Let there be reconciliation where there has been estrangement. Work peace into anything that needs to be worked out.

I pray that in his heart he will honor his father and mother so that he will live long and be blessed in his life (Exodus 20:12). Enable him to be a forgiving person and not carry grudges or hold things in his heart against others. Lord, You've said in Your Word that "he who hates his brother is in darkness and walks in darkness, and does not know where he is going, because the darkness has blinded his eyes" (1 John 2:11). I pray that my husband would never be blinded by the darkness of unforgiveness, but continually walk in the light of forgiveness. May he not judge or show contempt for anyone but remember that "we shall all stand before the judgment seat of Christ" (Romans

14:10). Enable him to love his enemies, bless those who curse him, do good to those who hate him, and pray for those who spitefully use him and persecute him (Matthew 5:44). I pray that I will be counted as his best friend and that our friendship with one another will continue to grow. Show him what it means to be a true friend and enable him to be one.

POWER TOOLS

Let us consider one another in order to stir up love and good works, not forsaking the assembling of ourselves together, as is the manner of some, but exhorting one another.
HEBREWS 10:24,25

If you bring your gift to the altar, and there remember that your brother has something against you, leave your gift there before the altar, and go your way. First be reconciled to your brother, and then come and offer your gift.
MATTHEW 5:23,24

If we walk in the light as He is in the light, we have fellowship with one another.
1 JOHN 1:7

Take heed to yourselves. If your brother sins against you, rebuke him; and if he repents, forgive him. And if he sins against you seven times in a day, and seven times in a day returns to you, saying, "I repent," you shall forgive him.
LUKE 17:3,4

A new commandment I give to you, that you love
one another; as I have loved you, that you also love
one another. By this all will know that you are My
disciples, if you have love for one another.

JOHN 13:34,35

CHAPTER EIGHTEEN

His Fatherhood

When I asked my husband to share with me his deepest fears, one of the things he mentioned was the fear of not being a good father. "I believe it's something men in general tend to fear," he said. "We get so caught up in doing what we do in our work that we're afraid we haven't done enough with our children. Or we're afraid we haven't done it *well* enough, or we're missing something. It becomes even more of a problem with teenagers. We fear we can't communicate with them because we'll be perceived as old and irrelevant."

I was touched by his perspective and resolved to pray for him to be a good father. I believe my prayers made a difference because I saw him become more patient with our children and less insecure about his own parenting skills. He grew increasingly relaxed and able to enjoy them. He became less guilt-ridden or angry when it was necessary to discipline them and more able to speak wisdom powerfully into their lives. He now sees that any flaw in our children is not necessarily a reflection of his value as a father.

Thoughts of failure and inadequacy are what cause so many fathers to give up, leave, become overbearing from trying too hard, or develop a passive attitude and fade into the background of their children's lives. It can be especially overwhelming to a man who already feels like a failure in other areas. Mothers get overwhelmed with feelings of inadequacy, too, but only the most deeply disturbed ever abandon, ignore, or hurt their children. That's because we have the opportunity from the moment of conception to pour so much of ourselves into our children's lives. We carry them in the womb, we nurse and nurture them as newborns, we guide and teach and love them so much that we have a full sense of bonding from the start. Fathers don't have that privilege and often feel they are starting on the outside, trying to work their way in. If they are also spending a great amount of time and energy trying to establish their careers, they can easily feel hopelessly removed and ineffectual. Our prayers can help redeem this situation.

Have you ever had someone pray for you when you couldn't think straight, and after they prayed you had complete clarity and vision? I've experienced that countless times. I believe this is what can happen for our husbands when we pray about their parenting. If they are tortured with doubt and burdened by a sense of responsibility, we can minimize these feelings with our prayers. Prayer can help them gain a clear perspective of what it means to be a good father, and open the door to Holy Spirit guidance on how to handle the parenting challenges that arise.

My husband recalled a specific incident where he knew my prayers for him regarding his fatherhood had made a big difference. It happened when our son, Christopher, was about seven and we had caught him in a lie. We knew we had to deal with it, but we wanted a full confession from him along with a repentant heart. Neither was forthcoming at that moment. Michael wanted to teach him a lesson but didn't know what to do, so he asked me to pray. While I was praying, it became very clear to him. As Chris watched, Michael drew a triangle and a picture of Satan, God, and Christopher, one at each of the points. He then described Satan's plan for Chris, and God's plan for Chris. He illustrated how lying was part of Satan's plan that Chris was going along with. He described in detail the ultimate consequences of going along with Satan's plans—which meant traveling on a spectrum away from God—and it shook Christopher up so badly that he broke down and confessed the lie with a completely repentant heart. Michael said he knew that without that clear picture from God he would not have been able to get through to his son with the depth he needed to.

The best way for a man to be a good father is to get to know his heavenly Father and learn to imitate Him. The more time he spends in the Lord's presence, being transformed into His likeness, the better influence he will be when he spends time with his children. He will have a father's heart because he understands *The Father's* heart. This can be difficult if your husband didn't have a good relationship with his earthly father. The way a man relates to his dad will often affect how he relates to his Father God. If he was abandoned by him, he may fear being abandoned by God. If his father was distant or uncaring, he may see God as distant and uncaring. If he doubted his father's love, he may doubt his heavenly Father's love. If he is angry with his father, he may be angry with his Father God as well. Events of the past with regard to his own dad can serve as a barrier that keeps him from truly knowing the Father's love. This will carry over into his relationship with his children.

Pray that your husband grows into a greater understanding of his heavenly Father's love and be healed of any misconceptions he has in his heart and mind about it. Where his father has failed him and he has blamed God, ask the Lord to heal that enormous hurt. The Bible says, "Whoever curses his father or his mother, his lamp will be put out in deep darkness" (Proverbs 20:20). Unless forgiveness happens in his heart for his dad, he will be in the dark as to how to be the best father for his children. His father doesn't have to be alive in order to right that relationship, because it's what is in his own heart regarding his dad that matters. Pray that he will gain a right attitude toward his earthly father so nothing will stand in the way of his relationship with his Father God.

Men don't always realize how important they are to their children. They sometimes feel they are only there to provide materially for them. But the importance of a father's influence can never be underestimated. How he relates to his children will shape their lives for bad or for good. It will change *his* life forever, too. For if he fails as a father, he will always carry that sense of failure with him. If he succeeds, there will be no greater measure of success in his life.

Prayer

Lord, teach __(husband's name)__ to be a good father. Where it was not modeled to him according to Your ways, heal those areas and help him to forgive his dad. Give him revelation of You and a hunger in his heart to really know You as his heavenly Father. Draw him close to spend time in Your presence so he can become more like You, and fully understand Your Father's heart of compassion and love toward him. Grow that same heart in him for his children. Help him to balance mercy, judgment, and instruction the way You do. Though You require obedience, You are quick to acknowledge a repentant heart. Make him that way, too. Show him when to discipline and how. Help him to see that he who loves his child disciplines him promptly (Proverbs 13:24). May he never provoke his "children to wrath, but bring them up in the training and admonition of the Lord" (Ephesians 6:4). I pray we will be united in the rules we set for our children and be in full agreement as to how they are raised. I pray that there will be no strife or argument over how to handle them and the issues that surround their lives.

Give him skills of communication with his children. I pray he will not be stern, hard, cruel, cold, abusive, noncommunicative, passive, critical, weak, uninterested, neglectful, undependable, or uninvolved. Help him instead to be kind, loving, softhearted, warm, interested, affirming, affectionate, involved, strong, consistent, dependable, verbally communicative, understanding, and patient. May he require and inspire his children to honor him as their father so that their lives will be long and blessed.

Lord, I know we pass a spiritual inheritance to our children. Let the heritage he passes on be one rich in the fullness of Your Holy Spirit. Enable him to model clearly a walk of submission to Your laws. May he delight in his children and long to grow them up Your way. Being a good father is something he wants very much. I pray that You would give him the desire of his heart.

POWER TOOLS

Children's children are the crown of old men, and
the glory of children is their father.
PROVERBS 17:6

For whom the LORD loves He corrects, just as a
father the son in whom he delights.
PROVERBS 3:12

The father of the righteous will greatly rejoice, and
he who begets a wise child will delight in him.
PROVERBS 23:24

Correct your son, and he will give you rest; yes, he
will give delight to your soul.
PROVERBS 29:17

I will be a Father to you, and you shall be My sons
and daughters, says the LORD Almighty.
2 CORINTHIANS 6:18

CHAPTER NINETEEN

His Past

Michael was nineteen when he collapsed from nervous exhaustion. He was attending college full time during the day and writing, arranging, playing piano and drums in local clubs in the afternoons and evenings. He had high stress, little sleep, and was rapidly working himself to death. The family doctor suggested he be placed in a nearby mental hospital where he could get the rest he needed. His mother later told me that she *and* the doctor regretted that decision, but at the time they didn't know what else to do. Michael described his two weeks of "rest" there as the most frightening experience of his life. He observed so much strange and horrifying behavior in the other patients that it traumatized him with fear that he might never get out. He went back to college with a less-stressful work schedule, but also great fear.

Throughout the years we've been married, there have been times when he was so overworked and pressured that he experienced that same kind of exhaustion. It always reminded him of what had happened when he was a teenager.

The past would come upon him like a specter and threaten him with the thought, *You're going to end up in a mental hospital again.* It's been at those times, he said, that my prayers for him have meant the most. I always prayed that he would know the truth, and the truth would set him free (John 8:32). I prayed for God to deliver him from his past. This has been a gradual process, but I saw strides forward every time I prayed.

The past should not be a place where we live, but something from which we learn. We are to forget "those things which are behind" and reach "forward to those things which are ahead," and we're to "press toward the goal for the prize of the upward call of God in Christ Jesus" (Philippians 3:13,14). God is a redeemer and a restorer. We need to allow Him to be both. He can redeem the past and restore what was lost. He can make up for the bad things that have happened (Psalm 90:15). We must trust Him to do those things. We can never move out of the present into the future of what God has for us if we cling to and live in the past.

Your husband's past not only affects him, it affects your offspring as well. More is passed down to your children and grandchildren than just the color of your hair and eyes. We can leave a legacy as painful and damaging as the one we experienced ourselves. We can bequeath a heritage of divorce, anger, anxiety, depression, and fear, to name a few. Whatever you and your husband can free yourselves from will mean more freedom for them. As long as you dwell in the past, you not only lose some of what God has for your future, but for your children's future as well.

The events of your husband's past that most affect his life today probably occurred in his childhood. Bad things that happened or good things that *didn't* happen with family members are the most significant. Being labeled in a certain way by a relative or peer carries over into adulthood. Such words as "fat," "stupid," "uncoordinated," "failure," "poor," "loser," "slob," "four-eyes," "slow," or "idiot" take their toll and imprint themselves into the mind and emotions well into adulthood. While no one can pretend the past didn't happen, it's possible to pray that all the effects of it are removed. No one is destined to live with them forever.

God says we are to cry out for deliverance, walk in His ways, proclaim His truth, and then we will find freedom from our past. But sometimes there are *levels* of freedom to go through. Your husband may think he's gotten free of something and it will rear its head again, leaving him feeling like he's right back where he started. Tell him not to be discouraged by that. If he has been walking with the Lord, he is probably moving into a deeper level of liberty that God wants to work in his life. Your prayers will surely gird him for the journey to greater freedom.

Being set free from the past can happen quickly or it can be a step-by-step process, depending on what God is teaching. The problem is, you can't make it happen on your timetable. You have to be patient and pray for as long as it takes to keep the voices of the past at bay so that your husband can make the decision to not listen to them.

Prayer

Lord, I pray that You would enable (husband's name) to let go of his past completely. Deliver him from any hold it has on him. Help him to put off his former conduct and habitual ways of thinking about it and be renewed in his mind

(Ephesians 4:22,23). Enlarge his understanding to know that You make all things new (Revelation 21:5). Show him a fresh, Holy Spirit-inspired way of relating to negative things that have happened. Give him the mind of Christ so that he can clearly discern Your voice from the voices of the past. When he hears those old voices, enable him to rise up and shut them down with the truth of Your Word. Where he has formerly experienced rejection or pain, I pray he not allow them to color what he sees and hears now. Pour forgiveness into his heart so that bitterness, resentment, revenge, and unforgiveness will have no place there. May he regard the past as only a history lesson and not a guide for his daily life. Wherever his past has become an unpleasant memory, I pray You would redeem it and bring life out of it. Bind up his wounds (Psalm 147:3). Restore his soul (Psalm 23:3). Help him to release the past so that he will not live in it, but learn from it, break out of it, and move into the future You have for him.

POWER TOOLS

Do not remember the former things, nor consider the things of old. Behold, I will do a new thing, now it shall spring forth; shall you not know it? I will even make a road in the wilderness and rivers in the desert.

ISAIAH 43:18,19

If anyone is in Christ, he is a new creation; old things have passed away; behold, all things have become new.

2 CORINTHIANS 5:17

Put off, concerning your former conduct, the
old man which grows corrupt according to the
deceitful lusts, and be renewed in the spirit of
your mind, and . . . put on the new man
which was created according to God,
in true righteousness and holiness.
EPHESIANS 4:22-24

Even though our outward man is perishing, yet the
inward man is being renewed day by day.
2 CORINTHIANS 4:16

God will wipe away every tear from their eyes;
there shall be no more death, nor sorrow, nor crying;
and there shall be no more pain, for the former
things have passed away.
REVELATION 21:4

CHAPTER TWENTY

His Attitude

No one wants to be around a person with a bad attitude. Life is hard enough without listening to someone constantly complaining in your ear. I know a man who is so in the habit of being angry and miserable that it is his first reaction to everything—even good news. When great things happen, he finds something to be upset about. Unfortunately, this was modeled to him as a child, so it was probably a learned response. Perhaps no one ever showed him how to enjoy life. But allowing the past to control today is still a choice he makes. Because of that, not only will he never be happy, but neither will those around him. We don't want to be that kind of person, nor do we want to live with one.

Without naming names, let me assure you that I am an expert when it comes to praying for someone with a bad attitude. It took me a long time, however, to stop reacting to the negativity and start praying about it instead. It has paid off, but I'm still perfecting this mode of operation. Every time I prayed for a spirit of joy to arise in this person's heart, I saw visible changes and my reaction was better as well.

An angry, dour, unforgiving, negative person can get that way for various reasons. He *stays* that way because of a stubborn will that refuses to receive God's love. The Bible says we have a choice as to what we will allow into our heart (Psalm 101:4), and whether we will harden it to the love of God or not (Proverbs 28:14). We choose our attitude. We choose to receive the love of the Lord. We permit an attitude of thankfulness to rise in us.

If your husband allows himself to wallow in a consistently bad attitude, it will make a good marriage miserable, and a shaky marriage intolerable. A habit of responding negatively will adversely affect every aspect of his life. Of course you can't rule over your husband's will, but you can pray that his will lines up with God's. Pray that his heart becomes pure, because the Bible promises a person who has a pure heart will see God (Matthew 5:8) and have a cheerful countenance (Proverbs 15:13). (Who doesn't wish her husband could see God and have a cheerful countenance?) Pray for his heart to be filled with praise, thanksgiving, love, and joy, because "a good man out of the good treasure of his heart brings forth good things" (Matthew 12:35). Even if there are no major changes immediately, he is certain to be softened by your prayers. And that, at least, can give *you* a better attitude while you wait for his to improve.

Prayer

Lord, fill <u>(husband's name)</u> with Your love and peace today. May there be a calmness, serenity, and sense of well-being established in him because his life is God-controlled, rather than flesh-controlled. Enable him to walk in his house with a clean and perfect heart before You (Psalm 101:2). Shine the light of Your Spirit upon him and fill him with Your love.

I pray that he will be kind and patient, not selfish or easily provoked. Enable him to bear all things, believe all things, hope all things, and endure all things (1 Corinthians 13:7). Release him from anger, unrest, anxiety, concerns, inner turmoil, strife, and pressure. May he not be broken in spirit because of sorrow (Proverbs 15:13), but enjoy the continual feast of a merry heart (Proverbs 15:15). Give him a spirit of joy and keep him from growing into a grumpy old man. Help him to be anxious for nothing, but give thanks in all things so he can know the peace that passes all understanding. May he come to the point of saying, "I have learned in whatever state I am, to be content" (Philippians 4:11). I say to <u>(husband's name)</u> this day, "The LORD bless you and keep you; the LORD make His face shine upon you, and be gracious to you; the LORD lift up His countenance upon you, and give you peace" (Numbers 6:24-26).

POWER TOOLS

Be anxious for nothing, but in everything by prayer
and supplication, with thanksgiving, let your requests
be made known to God; and the peace of God,
which surpasses all understanding, will guard your
hearts and minds through Christ Jesus.
PHILIPPIANS 4:6,7

Cast away from you all the transgressions which
you have committed, and get yourselves a
new heart and a new spirit.
EZEKIEL 18:31

Whoever has no rule over his own spirit is
like a city broken down, without walls.
PROVERBS 25:28

Though I have the gift of prophecy, and understand
all mysteries and all knowledge, and though I have
all faith, so that I could remove mountains,
but have not love, I am nothing.
1 CORINTHIANS 13:2

Enter into His gates with thanksgiving,
and into His courts with praise.
Be thankful to Him, and bless His name.
PSALM 100:4

CHAPTER TWENTY-ONE

His Marriage

Before I was married, one of the traits I knew I wanted in a husband was an avid disinterest in sports. I detested the thought of being with someone the rest of my life who spent every spare moment on a couch with remote in hand, watching football, baseball, basketball, and golf. One of the things I admired most about Michael when we first started dating was that he never mentioned sports when we were together. In fact, he claimed to be completely bored with them. You can imagine how shocked I was when, several years after we were married, he became not merely interested in sports, but obsessed. If the Chicago Bears lost, so, ultimately, did the rest of the family. When the Cubs won, everyone around him went deaf from his screaming. He wasn't content to see an occasional game; he had to see *every* game. He wasn't a passive observer. He dressed up in Bear T-shirts and Cub hats and jumped up and down. I tried going to games with him, but I found more intrigue in the hot dogs. I tried watching sports with him on TV, but the boredom was excruciating. I gave in to resentment over the fact that it seemed he would rather watch a sporting event than spend time with his family.

It wasn't until years later, when I really started praying about our marriage, that things changed. For some reason unfathomable to me, God didn't take away my husband's interest in sports like I prayed. Instead, He gave me peace and a new perspective on it. We worked out a compromise where I wouldn't pressure him to deny himself sports, if he wouldn't put pressure on me to feign interest. I would not accuse him of tactical deception before we were married, if he would allow me the same courtesy. This may seem like a minor concern in a marriage, but these kinds of things add up and can become pivotal in determining whether a marriage stays together or falls apart.

Praying about all aspects of a marriage keeps the concept of divorce from gaining any hold. So we mustn't neglect the major issues, even if we think they don't apply to us. From the day we were married, I prayed that there would be no divorce or adultery in our future. Although there was no history of either of those in our family backgrounds, divorce and adultery had so saturated our culture and the business we were in that they were almost expected in some circles. I prayed that God would preserve our marriage from any such destruction. He has been faithful to answer those prayers.

Marriage is great when two people enter into it with a mutual commitment to keep it strong no matter what. But often a couple will have preconceived ideas about who the other is and how married life is supposed to be, and then reality hits. That's when their kingdom can become divided. You have to continually pray that any unreal expectations be exposed and all incompatibilities be smoothed out so that you grow together in a spirit of unity, commitment, and a bond of intimacy. Pray that your marriage is a place where two agree so God will be in the midst of it (Matthew 18:19,20). If either of you has been married before, pray that you do not bring any residue from that into your marriage now. Break any ties—good or bad, emotional or spiritual—with any former relationships. You can't move forward into the future if you have a foot stuck in the past.

Don't take your marriage for granted, no matter how great it is. "Let him who thinks he stands take heed lest he fall" (1 Corinthians 10:12). Pray for your marriage to be protected from any person or situation that could destroy it. Ask the Lord to do whatever it takes to keep the marriage intact, even if it means striking one of you with lightning when you think about giving it all up! Pray that God will make your marriage a source of joy and life to both of you, and not a drudgery, a thorn, a dread, an irritation, or a temporary condition.

Prayer

Lord, I pray You would protect our marriage from anything that would harm or destroy it. Shield it from our own selfishness and neglect, from the evil plans and desires of others, and from unhealthy or dangerous situations. May there be no thoughts of divorce or infidelity in our hearts, and none in our future. Set us free from past hurts, memories, and ties from previous relationships, and unrealistic expectations of one another. I pray that there be no jealousy in either of us, or the low self-esteem that precedes that. Let nothing come into our hearts and habits that would threaten the marriage in any way, especially influences like alcohol, drugs, gambling, pornography, lust, or obsessions.

Unite us in a bond of friendship, commitment, generosity, and understanding. Eliminate our immaturity, hostility, or feelings of inadequacy. Help us to make time for one another alone, to nurture and renew the marriage and remind ourselves of the reasons we were married in the first place. I pray that <u>(husband's name)</u> will be so committed to You, Lord, that his commitment to me will not waiver, no matter what storms come. I pray that our love for each other will grow stronger every day, so that we will never leave a legacy of divorce to our children.

POWER TOOLS

Two are better than one, because they have a good reward for their labor. For if they fall, one will lift up his companion. But woe to him who is alone when he falls, for he has no one to help him up.

ECCLESIASTES 4:9,10

Take heed to your spirit, and let none deal treacherously with the wife of his youth. For the LORD God of Israel says that He hates divorce, "for it covers one's garment with violence," says the LORD of hosts. Therefore take heed to your spirit, that you do not deal treacherously.

MALACHI 2:15,16

Marriage is honorable among all, and the bed undefiled; but fornicators and adulterers God will judge.

HEBREWS 13:4

If two lie down together, they will keep warm;
but how can one be warm alone?
ECCLESIASTES 4:11

Now to the married I command, yet not I but the
Lord: A wife is not to depart from her husband. But
even if she does depart, let her remain unmarried or
be reconciled to her husband. And a husband is not
to divorce his wife.
1 CORINTHIANS 7:10,11

CHAPTER TWENTY-TWO

His Emotions

Don used anger to control his family. Each family member was so concerned about his temper that they lived their lives on tiptoe, doing his bidding out of fear rather than love. When his wife, Jenny, learned she not only didn't have to tolerate his anger, but going along with it was disobedient to God, things began to change: "Make no friendship with an angry man, and with a furious man do not go, lest you learn his ways and set a snare for your soul" (Proverbs 22:24,25).

Jenny realized she could still love the man but not approve of his sin, so she began praying fervently for him on a regular basis, both alone and with a group of prayer partners. She prayed he would stop being controlled by his emotions, and instead be controlled by the Holy Spirit. Her prayers not only helped to clear his mind enough for him to see how he had been acting, but they paved the way for him to find strength and courage to alter his behavior. "A gift in secret pacifies anger" (Proverbs 21:14). The best gift a wife can give in secret to calm her husband's anger is to pray for him.

Chad was tormented for years by chronic depression. Although his wife, Marilyn, was an upbeat person, his negative emotions brought her down and made her feel hopeless and depressed just like he was. Then she read about King David's experiences and recognized they described exactly what her husband had been feeling. "My soul is full of troubles, and my life draws near to the grave. I am counted with those who go down to the pit; I am like a man who has no strength" (Psalm 88:3,4). "I am troubled, I am bowed down greatly; I go mourning all the day long". . . . "I am feeble and severely broken; I groan because of the turmoil of my heart" (Psalm 38:6,8).

Marilyn saw that in spite of such deep despair, David found his hope in the Lord and rose above it. "O LORD, You have brought my soul up from the grave; You have kept me alive, that I should not go down to the pit" (Psalm 30:3). "I will be glad and rejoice in Your mercy, for You have considered my trouble; You have known my soul in adversities" (Psalm 31:7). "Draw near to my soul, and redeem it" (Psalm 69:18). She felt God surely had compassion for Chad and it sparked hope in her that prayer was the key to his freedom from the grips of depression.

She told Chad she had committed to pray for him every day and wanted him to keep her informed as to how he was feeling. From the first day, they both noticed that every time she prayed, his spirit lifted. Soon he could no longer deny the power of prayer and he began to pray along with her. He has been steadily improving ever since. His depressions are less frequent now and he is able to rise above them far more quickly. The two of them are committed to seek God for Chad's total freedom.

Anger and depression are but two of the many negative emotions that can torment a man's soul. Often they are only an habitual way of thinking that has been given place over time. Men tend to believe it's part of their character that can't be altered, but these patterns can be broken. Don't stand by and watch your husband be manipulated by his emotions. Freedom may be just a prayer away.

Prayer

Lord, You have said in Your Word that You redeem our souls when we put our trust in You (Psalm 34:22). I pray that <u>(husband's name)</u> would have faith in You to redeem his soul from negative emotions. May he never be controlled by depression, anger, anxiety, jealousy, hopelessness, fear, or suicidal thoughts. Specifically I pray about <u>(area of concern)</u>. Deliver him from this and all other controlling emotions (Psalm 40:17). I know that only You can deliver and heal, but use me as Your instrument of restoration. Help me not to be pulled down with him when he struggles. Enable me instead to understand and have words to say that will bring life.

Free him to share his deepest feelings with me and others who can help. Liberate him to cry when he needs to and not bottle his emotions inside. At the same time, give him the gift of laughter and ability to find humor in even serious situations. Teach him to take his eyes off his circumstances and trust in You, regardless of how he is feeling. Give him patience to possess his soul and the ability to take charge of it (Luke 21:19). Anoint him with "the oil of joy" (Isaiah 61:3), refresh him with Your Spirit, and set him free from negative emotions this day.

~≈~

POWER TOOLS

He who trusts in his own heart is a fool, but
whoever walks wisely will be delivered.
PROVERBS 28:26

The eye of the LORD is on those who fear Him,
on those who hope in His mercy, to deliver
their soul from death.
PSALM 33:18,19

I waited patiently for the LORD; and He inclined to
me, and heard my cry. He also brought me up out of
a horrible pit, out of the miry clay, and set my feet
upon a rock, and established my steps. He has put a
new song in my mouth—praise to our God; many
will see it and fear, and will trust in the LORD.
PSALM 40:1-3

He restores my soul; He leads me in the paths of
righteousness for His name's sake.
PSALM 23:3

The LORD redeems the soul of His servants, and none
of those who trust in Him shall be condemned.
PSALM 34:22

CHAPTER TWENTY-THREE

His Walk

A man's walk is the way he journeys through life—his direction, his focus, the steps he takes. Every day he chooses a path. One path will take him forward. All others will take him back. The way he walks affects every aspect of his being—how he relates to other people, how he treats his family, how people view him, even how he looks. I've seen men who were unattractive by any standard change radically as they learned to walk with the Spirit of God. As His image became imprinted upon theirs, they developed a richness of soul, a glorious purity, and an inner confidence of knowing what direction they were going. This gave them a strength and a sense of purpose that is not only attractive and appealing, it's magnetic.

The Bible reveals much about the kind of walk we should have. We are to walk with *moral correctness* because "no good thing will He withhold from those who walk uprightly" (Psalm 84:11). We are to walk *without fault* because "whoever walks blamelessly will be saved" (Proverbs 28:18). We are to walk with *godly advisors* because "blessed is the man who walks not in the counsel of the ungodly" (Psalm 1:1). We are to walk in *obedience* because "blessed is every one who fears the LORD, who walks in His ways" (Psalm 128:1). We are to walk with *people of wisdom* because "he who walks with wise men will be wise" (Proverbs 13:20). We are to walk with *integrity* because "he who walks with integrity walks securely" (Proverbs 10:9). Most of all, we are to walk a path of holiness. "A highway shall be there, and a road, and it shall be called the Highway of Holiness. The unclean shall not pass over it, but it shall be for others. Whoever walks the road, although a fool, shall not go astray" (Isaiah 35:8). The best part about walking on the Highway of Holiness is that even if we end up doing something dumb, we still won't get thrown off the path.

Debra's husband, Ben, is a godly man who would not be considered a foolish person. However, he did make an impulsive investment of a rather large sum of money which, in hindsight, proved to be a very foolish move. All that money was lost, and more, because there were added expenses as a result. This matter could have destroyed their finances and possibly even their health and their marriage, but because Ben had a solid walk of obedience and holiness before the Lord, they were spared. The fact that he ran ahead on the path and foolishly didn't wait for God's direction got him into trouble, but not to his destruction.

Jesus said there is only one way to get on the right path, one door through which to enter. "I am the way," He says (John 14:6). The way that leads to destruction is wide and broad and many choose to go that route. But "narrow is the gate and difficult is the way which leads to life, and there are few who find it" (Matthew 7:14). Pray for your husband to find it. Pray that he is guided by God's Holy Spirit. Pray that he stays on the path by having faith in God's Word, a heart for obedience, and deep repentance for any actions he takes that are not God's will for his life. Faith and obedience will get him on the Highway of Holiness; walking in the Spirit, and not in the flesh, will keep him there.

God desires that your husband's every step be led by Him (Galatians 5:25), so He can walk with him and grow him into His image. A man who walks with God is very desirable indeed.

Prayer

O Lord, I know the way of man is not in himself; it is not in man who walks to direct his own steps" (Jeremiah 10:23). Therefore, Lord, I pray that *You* would direct my husband's steps. Lead him in *Your* light, teach him *Your* way, so he will walk in *Your* truth. I pray that he would have a deeper walk with You and an ever progressing hunger for Your Word. May Your presence be like a delicacy he never ceases to crave. Lead him on Your path and make him quick to confess when he strays from it. Reveal to him any hidden sin that would hinder him from walking rightly before You. May he experience deep repentance when he doesn't live in obedience to Your laws. Create in him a clean heart and renew a steadfast spirit within him. Don't cast him away from Your presence, and do not take Your Holy Spirit from him (Psalm 51:10,11).

Lord, Your Word says that those who are in the flesh cannot please You (Romans 8:8). So I pray that You will enable <u>(husband's name)</u> to walk in the Spirit and not in the flesh and thereby keep himself "from the paths of the destroyer" (Psalm 17:4). As he walks in the Spirit, may he bear the fruit of the Spirit, which is love, joy, peace, patience, kindness, goodness, faithfulness, gentleness, and self-control (Galatians 5:22,23). Keep him on the Highway of Holiness so that the way he walks will be integrated into every part of his life.

POWER TOOLS

Walk worthy of the calling with which you were called, with all lowliness and gentleness, with long-suffering, bearing with one another in love.

EPHESIANS 4:1,2

He who walks righteously and speaks uprightly, he who despises the gain of oppressions, who gestures with his hands, refusing bribes, who stops his ears from hearing of bloodshed, and shuts his eyes from seeing evil: he will dwell on high; his place of defense will be the fortress of rocks; bread will be given him, his water will be sure.

ISAIAH 33:15,16

Having these promises, beloved, let us cleanse ourselves from all filthiness of the flesh and spirit, perfecting holiness in the fear of God.

2 CORINTHIANS 7:1

LORD, who may abide in Your tabernacle? Who may dwell in Your holy hill? He who walks uprightly, and works righteousness, and speaks the truth in his heart.

PSALM 15:1,2

My eyes shall be on the faithful of the land,
that they may dwell with me; he who walks in
a perfect way, he shall serve me.
PSALM 101:6

CHAPTER TWENTY-FOUR

His Talk

Have you ever observed a man who is all talk and no action? There are some men who spend more time bragging about what they are going to do than actually doing it. They typically never get anywhere. "A dream comes through much activity, and a fool's voice is known by his many words" (Ecclesiastes 5:3). Dreams don't come true when more time is spent talking about them than praying and working toward achieving them.

Have you been around a man who is angry, crass, or ungodly in his speech? His bad language gives his listeners a sick, uncomfortable feeling and they don't want to be around him. "Let all bitterness, wrath, anger, clamor, and evil speaking be put away from you, with all malice" (Ephesians 4:31). The good things of life seem to overlook those who have nothing good coming out of their mouths.

Have you known a man who complains all the time? No matter what's happening, he finds something negative to grumble about. "Do all things without murmuring and disputing, that you may become blameless and harmless, children of God without fault in the midst of a crooked and perverse generation, among whom you shine as lights in the world" (Philippians 2:14,15). Negative words bring negative results and things seldom turn out right for a person who continually uses them.

Are you acquainted with a man who is quick to speak yet does not seriously consider what he is saying? He blurts out words without weighing the effect of them. "The heart of the righteous studies how to answer, but the mouth of the wicked pours forth evil" (Proverbs 15:28). "Do you see a man hasty in his words? There is more hope for a fool than for him" (Proverbs 29:20). Much grief is in the future of anyone who doesn't consider the consequences of his spoken words.

Have you seen a man speak discouragement and pain into someone—a spouse, a child, a friend, a coworker? "Death and life are in the power of the tongue, and those who love it will eat its fruit" (Proverbs 18:21). That man will bring *destruction* into his own life because of it.

Our words can justify us or condemn us (Matthew 12:37). They can bring us joy (Proverbs 15:23), or corrupt and dishonor us (Matthew 15:11). What we say can either build up or break down the soul of whomever we are speaking to (Proverbs 15:4). The consequences of what we speak are so great that our words can lead us to ruin or save our lives (Proverbs 13:3).

Everyone has a choice about what he or she says, and there are rewards for making the right one. "Whoever guards his mouth and tongue keeps his soul from troubles" (Proverbs 21:23). Listen to the way your husband talks. What comes out of his mouth has to do with the condition of his heart. "For out of the abundance of the heart the mouth speaks" (Matthew 12:34). If he complains, speaks negatively, talks like a fool, or speaks words that bring destruction and death into his or anyone else's life, he is suffering from negative heart overflow. Pray for the Holy Spirit to convict his heart, fill it with His love, peace, and joy, and teach him a new way to talk.

Prayer

Lord, I pray Your Holy Spirit would guard my husband's mouth so that he will speak only words that edify and bring life. Help him to not be a grumbler, complainer, a user of foul language, or one who destroys with his words, but be disciplined enough to keep his conversation godly. Your Word says a man who desires a long life must keep his tongue from evil and his lips from speaking deceit (Psalm 34:12-13). Show him how to do that. Fill him with Your love so that out of the overflow of his heart will come words that build up and not tear down. Work that in my heart as well.

May Your Spirit of love reign in the words we speak so that we don't miscommunicate or wound one another. Help us to show each other respect, speak words that encourage, share our feelings openly, and come to mutual agreements without strife. Lord, You've said in Your Word that when two agree, You are in their midst. I pray that the reverse be true as well—that You will be in our midst so that we two can agree. Let the words of our mouths and the meditations of our hearts be acceptable in Your sight, O Lord, our strength and our Redeemer (Psalm 19:14).

POWER TOOLS

Let no corrupt word proceed out of your mouth, but
what is good for necessary edification, that it may impart grace to the hearers.
EPHESIANS 4:29

For every idle word men may speak, they will give
account of it in the day of judgment.
MATTHEW 12:36

Who is the man who desires life, and loves many
days, that he may see good? Keep your tongue from
evil, and your lips from speaking deceit.
PSALM 34:12,13

The words of a wise man's mouth are gracious, but
the lips of a fool shall swallow him up.
ECCLESIASTES 10:12

Those things which proceed out of the mouth come
from the heart, and they defile a man.
MATTHEW 15:18

CHAPTER TWENTY-FIVE

His Repentance

Suzanne prayed every day for years that her husband, Jerry, would stop using drugs. Over and over she caught him doing the same thing. Each time he would confess it, say he was sorry, and swear he wasn't going to do it again. But time and again he fell. She never gave up praying for true repentance to happen in his heart—the kind that turns a man around to walk in a different direction. Unfortunately, Jerry had to learn some hard and painful lessons before God got his attention, but eventually there was a life-changing transformation. Today he is a new man, and together with Suzanne he has a public ministry helping people with similar problems. Suzanne was a praying wife who never stopped believing that God would bring her husband to repentance.

Everyone makes mistakes. That's not the issue. But there is an epidemic in the world today of people who can't admit they did something wrong. God says, "If we confess our sins, He is faithful and just to forgive us our sins and to cleanse us from all unrighteousness" (1 John 1:9). But first we have to be sorry about what we've done.

According to God's way of doing things, there are three steps to changing our behavior. First there is *confession*, which is *admitting* what we did. Next there is *repentance*, which is *being sorry* about what we did. Then there is *asking forgiveness*, which is *being cleansed and released* from what we did. The inability or resistance to do any of these three steps is rooted in pride. A man who can't humble himself to admit he's wrong before God and before man will have problems in his life that never go away. "Do you see a man wise in his own eyes? There is more hope for a fool than for him" (Proverbs 26:12).

Does your husband have trouble confessing his faults? Or is he the kind of person who can say "I'm sorry" twenty times a day, yet the behavior he apologizes for never changes? In either case, he needs a repentant heart. True repentance means having so much remorse over what you've done that you don't do it again. Only God can cause us to see our sin for what it is, and feel about it the same way He does. "The goodness of God leads you to repentance" (Romans 2:4). Repentance is a working of God's grace, and we can pray for it to be worked in our husbands.

Too many men have fallen because of pride and the inability to confess and repent. We see it all the time. We read about it in the newspapers. Unconfessed sin doesn't just go away. It becomes a cancer that grows and suffocates life. Pray for your husband to be convicted of his sin, to humbly confess it before God, then turn from his error and cease to do it. God is "not willing that any should perish but that all should come to repentance" (2 Peter 3:9). This kind of prayer can be very annoying to the one being prayed for, but it's far easier to have God shine His light upon our sin than it is to experience the consequences of it. Your husband will be thankful in the end, even if he won't admit it.

Prayer

Lord, I pray that You would convict my husband of any error in his life. Let there be "nothing covered that will not be revealed, and hidden that will not be known" (Matthew 10:26). Cleanse him from any secret sins and teach him to be a person who is quick to confess when he is wrong (Psalm 19:12). Help him to recognize his mistakes. Give him eyes to see Your truth and ears to hear Your voice. Bring him to full repentance before You. If there is suffering to be done, let it be the suffering of a remorseful heart and not because the crushing hand of the enemy has found an opening into his life through unconfessed sin. Lord, I know that humility must come before honor (Proverbs 15:33). Take away all pride that would cause him to deny his faults and work into his soul a humility of heart so that he will receive the honor You have for him.

POWER TOOLS

If our heart does not condemn us, we have confidence toward God. And whatever we ask we receive from Him, because we keep His commandments and do those things that are pleasing in His sight.

1 JOHN 3:21,22

He who covers his sins will not prosper, but whoever confesses and forsakes them will have mercy.

PROVERBS 28:13

Search me, O God, and know my heart; try me, and know my anxieties; and see if there is any wicked way in me, and lead me in the way everlasting.

PSALM 139:23,24

When I kept silent, my bones grew old through my
groaning all the day long. For day and night Your
hand was heavy upon me; my vitality was turned into
the drought of summer. I acknowledged my sin to
You, and my iniquity I have not hidden. I said, "I will
confess my transgressions to the LORD," and You forgave the iniquity of my sin.

PSALM 32:3-5

A servant of the Lord must not quarrel but be gentle
to all, able to teach, patient, in humility correcting
those who are in opposition, if God perhaps will
grant them repentance, so that they may know the
truth, and that they may come to their senses and
escape the snare of the devil, having been taken
captive by him to do his will.

2 TIMOTHY 2:24-26

CHAPTER TWENTY-SIX

His Deliverance

Melissa was concerned about her husband's attraction to alcohol. Mark wasn't exactly an alcoholic, but he was exhibiting symptoms reminiscent of his father, who *was* an alcoholic. She prayed for a breaking of any similar tendency that may have been passed on to her husband, and she also prayed that their children would not inherit the weakness either. She asked God to protect them all from even the *symptoms* of alcoholism. To this day her husband has not become an alcoholic and her teenagers show no signs of it. She feels the power of God in answer to her prayers has played a major part in keeping them from inheriting this condition.

Stephanie had been married to Jason only a short time before she realized he struggled with a spirit of lust. It wasn't that he didn't love her. He was dealing with the sins of his past—a promiscuous lifestyle from which he had never thoroughly distanced himself or renounced. Once she recognized it as something he was captive to, she prayed for his deliverance. Because he wanted that, too, it wasn't long before he was set free from it.

Everyone needs deliverance at certain times, because there are all kinds of things that can pull us into bondage. God knows this. Why would Jesus have come as the Deliverer if we didn't need one? Why would He have instructed us to pray, "Deliver us from the evil one" (Matthew 6:13) if we didn't need to be? Why does He promise to deliver us from temptation (2 Peter 2:9), the clutches of dangerous people (Psalm 140:1), our self-destructive tendencies (Proverbs 24:11), *all* of our troubles (Psalm 34:17), and death (2 Corinthians 1:10), if He doesn't intend to do it? He is ready and willing. We just have to ask. "Call upon Me in the day of trouble; I will deliver you, and you shall glorify Me" (Psalm 50:15).

Isn't it comforting to know that when we feel imprisoned by the death grip of our circumstances, God hears our cries for freedom? He sees our need. "He looked down from the height of His sanctuary; from heaven the LORD viewed the earth, to hear the groaning of the prisoner, to release those appointed to death" (Psalm 102:19,20). How glorious to embrace the certainty that when there seems to be no way out, God can miraculously lift us up and away from whatever is seeking to devour us (Psalm 25:15). Who doesn't need that?

Even if your husband finds it difficult to admit he needs help—some men feel like failures if they can't do it all themselves—your prayers can still be instrumental in his finding deliverance. You can pray to the Deliverer to set him free from anything that binds him. You can stand strong, through your prayers, against the enemy who seeks to put him into bondage. "Stand fast therefore in the liberty by which Christ has made us free, and do not be entangled again with a yoke of bondage" (Galatians 5:1). The best way I know to stand strong is to put on the whole armor of

God. That's the way I pray for myself and my husband and I have found it to be most effective. Rather than explain it, let me show you how to pray it.

Prayer

Lord, You have said to call upon You in the day of trouble and You will deliver us (Psalm 50:15). I call upon You now and ask that You would work deliverance in my husband's life. Deliver him from anything that binds him. Set him free from (name a specific thing). Deliver him quickly and be a rock of refuge and a fortress of defense to save him (Psalm 31:2). Lift him away from the hands of the enemy (Psalm 31:15).

Bring him to a place of understanding where he can recognize the work of evil and cry out to You for help. If the deliverance he prays for isn't immediate, keep him from discouragement and help him to be confident that You have begun a good work in him and will complete it (Philippians 1:6). Give him the certainty that even in his most hopeless state, when he finds it impossible to change anything, You, Lord, can change everything.

Help him understand that "we do not wrestle against flesh and blood, but against principalities, against powers, against the rulers of the darkness of this age, against spiritual hosts of wickedness in the heavenly places" (Ephesians 6:12). I pray that he will be strong in the Lord and put on the whole armor of God, so he can stand against the wiles of the devil in the evil day. Help him to gird his waist with truth and put on the breastplate of righteousness, having shod

his feet with the preparation of the gospel of peace.
Enable him to take up the shield of faith, with which
to quench all the fiery darts of the wicked one. I pray
that he will take the helmet of salvation, and the
sword of the Spirit, which is the Word of God, praying
always with all prayer and supplication in the Spirit,
being watchful and standing strong to the end (Ephesians 6:13-18).

POWER TOOLS

The LORD is my rock and my fortress and my deliverer; my God, my strength, in whom I will trust; my
shield and the horn of my salvation, my stronghold. I
will call upon the LORD, who is worthy to be praised;
so shall I be saved from my enemies.

PSALM 18:2,3

Because he has set his love upon Me, therefore I will
deliver him; I will set him on high, because he has
known My name.

PSALM 91:14

He sent from above, He took me; He drew me out of
many waters. He delivered me from my strong
enemy, from those who hated me, for they were too
strong for me. They confronted me in the day of my
calamity, but the LORD was my support. He also
brought me out into a broad place; He delivered me
because He delighted in me.

PSALM 18:16-19

You have delivered my soul from death. Have You not delivered my feet from falling, that I may walk before God in the light of the living?
PSALM 56:13

The Spirit of the LORD is upon Me, because He has anointed Me to preach the gospel to the poor; He has sent Me to heal the brokenhearted, to proclaim liberty to the captives and recovery of sight to the blind, to set at liberty those who are oppressed.
LUKE 4:18

CHAPTER TWENTY-SEVEN

His Obedience

isa was concerned that her husband, Jonathan, was not growing spiritually the way she was. Her relationship with the Lord was deepening every day while his appeared to be shrinking just as rapidly. She was frustrated with his lack of spiritual commitment, because she longed for them to grow together and have a shared experience in this vital area of their lives. She didn't want to be the spiritual heavyweight in the family. Whenever she said anything about it, Jonathan protested, saying his career kept him too busy to spend time with the Lord and read His Word. Even his business trips often took him out of town on weekends so he missed attending church with Lisa and their children.

The thing that bothered *her* most was that none of this seemed to bother *him*—that is until his work became more challenging than he could comfortably handle. As he grew increasingly stressed, Lisa could see how depleting it was for him. She knew that if he could make the connection between spending time with the Lord every day and finding spiritual strength, his life would be far better. She also was certain he wasn't ready to hear about it from her.

Even though Lisa knew that God was calling Jonathan to this step of obedience, she determined not to say anything. Instead she prayed every day for him to have the desire for more of God in his life. Although she prayed for months without any visible change, one morning he quietly announced, "I'm going to the office earlier today because I need time alone with the Lord before I do anything else."

She silently thanked God.

Since then, with only a few exceptions, he has left home early every week-day morning to read his Bible and pray in his office. That was two years ago and now this spiritual discipline has carried over into areas of physical discipline as well. He is exercising, eating right, losing the weight he wanted to lose, and gaining new stamina. Only God can do that.

If you clearly observe your husband walking down a wrong path, should you say something? If so, how much should you say and when is the right time to say it? The best way I've found to proceed is to take it to God *first* and weigh it on *His* scales. He may instruct you to just be quiet and pray, like He did with Lisa. But if He does direct you to speak to your husband about the matter, there will be a far greater chance of him hearing God's voice somewhere in your words if you've prayed *before* you speak. Anything perceived as nagging will be counterproductive and better left unsaid. Praying that his eyes be opened to the truth and his heart convicted will be far more effective than you telling him what to do. You can *encourage* him to do what's right and *pray* for him to do what's right, but ultimately it's God's voice that will have the greatest impact.

No man can receive all God has for him if he is not living in obedience. Jesus, who was never one to beat around the bush, said, "If you want to enter into life, keep the commandments" (Matthew 19:17). He knew that nothing would give a man more peace and confidence than knowing he is doing what God wants him to do. God's Word promises that by being obedient to His ways your husband will find mercy (Psalm 25:10), peace (Psalm 37:37), happiness (Proverbs 29:18), plenty (Proverbs 21:5), blessings (Luke 11:28), and life (Proverbs 21:21). *Not* living in obedience brings harsh consequences (Proverbs 15:10), unanswered prayers (Proverbs 28:9), and the inability to enter into the great things God has for him (1 Corinthians 6:9).

Walking in obedience has to do not only with keeping God's commandments, but also with heeding God's *specific* instructions. For example, if God has instructed your husband to rest and he doesn't do it, that's disobedience. If He has told him to stop doing a certain type of work and he keeps doing it, that's disobedience. If He has told him to move to another place and he doesn't move, that's disobedience, too.

A man who does what God asks, builds his house on a rock. When the rain, floods, and wind come and beat on the house, it won't fall (Matthew 7:24-27). You don't want to witness the downfall of your house because of your husband's disobedience in any area. While it's not your place to be either his mother or the gestapo, it is your job to pray, and speak *after* you've gotten your orders from God.

If your husband's disobedience to God's ways has already brought down your house in some manner, know that God will honor *your* obedience and He will see that you will not be destroyed. He will pour His blessings on you and restore what has been lost. Just keep praying that your husband not have a hearing problem when it comes to the voice of God, and that he has the strength, courage, and motivation to act on what he hears.

Prayer

Lord, You have said in Your Word that if we regard iniquity in our hearts, You will not hear (Psalm 66:18). I want You to hear my prayers, so I ask You to reveal where there is any disobedience in my life, especially with regard to my husband. Show me if I'm selfish, unloving, critical, angry, resentful, unforgiving, or bitter toward him. Show me where I have not obeyed You or lived Your way. I confess it as sin and ask for Your forgiveness.

I pray that You would give (husband's name) a desire to live in obedience to Your laws and Your ways. Reveal and uproot anything he willingly gives place to that is not of You. Help him to bring every thought and action under Your control. Remind him to do good, speak evil of no one, and be peaceable, gentle, and humble (Titus 3:1,2). Teach him to embrace the stretching pain of discipline and discipleship. Reward him according to his righteousness and according to the cleanness of his hands (Psalm 18:20). Show him Your ways, O Lord; teach him Your paths. Lead him in Your truth, for You are the God of his salvation (Psalm 25:4,5).

Make him a praising person, for I know that when we worship You we gain clear understanding, our lives are transformed, and we receive power to live Your way. Help him to hear Your specific instructions to him and enable him to obey them. Give him a heart that longs to do Your will and may he enjoy the peace that can only come from living in total obedience to Your commands.

POWER TOOLS

My son, do not forget my law, but let your heart
keep my commands; for length of days and long life
and peace they will add to you. Let not mercy and
truth forsake you; bind them around your neck, write
them on the tablet of your heart.
PROVERBS 3:1-3

Not everyone who says to Me, "Lord, Lord," shall
enter the kingdom of heaven, but he who does the
will of My Father in heaven.
MATTHEW 7:21

One who turns away his ear from hearing the law,
even his prayer shall be an abomination.
PROVERBS 28:9

Obey My voice, and I will be your God, and you
shall be My people. And walk in all the ways that I
have commanded you, that it may be well with you.
JEREMIAH 7:23

CHAPTER TWENTY-EIGHT

His Self-Image

W hy do some very capable and talented men consistently find doors of opportunity and acceptance closed to them, while others with equal or less ability have seemingly unlimited opportunities and success in every area of their lives? It doesn't seem fair. Timing, of course, has something to do with it. God has a time for everything and He works in us what needs to be done to prepare us for what is ahead. Having a sense of God's timing brings the peace to wait on the Lord for it.

There can be another important reason for the struggle, however, and that is a man's perception of himself. If he has a poor self-image, he will have doubts about his value that creep into everything he does—even into his relationships. People who are uncomfortable with his insecurity may avoid him, and this will in turn affect how he relates to his family, friends, coworkers, and even strangers. Expecting to be rejected, he will be.

Dan experienced great frustration trying to find his way in life. He didn't know who he was or where he fit in, or if in fact he fit in anywhere. His preoccupation with trying to figure it all out caused great friction between him and his wife, Cindy. She tried to help him, but he resented her advice. He perceived her thoughts and suggestions as mocking his ability to figure things out for himself. His reaction was to dismiss her words, which caused her to strive even more to assert herself. The harder Cindy fought to not feel devalued, the more Dan retaliated, until in the frustration of his own insecurity he rejected her input altogether.

This kind of ever-deepening strife could have led to divorce, but Cindy learned how to pray rather than fight. She asked the Lord to help her understand what was happening with Dan. She wanted to know why he was rejecting her when she was only trying to help. God revealed that Dan's diminished self-image had been learned from his father. He, too, had experienced that same kind of insecurity all of his life. Whatever the source of Dan's behavior, Cindy knew God had the power to change it.

She set herself to pray as long as it would take for God to break the bonds of self-loathing and mold her husband into *His* image. She asked God to help Dan find his identity in the Lord. She also prayed for God to enable her to speak to Dan in the Spirit and not in her flesh, so that her words would be received as encouragement to his soul rather than criticism.

It took a number of months before she saw any changes, but eventually there were major ones. First, Dan learned to trust that his wife was on the same team with him and not his opponent. They agreed to stop fighting and committed to work together. He started going to church more, and she could see he was praying and reading the Bible with new faith. He gradually began to see himself as one of God's much-loved sons and not an evolutionary mistake. The more he sensed his own worth and grew accepting of who he was, the more he was appreciated by everyone else. Not coincidentally, doors of opportunity began to open for him and Dan soon found the kind of acceptance and success he had always dreamed of having.

If your husband's self-image needs a makeover, be patient. The answers don't come overnight when a long-held pattern of thinking has to be broken. But you can appropriate the power of God to fight the enemy that feeds him familiar lies, so he can be free to hear God's truth. You'll find that as you intercede, God will reveal glimpses of the key to unlocking that particular thing in your husband. In other words, as you pray He'll show you *how* to pray.

I firmly believe that the tendency toward a midlife crisis can be hindered by praying along this same line. Any toxicity still in a man's soul after he reaches his fifties will eventually pour out of him like a poison. It's as if the invisible dam holding it back weakens with age. When it breaks, the flood can be strong enough to carry him away. Having his identity soundly established in the Lord will make a major difference in how he gets through that time.

God says our first steps are to be toward Him: seeking His face, following His laws, putting Him first and our self-centered pursuits last. When we line up with Him, He leads the way and all we have to do is follow. As we look to Him, the glory of His image gets imprinted upon us. When our self-image gets so wrapped up in God that we lose ourselves in the process, we're free. We want that liberty for our husbands, as well as ourselves.

Your husband will never see who *he* really is until he sees who *God* really is. Pray that he finds his true identity.

Prayer

Lord, I pray that (husband's name) will find his identity in You. Help him to understand his worth through Your eyes and by Your standards. May he recognize the unique qualities You've placed in him and be able to appreciate them. Enable him to see himself the way You see him, understanding that "You have made him a little lower than the angels, and You crowned him with glory and honor. You have made him to have dominion over the works of Your hands; You have put all things under his feet" (Psalm 8:4-6). Quiet the voices that tell him otherwise and give him ears to hear Your voice telling him that it will not be his perfection that gets him through life successfully, it will be Yours.

Reveal to him that "he is the image and glory of God" (1 Corinthians 11:7), and he is "complete in Him, who is the head of all principality and power" (Colossians 2:10). Give him the peace and security of knowing that he is accepted, not rejected, by You. Free him from the self-focus and self-consciousness that can imprison his soul. Help him to see who *You* really are so he'll know who *he* really is. May his true self-image be the image of Christ stamped upon his soul.

POWER TOOLS

Whom He foreknew, He also predestined to be conformed to the image of His Son, that He might be the firstborn among many brethren.

ROMANS 8:29

We all, with unveiled face, beholding as in a mirror
the glory of the Lord, are being transformed into the
same image from glory to glory, just as by the Spirit
of the Lord.
2 CORINTHIANS 3:18

You have put off the old man with his deeds,
and have put on the new man who is
renewed in knowledge according
to the image of Him who
created him.
COLOSSIANS 3:9,10

If anyone is a hearer of the word and not a doer, he is
like a man observing his natural face in a mirror; for
he observes himself, goes away, and immediately forgets what kind of man he was. But he who looks into
the perfect law of liberty and continues in it, and is
not a forgetful hearer, but a doer of the work, this
one will be blessed in what he does.
JAMES 1:23-25

Arise, shine; for your light has come! And the
glory of the LORD is risen upon you.
ISAIAH 60:1

CHAPTER TWENTY-NINE

His Faith

always smile when someone tells me he or she has no faith, because I know it's probably not true. Everyone lives by faith to a certain extent. When you go to a doctor, you need faith to trust his diagnosis. When the pharmacy fills your prescription, you have faith that you'll receive the appropriate medicine. When you eat at a restaurant, you trust that the people serving you have not contaminated or poisoned the food. (Some restaurants require more faith than others.) Every day is a walk of faith on some level. Everyone believes in something. "God has dealt to each one a measure of faith" (Romans 12:3).

We choose what we will believe in. Some people choose to believe in themselves, some in government, some in evil, some in science, some in the newspaper, some in hard work, some in other people, and some in God. The only person I have ever known who didn't believe in anything ended up in a mental hospital because it drove her crazy. Faith is something we can't live without.

Faith is something we can't *die* without either. Our faith determines what happens to us after we leave this world. If you have faith in Jesus, you know that your eternal future is secure. That's because "the Spirit of Him who raised Jesus from the dead . . . will also give life to your mortal bodies through His Spirit who dwells in you" (Romans 8:11). In other words, if the same Spirit who raised Jesus from the dead dwells in you, He will raise you up as well. Having certainty about what happens to us when we die will greatly affect how we live today. Confidence in our eternal future gives us a perspective on living in the present that is laced with confidence as well.

Here's a scary thought! When healing some blind men, Jesus said, "According to your faith let it be to you" (Matthew 9:29). Doesn't that make you want to reevaluate your level of trust in God? The good news is that this means we have a certain amount of control over our lives and can, to some extent, determine how things are going to turn out for us. Our lives don't have to be left up to chance, or allowed to go flapping in the breeze according to whatever wind is blowing at the moment. Our faith will help determine our outcome.

We all have times of doubt. Even Jesus wondered why God had forsaken Him. It wasn't that He doubted God's existence or ability to come to His rescue, He just didn't expect to feel forsaken. Sometimes we don't doubt God's existence, or whether He is *able* to help us, we just doubt His desire to have any immediate impact on our lives. *Surely He is too busy for my problems*, we think. But the truth is, He's not.

Does your husband have times of doubt? If so, your prayers for him to have ever-increasing faith will make a big difference in his life. Even if he doesn't know the Lord, you can still pray for faith to rise in his heart and look for an improvement in his level of peace. There is nothing in your husband's life that can't be conquered or positively affected with an added measure of faith in God. Jesus said of any man who has faith to believe in Him, "out of his heart will flow rivers of living water" (John 7:38). That alone can be enough to wash away a lifetime of pain, trouble, fear, sorrow, apathy, hopelessness, failure, and doubt. Shall we pray?

Prayer

Lord, I pray that You will give (husband's name) an added measure of faith today. Enlarge his ability to believe in You, Your Word, Your promises, Your ways, and Your power. Put a longing in His heart to talk with You and hear Your voice. Give him an understanding of what it means to bask in Your presence and not just ask for things. May he seek You, rely totally upon You, be led by You, put You first, and acknowledge You in everything he does.

Lord, You've said that "faith comes by hearing, and hearing by the word of God" (Romans 10:17). Feed his soul with Your Word so his faith grows big enough to believe that with You all things are possible (Matthew 19:26). Give him unfailing certainty that what You've promised to do, You will do (Romans 4:21). Make his faith a shield of protection. Put it into action to move the mountains in his life. Your Word says, "the just shall live by faith" (Romans 1:17); I pray that he will live the kind of faith-filled life You've called us all to experience. May he know with complete certainty "how great is Your goodness, which You have laid up for those who fear You, which You have prepared for those who trust in You" (Psalm 31:19).

POWER TOOLS

Let him ask in faith, with no doubting, for he who
doubts is like a wave of the sea driven and tossed by
the wind. For let not that man suppose that he will
receive anything from the Lord; he is a double-
minded man, unstable in all his ways.

JAMES 1:6-8

Whatever is not from faith is sin.

ROMANS 14:23

If you have faith as a mustard seed, you will say to
this mountain, "Move from here to there," and it will
move; and nothing will be impossible for you.

MATTHEW 17:20

I have been crucified with Christ; it is no longer I
who live, but Christ lives in me; and the life which I
now live in the flesh I live by faith in the Son of
God, who loved me and gave Himself for me.

GALATIANS 2:20

Therefore, having been justified by faith, we have
peace with God through our Lord Jesus Christ.

ROMANS 5:1

CHAPTER THIRTY

His Future

None of us can live without a vision for our future. If we don't have one, we flounder aimlessly. Without it, life seems pointless and we die a little every day. "Where there is no vision, the people perish" (Proverbs 29:18 KJV).

Having a vision doesn't necessarily mean knowing the specifics about what is going to happen next. It has to do with sensing the general direction you're moving in and having hope that something good is on the horizon. It's knowing that you *do* have a future and a purpose, and that it is bright.

Not every man has that certainty. When he doesn't, you can almost see life draining from him. Even the ones who do, don't necessarily have it all the time. Even the most spiritual man can get overtired, burned out, beaten down, distanced from God, confused about who he is and why he is here, and lose his vision for the future. He can misplace his sense of purpose and become overwhelmed and hopeless because of it. If he loses sight of his dreams and forgets the truth about himself and his situation, he can end up believing destructive lies about his future. "My people are destroyed for lack of knowledge" (Hosea 4:6).

God says not to listen to voices that speak lies, for "they speak a vision of their own heart, not from the mouth of the LORD" (Jeremiah 23:16). Any vision for the future that is full of failure and empty of hope is not from God (Jeremiah 29:11). But God can restore vision where it has been lost. He can give hope to dream again. He can bring His truth to bear upon the lies of discouragement. He can give assurance of a promising future. Prayer is the avenue through which He can accomplish it.

My husband said that one of the times my prayers meant the most to him was when we moved from Los Angeles to Nashville. It was very hard for all of us to leave the people we loved and start over again. There was so much at stake and it was a difficult transition, not to mention a big step of faith. We didn't know how it would all work out, but we moved in certainty that we were following God's leading. We trusted that our lives were safe in His hands. My prayer for Michael during that season was that he not lose the vision God had given him for the future. When circumstances caused him to temporarily lose his spiritual sight, he said my prayers were instrumental in restoring it.

We have to remember that Father God has drawn up His will. His estate is divided equally among His children. All that *He* has, *we* will have. We are "heirs of God and joint heirs with Christ" (Romans 8:17). I've read my copy of the will and it says we don't have any idea of all God has for us, because He has more for us than we ever imagined. "Eye has not seen, nor ear heard, nor have entered into the heart of man the things which God has prepared for those who love Him" (1 Corinthians 2:9). It promises that "the blameless will inherit good" (Proverbs 28:10). It says that not only will we have everything we need in *this* life, but the most significant portion of it will be ours after we die. Then we will be with Him and we will want nothing more.

If your husband's eyes get so focused on the day-to-day details of living that he loses his vision for the future, your prayers can lift his sights. They can help him see that *God* is his future and he needs to run his life in a way that invests in that. "Do you not know that those who run in a race all run, but one receives the prize? Run in such a way that you may obtain it" (1 Corinthians 9:24). You don't want your husband to be a man who speaks a vision of his own heart and loses the prize. You want him to be able to see from God's perspective.

God doesn't want us to know the future, He wants us to know *Him.* He wants us to trust Him to guide us into the future one step at a time. In order to understand God's leading, we must seek Him for every step. "Those who seek the LORD understand all" (Proverbs 28:5). We must also stay close enough to hear His answer. The Lord is the giver of vision; pray that your husband looks to Him for it. With God, his future is secure.

Prayer

Lord, I pray that You would give (husband's name) a vision for his future. Help him to understand that Your plans for him are for good and not evil—to give him a future and a hope (Jeremiah 29:11). Fill him with the knowledge of Your will in all wisdom and spiritual understanding; that he may have a walk worthy of You, fully pleasing You, being fruitful in every good work and increasing in the knowledge of

You (Colossians 1:9,10). May he live with leading from the Holy Spirit and not walk in doubt and fear of what may happen. Help him to mature and grow in You daily, submitting to You all his dreams and desires, knowing that "the things which are impossible with men are possible with God" (Luke 18:27). Give him God-ordained goals and show him how to conduct himself in a way that always invests in his future.

I pray that he will be active in service for You all the days of his life. Keep him from losing his sense of purpose and fill him with hope for his future as an "anchor of the soul, both sure and steadfast" (Hebrews 6:19). Give him "his heart's desire" (Psalm 21:2) and "the heritage of those who fear Your name" (Psalm 61:5). Plant him firmly in Your house and keep him fresh and flourishing and bearing fruit into old age (Psalm 92:13,14). And when it comes time for him to leave this earth and go to be with You, may he have such a strong vision for his eternal future that it makes his transition smooth, painless, and accompanied by peace and joy. Until that day, I pray he will find the vision for his future in You.

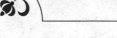

POWER TOOLS

I know the thoughts that I think toward you,
says the LORD, thoughts of peace and not of evil,
to give you a future and a hope.

JEREMIAH 29:11

Mark the blameless man, and observe the upright; for
the future of that man is peace. But the
transgressors shall be destroyed together;
the future of the wicked shall be cut off.
PSALM 37:37,38

Those who are planted in the house of the LORD
shall flourish in the courts of our God. They shall
still bear fruit in old age; they shall be fresh and
flourishing, to declare that the LORD is upright; He is
my rock, and there is no unrighteousness in Him.
PSALM 92:13-15

One thing I have desired of the LORD, that will I
seek: that I may dwell in the house of the LORD all
the days of my life, to behold the beauty of the LORD,
and to inquire in His temple.
PSALM 27:4

There is hope in your future.
JEREMIAH 31:17

THE
POWER
OF A
Praying®
Parent

STORMIE
OMARTIAN

HARVEST HOUSE PUBLISHERS
EUGENE, OREGON

Cover by Koechel Peterson & Associates, Minneapolis, Minnesota

THE POWER OF A PRAYING® PARENT

Copyright © 1995 by Stormie Omartian
Eugene, Oregon 97402
www.harvesthousepublishers.com

Library of Congress Cataloging-in-Publication Data
Omartian, Stormie
  The power of a praying parent / by Stormie Omartian
    p. cm.

Trade Edition
ISBN 10: 0-7369-1598-2
ISBN 13: 978-0-7369-1598-4

Deluxe Edition
ISBN 10: 0-7369-1710-1
ISBN 13: 978-0-7369-1710-0

1. Prayer—Christianity. 2. Parents—Prayer-books and devotions—English. 3. Devotional Calendars. I. Title.
BV220.O53   1995
248.3'2'0240431—dc20   95-8627
                                                                          CIP

Contents

Acknowledgments

With special thanks:

To my daughter, Amanda, and my son, Christopher, for filling my life with joy and giving me so much to pray about.

To my husband, Michael, for his willingness to spend countless hours with me over the last thirty years covering our children in prayer.

To my secretary, Susan Martinez, for being a gifted and valuable helper, encourager, comforter, sister, and friend.

To my Harvest House family, Bob Hawkins Jr., Carolyn McCready, Julie McKinney, Terry Glaspey, LaRae Weikert, Betty Fletcher, Mary Cooper, John Constance, and Kim Moore, for their dedication along with me to helping bring hope to concerned parents everywhere.

To my wonderful prayer partners, Susan Martinez, Roz Thompson, Donna Summer, and Jan Williamson, for the many hours of prayer time they've invested in this project, in my children, and in my life.

To my pastor for twenty-three years and spiritual father for over thirty, Pastor Jack Hayford, for teaching me how to pray.

To Pastors Rice Broocks, Tim Johnson, Jim Laffoon, John Rohr, and Dale and Joan Evrist, for reminding me that my treasure can only be found in the face of God.

To my spiritually adopted son, John Kendrick, for letting me be his mom on earth ever since his first mom and dad went to heaven.

To my housekeeper, Telma Lopez, for twenty-seven years of faithful service and for showing me that a mother's heart has no language barrier.

Foreword

My mom has been a great mother to me. She encourages me and tries to help me with everything. I am very thankful for her prayers and love. She prays for me daily, and I think that is one of the reasons I make it through school and life. Her prayers have made a difference to me, and because of them, I am alive on this earth. One time her prayers made a big and wonderful change in my life that I never imagined could possibly happen. At my school, I had a classmate who was very mean and I never wanted to go near her because she scared me. When I told my mom, she decided we should pray together for this girl. I thought that was a good idea and so we prayed nearly every day until school was out and through the summer too. The following school year, a miracle happened and that girl changed completely, and she became one of my best friends. It affected my life and it was one of the greatest things that ever happened to me.

Mom's praying worked. It doesn't always work, but even when our prayers aren't answered right away, just praying or being prayed for makes me feel better. I am thankful for God and my mother. Thank you, Mom.

Amanda Omartian (13 years old)

Amanda, Ten Years Later

Over the last ten years I have felt my mother's prayers every day. And I am now enjoying answers to the countless prayers she has prayed for me all my life. Even if I didn't realize it at the time, I know her prayers were covering me—no matter where I was and what foolish thing I may have been doing. I wish one day to be half the woman she is. She has held this family together with her prayers. She has grabbed a hold of God so tightly in prayer every day that the enemy couldn't have any of us, no matter how hard he tried to gain a foothold in each of our lives. I have been in situations where I knew I was close to danger or disaster, where all I could do was desperately cry to God at that very moment. I can see now what might have happened if my parents had not been praying for me all along, and especially at that time of crisis in my life. Their prayers protected, strengthened, and guided me, even when I didn't know I needed protection, strength, or guidance. Without them I'm certain that I would not be as whole, happy, or hopeful a person. Prayer has become such an important part of my life that I am now a faithful prayer partner in my mom's weekly prayer group of women. I know that prayer is something I cannot live without.

Amanda Omartian (23 years old)

Well, I must say that I have truly been blessed with a couple of parents who are very loving and caring, very understanding, and, yes, even occasionally funny. But of the many wonderful qualities my parents possess, the one that I respect most is their persistence in prayer for me and my sister and our everyday lives. If I were to tell you how much their prayers have meant to me and made a difference in my life, I would probably end up writing more than my mother. But since you probably did not pick up this book to read my writings, I will pinpoint the most memorable time in my life where having praying parents really paid off.

Throughout all of my eighteen years, both of my parents have constantly been in prayer for my safety. While growing up in the "peaceful" city of Los Angeles, those prayers kept me shielded from danger. I clearly remember one particular time during my freshman year in high school when God protected me in a serious auto accident. Two other boys and I were driving to school one morning and were not wearing seat belts when we collided nearly head-on with another car turning left in the intersection. One of my friends was severely injured when he went through the windshield, and the other boy hit the steering wheel with his face. I was in the back seat and ended up with only a minor injury to my lower back. In a situation where everyone could have died, God put His protection over the car and spared all three of us. It was at that point in my life when I realized just how important prayer is, and I gained a clearer perspective of God's awesome power in the midst of disastrous situations.

I am eternally grateful to my parents for their persistence in praying over my life. It has truly made a difference in not only sparing me from danger, but also keeping me on the right path as an honest, moral person.

I guess now that I am eighteen years old, the prayers of my parents will probably change somewhat. I suspect they may be praying that I will hurry up and get married so they can have the house to themselves.

Christopher Omartian (18 years old)

Christopher, Ten Years Later

When I look back over the past ten years, I cannot deny the awesome power of prayer and where I am today as a result of it. I am still blessed by the same loving and caring parents and, yes, they still struggle to be funny. But I know more than ever that having parents who cared enough to take the time to pray continually for my well-being has proven to be extremely valuable to me. Without the prayers of my family, who defined what it means to pray without ceasing, I don't know where I would be.

A few years ago, I found myself in a difficult place. The time I was spending in the Word and prayer had become more of a daily routine than the powerful life-changing experience it should be. And as a result, there were major deficiencies in my life. I was stuck in a financial crisis. I also had been stabbed in the back by someone I had trusted for years. But most importantly, I had lost my joy and peace. I remember calling my mother one night explaining my situation and asking her to pray for me. She responded by telling me that God had brought me to this place for a reason and that He was trying to get my attention. The following day when I opened the Word, I was stunned by the scripture "Seek first the kingdom of God and His righteousness, and all these things shall be added to you" (Matthew 6:33). I had read it so many times before but never realized the profound simplicity of the passage. I had become so sidetracked by my own personal challenges that I was constantly asking God to make something happen in my life rather than truly seeking the Spirit of God to *empower* my life. It was at that point I fell on my face before the Lord with no other agenda than to seek Him.

All this to say that God will often allow us to dig ourselves into our own stress-filled situations while waiting patiently for us to embrace His will first and foremost. And those miserable times become the very vehicle God uses to bring us into a deeper relationship with Him. I don't doubt that God was calling me to trust Him beyond my own comfort zone. Had I not gotten to that low point, I know I could not have come to the place where I would now be able to handle a recent abundance of work, the launching of a new and exciting business, and a forthcoming marriage to the most wonderfully beautiful and godly woman, the absolute love of my life. Each of these things is a tremendous blessing from the Lord that He has poured out on me far beyond what I deserve. And I can truly say that the fervent prayers of my parents for me to have a deeper walk with the Lord are what brought it all to fruition. Of course, I am referring mainly to my mother since half of my father's prayers are allocated toward the success of the Chicago Bears.

Christopher Omartian (28 years old)

Introduction

When I first wrote *The Power of a Praying Parent* ten years ago, I never dreamed it would sell over a million copies. All I thought about was how the Lord had taught me a way to pray for my children that was powerful and effective—and that I wanted to share this with other parents. What had begun as a group of families who got together regularly in our home to pray for our collective children became a way of life for all of us. We felt the power of our prayers and saw their wonderful effects and amazing results. The answers to the prayers we prayed over the years fueled our faith and inspired us to be persistent and diligent to *continue* to pray even as, one by one, our children grew up and left home to build their own lives.

In this latest edition I have included an additional chapter called "Praying for Your Adult Children." That's because as a parent you will always care about what happens to your children and so you will never stop praying for them, no matter what age they are or where they live. And it is never too late to *start* praying. Even if your children are already grown and you have not prayed for them before, you can still use this book to pray for them today. My children are in their twenties now, and I continue to use this book as a guide for prayer. Of course, I pray about other things that are specific to their needs as well, just as you will want to do for your children, but this book reminds me of things I might not remember to pray about unless it became an urgent issue. In the last chapter, I have given you simple prayer suggestions to add to the prayers at the end of each of the other chapters so you can pray more specifically about your adult children.

As you embark on this adventure of praying for your children, you will find it to be an unending habit of your heart. Being able to positively affect your children in prayer will keep you in close contact with them and actively involved in their lives, even after they leave home. And it will continually contribute to your joy as a parent.

Stormie Omartian

*Pour out your heart like water
before the face of the Lord.*

*Lift your hands toward Him for the
life of your young children.*

LAMENTATIONS 2:19

CHAPTER ONE

Becoming a Praying Parent

*I*t's the best of jobs. It's the most difficult of jobs. It can bring you the greatest joy. It can cause the greatest pain. There is nothing as fulfilling and exhilarating. There's nothing so depleting and exhausting. No area of your life can make you feel more like a success when everything is going well. No area of your life can make you feel more like a failure when things go wrong.

PARENTING!

The word itself can bring contradictory emotions to the surface. We try to do the best we can raising our children. Then, just when we think we've got the parenting terrain all figured out, we suddenly find ourselves in new territory again as each new age and stage presents another set of challenges. Sometimes we sail through smoothly. Sometimes we encounter tempests and tidal waves. Sometimes we get so tired that we just want to give up—let the storm take us where it will.

But I have good news. We don't have to be tossed and turned by these winds of change. *Our children's lives don't ever have to be left to chance.*

We don't have to pace the floor anxiously, biting our nails, gnawing our knuckles, dreading the terrible twos or torturous teens. We don't have to live in fear of what each new phase of development may bring, what dangers might be lurking behind every corner. Nor do we have to be perfect parents. We can start right now—this very minute, in fact—making a positive difference in our child's future. It's never too early and never too late. It doesn't matter if the child is three days old and perfect, or thirty years old and going through a third divorce because of an alcohol problem. At every stage of their lives our children need and will greatly benefit from our prayers. The key is not trying to do it all by ourselves all at once, but rather turning to the expert parent of all time—our Father God—for help. Then, taking one step at a time, we must cover every detail of our child's life in prayer. There is great *power* in doing that, far beyond what most people imagine. In fact, don't ever under-estimate the power of a praying parent.

I didn't have the best role model for parenting because I was raised by a mother who was mentally ill and very abusive. I wrote about that abuse and my miraculous recovery from its effects in my book *Stormie* (Harvest House Publishers). I also related how having my first child, our son Christopher, caused me to realize that I had the potential in me to be an abusive parent. I discovered that without God we are destined to repeat the mistakes of our past and to mimic what we've observed. A scene from childhood can flash across the screen of your mind and play itself out on the stage of your life in a moment of weakness—before you even realize what has happened. It may occur so quickly that you feel powerless to control it, and it can make you do and say destructive things to your children. This becomes compounded by the guilt that inevitably takes root and grows to often paralyzing proportions. Thankfully I had good counseling and support and was able to overcome this problem before any damage happened to my child, but many people have not been so fortunate.

Because I was painfully aware that I didn't have a positive parenting experience to imitate, I was nervous and anxious when my first child was born. I feared I would do to him what had been done to me. I read every book available on the subject of parenting and attended each Christian child-rearing seminar I could find. I tried to do my best with all this good and helpful information, but it was never enough. I had countless agonizing concerns for my son's social, spiritual, emotional, and mental growth, but most compelling of all, I feared that something bad might happen to him. Kidnapping, drowning, disfiguring accidents, irreparable injuries, diseases, sexual molestation, abuse, rape, or death all played across my mind as possibilities for his future. As much as I tried not to be an overreacting parent, every newspaper, magazine article, or TV newscast on crime made me more concerned for his welfare. Plus we lived in Los Angeles, a city where crime was rampant. It was more than I could handle.

One day in prayer I cried out to God, saying, "Lord, this is too much for me. I can't keep a twenty-four-hours-a-day, moment-by-moment watch on my son. How can I ever have peace?"

Over the next few weeks the Lord spoke to my heart about entrusting Christopher to Him. My husband and I had dedicated our son to God in a church service, but God wanted more than that. He wanted us to continue giving Christopher to Him on a daily basis. This didn't mean that we would now abdicate all responsibility as parents. Rather, we would declare ourselves to be in full partnership with God.

He would shoulder the heaviness of the burden and provide wisdom, power, protection, and ability far beyond ourselves. We would do *our* job to discipline, teach, nurture, and "train up a child in the way he should go" knowing that "when he is old, he will not depart from it" (Proverbs 22:6). We were to depend on God to enable us to raise our child properly, and He would see to it that our child's life was blessed.

An important part of our job was to keep the details of our child's life covered in prayer. In doing this, I learned to identify every concern, fear, worry, or possible scenario that came into my mind as a prompting by the Holy Spirit to pray for that particular thing. As I covered Christopher in prayer and released him into God's hands, God released my mind from that particular concern. This doesn't mean that once I prayed for something I never prayed about it again, but at least for a time I was relieved of the burden. When it surfaced again, I prayed about it again. God didn't promise that nothing bad would *ever* happen to my child, but praying released the power of God to work in his life, and I could enjoy more peace in the process.

I also learned that I should not try to force my own will on my child in prayer. This only leads to frustration and disappointment for all concerned. You know the kind of prayer I mean, because we're all prone to it: "God, I pray that Christopher will grow up and marry my best friend's daughter." (*Her parents would be great in-laws.*) Or, "Lord, let Amanda get accepted at this school." (*Then I can feel better about myself.*) Of course we may never consciously acknowledge the words in parentheses, but they are there in the back of our mind, subtly inspiring us to impose our will in God's ear. I have found it's better to pray more along the lines of "Lord, show me how to pray for this child. Help me to raise him Your way, and may Your will be done in his life."

By the time our daughter, Amanda, was born four and a half years after Christopher, God had taught me what it means to pray in great depth and to really intercede for my child's life. Over the next twelve years God answered my prayers in many wonderful ways, and today I see the results.

My husband and I recognize the hand of God on our children's lives, and they readily acknowledge it as well. For it's the power of God that penetrates a child's life when a parent prays.

What Is Prayer and How Does It Work?

Prayer is much more than just giving a list of desires to God, as if He were the great Sugar Daddy/Santa Claus in the sky. Prayer is acknowledging and experiencing the presence of God and inviting His presence into our lives and circumstances. It's seeking the *presence* of God and releasing the *power* of God which gives us the means to overcome any problem.

The Bible says, "Whatever you bind on earth will be bound in heaven, and whatever you loose on earth will be loosed in heaven" (Matthew 18:18). God gives us authority on earth. When we take that authority, God releases power to us from heaven. Because it's God's power and *not* ours, we become the vessel through which His power flows. When we pray, we bring that power to bear upon everything we are praying about, and we allow the power of God to work through our powerlessness. When we pray, we are humbling ourselves before God and saying, "I need Your presence and Your power, Lord. I can't do this without You." When we don't pray, it's like saying we have no need of anything outside of ourselves.

Praying in the name of Jesus is a major key to God's power. Jesus said, "Most assuredly, I say to you, whatever you ask the

Father in My name He will give you" (John 16:23). Praying in the name of Jesus gives us authority over the enemy and proves we have faith in God to do what His Word promises. God knows our thoughts and our needs, but He responds to our prayers. That's because He always gives us a choice about everything, including whether we will trust Him and obey by praying in Jesus' name.

Praying not only affects *us*, it also reaches out and touches those for whom we pray. When we pray for our children, we are asking God to make His presence a part of their lives and work powerfully in their behalf. That doesn't mean there will always be an *immediate* response. Sometimes it can take days, weeks, months, or even years. But our prayers are never lost or meaningless. If we are praying, something is happening, whether we can see it or not. The Bible says, "The effective, fervent prayer of a righteous man avails much" (James 5:16). All that needs to happen in our lives and the lives of our children cannot happen without the presence and power of God. Prayer invites and ignites both.

Begin with a Personalized List

I actually started praying for each of my children from the time they were conceived because the Bible says, "He has blessed your children within you" (Psalm 147:13). I believed in the power of prayer. What I *didn't* realize at that time was how important each detail of our lives is to Him. It's not enough to pray only for the concerns of the moment; we need to pray for the future, and we need to pray against the effects of past events. When King David was depressed over what had happened in his life and fearful about future consequences (Psalm 143), he didn't just say, "Oh, well, whatever will be will be." He cried out to God about the past, present, and future of his life. He prayed about *everything*. And that is exactly what we must do as well.

To do this effectively, I found I had to make an extensive personalized list for each child. This wasn't some legalistic obsession that said, "If I don't pray for each specific detail, God won't cover it." I was simply more at peace when I knew God had heard each of my many concerns. So once a year, when we went to the beach for our family vacation, I used those cherished early morning hours before anyone else was up to spend time with God making a master prayer list. I would sit and gaze out over the ocean, pencil and paper in hand, and ask God to show me how to pray for each child over the next twelve months. After all, He was the only one who truly knew what each child needed and what challenges they would face in the future. The Bible says, "The secret of the Lord is with those who fear Him" (Psalm 25:14). He reveals things to us when we ask. God always met me there with good instructions, and I came home with prayer lists for each of my children. Then, throughout the year, I added to them whenever I needed to do so.

I kept many of those lists, and as I look back at them now and see all the answers to my prayers, I'm overcome with the faithfulness of God to work in the lives of our children when we pray.

God's Word as Your Weapon

The battle for our children's lives is waged on our knees. When we don't pray, it's like sitting on the sidelines watching our children in a war zone getting shot at from every angle. When we *do* pray, we're in the battle alongside them, appropriating God's power on their behalf. If we also declare the Word of God in our prayers, then we wield a powerful weapon against which no enemy can prevail.

God's Word is "living and powerful, and sharper than any two-edged sword" (Hebrews 4:12) and it pierces everything it touches. God says His Word, "shall not return to Me void, but it shall accomplish what I please, and it shall prosper in the thing for which I sent it" (Isaiah 55:11). In other words, His Word is *never* ineffectual or without fruit. That's why I've included a number of Bible verses following each of the prayer examples. When you are praying for your child, include an appropriate Scripture verse in your prayer. If you can't think of a verse at the moment you're praying, don't let that stop you, but quote a verse or two whenever you can and you'll see mighty things happen.

As you read the Word during your own devotional time and as you pray for your children with the Holy Spirit's leading, you'll find many more Scriptures to include. And you don't have to have a different verse for each prayer. You may have one or two verses that you use repeatedly during a specific season of intercession for your child. For example, when my daughter went through a period of struggle in school, every time we prayed about it together I encouraged her to quote, "I can do all things through Christ who strengthens me" (Philippians 4:13). When I prayed about the matter by myself, I incorporated the verse, "The righteous cry out, and the LORD hears, and delivers them out of all their troubles" (Psalm 34:17).

When we employ God's Word in prayer, we are laying hold of the promises He gives us and appropriating them into the lives of our children. Through His Word, God guides us, speaks to us, and reminds us He is faithful. In that way, He builds faith in *our* hearts and enables us to understand *His* heart. This helps us to pray boldly in faith, knowing exactly what is *His* truth, *His* will, and *our* authority.

When Jesus spoke to the devil, He rebuked him. Sometimes in doing this He quoted Scripture. For example, when Satan said to Jesus, "If You will worship before me, all will be Yours," Jesus replied, "Get behind Me, Satan! For it is written, 'You shall worship the Lord your God and Him only you shall serve'" (Luke 4:7–8 NKJV/KJV).

Jesus is our role model. We are to observe Him and do what He does. He said, "Most assuredly I say to you, he who believes in Me, the works that I do he will do also; and greater works than these he will do, because I go to My Father" (John 14:12). He also said, "If you abide in Me, and My words abide in you, you will ask what you desire, and it shall be done for you" (John 15:7). We can resist the devil more effectively if we pray to God according to His directions found in the Scriptures, and if we understand the power and authority given to us through Jesus Christ. If we . . .

WATCH Him,
WALK with Him,
WAIT on Him,
WORSHIP Him,
and LIVE in His word,
WE WILL WIN this battle for our children.

Whenever you pray for your child, do it as if you are interceding for his or her life—because that is *exactly* what you are doing. Remember that while God has a perfect plan for our children's lives, Satan has a plan for them too. Satan's plan is to destroy them, and he will *try* to use any means possible to do so: drugs, sex, alcohol, rebellion, accidents, disease. But he won't be able to successfully use any of those things if his power has been dissipated by prayer. The Bible says, "How can one enter a strong man's house and plunder his goods unless he first binds the strong man?"

(Matthew 12:29). In other words, we can't have any effect in the devil's territory unless we first bind him and forbid him any authority there. Thus, we can also forbid him access to our children's lives.

Of course, Satan can do a lot of damage if we don't teach our children God's ways and God's Word and help them to respect God's laws, and if we don't discipline them, guide them, and help them learn to make godly choices. The Bible tells us, "Train up a child in the way he should go, and when he is old he will not depart from it" (Proverbs 22:6). When we don't do those things, our children can fall into rebellion and make choices that take them out from under the umbrella of God's protection. Prayer and proper instruction in the ways and words of God will make sure that does not happen and that God's plan succeeds—not the devil's. The Bible says, "Resist the devil and he will flee from you" (James 4:7). Binding Satan's plans in prayer is part of resisting the devil. Resisting him on behalf of our children can free them to make godly choices.

Satan will always try to make a case against our children so that he can have access into their lives. If we are armed with Scripture, however, he will have to contend with the Word of God. The Bible says, "Now salvation, and strength, and the kingdom of our God, and the power of His Christ have come, for the accuser of our brethren, who accused them before God day and night, has been cast down" (Revelation 12:10). Jesus' death on the cross broke the back of the accuser, but the evil one will still harass all who don't know their God-given authority over him. This is where our prayers come in. Our children will stand accused until we break the stronghold of the accuser in prayer, using the Word of God as hard evidence against him.

A Good Example of Answered Prayer

From the time our son was about two years old, my husband and I had regular prayer groups in our home. Our church had organized small home groups and we led one of them. Gradually we realized that the needs of our group were too great to handle in one monthly meeting, so we added another night each month just for prayer with the adults. During that time we prayed for every kind of need, but the volume of prayer requests for our children was enormous. As a result, I felt that we needed to have an entire day devoted specifically to praying with and for each of our children. This time of intercession, which we called "Interceding for Our Children's Lives," became so popular that people requested it again and again. In fact, the foundation for this book began more than twenty years ago in those very prayer groups. None of us had any idea how important they would become. We only knew we were following the leading of the Lord as we learned how to intercede, and we rejoiced together when we witnessed the many answers to our prayers. (See the Appendix, "Praying Together with Other Parents," for suggestions on how to organize your own time of group intercession for children.)

The Bible says, "If two of you agree on earth concerning anything that they ask, it will be done for them by My father in heaven" (Matthew 18:19). Also, one can put a thousand to flight and two can put ten thousand to flight (Deuteronomy 32:30). It doesn't take much of a mathematical mind to figure out, then, how powerful ten to twelve parents can be when they join in prayer and cry out to God for their children.

In the Scripture I used as the guiding verse for this entire book, God commands, "Pour out your heart like water before the face of the Lord. Lift your hands toward Him for the life of your young children" (Lamentations 2:19). How much clearer can it be that we are to pray with *fervency* and *passion* for our young ones, and look forward to those prayers being answered?

We have had so many answers to the prayers offered during our group times over the last twenty years that I could write a book on those alone, testified to by the parents and children who were involved. However, one specific instance stands out in my mind because it was a direct result of our very *first* prayer time and it was a compelling request for all of us in the group.

Nancy, a single mom, requested prayer for her daughter, Janet, who knew the Lord but was walking away from Him because of her disappointment and hurt over her parents' divorce. One of the specific things we prayed for was Janet's protection, for we knew that children who choose to walk out from under the umbrella of God's blessing open themselves up to all kinds of harm. Within a few weeks of that prayer time, Janet was driving on the freeway late at night and was hit head-on by a drunk driver who had driven up the off-ramp and was traveling full speed in the wrong direction. The doctors said it was a miracle she wasn't killed, but she did have severe injuries to her head, neck, shoulders, and back.

Eventually, through continued prayer and physical therapy, Janet recovered completely, physically and spiritually. She and her mother and all of us who prayed believe she would not be alive had we not interceded for her life before the accident. Today, Janet is happily married, with a beautiful daughter of her own, and she is a devoted Christian woman. She was our secretary and assistant for eight years, and she will always be our most wonderful reminder of the power of a praying parent.

When the Answers Don't Come

Possibly the hardest part of praying for our children is waiting for our prayers to be answered. Sometimes the answers come quickly, but many times they do not. When they don't, we can become discouraged, despairing, or angry at God. Everything seems hopeless, and we want to give up. Sometimes, in spite of all we've done for them and all our prayers for them, our children make poor choices and then reap the consequences. Those times are hard for a parent to watch, no matter how old the child.

If your child has made poor choices, don't berate yourself and stop praying. Keep communication lines open with your child, continue interceding for him or her, and declare God's Word. Instead of giving up, resolve to be even *more* committed to prayer. Pray with other believers. Stand strong and say, "I've only begun to fight," keeping in mind that *your* part of the fight is to pray. God actually fights the battle. Remember, too, that your fight is not with your child, it's with the devil. *He* is your enemy, not your child. Stand strong in prayer until you see a breakthrough in your child's life.

One of the most encouraging Scriptures I have read with regard to such perseverance is when David said, "I have pursued my enemies and overtaken them; neither did I turn back again till they were destroyed. I have wounded them, so that they were not able to rise; they have fallen under my feet. For You have armed me with strength for the battle" (Psalm 18:37–39). He didn't stop until the job was done and neither should we. We should pray through until we see the answer.

If you have anger or unforgiveness toward God or your child—yes, even loving parents can have these feelings—tell God. If you feel disappointment and hopelessness, state it clearly. Don't live with negative emotions and guilt that can separate you from God. Share all of your feelings honestly with Him and then ask Him to forgive you and show you what your next step should be. Above all, don't let any disappointment over unanswered prayer cause you to stop praying.

I Said "Praying," Not "Perfect"

When things go wrong in our children's lives, we blame ourselves. We beat ourselves up for not being perfect parents. But it's not being a perfect parent that makes the difference in a child's life, because there are no perfect parents. None of us are perfect, so how can we be perfect parents? It's being a *praying* parent that makes the difference. And that's something we *all* can be. In fact, we don't even have to be parents. We can be a friend, a teacher, a grandparent, an aunt, a cousin, a neighbor, a guardian, or even a stranger with a heart of compassion or concern for a child. The child may be someone we hear of or read about in the newspaper; the child may even be an adult for whom we have a mother's or father's heart.

If you're aware of a child who doesn't have a praying parent, you can step into the gap right now and answer that need. You can effect a change in the life of any child you care about. All it takes is a heart that says, "God, show me how to pray in a way that will make a difference in this child's life." Then begin with the prayers in this book and see where the Holy Spirit leads you.

At the end of each chapter I have included prayer suggestions for you to use. You may want to pray one each day for a month, or pray one specific prayer for a week, or concentrate on your most pressing concern of the moment until you feel released to move on to another.

Repeat these prayers as often as you like. God didn't say, "Don't come to Me over and over with the same request." In fact, He said to keep on praying, but don't make empty repetitions in your prayers.

And remember, you don't have to keep to any schedule or pray these specific prayers. They are simply a guide to get you going. Begin by submitting yourself to God and asking Him to help you be the parent and intercessor He wants you to be. Pray as the Holy Spirit leads *you*, as you listen to His prompting in *your* heart for *your* child.

I look forward to hearing about the answers to your prayers.

❧ ❧

PRAYER

Lord,

I submit myself to You. I realize that parenting a child in the way You would have me to is beyond my human abilities. I know I need You to help me. I want to partner with You and partake of Your gifts of wisdom, discernment, revelation, and guidance. I also need Your strength and patience, along with a generous portion of Your love flowing through me. Teach me how to love the way You love. Where I need to be healed, delivered, changed, matured, or made whole, I invite You to do that in me. Help me to walk in righteousness and integrity before You. Teach me Your ways, enable me to obey Your commandments and do only what is pleasing in Your sight. May the beauty of Your Spirit be so evident in me that I will be a godly role model. Give me the communication, teaching, and nurturing skills that I must have. Make me the parent You want me to be and teach me how to pray and truly intercede for the life of this child. Lord, You said in Your Word, "Whatever things you ask in prayer, believing, you will receive" (Matthew 21:22). In Jesus' name I ask that You will increase my faith to believe for all the things You've put on my heart to pray for concerning this child.

~∞ ∞~

WEAPONS OF WARFARE

You did not choose Me, but I chose you and
appointed you that you should go and bear fruit, and
that your fruit should remain, that whatever you ask
the Father in My name He may give you.
JOHN 15:16

The righteous man walks in his integrity;
his children are blessed after him.
PROVERBS 20:7

Whatever you ask in My name, that I will do,
that the Father may be glorified in the Son. If you
ask anything in My name, I will do it.
JOHN 14:13–14

Do not provoke your children to wrath, but bring
them up in the training and admonition of the Lord.
EPHESIANS 6:4

Take the helmet of salvation, and the sword
of the Spirit, which is the word of God; praying
always with all prayer and supplication in the Spirit,
being watchful to this end with all perseverance
and supplication for all the saints.
EPHESIANS 6:17–18

CHAPTER TWO

Releasing My Child into God's Hands

I didn't have peace when my first child, Christopher, was born because I was concerned about everything. I was afraid that someone might drop him, that he might drown in the bathtub, that he might get deathly ill, that I would forget to feed him, that he would be bitten by a dog, injured in a car accident, kidnapped, or lost. In an act more of desperation than obedience, I cried out to God concerning this. He immediately reminded me that Christopher was a gift to us from Him and that *He* cared even more about our son than we did. I was reminded of the biblical instruction to cast "all your care upon Him" (1 Peter 5:7), and so I did.

"Lord, my son is the biggest 'care' I have, and I release him into Your hands. Only You can raise him right and truly keep him safe. I will no longer strive to do it all by myself but will enter into full partnership with You."

From that point on, whenever I had fear about anything, I immediately took it as a sign to pray until I felt peace. If I didn't have peace right away, then I prayed about it with one or more prayer partners until I did. Daily I released my son to God and asked Him to be in charge of his life. This took the pressure off me and parenting became much more enjoyable.

Over the years I have prayed this kind of prayer many times for each of my children. I prayed it on the first Sunday morning I left them in the church nursery, when they stayed with a baby-sitter overnight, the day they started kindergarten, the times I had to leave them in an operating room so the doctor could stitch them up, their first weekend at a friend's house, the week they flew to Washington D.C. on a field trip, whenever they went away to camp, the morning my son first drove the family car by himself, and every time he played football.

Recently I had to release my son into God's hands again, this time as he left for college. I cried numerous times in the months leading up to that monumental moment of separation, for I realized that our lives would never be the same again. Then, just before the big day, God brought to life the words, "For you shall go out with joy, and be led out with peace; the mountains and the hills shall break forth into singing before you" (Isaiah 55:12). Along with that, He gave me the knowledge and assurance that after the initial pain of releasing our children there comes joy and peace, both for them *and* us. Because we know that no matter what stage of life our children are in, when we release them to God they are in *good hands*. We know that they will go forth in peace and joy and God will make a way for them. He will do the same for us, too. What greater comfort is there? Because of this, on the day we drove to the university to move Christopher into his freshman dorm, I had the joy and peace only God can give, and I was almost certain I heard the mountains and hills singing.

I still have many more times ahead when I will have to release my children into God's hands. One of the biggest of all will be when they marry. Whenever I think about this, I am reminded of the Bible story of Hannah, who prayed to God for a son. The Lord answered her prayer and she gave birth to Samuel. Afterward she said, "For this child I prayed, and the Lord has granted me my petition which I asked of Him. Therefore I also have lent him to the Lord; as long as he lives he shall be lent to the Lord" (1 Samuel 1:27–29).

Hannah did such a thorough job of lending him to the Lord that when Samuel was weaned, she took him to the house of the Lord to live with Eli the priest. She did that to fulfill a vow she had made to God concerning Samuel, so don't worry (or get your hopes up, as the case may be); God is not going to ask you to leave your child in the church office for the pastor and his wife to raise. The point is, Hannah released her child to God and then did as He instructed. The result was that Samuel became one of the greatest prophets of God the world has ever known.

We don't want to limit what God can do in our children by clutching them to ourselves and trying to parent them alone. If we're not positive that God is in control of our children's lives, we'll be ruled by fear. And the only way to be sure that God *is* in control is to surrender our hold and allow Him full access to their lives. The way to do that is to live according to His Word and His ways and pray to Him about everything. We can trust God to take care of our children even better than we can. When we release our children into the Father's hands and acknowledge that He is in control of their lives and ours, both we and our children will have greater peace.

We can't be everywhere. But God can. We can't see everything. But God can. We can't know everything. But God can. No matter what age our children are, releasing them into God's hands is a sign of our faith and trust in Him and is the first step toward making a difference in their lives. Prayer for our children begins there.

∾∾ ∾∾

PRAYER

Lord,

I come to You in Jesus' name and give (name of child) to You. I'm convinced that You alone know what is best for him (her). You alone know what he (she) needs. I release him (her) to You to care for and protect, and I commit myself to pray for everything concerning him (her) that I can think of or that You put upon my heart. Teach me how to pray and guide me in what to pray about. Help me not to impose my own will when I'm praying for him (her), but rather enable me to pray that Your will be done in his (her) life.

Thank You that I can partner with You in raising him (her) and that I don't have to do it alone. I'm grateful that I don't have to rely on the world's unreliable and ever-changing methods for child rearing, but that I can have clear directions from Your Word and wisdom as I pray to You for answers.

Thank You, Lord, for the precious gift of this child. Because Your Word says that every good gift comes from You, I know that You have given him (her) to me to care for and raise. Help me to do that. Show me places where I continue to hang on to him (her) and enable me to release him (her) to Your protection, guidance, and counsel. Help me not to live in fear of possible dangers, but in the joy and peace of knowing that You are in control. I rely on

You for everything, and this day I trust my child to
You and release him (her) into Your hands.

❧ ❧ ❧

WEAPONS OF WARFARE

If you then, being evil, know how to give
good gifts to your children, how much more will
your Father who is in heaven give good things to
those who ask Him!
MATTHEW 7:11

The mercy of the Lord is from everlasting to
everlasting on those who fear Him, and His
righteousness to children's children. To such as
keep His covenant, and to those who remember
His commandments to do them.
PSALM 103:17–18

They shall not labor in vain, nor bring forth children
for trouble; for they shall be the descendants of the
blessed of the Lord and their offspring with them.
ISAIAH 65:23

Behold, children are a heritage from the Lord,
The fruit of the womb is a reward.
PSALM 127:3

Whatever we ask we receive from Him, because
we keep His commandments and do those things
that are pleasing in His sight.
1 JOHN 3:22

CHAPTER THREE

Securing Protection from Harm

Often our most urgent and fervent prayers regarding our children are for their protection. It's hard to think about other aspects of their lives if we are worried sick over their personal safety. How can we pray about future events when we're concerned about them even having a future?

Living in Los Angeles as we did for the first seventeen years of my son's life and the first twelve years of my daughter's, I had good reason to fear for their safety. Crime rose steadily during those years, and even our "good" neighborhood was no protection against that. So I prayed for God's protection on a daily basis. Actually, I started interceding for my children's safety even *before* they were born, praying for protection from such things as crib death and infant diseases. As they grew, I prayed for protection from violence, molestation, and accidents. I prayed alone, I prayed with my husband, and I prayed with my prayer partners: "Hide (them) under the shadow of Your wings, from the wicked who oppress (them), from (their) deadly enemies who surround them" (Psalm 17:8–9).

Both children suffered their share of minor scrapes, cuts, and common childhood injuries, including a couple that required an emergency room and stitches. However, nothing happened to them that came close to being permanently damaging or serious. That is, until my son was in the car accident which he related to you in the foreword of this book.

Early one morning, shortly after getting fifteen-year-old Christopher and ten-year-old Amanda into their respective carpools and off to school, I received the call that every parent fears.

"Mrs. Omartian, your son is okay, but he's been in a serious car accident and is in the emergency room. It was nearly a head-on collision and none of the three boys in the car were wearing seat belts."

On the way to the hospital, my husband and I prayed for the three boys. As we did, I remembered the times we had laid our hands on Christopher and prayed for him to be protected from car accidents. I remembered the Scripture we had often quoted over him: "For He shall give His angels charge over you, to keep you in all your ways. In their hands they shall bear you up, lest you dash your foot against a stone" (Psalm 91:11–12). God answers prayer and His promises are true. I knew that. If Christopher was in a car accident, God and His angels must have been there protecting him. Then, as I also remembered what the Bible says about the righteous person who fears God—"He will not be afraid of evil tidings; his heart is steadfast, trusting in the Lord" (Psalm 112:7)—I began to feel the peace of God which passes all understanding.

When we arrived at the hospital, we learned that Christopher had been sitting in the backseat of the car with a large duffle bag full of football uniforms on his lap. This cushioned his impact with the back of the front seat and, as a result, he sustained only a bruised knee and a sore back. The boy in the front passenger seat had been thrown through the windshield and was seriously injured. The driver hit the steering wheel and had facial lacerations. The car was totally destroyed.

We and the parents of the other boys could not believe that after all the serious talks we'd had with our sons on the importance of wearing seat belts, they were still not wearing them. Had they obeyed the rules, they might not have been hurt at all. But the good news was that if we had not been praying, they might have been killed or sustained serious and permanent injuries. We *all* knew our sons had been spared because of our prayers in Jesus' name on their behalf, and we were grateful to God.

Being a praying parent doesn't mean that nothing bad will ever happen to your children or that they will never experience pain. They *will*, because pain is a part of life in this fallen world. But the Bible assures us that our prayers play a vital part in keeping trouble from them. And when a painful thing does happen, they will be protected in the midst of it so it will be to their betterment and not their destruction.

This is where the Word of God again plays a vital part in your prayers and your peace. I can't even estimate the number of times I prayed for protection for my family and myself while living in Los Angeles. Every time I asked God to protect us from the random violence that seemed to be everywhere, I quoted these Scriptures: "He delivers me from my enemies. You also lift me up above those who rise against me; You have delivered me from the violent man" (Psalm 18:48). "Blessed be the Lord for He has shown me His marvelous kindness in a strong city!" (Psalm 31:21).

Earthquakes were another major concern in California. I prayed about them all the time, but especially at night before

I went to bed. Every bad earthquake I have ever experienced jolted me out of a sound sleep. When that happens you awaken suddenly in pitch blackness with everything around you shaking and a loud noise more frightening than thunder at its mightiest roaring in your ears. That only has to happen once to be implanted in your memory forever. I never went to bed without thinking about earthquakes and praying over our entire family, and I always quoted: "God is our refuge and strength, a very present help in trouble. Therefore we will not fear, even though the earth be removed, and though the mountains be carried into the midst of the sea; though its waters roar and be troubled, though the mountains shake with its swelling" (Psalm 46:1–3).

Even though that Scripture promises safety in the *midst* of the problem, I actually asked for more than that: "Lord, I pray that there would *not* be an earthquake. But if there is one, I pray that we will not be here. Even so, Lord, if it's Your will for us to be here, I pray that You will protect us in it."

I believe God answered that prayer when we moved from Northridge before the earthquake hit that area on January 17, 1994. A few months afterward when my children and I walked through the ruins, we were horrified over how much damage had been done. The house that had been our home was destroyed. But we were most in awe of how God had rescued us and that His hand was on us in response to prayer.

If we had been in the earthquake, I trust that God would have protected us in it, just as He miraculously did for so many others. Disasters can occur anywhere. The point is to pray and trust God to answer.

Things happen when we pray that will not happen when we don't. What might happen, or might *not* happen, to our children if we don't pray today? Let's not wait to find out. Let's get on our knees now.

~~❧ ❧~~

PRAYER

Lord,

I lift (name of child) up to You and ask that You would put a hedge of protection around her (him). Protect her (his) spirit, body, mind, and emotions from any kind of evil or harm. I pray specifically for protection from accidents, disease, injury, or any other physical, mental, or emotional abuse. I pray that she (he) will make her (his) refuge "in the shadow of Your wings" until "these calamities have passed by" (Psalm 57:1). Hide her (him) from any kind of evil influences that would come against her (him). Keep her (him) safe from any hidden dangers and let no weapon formed against her (him) be able to prosper. Thank You, Lord, for Your many promises of protection. Help her (him) to walk in Your ways and in obedience to Your will so that she (he) never comes out from under the umbrella of that protection. Keep her (him) safe in all she (he) does and wherever she (he) goes. In Jesus' name, I pray.

❧ ❧

WEAPONS OF WARFARE

He who dwells in the secret place of the Most
High shall abide under the shadow of the Almighty.
I will say of the Lord, "He is my refuge and my for-
tress; my God, in Him I will trust.
PSALM 91:1–2

When you pass through the waters, I will be with you;
and through the rivers, they shall not overflow you.
When you walk through the fire, you shall not be
burned, nor shall the flame scorch you.
ISAIAH 43:2

No weapon formed against you shall prosper, and every
tongue which rises against you in judgment you shall
condemn. This is the heritage of the servants of the
Lord, and their righteousness is from Me, says the Lord.
ISAIAH 54:17

Because you have made the Lord, who is my refuge,
even the Most High, your dwelling place, no evil
shall befall you, nor shall any plague come
near your dwelling.
PSALM 91:9–10

I will both lie down in peace, and sleep; for You alone,
O Lord, make me dwell in safety.
PSALM 4:8

❧ CHAPTER FOUR ❧

Feeling Loved and Accepted

*O*ne of the difficult things children must deal with are the lies that can come into their minds masquerading as truth: "I'm not loved," "I'm not accepted," "I'm not appreciated," "I'm not attractive," "I'm not good enough," "I'm too fat," "too thin," "too tall," "too short," "too dumb," "too smart," "too everything." These lies escalate as children move into their teenage years and often are carried into adulthood. That's why I'm convinced it's never too soon to start praying for a child to feel loved and accepted—first by God, then by family, then by peers and others. We can start when they are babies, or whatever age your child is at this moment, and pray about this concern throughout their lives.

The opposite of being loved and accepted is being rejected—something we've all experienced at one time or another in our lives. Who among us has never felt embarrassment, humiliation, failure, fault, or someone's disapproval over something we've done? Whether it be by a family member, a friend, or a complete stranger, rejection happens to all of us. Some people can let such incidents roll off their backs, because they know, deep within, that they are accepted. Others, however, may bear deep emotional wounds from incident after incident of rejection, so any perceived lack of acceptance can transform their personalities into something ugly. That's why rejection is at the root of so much of the evil we read about in the newspapers every day. A rejected worker goes back to his former place of employment and shoots his boss and co-workers. A rejected husband beats or kills his wife. A mother who has been rejected by others abuses her child. Rejection brings out the worst in people. Love and acceptance bring out the best. A person who already feels rejected interprets everything as rejection—a mere look, a harmless word, an insignificant action—while someone who feels loved and accepted thinks nothing of the same look, word, or action. A person may *not* actually be rejected, but if he (she) *believes* he (she) is, the effect is just as damaging as if it were true.

The love of God, however, can change all this. Knowing that God loves and accepts us changes our lives. He says, "I have chosen you and not cast you away" (Isaiah 41:9). "I have loved you with an everlasting love" (Jeremiah 31:3). And He proves His love because "God demonstrates His own love toward us, in that while we were still sinners, Christ died for us" (Romans 5:8). On top of that, the Bible assures us that "neither death nor life, nor angels nor principalities nor powers, nor things present nor things to come, nor height nor depth, nor any other created thing, shall be able to separate us from the love of God which is in Christ Jesus our Lord (Romans 8:38–39).

We must pray that our children understand these truths; they are the solid ground upon which love and acceptance are established in their character.

Even though it is God's love that is ultimately most important in anyone's life, a parent's love (or lack thereof) is perceived and felt first. Parental love is the first love a child experiences and the first love he (she) understands. In fact, parental love is often the means by which children actually open themselves to God's love and come to understand it early in life. That's why from the time our children are born, we should pray, "God help me to really love my child the way You want me to and teach me how to show it in a way he (she) can understand." If, however, your child is now older and you realize for one reason or another that he (she) doesn't feel loved, you can begin right now asking God to penetrate his (her) heart with His love and open it to receive *your* love and the love of others.

Ask God to show you what you can do to communicate love to your child—and don't listen to the devil weighing *you* down with guilt about past failure. You know his tactics:

"Your child doesn't feel loved because you're a terrible parent."

"If you weren't so dysfunctional you'd be able to communicate love to your child."

"No one ever loved you, so how can you love anyone else?"

These are lies from the pit of hell and part of Satan's plan for your child's life.

If you are being tormented by guilt or feelings of failure in this area, confess your thoughts to God, pray about it, put it in God's hands, and then stand up and proclaim the truth. Say, "God loves my child. I love my child. Other people love my child. If my child doesn't feel loved it's because he (she) has believed the lies of the enemy. We refuse to live according to Satan's lies." Although you may have to persist for a while on this, don't give up resisting the devil's lies by speaking God's truth. Then pray for God's love to penetrate your child's heart, as well as for your love to be perceived and received.

Along with prayer, children need to see love manifested toward them with eye contact, physical touch (a pat, a hug, a kiss), and with loving acts, deeds, and words. I found that when I made a deliberate effort to look my children directly in the eye with my hands gently touching them and with a smile say, "I love you and I think you're great," I could *always* see an immediate and noticeable change in their face and demeanor. Try it and you'll see what I mean. It may feel awkward at first if you've never done it before, or if your child is older or even an adult, but go ahead and do it anyway. If you are hesitant, pray that God will enable you to do it and that it will be well received.

If you feel you don't have the love you need to give your child, ask the Holy Spirit for it. The Bible says, "The love of God has been poured out in our hearts by the Holy Spirit who was given to us" (Romans 5:5). One of God's main purposes for your life is to fill you with so much of His love that it overflows onto others. Praying for your child will not only be a sign of that love in your heart, it could also be the very means by which that love is multiplied to overflowing.

~~ ⚜ ~~

PRAYER

Lord,

I pray for (name of child) to feel loved and accepted. Penetrate his (her) heart with Your love right now and help him (her) to fully understand how far-reaching and complete it is. Your Word says You loved us so much that You sent Your Son to die for us (John 3:16). Deliver him (her) from any lies of the enemy that may have been planted in his (her) mind to cause him (her) to doubt that. Jesus said, "As the Father loved Me, I also have loved you; abide in My love" (John 15:9–10). Lord, help (name of child) to abide in Your love. May he (she) say as David did, "Cause me to hear Your lovingkindness in the morning, for in You do I trust" (Psalm 143:8). Manifest Your love to this child in a real way today and help him (her) to receive it.

I pray also that You would help me to love this child unconditionally the way You do, and enable me to show it in a manner he (she) can perceive. Reveal to me how I can demonstrate and model Your love to him (her) so that it will be clearly understood. I pray that all my family members will love and accept him (her), and may he (she) find favor with other people as well. With each day that he (she) grows in the confidence of being loved and accepted, release in him (her) the capacity to easily *communicate* love to others. Enable him (her) to reach out in love in a way that is appropriate. As he (she) comes to fully understand the depth of Your love for him (her) and receives it into his (her) soul, make him (her) a vessel through which Your love flows to others. In Jesus' name I pray.

~~~

WEAPONS OF WARFARE

In this the love of God was manifested toward us, that God has sent His only begotten Son into the world, that we might live through Him. In this is love, not that we loved God, but that He loved us and sent

His Son to be the propitiation for our sins. Beloved, if
God so loved us, we also ought to love one another.
1 JOHN 4:9–11

For you are a holy people to the Lord your God;
the Lord your God has chosen you to be a people
for Himself, a special treasure above all the
peoples on the face of the earth.
DEUTERONOMY 7:6

We have known and believed the love that God
has for us. God is love, and he who abides in
love abides in God, and God in him.
1 JOHN 4:16

We are bound to give thanks to God always for you,
brethren beloved by the Lord, because God from the
beginning chose you for salvation through sanctification by the Spirit and belief in the truth.
2 THESSALONIANS 2:13

Blessed be the God and Father of our Lord Jesus
Christ, who has blessed us with every spiritual blessing in the heavenly places in Christ, just as He chose
us in Him before the foundation of the world, that we
should be holy and without blame before Him in love,
having predestined us to adoption as sons by Jesus
Christ to Himself, according to the good pleasure of
His will, to the praise of the glory of His grace, by
which He has made us accepted in the Beloved.
EPHESIANS 1:3–6

CHAPTER FIVE

Establishing an Eternal Future

bove all else, we want our children to come to a knowledge of who God really is and to know Jesus as their Savior. When that happens, we know their eternal future is secure; we know that when they die, we will see them again in heaven. What a wonderful hope that is!

Debby Boone and her husband, Gabri, who participated in some of the "Interceding for Your Child's Life" prayer groups, asked me to write a song for one of Debby's albums that she could sing as an anthem of the heart to her children. I wrote the following lyrics to a song called "Above All Else," which my husband put to music and Debby recorded and now sings in her concerts. These words, I believe, sum up what is in every believing parent's heart.

So much to say and just a lifetime left to say it.
How quickly time passes.
If I had my way, I'd keep you safe within my arms
While the storm of life crashes.
I won't always be with you, my child, but words I can give.

When the winds of hope are dying down, these words
   will live.
Above all else, know God's the One who'll never leave
   you.
Look to Him above all else.
He is love you can depend upon, a heart set to care.
If in the darkest night you should be lost, He will be
   there.
He's the Everlasting Father,
In His hands you'll never fall.
He's the One who holds it all,
Above all else.
He's the Author of your laughter,
He's the Keeper of your tears,
He's the One who you must fear
Above all else.
He's the Giver of the kingdom
Bought for you right from the start,
And He'll ask you for your heart
Above all else.

So much to say
And not enough time left to say it.
Just love the Lord
Above all else.

My son and daughter both made a decision to receive
Jesus into their lives when they were around five years of
age. We had taught them about the things of God, read
Bible stories to them, prayed with them daily, and took them

regularly to church, where they were instructed in God's ways. They had much exposure to the idea of receiving Jesus, but we never forced it on them or asked them to make a decision. Instead, we prayed that what they learned would penetrate their heart and give them a desire for a close relationship with God. We wanted that decision to come from their heart and be theirs alone. When that moment occurred, each child started a conversation with us by asking questions about Jesus and ended up wanting us to pray with them to receive Him as Savior. My husband and I have great peace knowing our son's and daughter's eternal future is joy-filled and secure.

No matter what age your children are, it's never too early or too late to start praying for their salvation. Jesus said, "Most assuredly, I say to you, unless one is born again, he cannot see the kingdom of God" (John 3:3). He also said, "Behold, I stand at the door and knock. If anyone hears My voice and opens the door, I will come in to him and dine with him, and he with Me" (Revelation 3:20). We want our children to open the door of their hearts to Jesus and experience God's kingdom, both in this life and forever after. Remember, if *you* don't pray for your children's eternal future, they may not have the kind you want them to have.

Once our children have received the Lord, we must continue praying for their relationship with Him. How many times have we heard of children who walk with God when they're young, but turn away from Him in their teens or adulthood? We want our children to always be "filled with the knowledge of His will in all wisdom and spiritual understanding" and to "walk worthy of the Lord, fully pleasing Him, being fruitful in every good work and increasing in the knowledge of God" (Colossians 1:9–10). Paul and Timothy prayed this for the children of God in Colosse, and we should pray it for our children. There is always more and more of the life of the Lord for each of us to open up to and experience. Praying for the Lord to pour out His Spirit upon our children must be our ongoing prayer.

∽◌ ◌∾

PRAYER

Lord,

I bring (name of child) before You and ask that You would help her (him) grow into a deep understanding of who You are. Open her (his) heart and bring her (him) to a full knowledge of the truth about You. Lord, You have said in Your Word, "If you confess with your mouth the Lord Jesus and believe in your heart that God has raised Him from the dead, you will be saved" (Romans 10:9). I pray for that kind of faith for my child. May she (he) call You her (his) Savior, be filled with Your Holy Spirit, acknowledge You in every area of her (his) life, and choose always to follow You and Your ways. Help her (him) to fully believe that Jesus laid down His life for her (him) so that she (he) might have life eternally and abundantly now. Help her (him) to comprehend the fullness of Your forgiveness so that she (he) will not live in guilt and condemnation.

I pray that she (he) will live a fruitful life, ever increasing in the knowledge of You. May she (he) always know Your will, have spiritual understanding, and walk in a manner that is pleasing in Your sight. You have said in Your Word that You will pour out Your Spirit on my offspring (Isaiah 44:3). I pray that

You would pour out Your Spirit upon (name of child) this day.

Thank You, Lord, that You care about her (his) eternal future even more than I do and that it is secure in You. In Jesus' name I pray that she (he) will not doubt or stray from the path You have for her (him) all the days of her (his) life.

~ ~

WEAPONS OF WARFARE

This is the will of Him who sent Me, that
everyone who sees the Son and believes
in Him may have everlasting life; and I
will raise him up at the last day.
JOHN 6:40

For this is good and acceptable in the sight of God
our Savior, who desires all men to be saved and to
come to the knowledge of the truth.
1 TIMOTHY 2:3–4

We know that the Son of God has come and has
given us an understanding, that we may know Him
who is true; and we are in Him who is true, in His
Son Jesus Christ. This is the true God and eternal life.
1 JOHN 5:20

This is the testimony: that God has given us eternal
life, and this life is in His Son.
1 JOHN 5:11

And I will pray to the Father, and He will give
you another Helper, that He may abide with you
forever—the Spirit of truth, whom the world
cannot receive, because it neither sees Him nor
knows Him; but you know Him, for He
dwells with you and will be in you.
JOHN 14:16–17

Honoring Parents and Resisting Rebellion

*I*t seems odd to *require* someone to honor us, doesn't it? If it's really honor, shouldn't they do it without being told? Well, this may be true concerning other people in our lives, but not our children. They must be taught.

The Bible says, "Children, obey your parents in the Lord, for this is right. Honor your father and mother, which is the first commandment with promise: that it may be well with you and you may live long on the earth" (Ephesians 6:1–3). If our children disobey this command of the Lord, they could not only be cut off from all God has for them, but their lives could be cut short as well. The Bible also says, "Whoever curses his father or his mother, his lamp will be put out in deep darkness" (Proverbs 20:20). The fact that we can affect the length and quality of our children's lives is reason enough to pray, instruct, and discipline them. Along with that, we must recognize and resist any rebellion that threatens to creep into their minds and cause them to do other than God commands.

Rebellion is actually pride put into action. Rebellious thoughts say, "I'm going to do what I want, no matter what

God or anyone else says about it." The Bible says "rebellion is as the sin of witchcraft" (1 Samuel 15:23) because its ultimate end is total opposition to God. That same verse also says that "stubbornness is as iniquity and idolatry." Pride gets us into rebellion, but stubbornness is what *keeps* us there. Anyone who walks in rebellion has a stubborn idol in his or her life. When children do not honor their father or mother, it is often the first sign that the idols in a child's heart—a child of any age—are pride and selfishness. That's why children who are not taught to obey their parents become rebellious. They say, "I want what I want when I want it."

"Woe to the rebellious children," says the Lord, "Who take counsel, but not of Me, and who devise plans, but not of My Spirit, that they may add sin to sin" (Isaiah 30:1). Identifying and destroying the idols of pride and selfishness through prayer can often be the key to breaking a child's rebellion.

The opposite of rebellion is obedience, or walking in the will of God. Obedience brings great security and the confidence of knowing you're where you're supposed to be, doing what you're supposed to do. The Bible promises that if we are obedient we will be blessed, but if we are not we will dwell in darkness and be destroyed. We don't want that for our children. We want our children to walk in obedience so that they will have confidence, security, long life, and peace. One of the first steps of obedience for children is to obey and honor their parents. This is something a child must be taught, but teaching becomes easier when prayer paves the way.

When my son was fourteen years old, he covered his bedroom walls with posters of the musicians he admired most. The problem was that in some of the pictures both the attire and the music being represented were offensive to his father and me and not glorifying to God. When we asked Christopher to take those particular posters down and explained why, he balked and then with a less than humble spirit did what we asked. A short time later, however, he replaced them with new ones which were just as bad. We again confronted him, took appropriate disciplinary measures, and this time *we* took them *all* down for him.

Christopher was not happy, and we recognized we were dealing with the early manifestations of a rebellious spirit. So we decided to do as the Bible says and "put on the whole armor of God that you may be able to stand against the wiles of the devil" (Ephesians 6:11). We prayed, we employed the Word of God, and we professed our faith in God's ability to make us overcomers. We did battle in the Spirit and witnessed the peace of God take control of the situation. Our son's attitude changed, and the next time he put up posters they met the requirements we, as his parents, had established. This was the power of God in action, employed by praying parents.

Wall posters seem like such a minor issue now, but at the time we were dealing with a strong will that was exalting itself over parents and God. And by resisting that display of rebellion, we were able to stop it before it became something major. We were determined to win the struggle because we knew we had God and His Word on our side and because, for our son, something eternal was at stake.

If your child is older, an adolescent or even an adult, and rebellion is already clearly manifested in his or her behavior, the discipline and teaching part will be harder, but you still have the power of prayer. Remember, your battle is not with your son or daughter. "For we do not wrestle against flesh and blood, but against principalities, against powers, against the rulers of the darkness of this age, against spiritual hosts of wickedness in the heavenly places" (Ephesians 6:12). Your battle is with the enemy. The good news is that Jesus has given you authority "over all the power of the enemy" (Luke 10:19). Don't be afraid to take advantage of that.

Rebellion will surface in your child at one time or another. Be ready to meet the challenge with prayer and the Word of God, along with correction, discipline, and teaching. Don't be intimidated by a rebellious spirit. Jesus is Lord above that, too.

❦ ❦

PRAYER

Lord,

I pray that You would give (name of child) a heart that desires to obey You. Put into him (her) a longing to spend time with You, in Your Word and in prayer, listening for Your voice. Shine Your light upon any secret or unseen rebellion that is taking root in his (her) heart, so that it can be identified and destroyed. Lord, I pray that he (she) will not give himself (herself) over to pride, selfishness, and rebellion, but that he (she) will be delivered from it. By the authority You've given me in Jesus' name, I "stand against the wiles of the devil" and I resist idolatry, rebellion, stubbornness, and disrespect; they will have no part in my son's (daughter's) life, nor will my child walk a path of destruction and death because of them.

Your Word instructs, "Children, obey your parents in all things, for this is well pleasing to the Lord" (Colossians 3:20). I pray that You would turn the heart of this child toward his (her) parents and enable him (her) to honor and obey father and mother so that his (her) life will be long and good. Turn his (her) heart toward You so that all he (she) does is pleasing in Your sight. May he (she) learn to identify and confront pride and rebellion in himself (herself) and be willing to confess and repent of it. Make him (her) uncomfortable with sin. Help him (her) to know the beauty and simplicity of walking with a sweet and humble spirit in obedience and submission to You.

∽ ⁓

WEAPONS OF WARFARE

If you are willing and obedient, you shall eat the good of the land; but if you refuse and rebel, you shall be devoured by the sword; for the mouth of the Lord has spoken.
ISAIAH 1:19–20

Those who sat in darkness and in the shadow of death, bound in affliction and irons—because they rebelled against the words of God, and despised the counsel of the Most High, therefore He brought down their heart with labor; they fell down, and there was none to help.
PSALM 107:10–12

The eye that mocks his father, and scorns obedience to his mother, the ravens of the valley will pick it out, and the young eagles will eat it.
PROVERBS 30:17

My son, hear the instruction of your father, and do
not forsake the law of your mother; for they will
be graceful ornaments on your head, and
chains about your neck.

PROVERBS 1:8–9

Nevertheless they were disobedient and rebelled
against You. . . . Therefore You delivered them
into the hand of their enemies who
oppressed them.

NEHEMIAH 9:26–27

CHAPTER SEVEN

Maintaining Good
Family Relationships

My sister and I experienced a major breach in our relationship a number of years ago and ended up not communicating with each other for two years. All this was due to a complete misunderstanding. Our own individual hurts had masked our ability to see clearly what was happening in each other's personality and lives. We were in two different worlds, even though we had been raised in the same house within the same family. This whole episode was very upsetting to me, and I didn't stop praying about it until my sister and I were finally reconciled and our relationship restored. However, I believe if we'd had praying parents, it wouldn't have happened in the first place.

One of the things the enemy of our soul likes to do is get into the middle of God-ordained relationships and cause them to misfire, miscommunicate, short-circuit, fracture, or disconnect. The more a family can be splintered apart, the weaker and more ineffectual they become and the more the enemy has control of their lives. The way to avoid this is through prayer. When you cover your family relationships in prayer, whether it be with children, parents, stepparents, brothers, sisters, grandparents, aunts, uncles, cousins, husband, or wife, there will be far fewer instances of strained or severed relationships.

When my daughter was born, her brother was four and a half years old. I prayed from the beginning that Christopher and Amanda would have a close relationship with each other, and I did all I could to see that happen. Their friendship was so tight in their early years that other people noticed and remarked about it. Then one day Christopher became a teenager and everything changed. He suddenly had places to go and people to see and no longer had time for his little sister. The humorous put downs he enjoyed with his friends were not well received by his younger female sibling. Feeling rejected and hurt, she would retaliate. I became a referee and it grieved my heart to see what was happening.

Then one day I realized something important: because everything had been going so well between Amanda and Christopher, I had stopped praying about their relationship. So I began praying about it again, wishing I had never stopped. It took some time, but little by little I observed a softening in their attitude toward one another. I know that if I had done nothing there would most likely have been the same permanent breach between them as there have been in too many relationships in my family's past. Although my children's relationship is still not where I want it to be, it's getting stronger all the time. And I will continue to hold up this matter in prayer as long as I'm alive.

How many family relationships are left to chance because no one prays about them? Far too many, I suspect. It's sad to see families split apart and individual members have nothing to do with one another when they are grown. It's heartbreaking to think of that happening with our own children. Yet it doesn't have to be that way.

In Isaiah 58, God tells of all the wonderful things that will happen when we fast and pray. He says, "You shall raise up the foundations of many generations; and you shall be called the Repairer of the Breach" (Isaiah 58:12). God wants us to restore unity, to maintain the family bonds in the Lord, and to leave a spiritual inheritance of solidarity that can last for generations.

The Bible also says, "Be of the same mind toward one another. Do not set your mind on high things, but associate with the humble. Do not be wise in your own opinion" (Romans 12:16). We need to pray for humility and unity.

Jesus said, "Blessed are the peacemakers, for they shall be called the sons of God" (Matthew 5:9). I say, let's be peacemakers. There are obviously not enough of us in the world. "Let us pursue the things which make for peace and the things by which one may edify another" (Romans 14:19). Let's begin by praying for those closest to us—our children—and branch out from there.

~~~

PRAYER

Lord,

I pray for (name of child) and her (his) relationship with all family members. Protect and preserve them from any unresolved or permanent breach. Fill her (his) heart with Your love and give her (him) an abundance of compassion and forgiveness that will overflow to each member of the family. Specifically, I pray for a close, happy, loving, and fulfilling relationship between (name of child) and (name of family member) for all the days of their lives. May there always be good communication between them and may unforgiveness have no root in their hearts. Help them to love, value, appreciate, and respect one another so that the God-ordained tie between them cannot be broken. I pray according to Your Word, that they "be kindly affectionate to one another with brotherly love, in honor giving preference to one another" (Romans 12:10).

Teach my child to resolve misunderstandings according to Your Word. And if any division has already begun, if any relationship is strained or severed, Lord, I pray that You will drive out the wedge of division and bring healing. I pray that there be no strain, breach, misunderstanding, arguing, fighting, or separating of ties. Give her (him) a heart of forgiveness and reconciliation.

Your Word instructs us to "be of one mind, having compassion for one another; love as brothers, be tenderhearted, be courteous" (1 Peter 3:8). Help her (him) to live accordingly, "endeavoring to keep the unity of the Spirit in the bond of peace" (Ephesians 4:3). In Jesus' name I pray that You would instill a love and compassion in her (him) for all family members that is strong and unending, like a cord that cannot be broken.

WEAPONS OF WARFARE

Blessed are the peacemakers, for they shall
be called sons of God.
MATTHEW 5:9

Behold, how good and how pleasant it is for
brethren to dwell together in unity!
PSALM 133:1

Now may the God of patience and comfort grant you
to be like-minded toward one another, according
to Christ Jesus, that you may with one mind and
one mouth glorify the God and Father of
our Lord Jesus Christ.
ROMANS 15:5–6

If it is possible, as much as depends on you, live
peaceably with all men.
ROMANS 12:18

Now I plead with you, brethren, by the name of our
Lord Jesus Christ, that you all speak the same thing,
and that there be no divisions among you, but that
you be perfectly joined together in the same mind
and in the same judgment.
1 CORINTHIANS 1:10

CHAPTER EIGHT

Attracting Godly Friends and Role Models

I have always prayed for my children's friends and, for the most part, they've had great ones. Occasionally they've made friends that, as a parent, I had reservations about. Not because I didn't like them; actually, in every instance, I liked them very much. What I didn't like was the type of influence they were on my child, and what the combination of that child and mine produced. The way I always handled this situation was to pray. I prayed for that child to be changed or else be taken out of my child's life. In every case that prayer was answered. In several instances, the passage of time revealed the accuracy of my apprehension. The children I was concerned about turned out to have trouble-filled lives.

Parents often have gut-level feelings about their children's friends. When that happens, ask God for Holy Spirit-inspired discernment and pray accordingly.

One of my most fervent times of intercession regarding my children's friends came when we moved from California to Tennessee. We made the move just as my son was starting his senior year of high school and my daughter was beginning seventh grade—the two worst times for children to change schools. Normally I wouldn't have wanted my children to change schools at that time, but in this instance my husband and I felt the clear leading of the Lord to make the move. Because I knew how difficult this time could be for my children, every day in the months before and after we moved I prayed, "Lord, help my children to make godly friends. I know that *You* brought us here and You will not leave my children forsaken. I'm concerned that in their need for acceptance they'll end up with friends whose moral standards are not as high as Yours. Bring godly role models into their lives."

The first six months were very lonely times for both Christopher and Amanda, and I often lay awake at night praying on their behalf. There was nothing else I could do. I couldn't intervene and hook them up with good friends as I might have when they were younger. But even if I'd been able to do that, I never would have done as good a job as God did in answer to my prayers. Eventually people came into their lives who have become some of the greatest friends they've ever had. This is not just a coincidence or a fairy tale ending. This is a result of intercessory prayer. This is the result of crying out to God, saying, "God, help my children to attract godly friends and role models."

God's Word clearly instructs us: "Do not be unequally yoked together with unbelievers. For what fellowship has righteousness with lawlessness? And what communion has light with darkness? And what accord has Christ with Belial? Or what part has a believer with an unbeliever?" (2 Corinthians 6:14–15). That doesn't mean our children can never have a non-believing friend. But there is clear implication that their closest friends, the ones to whom they have strong ties, should be believers. "Can two walk together, unless they are agreed?" (Amos 3:3). No, they can't. That means if they are not agreed, somebody has to change. And that's why "The righteous should choose his friends carefully, for the way of the wicked leads them astray" (Proverbs 12:26).

If your child doesn't have close believing friends, begin to pray right now toward that end. Pray for the unbelieving friends to receive the Lord and for strong believing friends to come into their lives. Too often parents feel helpless to do anything about the bad influence of certain people in their children's lives. But we are not helpless. We have the *power of God* and the *truth of His Word* behind us. Don't stand for someone leading your child astray. There is too much written in Scripture about the importance of the company we keep to take a passive approach to this issue.

One of the greatest influences in our children's lives will be their friends and role models. How can we *not* pray about them?

∾ ❧ ∽

PRAYER

Lord,

I lift up (name of child) to You and ask that You would bring godly friends and role models into his (her) life. Give him (her) the wisdom he (she) needs to choose friends who are godly and help him (her) to never compromise his (her) walk with You in order to gain acceptance. Give me Holy Spirit-inspired discernment in how I guide or influence him (her) in the selection of friends. I pray that You would take anyone who is not a godly influence out of his (her) life or else transform that person into Your likeness.

Your Word says, "He who walks with wise men will be wise, but the companion of fools will be destroyed" (Proverbs 13:20). Don't let my child be a companion of fools. Enable him (her) to walk with wise friends and not have to experience the destruction that can happen by walking with foolish people. Deliver him (her) from anyone with an ungodly character so he (she) will not learn that person's ways and set a snare for his (her) own soul.

Whenever there is grief over a lost friendship, comfort him (her) and send new friends with whom he (she) can connect, share, and be the person You created him (her) to be. Take away any loneliness or low self-esteem that would cause him (her) to seek out less than God-glorifying relationships.

In Jesus' name I pray that You would teach him (her) the meaning of true friendship. Teach him (her) how to be a good friend and make strong, close, lasting relationships. May each of his (her) friendships always glorify You.

WEAPONS OF WARFARE

Do not enter the path of the wicked, and do
not walk in the way of evil.
PROVERBS 4:14

I have written to you not to keep company with
anyone named a brother, who is sexually immoral, or
covetous, or an idolater, or a reviler, or a drunkard, or
an extortioner—not even to eat with such a person.
1 CORINTHIANS 5:11

My son, fear the Lord and the king; do not associate
with those given to change; for their calamity will
rise suddenly, and who knows the ruin those
two can bring?
PROVERBS 24:21–22

Make no friendship with an angry man, and with
a furious man do not go, lest you learn his ways
and set a snare for your soul.
PROVERBS 22:24–25

Blessed is the man who walks not in the counsel of
the ungodly, nor stands in the path of sinners,
nor sits in the seat of the scornful.
PSALM 1:1

CHAPTER NINE

Developing a
Hunger for the Things
of God

W hen we read in the newspaper about young people stealing, killing, destroying property, or being sexually promiscuous, we can be sure that those individuals do not have a healthy fear of the Lord, nor a good understanding of His ways, nor a hunger for the things of God. Some of these young people may even be from Christian families and have received Jesus, but because they haven't been taught to fear God and desire His presence they are controlled by their flesh.

Fearing God means having a deeply committed respect, love, and reverence for God's authority and power. It means being afraid of what life would be like without Him and being grateful that because of His love we'll never have to experience such despair. It means hungering for all that God is and all that He has for us.

There is so much in the world to divert our children's attention away from the things of God, and the devil will come to each child with his agenda and plan to see if they will buy into it. But when we do our part to teach, instruct, discipline, and train our children in the ways of God...

when we read them stories from God's Word,

when we teach them how to pray and have faith that God is who He says He is and will do what He says He'll do,

when we help them get plugged in with godly friends,

when we show them that walking with God brings joy and fulfillment, not boredom and restrictions,

when we pray with and for them about everything, . . . then our children will develop a hunger for the things of God.

They will know that the things of God are top priority.

They will become God-controlled and not flesh controlled.

They will long for His ways, His Word, and His presence.

They will fear God and live a longer and better life.

For "The fear of the Lord prolongs days, but the years of the wicked will be shortened" (Proverbs 10:27).

When my husband and I knew we were moving from California to Tennessee, the first thing we prayed about was finding a great church with an excellent youth group. That prayer was answered, and it was the main reason our children were able to make this major adjustment successfully; for it was in their new church and youth group that they found godly friends and continued growing in their relationship with the Lord. Finding a church that is actively teaching God's Word, showing God's love, and sharing God's joy with its children and young people will make a big difference in helping your children develop a hunger for the things of God.

Start right now by praying for your child to fear God, have faith in Him and His Word, and develop the kind of heart that seeks after Him. This could be the determining factor in whether your child will have a constant struggle living in the flesh or be fulfilled and blessed living in the Spirit. Remember, "there is no want to those who fear Him" (Psalm 34:9). It's never too early to begin praying about this. Don't wait another moment.

~~~~~

PRAYER

Lord,

I pray for (name of child) to have an ever-increasing hunger for more of You. May she (he) long for Your presence—long to spend time with You in prayer, praise, and worship. Give her (him) a desire for the truth of Your Word and a love for Your laws and Your ways. Teach her (him) to live by faith and be led by the Holy Spirit, having an availability to do what You tell her (him) to do. May she (he) be so aware of the fullness of Your Holy Spirit in her (him) that when she (he) is depleted in any way she (he) will immediately run to You to be renewed and refreshed.

I pray that her (his) heart will not have any allegiances or diversions away from You, but rather that she (he) would be repulsed by ungodliness and all that is in opposition to You. May a deep reverence and love for You and Your ways color everything she (he) does and every choice she (he) makes. Help her (him) to understand the consequences of her (his) actions and know that a life controlled by the flesh will only reap death. May she (he) not be wise in her (his) own eyes, but rather "fear the Lord and depart from evil" (Proverbs 3:7).

I pray that she (he) will be reliable, dependable, responsible, compassionate, sensitive, loving, and giving to others. Deliver her (him) from any pride, laziness, slothfulness, selfishness, or lust of the flesh. I pray that she (he) will have a teachable and submissive spirit that says "Yes" to the things of God and

"No" to the things of the flesh. Strengthen her (him) to stand strong in her (his) convictions.

I pray that she (he) will always desire to be an active member of a Christian church that is alive to the truth of Your Word and the power of Holy Spirit-led worship, prayer, and teaching. As she (he) learns to read Your Word, write Your law in her (his) mind and on her (his) heart so that she (he) always walks with a confident assurance of the righteousness of Your commands. As she (he) learns to pray, may she (he) also learn to listen for Your voice. I pray that her (his) relationship with You will never become lukewarm, indifferent, or shallow. May there always be a Holy Spirit fire in her (his) heart and an unwavering desire for the things of God.

WEAPONS OF WARFARE

Blessed are those who hunger and thirst for
righteousness, for they shall be filled.
MATTHEW 5:6

The fear of the Lord is a fountain of life, to
turn one away from the snares of death.
PROVERBS 14:27

I have been crucified with Christ; it is no longer I
who live, but Christ lives in me; and the life which I
now live in the flesh I live by faith in the Son of God,
who loved me and gave Himself for me.
GALATIANS 2:20

Blessed are those who keep His testimonies,
who seek Him with the whole heart!
PSALM 119:2

Teach me Your way, O Lord; I will walk in Your truth;
unite my heart to fear Your name. I will praise You,
O Lord my God, with all my heart, and I will
glorify Your name forevermore.
PSALM 86:11–12

CHAPTER TEN

Being the Person God Created

I know a man who gave up his high-paying job as an engineer for a large company in order to become an auto mechanic. He did it because he loved doing auto repair more than anything else. He was not only the best mechanic in town, but also a happy and fulfilled person. I know another man who refused to follow the call of God to be a pastor because he wanted to be a successful businessman instead. He eventually lost his family through divorce, suffered the death of his young son, and saw his life dissipate into sadness and loss. How different it all might have been if he'd had a praying parent or someone helping him to understand who God made him to be.

Not knowing who God made us to be, trying to be who we are *not*, or even just *desiring* to be someone else, can only lead to a life of misery, frustration, and unfulfillment. We see examples of this in adults who work at jobs they hate, living miserable lives that always fall short of their expectations. You can be sure that at some point such persons bought into a lie that says, "Who I am is not good enough. I need to be someone else." Perhaps they've never been encouraged to recognize their God-given strengths and talents. Certainly they've not realized who God made them to be.

We become the person God created us to be when we ask God for guidance and then do what He tells us to do. The prophet Jeremiah kept telling the people of Israel what God wanted them to hear, but they refused to listen. Finally, the Lord said, "Behold, I will bring on Judah and on all the inhabitants of Jerusalem all the doom that I have pronounced against them; because I have spoken to them but they have not heard, and I have called to them but they have not answered" (Jeremiah 35:17). Destructive things happen to us when we don't respond to God's voice. We can pray that our children have ears to hear God's voice so such misery doesn't happen to them.

One of the devil's plans for young people is to get them to compare themselves with others, judge themselves as deficient, and then seek to be someone they were not created to be. Young girls compare themselves to other girls and see them as having prettier hair, nicer clothes, a better house, greater popularity, higher scholastic achievement, or more talent and beauty. Young boys look at other boys and see them as taller, better looking, greater athletes, having more friends, more hair, more possessions, or more skills and ability. This day after day comparing and falling short can attack the true identity of a child. I've known far too many young people who, by the time they reach their teens, long to be someone other than who they are. Instead of appreciating who God made them to be and spending their energies trying to be their best at that, they strive and strain to be something they can't be, doing something that will never fulfill them. Our prayers can block this plan of the enemy and give our children a clear vision of themselves and their future.

From the time my children were small I prayed for God to reveal to us what their gifts and talents are. Along with that I asked for wisdom as to how to best encourage, nurture, develop, and train them to be all God made them to be. Helping them to appreciate their strengths and not dwell on their weaknesses was part of that; and since this wasn't easy during their teen years, it was a frequent focus of my prayers.

The biggest part of helping my son and daughter understand who God created them to be was encouraging their relationship with the Lord. I know they will never fully understand who *they* are until they understand who God is.

In the Bible where God promises to pour out His Spirit on our children, He says of them, "They will spring up among the grass like willows by the watercourses. One will say, 'I am the Lord's'; another will write with his hand, 'The Lord's'" (Isaiah 44:4–5). These children will know who they are. They will be filled with His Spirit and have that inner confidence of knowing they are His. You will see a confident and radiant expression on the face of any child who can say with conviction, "I am the Lord's." Do you want that for your child enough to pray for it?

❧ ❧

PRAYER

Lord,

I pray that You would pour out Your Spirit upon (name of child) this day and anoint him (her) for all that You've called him (her) to be and do. Lord, You have said, "Let each one remain with God in that state in which he was called" (1 Corinthians 7:24). May it be for this child according to Your Word, that he (she) never stray from what You have called him (her) to be and do, or try to be something he (she) is not.

Deliver him (her) from any evil plan of the devil to rob him (her) of life, to steal away his (her) uniqueness and giftedness, to compromise the path you've called him (her) to walk, or to destroy the person You created him (her) to be. May he (she) not be a follower of anyone but You, but may he (she) be a leader of people into Your kingdom. Help him (her) to grow into a complete understanding of his (her) authority in Jesus, while retaining a submissive and humble spirit. May the fruit of the Spirit, which is love, joy, peace, patience, kindness, goodness, faithfulness, gentleness, and self-control grow in him (her) daily (Galatians 5:22). May he (she) find his (her) identity in You, view himself (herself) as Your instrument, and know that he (she) is complete in You. Give him (her) a vision for his (her) life when setting goals for the future and a sense of purpose about what You've called him (her) to do. Help him (her) to see himself (herself) as You do—from his (her) future and not from his (her) past. May he (she) be convinced that Your thoughts toward him (her) are thoughts of peace and not of evil, to give him (her) a future and a hope (Jeremiah 29:11). Teach him (her) to look to You as his (her) hope for the future. May he (she) understand it is You "who has saved us and called us with a holy calling, not according to our works, but according to His own purpose and grace which was given to us in Christ Jesus before time began" (2 Timothy 1:9). May his (her) commitment to being who You created him (her) to be enable him (her) to grow daily in confidence and Holy Spirit boldness.

WEAPONS OF WARFARE

You are a chosen generation, a royal priesthood, a
holy nation, His own special people, that you may
proclaim the praises of Him who called you out
of darkness into His marvelous light.
1 PETER 2:9

Eye has not seen, nor ear heard, nor have entered
into the heart of man the things which God has
prepared for those who love Him.
1 CORINTHIANS 2:9

Be even more diligent to make your calling and
election sure, for if you do these things you
will never stumble.
2 PETER 1:10

We know that all things work together for good to
those who love God, to those who are the called
according to His purpose. For whom He foreknew,
He also predestined to be conformed to the image
of His Son, that He might be the firstborn among
many brethren. Moreover whom He predestined,
these He also called; whom He called, these
He also justified; and whom He justified,
these He also glorified.
ROMANS 8:28–30

Arise, shine; for your light has come! and the
glory of the Lord is risen upon you.
ISAIAH 60:1

Following Truth, Rejecting Lies

In our house, our children know that while it might be possible to cut a deal on the punishment for certain infractions, if lying is part of the offense, the punishment will be swift, immediate, unpleasant, and nonnegotiable. We consider telling a lie to be the worst offense because it is foundational for all other evil acts. Every sin or crime begins with someone believing or speaking a lie. Even if the lie is as simple as "I can get what I want if I lie," it paves the way for evil.

Early on, my daughter tested the water with "little white lies." But it didn't take long for her to see that the punishment for lying greatly overshadowed any possible advantage she thought she might gain as a result of telling a lie. My son, on the other hand, didn't just dabble. If he was going to tell a lie, he went for a big one.

When Christopher was seven, he was playing baseball with his friend Steven out in front of Steven's house. The ball struck the large front picture window with a loud crack, which immediately brought Steven's mother to the front door.

"Who did this?" she asked.

"I didn't do it," said Steven.

"I didn't do it," said Christopher.

"Steven, you mean to tell me you did not strike the window with this ball?" she said.

"No, I didn't," answered Steven emphatically.

"Christopher, did *you* strike the window with the ball?" she asked.

"If you saw me do it, I did it. If you didn't see me do it, I didn't do it," Christopher answered in his most matter-of-fact voice.

"I didn't see you do it," she said.

"Then I didn't do it," he replied.

When Steven's mom told us what happened, we knew we needed to deal with this matter immediately so Christopher would not think he could get away with lying.

"Christopher, someone saw everything that happened. Would you like to tell us about it?" I said, wanting his full confession and a repentant heart.

He hung his head and said, "Okay, I did it."

We had a long talk about what the Word of God says about lying. "Satan is a liar," I told him. "All the evil he does begins with a lie. People who lie believe that lying will make things better for them. But actually, it does just the opposite. That's because telling a lie means you have aligned yourself with Satan. Every time you lie you give Satan a piece of your heart. The more lies you tell, the more you give place in your heart to Satan's lying spirit, until eventually you can't stop yourself from lying. The Bible says, "Getting treasures by a lying tongue is the fleeting fantasy of those who seek death" (Proverbs 21:6). In other words, you may *think* you're getting something by lying, but all you're really doing is bringing death into your life. The consequences of telling the truth have to be better than death. Even the punishment you receive from your parents for lying will be far more pleasant than the consequences of lying. For the Bible promises that "A false witness will not go unpunished, and he who speaks lies will not escape" (Proverbs 19:5).

It was quite some time after that incident before Christopher asked me who had seen him that day.

"It was God," I explained. "He saw you. I've always asked Him to reveal to me anything I need to know about you or your sister. He is the Spirit of Truth, you understand."

"Mom, that's not fair," was all he said. After that, though, on the few occasions when he told a lie, he always came to me immediately to confess it.

"I thought I better tell you before you heard it from God," he would explain.

Children will lie at one time or another. The question is not *if* they will, but whether or not lying will become something they believe they can get away with. How we handle their lying will determine the outcome. If we don't teach our children what God says about lying, they won't know why it's wrong. If we don't discipline them when they lie, they will think that lying has no consequence. If we don't pray about this issue now, there will be bigger issues to deal with later.

The Bible says of the devil, "He was a murderer from the beginning, and does not stand in the truth, because there is no truth in him. When he speaks a lie, he speaks from his own resources, for he is a liar and the father of it" (John 8:44). When you consider the source, there is no way you can sit by and allow the seed of a lie to take root in your child's heart.

Pray now that any lying spirit will be uprooted—not only in your children, but in *yourself* as well. Sometimes parents are soft on this subject with their children because they lie themselves. We need to reject the way of lying and follow the truth. We need to be an example to our children. *We* want to be able to say as John did, "I have no greater joy than to hear that my children walk in truth" (3 John 1:4). We don't want our children to be aligned with the father of lies. *We* want them to be aligned with the Father of Lights (James 1:17).

PRAYER

Lord,

I pray that You will fill (name of child) with Your Spirit of truth. Give her (him) a heart that loves truth and follows after it, rejecting all lies as a manifestation of the enemy. Flush out anything in her (him) that would entertain a lying spirit and cleanse her (him) from any death that has crept in as a result of lies she (he) may have spoken or thought. Help her (him) to understand that every lie gives the devil a piece of her (his) heart, and into the hole that's left comes confusion, death, and separation from Your presence. Deliver her (him) from any lying spirit. I pray that she (he) not be blinded or deceived, but always be able to clearly understand Your truth.

I pray that she (he) will never be able to get away with lying—that all lies will come to light and be exposed. If she (he) lies, may she (he) be so miserable that confession and its consequences will seem like a relief. Help me to teach her (him) what it means to lie, and effectively discipline her (him) when she (he) tests that principle. Your Word says that "when He, the Spirit of truth, has come, He will guide you into all truth" (John 16:13). I pray that Your Spirit of truth will guide her (him) into all truth. May she (he) never be a person who gives place to lies, but rather a person of integrity who follows hard after the Spirit of truth.

❧ ❧

WEAPONS OF WARFARE

Lying lips are an abomination to the Lord, but those who deal truthfully are His delight.
PROVERBS 12:22

My soul melts from heaviness; strengthen me according to Your Word. Remove from me the way of lying, and grant me Your law graciously.
PSALM 119:28–29

Let not mercy and truth forsake you; bind them around your neck, write them on the tablet of your heart, and so find favor and high esteem in the sight of God and man.
PROVERBS 3:3–4

The coming of the lawless one is according to the working of Satan, with all power, signs, and lying wonders, and with all unrighteous deception among those who perish, because they did not receive the love of the truth, that they might be saved.
2 THESSALONIANS 2:9–10

If you love Me, keep My commandments. And I will pray the Father, and He will give you another Helper, that He may abide with you forever—the Spirit of

truth, whom the world cannot receive, because it
neither sees Him nor knows Him; but you know
Him, for He dwells with you and will be in you.

JOHN 14:15–17

CHAPTER TWELVE

Enjoying a Life of Health and Healing

When my daughter was four years old she was diagnosed with an eye problem which the doctor said would require her to have surgery and wear thick glasses for the rest of her life.

"Lord, is this what You have for my daughter?" I prayed. "Show me if it is because I don't have any peace about it."

My husband felt as I did, so we prayed for Amanda's eyes to be healed. We also prayed that, if necessary, we would find another doctor who could help her. The next day, seemingly out of nowhere, I received a call from someone who had no idea about Amanda's situation, but had information about an excellent specialist in the eye clinic at Children's Hospital in Los Angeles. I took Amanda to see this doctor, and after he thoroughly tested her, he offered encouraging news. He believed that contact lenses would correct the problem and she wouldn't have to have surgery. We felt immediate peace about his diagnosis and placed Amanda in this doctor's care, although we never stopped praying for her healing.

For eight years she wore contact lenses under the doctor's strict supervision. We did tire of putting her contacts in every morning and taking them out every night, and I grew tired of having to run to school each time she lost one on the playground. But we persevered. Then one day when she was twelve years old, she went for her regular eye exam and the doctor said, "You no longer need contacts, glasses, or surgery. Your eyes are fine." We were ecstatic and so very grateful to God for His direction and His answer to prayer.

We have prayed our children through every cold, flu, fever, and injury, and the Lord has always answered. We never hesitate to take them to a doctor when they need it, of course, because we know God heals through doctors, too. But the Bible says, "Is anyone among you sick? Let him call for the elders of the church, and let them pray over him, anointing him with oil in the name of the Lord. And the prayer of faith will save the sick, and the Lord will raise him up" (James 5:14–15). The point is to pray first and see a doctor whenever necessary. And then, when we are healed, we are not to question or doubt.

After our son was in the car accident which I related earlier in this book, his back and knees were very sore. We, of course, prayed immediately for his healing and made sure he was x-rayed and checked thoroughly at the hospital. We continued to pray for complete healing, however, because we did not want him to have weakness in his back and knees that could be a problem for the rest of his life. When the insurance company for the driver of the other car, who was at fault in the accident, called to settle their responsibility, I felt *strongly* impressed by the Scripture, "'For I will restore health to you and heal you of your wounds,' says the Lord" (Jeremiah 30:17). I was certain that my son was healed and that we were to refuse any compensation whatsoever. It was as if I heard God say, "Do you want the money or do you want the healing?"

"I want the healing, Lord, and thank You," I answered without hesitation.

I'm not saying that it is a lack of faith to collect insurance. I don't believe that at all. But in this instance refusing compensation was the right thing for us to do. When we pray for healing and God heals, we shouldn't act like it didn't happen.

The Bible is full of healing promises. David said, "Bless the Lord, O my soul, and forget not all His benefits: who forgives all your iniquities, who heals all your diseases" (Psalm 103:2–3). One of the main things Jesus wants to be to us is the forgiver of our sins and the healer of our bodies. Let's lay hold of the health and healing He has for our children by praying for it even *before* the need arises.

❧ ❧

PRAYER

Lord,

Because You have instructed us in Your Word that we are to pray for one another so that we may be healed, I pray for healing and wholeness for (name of child). I pray that sickness and infirmity will have no place or power in his (her) life. I pray for protection against any disease coming into his (her) body. Your Word says, "He sent His word and healed them, and delivered them from their destructions" (Psalm 107:20). Wherever there is disease, illness, or infirmity in his (her) body, I pray that You, Lord, would touch him (her) with Your healing power and restore him (her) to total health.

Deliver him (her) from any destruction or injury that could come upon him (her). Specifically I ask You to heal (name any specific problem). If we are to see a doctor, I pray that You, Lord, would show us who that should be. Give that doctor wisdom and full knowledge of the best way to proceed.

Thank You, Lord, that You suffered and died for us so that we might be healed. I lay claim to that heritage of healing which You have promised in Your Word and provided for those who believe. I look to You for a life of health, healing, and wholeness for my child.

WEAPONS OF WARFARE

He was wounded for our transgressions, He was
bruised for our iniquities; the chastisement
for our peace was upon Him, and by His
stripes we are healed.

ISAIAH 53:5

Confess your trespasses to one another, and pray for
one another, that you may be healed. The effective,
fervent prayer of a righteous man avails much.

JAMES 5:16

But to you who fear My name the Sun of Righteousness shall arise with healing in His wings.

MALACHI 4:2

For to this you were called, because Christ also
suffered for us, leaving us an example, that you
should follow His steps . . . who Himself bore our
sins in His own body on the tree, that we, having
died to sins, might live for righteousness—by
whose stripes you were healed.
1 PETER 2:22,24

Your light shall break forth like the morning, your
healing shall spring forth speedily, and your
righteousness shall go before you; the glory
of the Lord shall be your rear guard.
ISAIAH 58:8

CHAPTER THIRTEEN

Having the Motivation for Proper Body Care

*L*eft to themselves in this junk-food world, children will be attracted to all the wrong foods. Much of what we eat has been so masked, processed, stripped, altered, added to, and taken away from, that it has little food value. But children don't care about that. They just want food that looks good, smells good, tastes good—and if they've seen it advertised on TV that's even better. And if you have a spouse, as I do, who loves junk food and brings it into the house for himself and the children, you have an even more difficult situation. I knew I was in trouble the day I came home, after leaving our ten-month-old son with his father for the afternoon, and found carbonated cola in his baby bottle. I realized then that prayer was my only hope.

I did my best to make healthy meals desirable, and I tried to teach my children proper eating habits. I was even willing to endure criticism from them.

"I hate this. We're the only people in the world who don't have any junk food in their kitchen," said my son in utter disgust.

"We're so healthy it makes me sick," said my daughter with tears in her eyes.

Because I believe that "better is a dry morsel with quietness, than a house full of feasting with strife" (Proverbs 17:1), I haven't made an issue of this nearly as much as I would like. I know I can't force my children to make healthful food choices when I'm not around to remind them. Only the power of God through prayer can make the difference.

Nearly everyone struggles somewhat in the area of proper body care. But because of the health books I've written and the exercise videos I've made, I have come in contact with countless people who seriously battle with this issue—even to the point of heartbreaking agony and defeat. We do our children a disservice if we don't support them in prayer, as well as guide and instruct them in healthy practices, so that they don't end up with this kind of misery.

If your children are young, start praying for them to be attracted to healthful food and to desire to exercise and take good care of their bodies. If you don't, by the time they are in their teens, they may have already developed bad habits and the situation can quickly get out of control. We see this in the eating disorders that are epidemic among teen and college-age girls and which are now being seen more and more in boys. Start praying before any such symptoms appear.

If your children are older, begin right now to intercede on their behalf. Many young women who suffer with anorexia and bulimia struggle against more than just the desires of the flesh; they face a spiritual battle as well. They are bound to obsessive eating habits which are deadly and completely opposed to the way God created them to live. I have known far too many young women who suffer in this regard. The ones who have parents who learn to intercede on their behalf later have success stories to tell. Others less fortunate do not.

Your child needs Holy Spirit guidance and strength to do what's right for his or her body. Your prayers can spare them much defeat, frustration, and heartbreak. Don't you wish you'd had someone praying about this for you? I know I do.

❦ ❦

PRAYER

Lord,

I lift (name of child) to You and ask that You would place in her (him) a desire to eat healthy food. I know that throughout her (his) life she (he) will be tempted to make poor food choices and eat that which brings death instead of life. Help her (him) to understand what's good for her (him) and what isn't, and give her (him) a desire for food that is healthful. Let her (him) be repulsed or dissatisfied with food that is harmful.

I pray that she (he) be spared from all eating disorders in any form. By the authority given me in Jesus Christ (Luke 10:19), on my daughter's (son's) behalf, I say "No to anorexia," "No to bulimia," "No to food addiction," "No to overeating," "No to starvation diets," "No to any kind of unbalanced eating habits."

Lord, Your Word says, "You shall know the truth, and the truth shall make you free" (John 8:32). Help her (him) to see the truth about the way she (he) is to live, so that she (he) can be set free from unhealthful habits. I pray that along with the desire to eat properly, You would give her (him) the motivation to exercise regularly, to drink plenty of pure water, and to control and manage stress in her (his) life by living according to Your Word. Whenever she (he) struggles in any of those areas may she (he) turn to You and say, "Teach me Your way, O Lord" (Psalm 27:11). Give her (him) a vision of her (his) body as the temple of Your Holy Spirit.

I pray that she (he) will value the body You've given her (him) and desire to take proper care of it. May she (he) not be critical of it, nor examine herself (himself) through the microscope of public opinion and acceptance. I pray that she (he) will not be bound by the lure of fashion magazines, television, or movies which try to influence her (him) with an image of what they say she (he) should look like. Enable her (him) to say, "Turn away my eyes from looking at worthless things" (Psalm 119:37). Help her (him) to see that what makes a person truly attractive is Your Holy Spirit living in her (him) and radiating outward. May she (he) come to understand that true attractiveness begins in the heart of one who loves God.

Establish Your vision of health and attractiveness in her (his) heart this day, and permanently instill in her (him) the desire to take proper care of her (his) body because it is the temple of your Holy Spirit.

◈◈ ◈◈

WEAPONS OF WARFARE

Do you not know that your body is the temple of
the Holy Spirit who is in you, whom you have from
God, and you are not your own? For you were
bought at a price; therefore glorify God in your
body and in your spirit, which are God's.
1 CORINTHIANS 6:19–20

If anyone defiles the temple of God, God will
destroy him. For the temple of God is holy,
which temple you are.
1 CORINTHIANS 3:17

I beseech you therefore, brethren, by the mercies
of God, that you present your bodies a living
sacrifice, holy, acceptable to God, which is
your reasonable service.
ROMANS 12:1

Put on the Lord Jesus Christ, and make no
provision for the flesh, to fulfill its lusts.
ROMANS 13:14

Therefore, whether you eat or drink, or whatever
you do, do all to the glory of God.
1 CORINTHIANS 10:31

CHAPTER FOURTEEN

Instilling the Desire to Learn

*S*chool was a frightening experience for me socially, but getting A's was easy. That's why I never thought to pray about my children having the ability or the motivation to learn. That is, until it became clear that one of my children had a form of dyslexia. Because this child was bright, intelligent, and exceptionally gifted, the possibility of a learning difficulty never crossed my mind. However, school was a struggle from the beginning, and we didn't understand what was happening until our child's learning difficulty was professionally diagnosed in the third grade. Although there have been many heartbreaking moments because of this problem, prayer has sustained us along the way. My husband and I and our prayer partners continue to pray that this child will either be totally healed or be completely at peace about it and accept it as part of our child's wonderful uniqueness.

In one way or another, of course, we all have deficiencies. Thankfully, God makes up for our deficiencies with His strength. His Word says, "Not that we are sufficient of ourselves to think of anything as being from ourselves, but our sufficiency is from God" (2 Corinthians 3:5). That is so true. God has gotten our child through each year of school successfully, and through the process, we are all learning that true knowledge and understanding begin with and come from the Lord.

The Bible teaches us that knowledge begins with a reverence for God and His ways. If we receive His words and treasure His commands in our heart, if we work at trying to understand and ask God to help us do so, if we seek understanding as fervently as we would search out hidden treasure, then we will find the knowledge of God (Proverbs 2:1–12). And what a vast knowledge it is. So grand, in fact, it is a shield that delivers and protects us from evil.

A child's ability and desire to learn cannot be taken for granted. Even while our child is still in the womb we can pray, "Lord, let this child be knit perfectly together with a good, strong, healthy mind and body and be taught by You forever." The earlier we start praying the better, of course, but no matter what age your child is, your prayers will make a positive and permanent difference.

$\sim\!\!\infty\!\!\sim$

PRAYER

Lord,

I pray that (name of child) will have a deep reverence for You and Your ways. May he (she) hide Your Word in his (her) heart like a treasure, and seek after understanding like silver or gold. Give him (her) a good mind, a teachable spirit, and an ability to learn. Instill in him (her) a desire to attain knowledge and skill, and may he (she) have joy in the process. Above all, I pray that he (she) will be taught by You, for Your Word says that when our children are taught by You they are guaranteed peace. You have also said, "The fear of the Lord is the beginning of knowledge, but fools despise wisdom and instruction" (Proverbs 1:7). May he (she) never be a fool and turn away from learning, but rather may he (she) turn to You for the knowledge he (she) needs.

I pray he (she) will respect the wisdom of his (her) parents and be willing to be taught by them. May he (she) also have the desire to be taught by the teachers You bring into his (her) life. Handpick each one, Lord, and may they be godly people from whom he (she) can easily learn. Take out of his (her) life any teacher who would be an ungodly influence or create a bad learning experience. Let him (her) find favor with his (her) teachers and have good communication with them. Help him (her) to excel in school and do well in any classes he (she) may take. Make the pathways of learning smooth and not something with which he (she) must strain and struggle. Connect everything in his (her) brain the way it is supposed to be so that he (she) has clarity of thought, organization, good memory, and strong learning ability.

I say to him (her) according to Your Word, "Apply your heart to instruction, and your ears to words of knowledge" (Proverbs 23:12). "May the Lord give you understanding in all things" (2 Timothy 2:7). Lord, enable him (her) to experience the joy of learning more about You and Your world.

❧ ❧

WEAPONS OF WARFARE

All your children shall be taught by the Lord, and
great shall be the peace of your children.
ISAIAH 54:13

A wise man will hear and increase learning, and a
man of understanding will attain wise counsel.
PROVERBS 1:5

My people are destroyed for lack of knowledge.
Because you have rejected knowledge, I also will
reject you from being priest for Me; because you
have forgotten the law of your God, I also will
forget your children.
HOSEA 4:6

Take firm hold of instruction, do not let go;
keep her, for she is your life.
PROVERBS 4:13

My son, if you receive my words, and treasure my
commands within you, so that you incline your ear to
wisdom, and apply your heart to understanding; yes, if
you cry out for discernment, and lift up your voice for
understanding, if you seek her as silver, and search for
her as for hidden treasures; then you will understand
the fear of the Lord, and find the knowledge of God.
PROVERBS 2:1–5

CHAPTER FIFTEEN

Identifying God-Given Gifts and Talents

From the time my children were born, I prayed for God to reveal to us the gifts, talents, and abilities He had placed in them and to show us how to best nurture and develop them for His glory. At a very early age both of our children showed signs of musical talent, so I asked God what to do about it and waited on Him for the answer.

When Christopher was four, we felt directed to give him piano lessons. He showed remarkable ability, but after a couple of years did not want to practice. God gave me clear indication, however, that I would not be a good steward of the gifts He had given my son if I let him stop at that point. So I devised an appropriate incentive for my six-year-old: I would pay him twenty-five cents every time he practiced. This payment plan must have been Holy Spirit inspired, because I never heard another complaint about practicing until Christopher was twelve. At that time I felt released to let him stop studying piano and start taking the drum lessons he wanted. And I've never had to ask him to practice drums. In fact, quite the opposite!

Today Christopher performs on electric keyboards, drums, bass, and guitar, but he writes all his songs and arrangements on the piano. His music instructors say that he does so well because his knowledge of piano has given him a good foundational understanding of music, which only confirms God's leading all those years ago.

I've sensed the same Holy Spirit leading for my daughter with regard to her singing ability. Because the enemy wants to use our children's gifts for *his* glory, or at the very least keep them from being used for God's purposes, we need to cover them in prayer. Praying for the development of our children's God-given gifts and talents is an ongoing process.

There was a time in both of my children's lives— between the ages of twelve and fourteen—when they were attracted to the world's music and the unacceptable appearance and behavior of certain popular artists. My husband and I knew our battle was with the devil, not with our children, but we also knew we had to confront them about the matter and establish rules about what music they could listen to and what was unacceptable. (This does not mean that we think our children should never have anything at all to do with secular music. But whatever they do, they must "do all to the glory of God" [1 Corinthians 10:31] because God has called them to do it.)

We prayed our children's eyes would be turned away from the world and focused on what God had called them to do. We prayed that God would *open the doors* they were to go through and *shut all doors* that they were not to enter. We've seen Him answer that prayer many times. For example, Christopher was asked to be a part of a number of different musical groups and tour with them on the road. We never felt peace about any of them being the right situation or timing for *him*. Then, when he was eighteen, he was offered the opportunity to produce, write, arrange, and play keyboards, bass, and drums on a worship album for Sparrow Records. We knew this was clearly from the Lord and an answer to our prayers concerning his talents being used for God's glory. This does not end our prayers in this regard, of course. My husband and I are well aware of what the music business is like and the temptations of road life, even for Christian artists, so we will continue to pray for Christopher's faithfulness to use his talents and life for God's glory.

What gifts and talents has God planted in *your* child? Every child has them. They are there, whether you can see them or not. The Bible says, "Each one has his own gift from God, one in this manner and another in that" (1 Corinthians 7:7). Sometimes it takes prayer to uncover them.

When God gives you a glimpse of your child's potential for greatness, love and pray him (her) into being that. The Bible says, "Do you see a man who excels in his work? He will stand before kings; he will not stand before unknown men" (Proverbs 22:29). Pray that your child will develop and excel in the gifts and talents God has given him (her), and let him (her) know he (she) has a unique purpose and significance in this world.

Each child has special gifts and talents. We need to pray for them to be identified, revealed, developed, nurtured, and used for God's glory.

◦◦◦ ◦◦◦

PRAYER

Lord,

I thank You for the gifts and talents You have placed in (name of child). I pray that You would develop them in her (him) and use them for Your glory. Make them apparent to me and to her (him), and show me specifically if there is any special nurturing, training, learning experience, or opportunities I should provide for her (him). May her (his) gifts and talents be developed in Your way and in Your time.

Your Word says, "Having then gifts differing according to the grace that is given to us, let us use them" (Romans 12:6). As she (he) recognizes the talents and abilities You've given her (him), I pray that no feelings of inadequacy, fear, or uncertainty will keep her (him) from using them according to Your will. May she (he) hear the call You have on her (his) life so that she (he) doesn't spend a lifetime trying to figure out what it is or miss it altogether. Let her (his) talent never be wasted, watered down by mediocrity, or used to glorify anything or anyone other than You, Lord.

I pray that You would reveal to her (him) what her (his) life work is to be and help her (him) excel in it. Bless the work of her (his) hands, and may she (he) be able to earn a good living doing the work she (he) loves and does best.

Your Word says that, "A man's gift makes room for him, and brings him before great men" (Proverbs 18:16). May whatever she (he) does find favor with others and be well received and respected. But most of all, I pray the gifts and talents You placed in her (him) be released to find their fullest expression in glorifying You.

WEAPONS OF WARFARE

For the gifts and the calling of God are irrevocable.
ROMANS 11:29

To each one of us grace was given according to the
measure of Christ's gift.
EPHESIANS 4:7

As each one has received a gift, minister it to
one another, as good stewards of the
manifold grace of God.
1 PETER 4:10

Every good gift and every perfect gift is from above,
and comes down from the Father of lights, with whom
there is no variation or shadow of turning.
JAMES 1:17

I thank my God always concerning you for the grace
of God which was given to you by Christ Jesus, that
you were enriched in everything by Him in all utter-
ance and all knowledge, even as the testimony of
Christ was confirmed in you, so that you come short
in no gift, eagerly waiting for the revelation
of our Lord Jesus Christ.
1 CORINTHIANS 1:4–7

Learning to Speak Life

After school one afternoon I heard my son say a couple of swear words.

"That kind of language is not acceptable," I told him. "Why are you using those words when you know you shouldn't?"

"The kids at school talk that way," he explained.

"Other people do it, so it's okay for you?" I questioned. Then in my next sentence I rattled off a string of four-letter words I used to say before I met the Lord and was refined by His Spirit.

With a look of horror and shock he exclaimed, "Mom! Why are you talking like that?"

"Other people talk that way," I said. "How does it make you feel when I talk like that?"

"It makes me feel awful."

"You know, I can talk like that any time I want. But I choose not to. When I say those words it makes you feel bad because it hurts your spirit. When you talk like that, it hurts my spirit. Imagine what it does to God's Spirit. You have a choice whether to grieve God's Spirit with the words you say or to glorify Him. He'll love you either way and so will I. But one way will bless and one way will hurt."

I didn't hear Christopher say any words like that again until he was a teenager. Then we had this conversation all over again. I pray to this day he will remember it.

I know my teaching method may seem shocking. It shocked me, too, and I asked God to cleanse me from the contamination I felt for even speaking those words. But those words did not come from my heart. I said them only as a means of demonstrating their destructiveness. I'm not recommending that you adopt my methods of teaching, but that you accept my experience as a valid example of the power of what we speak.

We create a world for ourselves by what we speak. Words have power, and we can either speak life or death into a situation. The Bible says that what we say can get us *into* trouble or keep us *away* from it. It can even save our lives. "He who guards his mouth preserves his life, but he who opens wide his lips shall have destruction" (Proverbs 13:3). We need to ask God to put a guard over our own mouth as well as the mouth of our child.

Speech that is not godly or not of the Lord, such as, "I'm no good," "I wish I was dead," "Life is terrible," "People are horrible," "I'll never be anything special," does not reflect a heart filled with the Holy Spirit. It reflects the work of darkness. And that is exactly what will play itself out on the stage of your child's life if you don't help him monitor what he says.

The Bible says that when we go to be with the Lord we will have to account for every careless word we have spoken. We pay for them here on earth also. I believe the price is too high to pay for something that can easily be controlled by our own will. We can speak love, joy, and peace into our world, or we can speak strife, hatred, deception, and all other manifestations of evil.

We want our children to speak life. This doesn't mean they can't be honest about negative feelings. But those words should be spoken for the purpose of confession, understanding, and submission to God for healing, not as tools of destruction.

When our children's words reflect negatively on themselves, others, their situation, or the world around them, we must encourage them to see in God's Word all that could be better said. The best way to improve speech is to improve the heart, "For out of the abundance of the heart the mouth speaks" (Matthew 12:34). A heart filled with the Holy Spirit and the truth of the Word of God will produce godly speech that brings life to the speaker as well as the listener. This is where our point of prayer should begin.

❧❧ ❦❧

PRAYER

Lord,

I pray that (name of child) will choose to use speech that glorifies You. Fill his (her) heart with Your Spirit and Your truth so that what overflows from his (her) mouth will be words of life and not death. Put a monitor over his (her) mouth so that every temptation to use profane, negative, cruel, hurtful, uncaring, unloving, or compassionless language would pierce his (her) spirit and make him (her) feel uncomfortable. I pray that obscene or foul language be so foreign to him (her) that if words like that ever do find their way through his (her) lips, they will be like gravel in his (her) mouth and he (she) will be repulsed by them. Help him (her) to hear himself (herself) so that words don't come out carelessly or thoughtlessly.

Keep him (her) from being snared by the words of his (her) mouth. You've promised that "whoever guards his mouth and tongue keeps his soul from troubles" (Proverbs 21:23). Help him (her) to put a guard over his (her) mouth and keep far away from adversity. Your Word says that "death and life are in the power of the tongue, and those who love it will eat its fruit" (Proverbs 18:21). May he (she) speak life and not death. May he (she) be quick to listen and slow to speak so that his (her) speech will always be seasoned with grace. Equip him (her) to know how, what, and when to speak to anyone in any situation. Enable him (her) to always speak words of hope, health, encouragement, and life, and to resolve that his (her) mouth will not sin.

※ ✌

WEAPONS OF WARFARE

Let the words of my mouth and the meditation of
my heart be acceptable in Your sight, O Lord,
my strength and my redeemer.
PSALM 19:14

A good man out of the good treasure of his heart
brings forth good things, and an evil man out of
the evil treasure brings forth evil things.
MATTHEW 12:35

But I say to you that for every idle word men may
speak, they will give account of it in the day of
judgment. For by your words you will be justified,
and by your words you will be condemned.
MATTHEW 12:36–37

Pleasant words are like a honeycomb, sweetness
to the soul and health to the bones.
PROVERBS 16:24

There is one who speaks like the piercings of a sword,
but the tongue of the wise promotes health.
PROVERBS 12:18

CHAPTER SEVENTEEN

Staying Attracted to
Holiness and Purity

C hildren who are taught to live in purity and holiness have distinctly radiant faces and a compelling attractiveness. The Bible says, "Even a child is known by his deeds, whether what he does is pure and right" (Proverbs 20:11). We want our children to be known for their goodness. We want our children to be attractive to others because of their purity. This doesn't just happen. It must be taught. And although we can do much to teach our children about living purely in the ways of the Lord and model this to the best of our ability, the real teacher is the Holy Spirit. Holiness begins with a love for Him. "Keep yourself pure" (1 Timothy 5:22), the Bible instructs us. That's a hard assignment for anyone, but especially for a child. It can only be accomplished by total submission to God and His law and the enabling power of the Holy Spirit.

When my son started his senior year in high school, he was at a new school, in a different state, and in a different culture—a tough assignment for any young person, no matter how grounded or godly. The school he attended was a small private Christian school, so within the first week he had met all the senior boys. One of the young men stood out, however. His name was Sandy, and he was a sports star, excelled in his studies, and had received award after award for outstanding achievement. But Sandy was outstanding in another, more important way: his words and his actions reflected his deep respect for God and His laws.

One day at lunch when all the guys were together, one of them told an off-color joke and everyone laughed. Everyone, that is, except Sandy. My son admitted that he laughed, too.

"I was the new guy and I didn't want everyone to think I was from another planet," he sheepishly explained when he told us about it later.

What Christopher soon came to realize was that Sandy never laughed at obscene humor. Nor did he smoke or drink or use bad language. Yet, amazingly, everyone liked and respected him.

One day, shortly after a parents' meeting at the school, I came home and told Christopher about a wonderful woman I had met there.

"She stands out," I told him. "She's very warm and loving—a godly woman with a wonderful sense of humor. And she made me feel so welcome, like I've known her forever." As I went on to describe her, I mentioned her name.

"That's Sandy's mother," he said.

"Of course," I replied. "I should have known that Sandy would have strong, exceptional, believing, and praying parents. No child turns out like that by accident."

Throughout Christopher's senior year we observed that whole family and saw how exceptional each member was; and we noticed that people were not turned off by their goodness. Why? Because the way they lived was not a legalistic attempt to be perfect or to impress others; it was done from hearts that had a deep reverence for God and a desire to live His way—in holiness and purity.

My son is no longer at that school and we don't see Sandy or his family any more because our lives have gone different directions. But we will never forget them. They raised our personal standards, gave us something higher to aim for, and allowed us to see how attractive holiness is.

Let's pray for our children to be attracted to holiness and purity like a magnet, so that when anything entices them that isn't holy or pure, they detect the pull immediately and are made uncomfortable enough to thoroughly reject it. "For God did not call us to uncleanness, but to holiness" (1 Thessalonians 4:7). To live purely within the boundaries of God's law is to find wholeness in the total person. That wholeness is what holiness is all about. Children who have a desire for holiness and seek God's enabling power to help them achieve it can never be anything but blessed and fulfilled.

Sandy exemplified the Scripture that says, "Let no one despise your youth, but be an example to the believers in word, in conduct, in love, in spirit, in faith, in purity" (1 Timothy 4:12). There is nothing more compelling than children who walk in holiness and purity. Let's pray for our children to be among those who do.

❧❦

PRAYER

Lord,

I pray that You would fill (name of child) with a love for You that surpasses her (his) love for anything or anyone else. Help her (him) to respect and revere Your laws and understand that they are there for her (his) benefit. May she (he) clearly see that when Your laws are disobeyed, life doesn't work. Hide Your Word in her (his) heart so that there is no attraction to sin. I pray she (he) will run from evil, from impurity, from unholy thoughts, words, and deeds, and that she (he) will be drawn toward whatever is pure and holy. Let Christ be formed in her (him) and cause her (him) to seek the power of Your Holy Spirit to enable her (him) to do what is right.

You have said, "Blessed are the pure in heart, for they shall see God" (Matthew 5:8). May a desire for holiness that comes from a pure heart be reflected in all that she (he) does. Let it be manifested in her (his) appearance as well. I pray that the clothes she (he) wears and the way she (he) styles her (his) hair and chooses to adorn her (his) body and face will reflect a reverence and a desire to glorify You, Lord.

Where she (he) has strayed from the path of holiness, bring her (him) to repentance and work Your cleansing power in her (his) heart and life. Give her (him) understanding that to live in purity brings wholeness and blessing, and that the greatest reward for it is seeing You.

❧ ❧

WEAPONS OF WARFARE

Who may ascend into the hill of the Lord? Or who may stand in His holy place? He who has clean hands and a pure heart, who has not lifted up his soul to an idol, nor sworn deceitfully. He shall receive blessing

from the Lord, and righteousness from the
God of his salvation.
PSALM 24:3–5

In a great house there are not only vessels of gold and
silver, but also of wood and clay, some for honor and
some for dishonor. Therefore if anyone cleanses
himself from the latter, he will be a vessel for
honor, sanctified and useful for the Master,
prepared for every good work.
2 TIMOTHY 2:20–21

Every branch in me that does not bear fruit He takes
away; and every branch that bears fruit He prunes,
that it may bear more fruit.
JOHN 15:2

A highway shall be there, and a road, and it shall be
called the Highway of Holiness. The unclean shall
not pass over it, but it shall be for others. Whoever
walks the road, although a fool, shall not go astray…
the redeemed shall walk there, and the
ransomed of the Lord shall return, and come to
Zion with singing, with everlasting joy on their heads.
They shall obtain joy and gladness, and sorrow
and sighing shall flee away.
ISAIAH 35:8–10

There is a generation that is pure in its own eyes,
yet is not washed from its filthiness.
PROVERBS 30:12

CHAPTER EIGHTEEN

Praying Through a Child's Room

When my son was about eleven, he suddenly started having nightmares for no apparent reason. He hadn't seen anything frightening in a movie or on TV, and he gave us no indication that anything out of the ordinary had happened to him. We prayed with him several times, but night after night the bad dreams persisted.

As I was praying alone about this one morning, I asked God to show me what was causing these nightmares. As I did, I felt strongly led to go to my son's room.

"Lord, if there is anything in Christopher's room that shouldn't be here, show me," I prayed. Immediately, I felt prompted to go to his computer and look at his games. The first game I picked up was one he had borrowed from a friend at church. The outside of the box looked totally harmless; it was just a boy's action-adventure game. I opened the box and pulled out the small instruction booklet. The first few pages revealed nothing unusual, but in the back pages I found the worst kind of satanic garbage. I was shocked, but I said, "Thank You, Jesus," and took the game out of his room immediately.

If the game had been my son's property, I would have destroyed it immediately. But since it belonged to someone else, I called the boy's parents and told them what I had found. They were as surprised and unaware as we had been. When Christopher got home from school, I showed him what I had discovered. He said he hadn't gotten that far in the game yet and didn't realize what was in it. He had no hesitation about giving it back.

When my husband came home, we anointed our son's room with oil and thoroughly prayed through it. We knew the Bible said, "The yoke will be destroyed because of the anointing oil" (Isaiah 10:27). And although most of the biblical examples of that are of people being anointed, there are also examples of buildings or rooms being anointed to sanctify them. "You shall take the anointing oil, and anoint the tabernacle and all that is in it; and you shall hallow it and all its utensils, and it shall be holy" (Exodus 40:9). Because we wanted to break any yoke of the enemy and cleanse our son's room of anything unholy, we anointed the doorpost and prayed over his room, inviting the Holy Spirit to dwell there and crowd out anything that was not of God.

The proof to us that we had done the right thing was that Christopher's nightmares stopped immediately—just as suddenly as they began.

Everyone's house needs a spiritual housecleaning from time to time, especially in the rooms where our children sleep and play. The Bible says if we bring anything detestable into our homes, we bring destruction along with it. A holy housecleaning should be done periodically as a matter of principle, but definitely whenever you feel troubled by something in your child. If he or she is becoming fearful, rebellious, angry, depressed, distant, strange, a disciplinary problem, or having bad dreams and nightmares, sometimes simply praying through the room can change things quickly. Singing Christian songs, hymns, and worship choruses in the room is also very effective, and I've seen a change of spirit in my children after I have done so.

I know one mother and father who battled a heavy enemy stronghold of alcohol, drugs, rebellion, and occult involvement in their sixteen-year-old son by playing Christian worship songs and the Word of God on tape in his room while he was at school. His rebelliousness was eventually broken and he became a peaceful and godly person.

When you pray through your child's room, remove anything that is not glorifying to God: posters, books, magazines, pictures, photos, games, or articles of clothing depicting drug or alcohol use or any kind of blasphemy. Of course God's Word on this should be lovingly explained to the child and, if at all possible, he should be encouraged to remove the offensive articles himself. Explain that for his own peace and blessing he must clean the room of anything that is not of the Lord. Then pray over the room thoroughly. I've seen miraculous transformations as a result of doing that.

This is not a superstitious little ritual. This is a powerful claiming of your home, your child, and all aspects of his life for God. It's standing up and proclaiming, "As for me and my house, we will serve the Lord" (Joshua 24:15). It's saying, "My home is sanctified and set apart for God's glory."

Let's start our spiritual housecleaning by praying through our children's rooms even *before* the need arises.

PRAYER

Lord,

I invite Your Holy Spirit to dwell in this room, which belongs to (name of child). You are Lord over heaven and earth, and I proclaim that You are Lord over this room as well. Flood it with Your light and life. Crowd out any darkness which seeks to impose itself here, and let no spirits of fear, depression, anger, doubt, anxiety, rebelliousness, or hatred (name anything you've seen manifested in your child's behavior) find any place here. I pray that nothing will come into this room that is not brought by You, Lord. If there is anything here that shouldn't be, show me so it can be taken out.

Put Your complete protection over this room so that evil cannot enter here by any means. Fill this room with Your love, peace, and joy. I pray that my child will say, as David did, "I will walk within my house with a perfect heart. I will set nothing wicked before my eyes" (Psalm 101:2–3). I pray that You, Lord, will make this room a holy place, sanctified for Your glory.

❦❦ ❦❦

WEAPONS OF WARFARE

Nor shall you bring an abomination into your house,
lest you be doomed to destruction like it.
DEUTERONOMY 7:26

Wash yourselves, make yourselves clean; put away
the evil of your doings from before My eyes.
Cease to do evil.
ISAIAH 1:16

Therefore, having these promises, beloved, let us
cleanse ourselves from all filthiness of the flesh and
spirit, perfecting holiness in the fear of God.
2 CORINTHIANS 7:1

Have mercy upon me, O God, according to Your
loving kindness; according to the multitude of Your
tender mercies, blot out my transgressions.
Wash me thoroughly from my iniquity,
and cleanse me from my sin.
PSALM 51:1–2

The curse of the Lord is on the house of the wicked,
but He blesses the habitation of the just.
PROVERBS 3:33

CHAPTER NINETEEN

Enjoying Freedom from Fear

*F*ear was a way of life for me as a child because I lived with a mother who was mentally ill. Her bizarre, erratic, and abusive behavior was a constant source of terror. When, as an adult, I came to know the Lord, I learned to identify the *true* source of fear and battle against it. I've employed the same tactics on behalf of my children.

In Los Angeles we lived through earthquakes, fires, floods, riots, and rampant crime. Fear could have controlled our lives if we'd let it. In fact, we found ourselves praying about fear and protection so often that this plea became part of every prayer. Whenever I saw fear begin to grip either of my children, we would pray, read the Bible, sing hymns and worship choruses, and play Christian music. Since we moved away from that area we don't have to deal with that kind of fear on a daily basis anymore, but the lessons we learned about God's perfect love casting out all fear have been etched forever in each of our hearts.

Fear is something that comes upon us the moment we don't believe that God is able to keep us, or all we care about, safe. FEAR—or False Evidence Appearing

Real—easily strikes children because they can't always discern what's real and what isn't. Our comfort, reassurance, and love can *help* them; but praying, speaking the Word of God in faith, and praising God for His love and power, can *free* them.

When Jesus was at sea with His disciples and a storm came up, He responded to their terror by saying, "Why are you fearful, O you of little faith" (Matthew 8:26). He wants us, like them, to believe that our boat won't sink if He's in it with us.

There are times, however, when fear is more than a passing emotion. It can grip a child's heart so strongly and so unreasonably that no actions or words can take it away. When that happens, the child is being harassed by a spirit of fear. And the Bible clearly tells us a spirit of fear does not come from God. It comes from the enemy of our soul.

Parents have the authority and power through Jesus Christ to resist that spirit of fear on their child's behalf. *Fear* doesn't have power over *them*. *We* have power over *it*. Jesus gave us authority over *all* the power of the enemy (Luke 10:19). Don't be deceived into thinking otherwise. If fear persists after you have prayed, ask two or more strong believers to pray with you. Where two or three are gathered together in the name of the Lord, He is there in the midst of them (Matthew 18:20). Fear and the presence of the Lord cannot occupy the same space.

Because we have Jesus, we and our children never have to live with or accept a spirit of fear as a way of life.

∽◦ ◦∾

PRAYER

Lord,

Your Word says, "I sought the Lord, and He heard me, and delivered me from all my fears" (Psalm 34:4). I seek You this day, believing that You hear me, and I pray that You will deliver (name of child) from any fear that threatens to overtake her (him). You said You have "not given us a spirit of fear, but of power and of love and of a sound mind" (2 Timothy 1:7). Flood her (him) with Your love and wash away all fear and doubt. Give her (him) a sense of Your loving presence that far outweighs any fear that would threaten to overtake her (him). Help her (him) to rely on Your power in such a manner that it establishes strong confidence and faith in You. Give her (him) a mind so sound that she (he) can recognize any false evidence the devil presents to her (him) and identify it as having no basis in reality.

Wherever there is real danger or good reason to fear, give her (him) wisdom, protect her (him), and draw her (him) close to You. Help her (him) not to deny her (his) fears, but take them to You in prayer and seek deliverance from them. I pray that as she (he) draws close to You, Your love will penetrate her (his) life and crowd out all fear. Plant Your Word in her (his) heart. Let faith take root in her (his) mind and soul as she (he) grows in Your Word.

Thank You, Lord, for Your promise to deliver us from all our fears. In Jesus' name I pray for freedom from fear on behalf of my child this day.

෨৯৩ ৩৪৩

WEAPONS OF WARFARE

Oh, how great is Your goodness, which You have laid
up for those who fear You, which You have prepared for
those who trust in You in the presence of the sons of men!
PSALM 31:19

Fear not, for I am with you; be not dismayed, for I am
your God. I will strengthen you, yes, I will help you, I
will uphold you with My righteous right hand.
ISAIAH 41:10

He shall cover you with His feathers, and under His
wings you shall take refuge; His truth shall be your
shield and buckler. You shall not be afraid of the terror by night, nor of the arrow that flies by day, nor of
the pestilence that walks in darkness, nor of the
destruction that lays waste at noonday.
PSALM 91:4–6

The Lord is my light and my salvation; whom shall I
fear? The Lord is the strength of my life;
of whom shall I be afraid?
PSALM 27:1

The pangs of death surrounded me, and the floods of
ungodliness made me afraid. The sorrows of Sheol surrounded me; the snares of death confronted me. In
my distress I called upon the Lord, and cried out to
my God; He heard my voice from His temple, and my
cry came before Him, even to His ears.
PSALM 18:4–6

There is no fear in love; but perfect love casts out fear,
because fear involves torment. But he who fears
has not been made perfect in love.

1 JOHN 4:18

CHAPTER TWENTY

Receiving
a Sound Mind

The world and the devil are making every effort to control your child's mind. The good news is that you have the authority to resist those efforts. If your child is young, you have authority over what he puts *into* his mind—the television, movies, and videos he watches, the radio programs, tapes, and CD's he listens to, the books and magazines he reads. You can also do much to help your child fill his mind with godly music, words, and pictures. But most important of all, you have the power of prayer. So, even if your child is beyond your daily influence, you can pray for his or her mind to be sound, protected, and freed.

One of the many wonderful things about receiving Jesus and being filled with the Holy Spirit is that, along with every other blessing, we gain sound-mindedness and a stability that cannot be acquired any other way. That's because we are given the mind of Christ. The Bible says, "Let this mind be in you which was also in Christ Jesus" (Philippians 2:5). We can resist the worldly mind and allow His mind to be in control, and we can continually renew our minds by taking every thought captive.

My mother suffered with mental illness from her early twenties until she died at age sixty-seven. I saw firsthand what it was like for someone to live in a fantasy world and have no control over the thoughts that came into her mind. It was a frightening experience. Once I came to know the Lord, I frequently prayed that neither my children nor I would inherit any of that mental instability. Whenever I felt concern I said, "For God has not given us a spirit of fear, but of power and of love and of a sound mind" (2 Timothy 1:7).

"God has given me a *sound mind*," I have said many times. "He has also given my son a sound mind and my daughter a sound mind. I will accept nothing less."

Mental illness does not have to be passed along from one generation to another, and mental imbalance is not God's will for our children. Neither is confused or unstable thinking.

A big part of having a sound mind has to do with what goes into it. Filling our minds with what is out in the world brings confusion. Filling our minds with the things of God—especially His Word—brings clarity of thought and peace of mind. The Bible says, "God is not the author of confusion but of peace" (1 Corinthians 14:33). We must do what we can to make sure our children have the Word of God in their minds so as to crowd out confusion and ensure they are soundminded.

God has *given* us a *sound mind*. Why should we accept anything less for our children? Ask God for it.

❧ ❧

PRAYER

Lord,

Thank You for promising us a sound mind. I lay claim to that promise for (name of child). I pray that his (her) mind be clear, alert, bright, intelligent, stable, peaceful, and uncluttered. I pray there will be no confusion, no dullness, and no unbalanced, scattered, unorganized, or negative thinking. I pray that his (her) mind will not be filled with complex or confusing thoughts. Rather, give him (her) clarity of mind so that he (she) is able to think straight at all times. Give him (her) the ability to make clear decisions, to understand all he (she) needs to know, and to be able to focus on what he (she) needs to do. Where there is now any mental instability, impairment, or dysfunction, I speak healing in Jesus' name. May he (she) be renewed in the spirit of his (her) mind (Ephesians 4:23) and have the mind of Christ (1 Corinthians 2:16).

I pray that he (she) will so love the Lord with all his (her) heart, soul, and mind that there will be no room in him (her) for the lies of the enemy or the clamoring of the world. May the Word of God take root in his (her) heart and fill his (her) mind with things that are true, noble, just, pure, lovely, of good report, virtuous, and praiseworthy (Philippians 4:8). Give him (her) understanding that what goes into his (her) mind becomes part of him (her), so that he (she) will weigh carefully what he (she) sees and hears.

You have said, "You will keep him in perfect peace, whose mind is stayed on You, because he trusts in You" (Isaiah 26:3). I pray that his (her) faith in You and Your Word will grow daily so that he (she) will live forever in peace and soundness of mind.

WEAPONS OF WARFARE

Do not be conformed to this world, but be transformed by the renewing of your mind, that you may prove what is the good and acceptable and perfect will of God.

ROMANS 12:2

Be anxious for nothing, but in everything by prayer and supplication, with thanksgiving, let your requests be made known to God; and the peace of God, which surpasses all understanding, will guard your hearts and minds through Christ Jesus.

PHILIPPIANS 4:6–7

For the weapons of our warfare are not carnal but mighty in God for pulling down strongholds, casting down arguments and every high thing that exalts itself against the knowledge of God, bringing every thought into captivity to the obedience of Christ.

2 CORINTHIANS 10:4–5

For to be carnally minded is death, but to be spiritually minded is life and peace.

ROMANS 8:6

This I say, therefore, and testify in the Lord, that you should no longer walk as the rest of the Gentiles walk, in the futility of their mind, having their understanding darkened, being alienated from the life of God, because of the ignorance that is in them, because of the blindness of their heart.

EPHESIANS 4:17–18

CHAPTER TWENTY-ONE

Inviting the Joy of the Lord

A young teenage girl came to me with very sad eyes, a furrowed brow, and a pinched and strained face. In the hour that followed she shared with me the pain of her life, crying as she talked. She was feeling nearly every negative emotion imaginable, including suicidal thoughts. I prayed with her about each matter of concern and then I asked God to give her "beauty for ashes, the oil of joy for mourning, the garment of praise for the spirit of heaviness" (Isaiah 61:3).

When we were done, I was amazed at the difference in her face. The joyless and tortured expression had been replaced by a radiant and calm beauty. A spirit of joy had already begun to take root, and she looked like a different person. Since then I have seen this girl blossom into such confidence and beauty that she is attractive to everyone around her.

Sadly, many young people today suffer with depression. And the worst part is that they carry it with them into adulthood. It comes and goes, putting a pall over their lives, affecting their work, upsetting their relationships, ruining their health, and even affecting how they view God.

This doesn't have to happen. No matter what kind of experiences a person has had, there is no need to live with depression or any other negative emotion. Don't allow your child to be stuck with a sad, depressed, angry, moody, or difficult personality. Pray them out of it.

It's easy to tell which people carry negative emotions inside and which ones have a spirit of joy. It's especially obvious in children, because they don't have the ability to hide their emotions the way we learn to do as adults.

Take a long look at your child. Is the common expression on his or her face one of peace, happiness, and joy? Or is it distress, frustration, dissatisfaction, anger, depression, or sadness? Does your child ever have a bad attitude for what seems to be no reason at all? Does your child ever seem down or moody and yet can't explain why? Take charge of that situation before it becomes a habit. Negative emotions are habit-forming if we don't put a stop to them by praying for our children to be overtaken by a spirit of joy.

Don't think for a moment that by praying for the joy of the Lord to fill your child you are creating a shallow person without compassion for the sufferings of others. This will never happen. The joy of the Lord is rich and deep and causes anyone who walks in it to be likewise. That's because joy doesn't have anything to do with happy circumstances; it has to do with looking into the face of God and knowing He's all we'll ever need.

I'm not saying that your child should never have a negative emotion or show emotional pain. I'm saying that negative emotions should not be a way of life. I'm saying that we should look to the Lord because "He brought forth His people with joy" (Psalm 105:43). He will bring forth our children in like manner if we ask it of Him.

PRAYER

Lord,

I pray that (name of child) be given the gift of joy. Let the spirit of joy rise up in her (his) heart this day and may she (he) know the fullness of joy that is found only in Your presence. Help her (him) to understand that true happiness and joy are found only in You.

Whenever she (he) is overtaken by negative emotions, surround her (him) with Your love. Teach her (him) to say, "This is the day that the Lord has made, we will rejoice and be glad in it" (Psalm 118:24). Deliver her (him) from despair, depression, loneliness, discouragement, anger, or rejection. May these negative attitudes have no place in (name of child), nor be a lasting part of her (his) life. May she (he) decide in her (his) heart, "My soul shall be joyful in the Lord; it shall rejoice in His salvation" (Psalm 35:9).

I know, Lord, that any negative emotions this child feels are lies, contrary to the truth of Your Word. Plant Your Word firmly in her (his) heart and increase her (his) faith daily. Enable her (him) to abide in Your love and derive strength from the joy of the Lord this day and forever.

❧❧ ❧❧

WEAPONS OF WARFARE

If you keep My commandments, you will abide in
My love, just as I have kept My Father's commandments and abide in His love. These things I have
spoken to you, that My joy may remain in you,
and that your joy may be full.

JOHN 15:10–11

You will show me the path of life; in Your presence
is fullness of joy; at Your right hand are
pleasures forevermore.

PSALM 16:11

Now may the God of hope fill you with all joy
and peace in believing, that you may abound in
hope by the power of the Holy Spirit.

ROMANS 15:13

His anger is but for a moment, His favor is
for life; weeping may endure for a night, but joy
comes in the morning.

PSALM 30:5

I will greatly rejoice in the Lord, my soul shall be
joyful in my God; for He has clothed me with the
garments of salvation, He has covered me with
the robe of righteousness, as a bridegroom decks
himself with ornaments, and as a bride
adorns herself with her jewels.

ISAIAH 61:10

CHAPTER TWENTY-TWO

Destroying an Inheritance of Family Bondage

We all know we can inherit our mother's eyes, our father's nose, or the color of our grandmother's hair. But did you know that we can also pick up character qualities from our parents, such as a bad temper, a propensity for lying, depression, self-pity, envy, unforgiveness, perfectionism, and pride? These and other characteristics that have a spiritual root can be passed along from our parents to us, and from us to our children. In a particular family there may be a tendency toward such things as divorce, infidelity, alcoholism, addiction, suicides or depression all mistakenly accepted as "the way I am."

The Bible talks about the influence our parents can have on us. It says God will visit "the iniquities of the fathers upon the children to the third and fourth generations of those who hate Me" (Exodus 20:5). This Scripture is referring to people who don't walk in a loving relationship with God. However, a parent who is a believer and loves God can still choose to sin. And his sin will profoundly affect his children.

The Bible says "if anyone is in Christ, he is a new creation; old things have passed away: behold, all things have become new" (2 Corinthians 5:17). That doesn't mean that when we receive Jesus we are suddenly perfect and incapable of sinning. It means we have been freed from the consequences of sin, which is death, and we have been given the power to resist it. But we must make choices everyday about whether we will live in that freedom and power or not.

The Bible also says, "Stand fast therefore in the liberty by which Christ has made us free, and do not be entangled again with a yoke of bondage" (Galatians 5:1). If it is not possible as a believer to become entangled again with a yoke of bondage, why does the Bible warn us about it? The answer is, even though Jesus set us free from sin we can still make choices that put us back into bondage to it.

The point is, sometimes we accept certain tendencies toward sin in ourselves and we don't have to. Sometimes we carry on a family tradition that we shouldn't and it affects our children. Unlike physical traits, tendencies toward sin are something we don't have to receive as an inheritance from our parents. That's because these tendencies are nothing more than the unquestioned acceptance of a firmly entrenched lie of the enemy. He wants us to believe that we are not a new creation in Christ and that we have not been set free from our old nature. He wants us to think that because dad or grandpa drank too much, or was a complainer, or cheated on his wife, or abused his family with his anger, or got divorced, or was dishonest in his business dealings, that's the way things are done in our family. But we can choose to break away from these old familial habits through prayer and the power of the Holy Spirit. And when we see things we don't like about ourselves reflected in our children, we can pray for them to be set free of that tendency as well.

"If God through His mercy has saved us, and the Holy Spirit has washed and renewed us, and we are justified by grace, then why am I still struggling with sin?" I asked my Christian counselor many years ago.

"It's because the sin is either unconfessed, or you are choosing to continue to do it," he answered.

"But I still have unforgiveness for various family members for things that have happened in the past," I said. "I've reconfessed it. I don't want to do it. Why can't I get beyond this?"

"Your mother was an unforgiving person, wasn't she?" he said.

"Very much so. She had unforgiveness for nearly every family member. That's why she distanced herself from most of them. She had few friends for the same reason—she pushed them away with her unforgiveness for the most minor infractions."

"Have you ever thought of the possibility that you could have acquired that tendency toward unforgiveness in your personality? Children pick up what their parents are," he suggested.

I'd never thought about the possibility of there being anything outside my own mind that was propelling me to stay locked in unforgiveness, but the more I thought about it, the more I remembered seeing that trait manifest seriously in other family members. Nearly every family has to deal with that at some point, but most get beyond it without allowing it to cause a major breach in the family ties.

"I know this doesn't relieve me of my responsibility to forgive, but I do see a pattern of this in my family," I said. "And what frightens me most is that it could happen in my own children. I see them now hanging on to unforgiveness toward one another for things that have happened. It would break my heart to think that after they've grown and left our house, or after my husband and I have gone to be with the Lord, they would have nothing to do with one another. I can see that I have to get free of this for them as well as for myself."

The counselor and I prayed that day that the sin of unforgiveness in my family would not be passed down from generation to generation, but would be stopped by the power of the Holy Spirit. I proclaimed the truth of God's Word, which says I am a new creation in Christ and I don't have to live according to the habits and sins of the past. Through that revelation, I resolved to confess unforgiveness the moment it appeared—even if that meant doing it on an hour by hour basis.

The more I have released unforgiveness through confession,

repentance, and prayer before God, the more I have seen my children become free of it too. And their relationship with one another has improved. Of course, my children's ability to forgive does not rely on me. It is their decision. But hopefully they will see forgiveness being modeled in a clear-enough manner as to make their decision to forgive easier.

A good way to see a negative trait broken in your child is to see it broken in you first. The best place to start is to identify any sin in your life. Wherever there is sin, you need to confess it. If that sin is given place time and again, it will become more and more entrenched. For example, a lie is a sin. By repeated lying, place is given for this trait to become entrenched, and soon lying gets out of control. Another example is wanting to die. This is a sin. When people say "I want to die" enough times, they can get to the point where they are plagued by suicidal thoughts.

If you see a place in your life where you have sinned or not lived God's way, repent of it immediately by going before the Lord and confessing it. Ask for God's forgiveness and say, "God, You be in control and help me not to live like that anymore."

Then identify any sin in your parents or grandparents that you feel could be affecting you or your children and pray about that also. The Bible says, "The Spirit Himself bears witness with our spirit that we are children of God, and if children, then heirs— heirs of God and joint heirs with Christ" (Romans 8:16–17). We want to be heirs of God, not of our family's sin.

In Jesus' name we can be set free from any family pattern of sin, and by the power of the Holy Spirit we can refuse to allow it any place in our children's lives. If you can think of any family traits you don't want your children to inherit, start praying now.

~~◆~~ ◆~~

PRAYER

Lord,

You have said in Your Word that a good man leaves an inheritance to his children's children (Proverbs 13:22). I pray that the inheritance I leave to my children will be the rewards of a godly life and a clean heart before You. To make sure that happens, I ask that wherever there is a sinful trait in me that I have acquired from my family, deliver me from it now in the name of Jesus. I confess my sins to You. I ask for forgiveness and restoration, knowing Your Word says, "If we confess our sins, He is faithful and just to forgive us our sins and cleanse us from all unrighteousness" (1 John 1:9). I know that cleansing from sin through confession lessens the possibility of passing the habit of sin on to my child.

Jesus said, "I give you the authority . . . over all the powers of the enemy" (Luke 10:19). If there is any work of the enemy in my past that seeks to encroach upon the life of my child, (name of child), I break it now by the power and authority given me in Jesus Christ. I pray specifically about (name something you see in yourself or your family that you don't want passed on to your child). Whatever is not Your will for our lives, I reject as sin.

Thank You, Jesus, that You came to set us free from the past. We refuse to live bound by it. Thank You, Father, that You have "qualified us to be partakers of the inheritance of the saints in the light" (Colossians 1:12). I pray that my son (daughter) will not inherit any sin trait from his (her) earthly family, but will "inherit the kingdom prepared for him (her) from the foundation of the world" (Matthew 25:34). Thank You, Jesus, that in You the old has passed away and all things are new.

⌘

WEAPONS OF WARFARE

Stand fast therefore in the liberty by which
Christ has made us free, and do not be entangled
again with a yoke of bondage.
GALATIANS 5:1

Blessed be the God and Father of our Lord Jesus
Christ, who according to His abundant mercy has
begotten us again to a living hope through the
resurrection of Jesus Christ from the dead, to an
inheritance incorruptible and undefiled and that does
not fade away, reserved in heaven for you, who are
kept by the power of God through faith for salvation
ready to be revealed in the last time.
1 PETER 1:3–5

The Spirit of the Lord God is upon Me, because the
Lord has anointed Me to preach good tidings to the
poor; He has sent Me to heal the brokenhearted, to
proclaim liberty to the captives, and the opening
of the prison to those who are bound.
ISAIAH 61:1

Therefore, if anyone is in Christ, he is
a new creation; old things have passed away;
behold, all things have become new.
2 CORINTHIANS 5:17

For we ourselves were also once foolish, disobedient,
deceived, serving various lusts and pleasures, living in
malice and envy, hateful and hating one another.
But when the kindness and the love of God our
Savior toward man appeared, not by works of
righteousness which we have done, but according to
His mercy He saved us, through the washing of
regeneration and renewing of the Holy Spirit,
whom He poured out on us abundantly through
Jesus Christ our Savior, that having been justified by
His grace we should become heirs according
to the hope of eternal life.
TITUS 3:3–7

CHAPTER TWENTY-THREE

Avoiding Alcohol, Drugs and Other Addictions

*S*atan wants our children, and he'll take them any way he can. Alcohol, drugs, and other addictions are some of his most successful lures. In fact, the attack against our children is so great that they cannot stand against it without our support. The good news is that *with* our support, prayer covering, and teaching, they can stand firm.

It's never too soon to start praying for our children to avoid alcohol and drugs, because the exposure to and possibility of addiction to these substances can happen at a very early age. It's also never too late to pray about it either, because temptation can happen to anyone at any point in their lives. I know someone who didn't become an alcoholic until he was in his fifties. He said he knew he had a weakness for it, but didn't give in to it until he was at a small dinner party where liquor was being served. He tried a little, and when he went home he didn't stop drinking. Perhaps if he'd had a praying parent or a prayer group interceding for him this would never have happened.

I've seen many Christian music ministries go under because of alcohol and drugs. These people are out on the front lines of battle and don't even realize it until they are shot down. They are prime targets for enemy attack, and they fall right into his traps because they are not covered in prayer. Granted, some of them willfully give in to temptation, but I believe that most of them want to do what's right. The point is, the draw of the flesh and the devil's plans are a lot stronger than we'd like to think. In a moment of weakness, such as is possible for all of us, we can end up doing something we never thought we would. Only the power of God, through prayer, can make the difference.

If your child *already* has a problem in this area and the devil has won some ground in the battle, stand up in the confidence of knowing who you are in the Lord and gain it back. Your children are *yours* and *not* the devil's, and you can make a case for them before the throne of God. *You* have the power *and* the authority. Satan doesn't. All he has to work with are lies and deception. Rebuke his lies by the power invested in you through Jesus Christ your Savior, who is Lord over everything in your life, including your child.

The Bible says, "Therefore, whether you eat or drink, or whatever you do, do all to the glory of God" (1 Corinthians 10:31). Let's pray that everything our children do with their bodies be done to God's glory.

❧ ❧ ❧

PRAYER

Lord,

I pray that You would keep (name of child) free from any addiction—especially to alcohol or drugs. Make her (him) strong in You, draw her (him) close and enable her (him) to put You in control of her (his) life. Speak to her (his) heart, show her (him) the path she (he) should walk, and help her (him) see that protecting her (his) body from things that destroy it is a part of her (his) service to You.

I pray that You, Lord, would thwart any plan Satan has to destroy her (his) life through alcohol and drugs, and take away anything in her (his) personality that would be drawn to those substances. Your Word says, "There is a way that seems right to a man, but its end is the way of death" (Proverbs 16:25). Give her (him) discernment and strength to be able to say "no" to things that bring death and "yes" to the things of God that bring life. May she (he) clearly see the truth whenever tempted and be delivered from the evil one whenever trapped. Enable her (him) to choose life in whatever she (he) does, and may her (his) only addiction be to the things of God.

In Jesus' name I pray that everything she (he) does with her (his) body be done to Your glory.

~~ಎಲ~ ~ಎಲ~

WEAPONS OF WARFARE

If you live according to the flesh you will die;
but if by the Spirit you put to death the
deeds of the body, you will live.
ROMANS 8:13

Therefore remove sorrow from your heart,
and put away evil from your flesh.
ECCLESIASTES 11:10

I have set before you life and death, blessing and
cursing; therefore choose life, that both
you and your descendants may live.
DEUTERONOMY 30:19

The righteousness of the upright will deliver them,
but the unfaithful will be caught by their lust.
PROVERBS 11:6

Therefore if the Son makes you free,
you shall be free indeed.
JOHN 8:36

Rejecting Sexual Immorality

Next to catastrophic injury, death, and eternal hell, sexual immorality is the most dreaded possibility for our children's lives. That's because the results of sexual sin last a lifetime—often for the parents as well as the child. Words like "abortion," "out-of-wedlock," "infidelity," "homosexuality," "sexually transmitted disease," and "AIDS" all make a parent shudder. And today, more than ever before, this is a life-and-death issue.

We are all well aware that there is no way out of sexual immorality without consequences. But it's not only what happens to our children's bodies that concerns us. The Bible says, "Abstain from fleshly lusts which war against the soul" (1 Peter 2:11). The consequences of sexual sin invade the soul as well.

This is something I've prayed diligently about from the time my children were little, and I pray as fervently today. I certainly don't want them dying from AIDS, nor do I want grandchildren before my children are married. Aside from those major points, I also do not want them to disobey God and miss out on all He has for them. I know that with sexual sin the fullness of God's presence, peace, blessing, and joy is sacrificed. The price is way too high.

We can't wait until our children are teenagers to pray about this, just as we can't wait until then to instruct them that life works better when we live God's way. Today is the day to pray. Sexual temptation is everywhere. It's in front of our children's eyes at every turn. It's on billboards, TV, and radio; it's in movies, popular music, books, and magazines—even such innocuous publications as those having to do with news, sports, health, and hobbies. Our children are bombarded by it, and we are living in denial if we think they cannot be tempted. They can, and the force will be strong. They need us interceding on their behalf. Even if your child has already failed in this area, it is never too late for them to confess and repent, and be forgiven, healed, and made new.

The Bible says, "He who trusts in his own heart is a fool, but whoever walks wisely will be delivered" (Proverbs 28:26). We must pray for our children to trust God and not their unreliable emotions, so that they will walk with wisdom and avoid this dangerous trap. We must pray for them to live God's way.

One of God's ways for our lives is sexual purity, and the foundation for it is laid at a very young age. No matter what age your child is—a toddler, a teenager, or a thirty-something—and whether a virgin or sexually active—start praying for him or her to live a life of sexual purity from this day forward.

PRAYER

Lord,

I pray that You will keep (name of child) sexually pure all of his (her) life. Give him (her) a heart that wants to do what's right in this area, and let purity take root in his (her) personality and guide his (her) actions. Help him (her) to always lay down godly rules for relationships and resist anything that is not Your best. Open his (her) eyes to the truth of Your Word, and help him (her) to see that sex outside of marriage will never be the committed, lasting, unconditional love that he (she) needs. Let his (her) personality not be scarred nor his (her) emotions damaged by the fragmentation of the soul that happens as a result of sexual immorality.

I pray that he (she) will have no premarital sex and no sex with anyone other than his (her) marriage partner. I pray that homosexuality will never take root in him (her) or even have an opportunity to express itself toward him (her). Keep him (her) away from the presence of anyone with evil intentions, or take that person out of his (her) life. Protect him (her) from any sexual molestation or rape. Turn his (her) eyes away from the sexual immorality that saturates the world and enable him (her) to understand that whoever "wants to be a friend of the world makes himself an enemy of God" (James 4:4). May he (she) long for Your approval, Lord, and not allow sexual sin in his (her) life at any time. Deliver him (her) from any spirit of lust bringing temptation to fail in this area. Put a Holy Spirit alarm in him (her) that goes off like a loud, flashing siren whenever he (she) steps over the line of what is right in Your sight.

Your Word says, "Blessed is the man who endures temptation; for when he has been proved, he will receive the crown of life which the Lord has promised to those who love Him" (James 1:12). Speak loudly to him (her) whenever there is temptation to do something he (she) shouldn't, and make him (her) strong enough in You to stand for what's right and say "No" to sexual immorality. May Your grace enable him (her) to be committed to staying pure so that he (she) will receive Your crown of life.

~~~~~

WEAPONS OF WARFARE

This is the will of God, your sanctification: that you should abstain from sexual immorality; that each of you should know how to possess his own vessel in sanctification and honor, not in passion of lust, like the Gentiles who do not know God.

1 THESSALONIANS 4:3–5

Flee sexual immorality. Every sin that a man does is outside the body, but he who commits sexual immorality sins against his own body.

1 CORINTHIANS 6:18

The body is not for sexual immorality but for the Lord, and the Lord for the body.

1 CORINTHIANS 6:13

No temptation has overtaken you except such as is common to man; but God is faithful, He will not allow you to be tempted beyond what you are able, but with the temptation will also make the way of escape, that you may be able to bear it.

1 CORINTHIANS 10:13

But each one is tempted when he is drawn away by his own desires and enticed. Then, when desire has conceived, it gives birth to sin; and sin, when it is full-grown, brings forth death.

JAMES 1:14–15

CHAPTER TWENTY-FIVE

Finding the Perfect Mate

Shortly after my son and daughter were born, I started praying for their respective wife and husband. I'm still praying, and will be until they are married. Along with that, I pray that a spirit of divorce will never have any place in either of their lives. Some may think these prayers premature. They are not. Next to their decision to receive Jesus, marriage is the most important decision our children will ever make. It will affect the rest of their lives, not to mention the lives of other family members. The wrong decision can bring misery and pain for everyone concerned. And since only God knows who will make the best marriage partner for anyone, He should be consulted first and He should give the final answer.

When I think of the people I know who have experienced miserable marriages, abusive spouses, marital infidelity, multiple marriages, being married too late to have children, or who are unhappily single, one thing stands out in my mind: none of them had parents who interceded on their behalf for their mate and their marriage relationship.

On the other hand, I know couples who are perfectly matched in the bond of marriage and who have suffered none of the aforementioned problems. Not surprisingly, all of these individuals had parents who prayed for them in this regard or the individuals themselves prayed and waited until they were certain they'd found the mate God had chosen for them. Also, these individuals did not flit from one affair to another or ignore God's rules for sexual purity. They kept themselves pure for the mate God had for them, and they have been greatly rewarded.

As a result of all these observations and my own experience, I now believe that marriages can literally be made in heaven when we pray to the ultimate matchmaker.

Magnificent weddings do not make perfect marriages. Only God can do that. The Bible says, "There are many plans in a man's heart, nevertheless the Lord's counsel—that will stand" (Proverbs 19:21). It's not bridal consultants and caterers who set the bride and groom on the right path. Consulting God and following His leading does that. And only prayer keeps our children continually seeking God's will instead of following their own emotions.

The Spirit of God keeps a marriage together; a spirit of divorce destroys it. Pray now that the Holy Spirit, not a spirit of divorce, will rule your child's future.

If your child is already married to someone, pray that he or she and his or her mate will "be perfectly joined together in the same mind" (1 Corinthians 1:10), because every "house divided against itself will not stand" (Matthew 12:25). Pray that they will be delivered from any spirit of divorce that would try to drive a wedge between them. If your child is already divorced, pray for all brokenness to be healed and that there will be no more divorce in his or her future.

No matter what age your child is, pray about this today. Divorce is a part of the spirit of this age, and it threatens everyone at one time or another. Let's stand together to resist it for ourselves and our children by the power of the Holy Spirit in us through Jesus Christ, God's Son.

⋙ ⋘

PRAYER

Lord,

I pray that unless Your plan is for her (him) to remain single, You will send the perfect marriage partner for (name of child). Send the right husband (wife) at the perfect time, and give her (him) a clear leading from You as to who it is. I pray that my daughter (son) will be submissive enough to hear Your voice when it comes time to make a marriage decision, and that she (he) will make that decision based on what You are saying and not just fleshly desire. I pray that she (he) will trust You with all her (his) heart and lean not on her (his) own understanding; that she (he) will acknowledge You in all her (his) ways so that You will direct her (his) path (Proverbs 3:5–6).

Prepare that person who will make the perfect husband (wife) for her (him). Help my daughter (my son) to know the difference between simply falling in love and knowing for certain this is the person with whom God wants her (him) to spend the rest of her (his) life. If she (he) becomes attracted to someone she (he) shouldn't marry, I pray that You, Lord, would cut off the relationship. Help her (him) to realize that unless You are at the center of the marriage, it will never stand. Unless You bless it, it won't be blessed. For Your Word says, "Unless the

Lord builds the house, they labor in vain who build it" (Psalm 127:1). I pray that You would build the marriage around which their house is established.

When she (he) does find the right one to marry, I pray that person will be a godly and devoted servant of Yours, who loves You and lives Your way, and will be like a son (daughter) to me and a blessing to all other family members. Once she (he) is married, let there be no divorce in her (his) future. May there never be mental, emotional, or physical abuse of any kind, but rather mental, emotional, and physical unity that is never touched by division. I pray for their deliverance from any spirit of divorce, separation, or disunity that would attempt to drive a wedge into their relationship. Give them each a strong desire to live in fidelity, and remove any temptation to infidelity.

May she (he) have one mate for life, who is also her (his) closest friend. May they be mutually loyal, compassionate, considerate, sensitive, respectful, affectionate, forgiving, supportive, caring, and loving toward one another all the days of their lives.

&

WEAPONS OF WARFARE

From the beginning of the creation, God made them male and female. For this reason a man shall leave his father and mother and be joined to his wife, and the two shall become one flesh; so then they are no longer two, but one flesh. Therefore what God has joined together, let not man separate.

MARK 10:6–9

Marriage is honorable among all, and
the bed undefiled; but fornicators and adulterers
God will judge.
HEBREWS 13:4

Whoever divorces his wife and marries another
commits adultery against her.
MARK 10:11

He who finds a wife finds a good thing, and
obtains favor from the Lord.
PROVERBS 18:22

You cover the altar of the Lord with tears, with
weeping and crying; so He does not regard the
offering anymore, nor receive it with good will from
your hands. Yet you say, "For what reason?"
Because the Lord has been witness between you
and the wife of your youth, with whom you have dealt
treacherously; yet she is your companion and your
wife by covenant. But did He not make them one,
having a remnant of the Spirit? And why one?
He seeks godly offspring. Therefore take heed to your
spirit, and let none deal treacherously with the wife
of his youth. For the Lord God of Israel says
that He hates divorce.
MALACHI 2:13–16

CHAPTER TWENTY-SIX

Living Free of Unforgiveness

Whenever I have to apologize to my children for something, I tell them I need to hear them say, "I forgive you." I don't do that just because *I* need to *hear* it; I do it because *they* need to *say* it and be completely released. Likewise, if my children argue with each other, I ask them to say "I'm sorry" and "I forgive you" to one another. Even if they don't wholeheartedly feel those things at the time, I know that what they say will eventually work its way into their soul. Of course it's best if they say these things and mean them without ever having to be told, but until that becomes a reality, this is far better than doing nothing and just waiting for forgiveness to happen.

"Forgiveness is a *choice* you make," I've instructed them. "If you don't forgive, it brings death into your life in one form or another. The best way to become forgiving is to pray for the person you need to forgive. Even though it may seem hard at first, once you get into it and find more and more things to pray about, you'll notice your heart becoming soft toward that person."

I've observed firsthand, as I'm sure you have, families who wait for forgiveness to happen. They don't forgive until they *feel like* forgiving. As a result, there are often serious rifts among family members. They habitually say unkind things *to* or *about* one another, or perhaps haven't even spoken in years. A distinct lack of graciousness and mutual appreciation undergirds every word and deed because a spirit of unforgiveness has been given a home there. A whole family suffers when one or more of its members walk in an unforgiving stance toward one another.

As a part of honoring father and mother and receiving the promise of long life and blessing that accompanies that commandment, every child needs to forgive both parents for their imperfections and anything they may have done that was hurtful. Along with that they also need to forgive sisters, brothers, aunts, uncles, cousins, grandparents, acquaintances, friends, enemies, and sometimes even themselves—and we need to encourage them to do it. If we don't teach our children to forgive, we're doing them a disservice that may have serious consequences.

One of the best things we can do to help our children stay free of unforgiveness, besides teaching *them* to be forgiving and praying that they walk in forgiveness, is to get free of unforgiveness ourselves. Unforgiveness can so easily become a part of our lives that we take it along with us wherever we go without even realizing we are carrying this excess baggage.

When I finally learned that forgiveness doesn't make the *other person right*, it makes *you free*, I found great breakthrough in that area. I always felt that forgiving someone meant I was saying, "What you did is okay." But that's not the case at all. Forgiveness is trusting that God is the God of justice He says He is and saying, "Father, I won't hold that person to myself with unforgiveness anymore." It's acknowledging that God knows the truth and allowing Him to be the judge, because He is the only one who knows the whole story.

The Bible says, "The Lord is a God of justice; blessed are all those who wait for Him" (Isaiah 30:18). We will be blessed if we confess our unforgiveness to Him, pray to be delivered from it, and then sit back and wait for God to do the right thing while we enjoy His blessings. Doesn't that sound a lot more enjoyable than living in the prison of unforgiveness and suffering the disease it brings into our souls, bodies, relationships, and lives?

How does the son forgive the father who beat him? How does the mother forgive the drunk driver who killed her daughter? How does the young girl forgive the uncle who molested her? How can anyone show mercy for someone who was merciless? They can't fully, unless they come into the presence of the Lord and understand His *complete* forgiveness. There is nothing like the tears of joy and release we feel when we come to that place of complete forgiveness before the Lord. It's life-giving because it renews our entire being. The Bible says, "One thing I do, forgetting those things which are behind and reaching forward to those things which are ahead, I press toward the goal for the prize of the upward call of God in Christ Jesus" (Philippians 3:13–14).

We cannot get on with our lives and all that God has for us as long as we are bound and tethered to the past. Neither can our children. Jesus said, "Blessed are the merciful, for they shall obtain mercy" (Matthew 5:7). Let's pray for our children to show mercy so nothing will limit God's mercy toward them. Let's pray for them to be people who say "I forgive you" whenever the opportunity presents itself.

Let's pray that bitterness and unforgiveness do not become a wall between us and God and hinder our prayers. We don't have time for that. There is too much praying to be done.

~~~

PRAYER

Lord,

I pray that You would enable (name of child) to live in ongoing forgiveness. Teach him (her) the depth of Your forgiveness toward him (her) so that he (she) can be freely forgiving toward others. Help him (her) to make the decision to forgive based on what You've asked us to do and not on what feels good at the moment. May he (she) understand that forgiveness doesn't justify the other person's actions; instead, it makes him (her) free. Help him (her) to understand that only You know the whole story about any of us, and that's why he (she) doesn't have the right to judge.

Lord, Your Word says, "He who loves his brother abides in the light, and there is no cause for stumbling in him. But he who hates his brother is in darkness and walks in darkness, and does not know where he is going, because the darkness has blinded his eyes" (1 John 2:10–11). Show me places where I walk in the darkness of unforgiveness. I don't want that in my life. I want to see clearly and know where I'm going. And I pray that for my child as well. May he (she) always walk in the light of love and forgiveness. Enable him (her) to forgive family members, friends, and all others as well. Teach him (her) to release the past to You so that he (she) can move into all that You have for him (her). Don't allow him (her) to harbor resentment, bitterness, and anger, but rather help him (her) to turn these feelings over to you immediately whenever they creep in.

I pray that he (she) will forgive himself (herself) for times of failure, and may he (she) never blame You, Lord, for things that happen on this earth and in his (her) life. According to Your Word I pray that he (she) will love his (her) enemies, bless those who curse him (her), do good to those who hate him (her), and pray for those who spitefully use and persecute him (her), so that he (she) may enjoy all Your blessings (Matthew 5:44-45). In Jesus' name, I pray that he (she) will live in the fullness of Your forgiveness for him (her) and walk in the freedom of forgiveness in his (her) own heart.

WEAPONS OF WARFARE

Let all bitterness, wrath, anger, clamor, and evil
speaking be put away from you, with all malice. And
be kind to one another, tenderhearted, forgiving one
another, just as God in Christ also forgave you.
EPHESIANS 4:31–32

If you forgive men their trespasses, your heavenly
Father will also forgive you. But if you do not
forgive men their trespasses, neither will your
Father forgive your trespasses.
MATTHEW 6:14–15

His master was angry, and delivered him to the
torturers until he should pay all that was due to him.
So My heavenly Father also will do to you if each
of you, from his heart, does not forgive
his brother his trespasses.
MATTHEW 18:34–35

The discretion of a man makes him slow to anger, and
it is to his glory to overlook a transgression.
PROVERBS 19:11

Whenever you stand praying, if you have anything
against anyone, forgive him, that your Father in
heaven may also forgive you your trespasses.
MARK 11:25

CHAPTER TWENTY-SEVEN

Walking in
Repentance

*H*ave you ever noticed children who live in guilt and condemnation because they have not been disciplined to confess, repent, and be forgiven of their sins? They don't have the same clear-eyed, confident faces that children who are free of condemnation have. The Bible says, "They looked to Him and were radiant and their faces were not ashamed" (Psalm 34:5). Children who admit their mistakes and are sorry enough about them to want to change their ways have an entirely different countenance than those who hide their sin and have no intention of being different.

Confession and repentance are two life principles we must insist upon for our children, because unconfessed sin will put a wall between them and God. Repentance, which literally means "turning away and deciding not to do it again," is manifested when the child says, in effect, "I did this, I'm sorry about it, and I'm not going to do it again." If sin is not confessed and repented of in that way, the child can't be free of the bondage that goes along with unconfessed sin, and that will show on his (her) face and in his (her) personality and actions.

God said to the Israelites who disobeyed Him and didn't repent of it, "You shall remember your ways and all your doings with which you were defiled; and you shall loathe yourselves in your own sight because of all the evils that you have committed" (Ezekiel 20:43). That self-loathing for unconfessed and unrepented sin is *our* lot as well, and one of its manifestations is a poor self-image. Such feelings of failure and guilt will wreak destruction in our children's lives if they are not taught to confess and repent.

I remember detecting sin on my children's faces before I ever discovered it in their actions. They used to tell me how irritating it was that they could never get away with anything for long.

"That's because I asked God to reveal to me anything I need to know," I told them, "and the Holy Spirit always tells me if you've done something wrong."

Whenever I saw their open, clear-eyed countenances clouded by a dishonest demeanor, I would ask God to show me any hidden sin. After they had confessed and repented and received the appropriate punishment, their faces looked totally different—as though a weight or a shadow had been lifted from them. Sin has a toxic effect. Unconfessed sin weighs us down; it distorts and darkens our image. Confessed sin and a repentant heart bring light, life, confidence, and freedom.

Because no child is perfect, we need to ask God to reveal, expose, or bring to light any hidden sin that has taken root in our children's hearts so it can be dealt with now rather than later when the consequences are far more serious. God will do that, "for He knows the secrets of the heart (Psalm 44:21). We've all heard stories of the "nice, likeable man" who beats his wife, abuses his children, or goes on a killing spree. You can be sure that he was a man who had hidden sin in his heart. We can be just as sure that any hidden sin in our children will eventually display itself in an undesirable way. The time to catch it is now. "Cast away from you all the transgressions which you have committed, and get yourselves a new heart and a new spirit. For why should you die?" (Ezekiel 18:31). Ask God to bring any hidden sin in you or your children to light so there won't be a physical and emotional price to pay for it.

Sin leads to death. Repentance leads to life. We don't confess so that God will find out something. He already knows. Confession is a chance for us to clear the slate. Repentance is an opportunity for us to start over. Our children, as do we, need both.

❧ ❧

PRAYER

Lord,

I pray that You would give (name of child) a heart that is quick to confess her (his) mistakes. May she (he) be truly repentant of them so that she (he) can be forgiven and cleansed. Help her (him) to understand that Your laws are for her (his) benefit and that the confession and repentance You require must become a way of life. Give her (him) the desire to live in truth before You, and may she (he) say as David did, "Wash me thoroughly from my iniquity, and cleanse me from my sin. Create in me a clean heart, O God, and renew a steadfast spirit within me. Do not cast me away from Your presence, and do not take Your Holy Spirit from me. Restore to me the joy of Your salvation" (Psalm 51:2,10–12).

Lord, bring to light any hidden sins so they can be confessed, repented of, and forgiven. Your Word says, "Blessed is he whose transgression is forgiven, whose sin is covered" (Psalm 32:1). I pray that my daughter (son) will never be able to contain sin within her (him), but rather let there be a longing to confess fully and say, "See if there is any wicked way in me, and lead me in the way everlasting" (Psalm 139:24). May she (he) not live in guilt and condemnation, but rather dwell with a clear conscience in the full understanding of her (his) forgiveness in Christ. I pray that she (he) will always look to You and wear a radiant countenance.

∽◇∾

WEAPONS OF WARFARE

Beloved, if our heart does not condemn us, we
have confidence toward God. And whatever we
ask we receive from Him, because we keep His
commandments and do those things that are
pleasing in His sight.
1 JOHN 3:21–22

Let the wicked forsake his way, and the unrighteous
man his thoughts; let him return to the Lord, and
He will have mercy on him; and to our God, for
He will abundantly pardon.
ISAIAH 55:7

"Therefore I will judge you, O house of Israel, every
one according to his ways," says the Lord God.
"Repent, and turn from all your transgressions, so
that iniquity will not be your ruin."
EZEKIEL 18:30

He who covers his sins will not prosper, but whoever
confesses and forsakes them will have mercy.
PROVERBS 28:13

Repent therefore and be converted, that your sins may
be blotted out, so that times of refreshing may come
from the presence of the Lord.
ACTS 3:19

CHAPTER TWENTY-EIGHT

Breaking Down Ungodly Strongholds

Have you ever observed something in your child that bothers you but you can't identify what it is? When that happens, don't ignore your God-given instincts. Ask God to reveal what it is you're sensing. We are aligned with the Creator of the universe, who understands perfectly what is going on, and we need to ask Him for wisdom and revelation.

Have you ever detected an expression on your child's face that you knew was guilt but you didn't know the reason for it? In other words, you suspected an offense worthy of some kind of discipline but you didn't have the hard evidence. Whenever that happened with either of my children, I prayed, "Lord, You know our foolishness and our sins are not hidden from You (Psalm 69:5). Reveal to me what I am sensing in this child." Each time He revealed an ungodly stronghold erecting itself in the flesh. For instance, one time one of the children was smuggling forbidden foods into the bedroom for secret consumption. Another time, a lie was being set in motion in order to achieve a desired result. In every case the sins were revealed *after* I prayed.

I always told my children it wasn't worth it for them to disobey their mom and dad because God would always reveal it to us. They soon believed me.

One particular instance stands out in my mind. It occurred when Amanda was about seven years old. Every morning I gave her three tiny vitamins to swallow. These had been prescribed by our doctor, and I always made sure she had them in a tiny dish by her plate at the breakfast table. In the beginning she protested every time she had to take them. After a while she became more cheerful about it, and eventually she stopped complaining altogether. Around the same time, I sensed something about Amanda that troubled me, but I couldn't put my finger on exactly what it was.

"Show me, Lord. Is there anything in Amanda I should be seeing?" I prayed.

Nothing happened over the next several days, and I didn't think much about it because I was busy packing our household goods for a move to another location. The day the moving company came to pack the large items, we started to remove the little cushions that were tied to the seats of the kitchen chairs. There, under Amanda's seat cushion, I found twenty-six little vitamins spread all around the seat. I couldn't believe my eyes. I called my husband in to show him what I'd found, and we both chuckled, even though we knew she'd have to be confronted when she arrived home from school.

We proceeded to untie the other five cushions and, much to our amazement, under all but one we discovered twenty to thirty vitamins. Only the chair furthest away from hers was empty. This time we rolled with laughter.

When Amanda arrived home from school, we wiped the smiles off our faces and presented her with well over a hundred vitamins and a cup of water. We told her that unless she wanted to take all those vitamins she had better do some explaining.

This incident seems humorous and minor, but if Amanda's deception had gone undetected and never dealt with, it could have led to bigger deceptions until deception had a foothold in her life. I'm grateful to God that He reveals such things to us *before* they become serious.

It doesn't necessarily have to be a child's sins you are sensing. It could be hurt or fear over something he (she) has thought, seen, or experienced. It could be hopelessness, confusion, envy, selfishness, or pride. It's impossible to guess, so it's best to ask God to reveal it to you. Even if you don't get a clear leading right away, you can still pray about it. Jesus instructed us to pray as a matter of course, "Deliver us from the evil one" (Matthew 6:13). Sometimes we don't have to be any more specific than praying for God to penetrate the lives of our children by the power of His Spirit and deliver them from evil. The point is, don't ignore these warnings.

Even if you don't sense anything in your child now, it's still a good preventative measure to pray the following prayer. Not that you have to be forever suspicious of your children, but you do have to be suspicious of the enemy lurking around waiting to erect a stronghold in their lives. "Be sober, be vigilant; because your adversary the devil walks about like a roaring lion, seeking whom he may devour" (1 Peter 5:8). The verse following that one gives us directions on how to deal with this: *"Resist him,"* it says. Shall we pray?

PRAYER

Lord,

Thank You that You have promised in Your Word to deliver us when we cry out to You. I come to You on behalf of (name of child) and ask that You would deliver him (her) from any ungodliness that may be threatening to become a stronghold in his (her) life. Even though I don't know what he (she) needs to be set free from, You do. I pray in the name of Jesus that You will work deliverance in his (her) life wherever it is needed. I know that although "we walk in the flesh, we do not war according to the flesh. For the weapons of our warfare are not carnal but mighty in God for pulling down strongholds, casting down arguments and every high thing that exalts itself against the knowledge of God" (2 Corinthians 10:3–5).

Give me wisdom and revelation regarding him (her). I know there are areas of enemy operation which I cannot see, so I depend on You, Lord, to reveal these to me as I need to know them. Speak to my heart. Show me how to pray when there is something deep in my spirit that is unsettled, disturbed, or troubled about him (her). Show me anything that I am not seeing, and let all that is hidden come to light. If there is any action I need to take, I depend on You to show me. Thank You that You help me parent this child.

Lord, I put (name of child) in Your hands this day. Guide, protect, and convict him (her) when sin is trying to take root. Strengthen him (her) in battle when Satan attempts to gain a foothold in his (her) heart. Make him (her) sensitive to enemy encroachment, and may he (she) run to You to be his (her) stronghold and refuge in times of trouble. May the cry of his (her) heart be, "Cleanse me from secret faults" (Psalm 19:12). According to Your Word I say that the Lord will deliver him (her) from every evil work and preserve him (her) for His heavenly kingdom (2 Timothy 4:18).

❧ ❦

WEAPONS OF WARFARE

I will give you the keys of the kingdom of heaven,
and whatever you bind on earth will be bound
in heaven, and whatever you loose on earth
will be loosed in heaven.
MATTHEW 16:19

There is nothing covered that will not be revealed,
and hidden that will not be known.
MATTHEW 10:26

Though they join forces, the wicked will not
go unpunished; but the posterity of the
righteous will be delivered.
PROVERBS 11:21

The Lord also will be a refuge for the oppressed,
a refuge in times of trouble.
PSALM 9:9

Call to Me, and I will answer you, and show you great
and mighty things, which you do not know.
JEREMIAH 33:3

CHAPTER TWENTY-NINE

Seeking Wisdom and Discernment

Will my child know not to get into a car with a stranger? Will she see that playing near deep water is dangerous? Will he just say "No" when peers offer him drugs? Will she remember to look both ways before crossing a street? Will he ask the wrong girl to marry him? Will they be able to sense danger when it is imminent? So much of our children's safety and well-being depends on decisions they alone will make. The possible outcome of those decisions can seem frightening to a parent.

We can't ever be sure they'll make the right decision unless they have the gifts of wisdom, revelation, and discernment, along with an ear tuned to God's voice. The only way to secure any of those things is to seek God for them. The Bible says, "If any of you lacks wisdom, let him ask of God, who gives to all liberally and without reproach, and it will be given to him" (James 1:5).

Have you ever had times in your life when you knew God's wisdom was in control and you made the right decision in spite of yourself? Perhaps you decided not to complete a left turn, even though the light was with you; and sure enough, an oncoming car ran the light. You did the right thing, but you can't take the credit. Some people may view that as a coincidence. I believe it is the wisdom and discernment of God. And more times than we even know, it saves our lives.

We want that same wisdom and discernment flowing in our children's lives, for as they grow older they make more and more important decisions without us. Certain decisions my son had to make after graduating from high school caused me to sit on the sidelines holding my breath and praying, "Give him wisdom, Lord. Let him have a clear leading from You." God answered those prayers, and we see now how right Christopher's decisions were—for reasons only God could have known.

The old proverb that says, "A wise son makes a glad father, but a foolish son is the grief of his mother" (Proverbs 10:1), is completely accurate. No one can be prouder than Dad when his child makes a wise decision. But when a child acts without wisdom, no one grieves more deeply than a mother. Proverbs also says if we cry out for discernment and seek it like a hidden treasure we will find all the knowledge of God (Proverbs 2:3–5). I believe that's all the knowledge, wisdom, and discernment we could possibly need. Let's cry out to God and save ourselves some grief, shall we?

∼⁀◌ ⌒∼

PRAYER

Lord,

I pray that You would give the gifts of wisdom, discernment, and revelation to (name of child). Help her (him) to trust You with all her (his) heart, not depending on her (his) own understanding, but acknowledging You in all her (his) ways so that she (he) may hear Your clear direction as to which path to take (Proverbs 3:5). Help her (him) to discern good from evil and be sensitive to the voice of the Holy Spirit saying, "This is the way, walk in it" (Isaiah 30:21). I know that much of her (his) happiness in life depends on gaining wisdom and discernment, which Your Word says brings long life, wealth, recognition, protection, enjoyment, contentment, and happiness. I want all those things for her (him), but I want them to come as blessings from You.

Your Word says, "The fear of the Lord is the beginning of wisdom, and the knowledge of the Holy One is understanding" (Proverbs 9:10). May a healthy fear and knowledge of You be the foundation upon which wisdom and discernment are established in her (him). May she (he) turn to You for all decisions so that she (he) doesn't make poor choices. Help her (him) to see that all the treasures of wisdom and knowledge are hidden in You and that You give of them freely when we ask for them. As she (he) seeks wisdom and discernment from You, Lord, pour it liberally upon her (him) so that all her (his) paths will be peace and life.

~∞ ∞~

WEAPONS OF WARFARE

The father of the righteous will greatly rejoice, and he
who begets a wise child will delight in him.
Let your father and your mother be glad,
and let her who bore you rejoice.
PROVERBS 23:24–25

Wisdom is the principal thing; therefore get wisdom.
And in all your getting, get understanding. Exalt her,
and she will promote you; she will bring you
honor, when you embrace her.
PROVERBS 4:7–8

The law of the Lord is perfect, converting the
soul; the testimony of the Lord is sure,
making wise the simple.
PSALM 19:7

When wisdom enters your heart, and knowledge is
pleasant to your soul, discretion will preserve you,
understanding will keep you, to deliver you from the
way of evil, from the man who speaks perverse things.
PROVERBS 2:10–12

Happy is the man who finds wisdom, and the man
who gains understanding; for her proceeds are better
than the profits of silver, and her gain than fine gold.
She is more precious than rubies, and all the things
you may desire cannot compare with her. Length of

days is in her right hand, in her left hand riches and
honor. Her ways are ways of pleasantness,
and all her paths are peace.
She is a tree of life to those who take hold of her,
and happy are all who retain her.
PROVERBS 3:13–18

CHAPTER THIRTY

Growing in Faith

*H*ow many times have I heard parents of teenagers or young adults say, "My son is not motivated to do anything." "My daughter mopes around the house like she is depressed all the time." "My son is flunking out of school and doesn't seem to care." "My daughter seems lost, as if her life has no purpose." In each instance, these children are struggling with a lack of vision for their lives because they have no faith in God and His Word.

Kids without faith have a harder time in life. Kids without faith have no positive motivation, no sense of purpose, and no hope for being any different than they are. Kids without faith sit in front of the TV hour after hour, day after day, month after month. Kids without faith roam the streets looking for trouble and usually find it. Kids without faith hang around with other kids without faith, and that's the main problem with kids who are in trouble today. They don't know that Jesus died for them (Romans 5:8) and that they are God's children (John 1:12), who are loved, and have a special purpose and calling (1 Corinthians 7:22), and a bright future (1 Corinthians 2:9), and because of that they are sure winners (Romans 8:37). They don't know that "all things are possible to him who believes" (Mark 9:23), and so they don't believe there are any possibilities for their future. All they see are their own limitations and the failings and struggles of the adults around them, and so they give up.

But it's even more than that, because sensing *our* limitations doesn't necessarily mean we don't have faith. It's feeling that *God* has limitations that indicates a lack of faith. And if children don't have faith in the only thing that is secure, unchanging, and all-powerful, how can they believe in themselves and their future, which they know is insecure, unstable, and powerless?

Having raised one child so far from birth to adulthood, I've come to realize that one of the main things our children will take with them when they leave our realm of influence is their faith. If we can be sure they have strong faith in God and His Word, and the love of God in their hearts, then we can know they are set for eternity. Our prayers can play a big part in helping them achieve that.

The apostles, who were with Jesus every day, hearing Him teach and watching what He did, still had to ask of Him, "Increase our faith" (Luke 17:5). Surely *we* can ask the same for our children. "Lord, increase their faith."

The Israelites, who witnessed more miracles than we may ever see, were not allowed to enter the Promised Land because of their unbelief (Hebrews 3:19). We don't want a lack of faith to keep our children from entering into all God has promised for them. We can teach them the Word of God, which plants faith in them, and we can pray that their faith will grow.

Children who have faith have distinctly different characteristics from those who don't. They are more confident, more motivated, happier, more positive about the future, and more giving of themselves. In fact, one of the main manifestations of a person strong in faith is the ability to give—not just in terms of money or possessions, but also time, love, encouragement, and help. A person of faith is filled with God's love and looks for opportunities to share that love with others.

The Bible says, "Now abide faith, hope, love, these three; but the greatest of these is love" (1 Corinthians 13:13). In heaven, faith won't be necessary because we'll see everything. Hope won't be needed because what more could we possibly hope for? Only love will last forever, because God is love and *He* is eternal. That's why it doesn't matter what great thing we do or how much we give; if it's not done out of love, it is meaningless. "Though I bestow all my goods to feed the poor, and though I give my body to be burned, but have not love, it profits me nothing" (1 Corinthians 13:3). Everything we do out of love will last forever and the rewards are eternal.

Love is the greatest virtue. It's even greater than faith. But faith is where it begins. That's why we need to pray that as faith increases in our children, they will become God's instruments of giving. One of the reasons people don't give is that they believe there won't be enough for them if they do; another is that they don't have the love of God in their hearts for others. Pray that the principle of giving—out of love, as to the Lord, in faith, *with wisdom* and Holy Spirit guidance—be instilled in the hearts and minds of your children, because as they live accordingly, they are guaranteed to be richly blessed and fulfilled.

In any area of concern, as we begin to seriously pray in depth for our child, we often come face to face with our own need for prayer, deliverance, and restoration. How can we pray effectively for our children to be forgiving people if we are harboring unforgiveness in our own hearts? How can we pray in power for them to be repentant if we have unconfessed sin? How can we ask God to make our children faith-filled when we struggle with doubt? How can we pray for them to be givers when we have a hard time giving? I get convicted of those things too. But I don't let that stop me from praying. I go before the Lord with a humble heart, confessing what I see in myself and asking Him for help.

If, for example, you feel you don't have enough faith, confess it to God and pray the prayer at the end of this chapter with *your* name in it before you pray for your child. The Bible says that "whatever is not from faith is sin" (Romans 14:23). If we doubt, we are not obeying God. If we have faith, we're being obedient. Doubt comes from believing that God is not all-powerful. Don't let your own lack of faith put a wall between you and God. Let it become an invitation to run to God in prayer, asking Him to increase *your* faith as well as *your child's*.

Even though this is the last of the categories for prayer focus in this book, I pray it is just the beginning for you as the Lord shows you new ways to pray for your child. Keep in mind that the power you have as a praying parent is God's power. Your prayers release that power to do God's will. It's always available, it's never in limited supply, and the only restrictions are due to lack of faith that God will answer. And even then, God's grace is such that when we don't feel we have much faith, the faith that we *do* have is like a mustard seed— enough to grow into something big.

Let's unite with other praying parents and say, "May the seeds of our faith, planted in prayer, bring forth life and grow our children into big people who follow after God's heart."

❦ ❦

PRAYER

Lord,

You have said in Your Word that You have "dealt to each one a measure of faith" (Romans 12:3). I pray that You would take the faith You have planted in (name of child) and multiply it. May the truth of Your Word be firmly established in his (her) heart so that faith will grow daily and navigate his (her) life. Help him (her) to trust You at all times as he (she) looks to You for truth, guidance, and transformation into Your likeness. I know that trusting in You is a choice we make. Enable him (her) to make that choice. I pray that he (she) will look to You for everything, knowing that he (she) is never without hope. May his (her) faith be the "substance of things hoped for, the evidence of things not seen" (Hebrews 11:1). I pray he (she) will have faith strong enough to lift him (her) above his circumstances and limitations and instill in him (her) the confidence of knowing that everything will work together for good (Romans 8:28).

I pray that he (she) will be so strong in faith that his (her) relationship with You supersedes all else in his (her) life—even my influence as a parent. In other words, may he (she) have a relationship with You, Lord, that is truly his (her) own—not an extension of mine or anyone else's. I want the comfort of knowing that when I'm no longer on this earth, his (her) faith will be strong enough to keep him (her) "steadfast, immovable, always abounding in the work of the Lord" (1 Corinthians 15:58).

As he (she) walks in faith, may he (she) have Your heart of love that overflows to others, a heart that is willing to give of self and possessions according to Your leading. May he (she) see that giving out of love is actually giving back to You in faith and that he (she) will never lose anything by doing so. I pray that he (she) will take the "shield of faith" in order to "quench all the fiery darts of the wicked one" (Ephesians 6:16), and thereby be able to stand strong in faith and say, "I thank Christ Jesus our Lord who has enabled me, because He counted me faithful" (1 Timothy 1:12). In Jesus' name, I pray all of these things.

WEAPONS OF WARFARE

Without faith it is impossible to please Him, for he who comes to God must believe that He is, and that He is a rewarder of those who diligently seek Him.

HEBREWS 11:6

Therefore I say to you, whatever things you ask when you pray, believe that you receive them, and you will have them.

MARK 11:24

If you have faith as a mustard seed, you will say to this mountain, "Move from here to there," and it will move; and nothing will be impossible for you.

MATTHEW 17:20

But let him ask in faith, with no doubting, for he who doubts is like a wave of the sea driven and tossed by the wind. For let not that man suppose that he will receive anything from the Lord; he is a double-minded man, unstable in all his ways.

JAMES 1:6–8

And let us not grow weary while doing good, for in due season we shall reap if we do not lose heart. Therefore, as we have opportunity, let us do good to all, especially to those who are of the household of faith.

GALATIANS 6:9–10

CHAPTER THIRTY-ONE

Praying for Your
Adult Children

*I*t doesn't make any difference how old your children become, they will always be your children. They will never outgrow their need for your love and approval, your admiration and respect, and your emotional and spiritual support. And you will continue to desire God's best for their lives. You'll always want them to be protected and provided for, to be growing in the things of the Lord, to be fulfilling the purpose God has for them, and to becoming all God created them to be. From the time your children become part of your life, a part of your heart will always be with them, no matter where they go or what they do.

In the years since I first wrote this book, my children have left home for college, come back, and left home again once they were financially able to support themselves. I have seen them grow up and take responsibility in their professional and personal lives. They have learned some hard lessons, gained wisdom from their mistakes, and have come to understand what works and what doesn't. They have stayed in church and grown in the Word of God. They understand the power of prayer and have become strong praying people on their own and as members of their own prayer groups. They have learned to make good choices—and none more impressive than with regard to the people they chose to marry. Our prayers have never been more profoundly answered, and we are grateful to God every day for that.

Over the past twenty-eight years, my husband and I have held countless prayer groups in our home to pray specifically for the children of those parents present, and we have not lost one child. I'm not saying that none of these children ever had problems. That wouldn't even be scriptural or healthy. If a child never experiences any trouble or disappointment, how would he understand his need for God? He would be in danger of becoming spoiled, over-protected, shallow, irresponsible, or uncommitted. We want our children to learn responsibility, compassion, and understanding. We want them to gain the skills necessary to handle what life throws at them. How will they ever know God as their helper, protector, provider, or rescuer if they never need Him to help, protect, provide, or rescue them? All these kids went through things, but they came through them stronger, wiser, and more compassionate toward the struggles of others. Prayer works!

How to Pray When Your Child Leaves Home

As your children leave home and go out into the world on their own, your prayers won't stop. In fact, they may even increase because you no longer have the day-to-day responsibility you once had for their lives. Prayer may very well be your only means of influence. But don't minimize the importance of that. Because your children are still your children, your prayers will always have impact in their lives.

You may no longer be able to tell them what to do, but you can sure tell the enemy what to do. And you can also tell him what he can't do in your children's lives. You can also tell God everything that is on your heart and how you would like to see Him move in your children's lives. In prayer you will be powerfully connected to your adult children, and they will experience the effects of your prayers. That's a lot of influence!

If you have a child who has grown up and left home either for college or to find his way in the world, add the following short prayers to the prayer at the end of each corresponding chapter. This is the way I pray for my own adult children, and it gives me peace to know that God hears my prayers.

~~~~~

PRAYERS

Chapter 1: Becoming a Praying Parent

Lord, show me how to pray specifically for my child now that I am not often with her (him). I depend on You to give me revelation. Show me things I need to see and how I should be praying. Help me communicate my love for her (him) and my commitment to pray consistently for her (him) in a way that is encouraging. Give her (him) the desire to communicate prayer needs to me, knowing that I can be trusted to treat that information with respect and confidentiality.

Chapter 2: Releasing My Child into God's Hands

Lord, the more my child establishes his (her) own independent life, the more I have no choice but to release him (her) into Your hands. The only way I can feel secure about him (her) is to know that he (she) continues to live under Your control. I have done all I can to raise him (her), so I release him (her) into Your hands and depend on You to be in charge of his (her) life. Even though I don't see him (her) every day, I know that You do. I trust You to keep him (her) on the path You have for him (her).

Chapter 3: Securing Protection from Harm

Lord, even though I don't always know where my child is, You do. Thank You that You always keep Your eyes on (name of child) to protect her (him) from harm. Thank You that no weapon formed against her (him) will prosper. Wherever she (he) drives, flies, or walks, keep her (him) surrounded with Your angels. Guide her (him) away from danger and far from any evil plans of ungodly influences.

Chapter 4: Feeling Loved and Accepted

Lord, I know that You give favor to those who love You. I pray that (name of child) will learn to love You more each day and enjoy Your favor in his (her) life. May he (she) find love and acceptance wherever he (she) goes. Enable him (her) to enjoy favor with all people, from family members, friends, and co-workers to casual acquaintances and strangers. May he (she) extend love and acceptance to others in a way that is pleasing to You.

Chapter 5: Establishing an Eternal Future

Lord, I continue to pray for the relationship (name of adult child) has with You. May it always be strong and unwavering. May it always be solid and without compromise. I pray that nothing in the world will blind her (his) eyes to who You are and to Your working in her (his) life. I pray that she (he) will never fall away from You and come to doubt or reject her (his) salvation in You, Jesus. May her (his) eternal future with You always be secure.

Chapter 6: Honoring Parents and Resisting Rebellion

Lord, I pray that (name of adult child) will not reject the good things he (she) was taught by doing anything to dishonor You or his (her) mother and father. Give him (her) the strength and wisdom to resist temptation to be rebellious in any of his (her) actions. May he (she) be obedient to the things he (she) knows are right in Your eyes. Give him (her) an attitude that willingly submits to all authority in his (her) life, and help him (her) to always obey the law.

Chapter 7: Maintaining Good Family Relationships

Lord, I pray that (name of adult child) will stay close to her (his) family members, even though she (he) lives apart from them. I pray that she (he) will take the time to maintain strong family ties. I also pray that she (he) will find favor with any in-laws, present or future, and that their relationships will be loving and positive. Wherever there is any broken relationship, I pray that she (he) will be the first to extend herself (himself) to seek reconciliation.

Chapter 8: Attracting Godly Friends and Role Models

Lord, I pray for (name of adult child) to have eyes to see the true character in people. Give him (her) discernment to spot anyone who is a bad influence so that he (she) can avoid establishing a close relationship with that person. Let him (her) not be misled by someone who talks a smooth talk but has less-than-pure motives. Give him (her) a desire to seek out brothers and sisters in the Lord to spend time with whenever possible. Bring people into his (her) life to mentor him (her) so that he (she) will always stay on the right path.

Chapter 9: Developing a Hunger for the Things of God

Lord, don't let (name of adult child) fall away from Your ways. As her (his) life gets busier with more and more responsibilities, may she (he) long for a deeper relationship and a closer walk with You. Don't let her (him) grow apathetic in her (his) commitment to serving You and living Your way. May she (he) always have a longing for Your presence and a desire to know You better.

Chapter 10: Being the Person God Created

Lord, I lift (name of adult child) up to You and ask that You would give him (her) new understanding about who You created him (her) to be. Don't let him (her) be tempted to compromise the life You have for him (her) in any way as he (she) seeks career opportunities and makes new friends. As new situations arise, keep him (her) from the intimidation that might cause him (her) to cast aside what he (she) knows to be true in order to impress others. Lead him (her) into the kind of work and activity that will fulfill the destiny You have for him (her).

Chapter 11: Following Truth, Rejecting Lies

Lord, I pray that (name of adult child) will not fall prey to believing lies. May she (he) have Your Spirit of Truth in her (him) as a barometer so that what is false is glaringly obvious. I also pray that she (he) will not be tempted to speak lies for personal gain. May she (he) not think for a moment that she (he) can get away with it just because other people appear to. May Your Spirit of Truth in her (him) be an ever-present reminder of what is true and right.

Chapter 12: Enjoying a Life of Health and Healing

Lord, help (name of adult child) always remember that You are his (her) healer. May he (she) never accept any kind of infirmity without seeking Your healing touch. Give him (her) faith to believe for miracles of healing in his (her) life. May he (she) be quick to pray for healing for others and be able to stand strong in faith with them as they wait upon You, Lord, for answers.

Chapter 13: Having the Motivation
for Proper Body Care

Lord, I pray that (name of adult child) will have a desire to take care of her (his) body. Remind her (him) that even though she (he) is on her (his) own, she (he) is still the temple of Your Holy Spirit. Because of that, she (he) should be diligent to take care of herself (himself). Convict her (him) when she (he) is tempted to do careless things that put her (his) health and safety at risk. Teach her (him) what she (he) needs to know with regard to taking care of her (his) body.

Chapter 14: Instilling the Desire to Learn

Lord, I pray that no matter how old (name of adult child) becomes, he (she) will always have a strong desire to learn and increase in knowledge. I know that in order for him (her) to keep up in the competitive world, he (she) must be ever-increasing in his (her) skills. I pray that he (she) will learn to develop his (her) abilities and knowledge more and more in each season of life. May he (she) especially increase in his (her) knowledge of You and Your ways.

Chapter 15: Identifying God-Given Gifts and Talents

Lord, I pray that (name of adult child) will continue to become more and more aware of the gifts and talents You have placed within her (him). Refine them for greater use in serving Your purposes here on earth. Release her (him) into the full use of her (his) gifts and abilities now, and let nothing hold her (him) back from using them as You created her (him) to do.

Chapter 16: Learning to Speak Life

Lord, I know that as (name of adult child) is out in the world each day, he (she) will hear bad language that is not edifying or glorifying to You. Put a barometer in him (her) that recognizes, measures, and is repulsed by anything that is not honoring of Your presence. Give him (her) strength to take the steps necessary, whenever possible, to distance himself (herself) from people who speak crudely or irreverently. Put a desire in his (her) heart to speak words that bring life. May the words of his (her) mouth and the meditations of his (her) heart always be acceptable in Your sight, O Lord, our strength and our redeemer (Psalm 19:14).

Chapter 17: Staying Attracted to Holiness and Purity

Lord, I pray that (name of adult child) will always have a pure heart. I pray that she (he) will cleanse herself (himself) from anything that would keep her (him) from being a vessel for Your honor and useful for Your purposes. Remove anything in her (his) life that keeps her (him) from bearing good fruit. May she (he) aim to not just be pure in her (his) own eyes or in the opinion of others, but most importantly, in Your eyes.

Chapter 18: Praying Through a Child's Room

(When praying the prayer at the end of Chapter 18 for your adult child, substitute the words "the home" in place of the words "this room," and then continue with this prayer.)

Lord, I pray that the home where (name of adult child) lives will be a dwelling for Your presence. Make him (her) aware of anything there that is not glorifying to You. Don't let him (her) bring anything that is an abomination to You into his (her) dwelling place. I pray that nothing will ever go on in that home that is not pleasing in Your sight. Protect the home from intruders or disasters of any kind.

Chapter 19: Enjoying Freedom from Fear

Lord, I pray that (name of adult child) will always remember that You are with her (him) wherever she (he) goes, and that You will continue to uphold and strengthen her (him). Remind her (him) that no matter how many frightening things go on around her (him), You are her (his) protector. Continue to perfect her (him) in Your love so that she (he) will not live in fear. Help her (him) know that she (he) can always take refuge in You.

Chapter 20: Receiving a Sound Mind

Lord, I pray that as (name of adult child) is more and more in the world, You will protect him (her) from the confused thinking that is there. Give him (her) clarity of thought and immunity from the voices of confusion that would like him (her) to conform to their ways. May his (her) mind be increasingly controlled by Your Spirit. May he (she) not be conformed to this world, but be transformed by the renewing of his (her) mind (Romans 12:2). Help him (her) to daily bring every thought into captivity in obedience to the Lord.

Chapter 21: Inviting the Joy of the Lord

Lord, I know that because of the way life is, the longer (name of adult child) lives, the more pain, suffering, and loss she (he) will experience either in her (his) life or in the lives of others. I pray that whenever that happens, You will keep her (him) from losing her (his) joy. Whenever her (his) spirit is grieved due to some loss, I pray that You would give her (him) the oil of joy for mourning and the garment of praise for the spirit of heaviness (Isaiah 61:3). Help her (him) run to You, knowing that in Your presence is where joy is found (Romans 15:13).

Chapter 22: Destroying an Inheritance of Family Bondage

Lord, I lift up (name of adult child) to You and ask that anything bad from my past or his (her) father's past will not be something with which he (she) will have to struggle or a burden he (she) will have to bear. I know that things from the past may try to raise their ugly heads in his (her) life as he (she) gets older, but I pray that he (she) will know that these things have been broken by the power of Your Spirit. May he (she) be strong enough in You to lay hold of the inheritance of freedom that was bought for him (her) on the cross. Thank You, Jesus, that You paid that price so we and our children don't have to.

Chapter 23: Avoiding Alcohol, Drugs, and Other Addictions

Lord, I know that it is never too late to become an alcoholic, get hooked on drugs, or develop any other kind of addiction. Please keep (name of adult child) protected from all those things. Wherever the enemy has gained ground in that area, set her (him) free.

Whenever something like this becomes a temptation or is thrown in her (his) face, deliver her (him) from it. Help her (him) to choose life and not the death that all of these things bring.

Chapter 24: Rejecting Sexual Immorality

Lord, I know that sexual temptation is everywhere and nearly impossible to avoid. It is increasingly accepted in our society as a whole. I also know it is one of the ways the enemy wants to destroy the life of (name of adult child). Gird up his (her) spirit, soul, and mind, and help him (her) stand strong against it. Whenever he (she) feels drawn away from what's right by his (her) own desires, help him (her) stand up and resist so that he (she) can preserve his (her) life in a way that is honoring to You.

Chapter 25: Finding the Perfect Mate

Lord, I pray that (name of adult child) will always be with the husband (wife) You have for her (him). Don't let her (him) make any mistakes with regard to that. Where mistakes have already been made, I pray that You will redeem the situation. During times of discouragement in that area, keep her (him) determined not to give in to the temptation to step outside of Your will for her (his) life. I pray that her (his) marriage will be godly and produce "godly offspring" just as You desire (Malachi 2:15-16).

Chapter 26: Living Free of Unforgiveness

Lord, I pray that no matter how old (name of adult child) becomes, or what happens in life, that he (she) will refuse to be bitter toward others. May he (she) always be willing to forgive another's offense against him (her), just as You have forgiven his (her) offenses against You. May he (she) be slow to anger and able to overlook a transgression (Proverbs 19:11). Give him (her) the ability to always be loving and generous of spirit toward others, even those who are not that way toward him (her).

Chapter 27: Walking in Repentance

Lord, I pray that You would give (name of adult child) a continually regenerating heart. May she (he) never get to the point where she (he) doesn't understand the value of confession and repentance in her (his) life. May she (he) never think because no one is watching that You aren't seeing all that she (he) does. Make her (him) quick to repent of any unrighteousness in her (his) thoughts and actions. May she (he) always be able to uncover her (his) sins before You, confessing and forsaking them, so that she (he) can enjoy Your mercy and prosperity (Proverbs 28:13).

Chapter 28: Breaking Down Ungodly Strongholds

Lord, I know the enemy likes to erect strongholds in our lives that in our busyness and preoccupation with the demands and pressures of life we don't even recognize. I pray that You will reveal anything like that in (name of adult child) and break down every negative stronghold in his (her) life. Show him (her) things he (she) has not seen, and let nothing be hidden that needs to be shown (Matthew 10:26).

Chapter 29: Seeking Wisdom and Discernment

Lord, I pray that You would give (name of adult child) a gift of wisdom today. Give her (him) the ability to see things she (he) has not been able to see before. Give her (him) wisdom for all decisions, especially quick decisions where there is not time to pray in-depth. May she (he) enjoy the long life, riches, honor, pleasantness, happiness, and peace You have for her (him) because of the wisdom You have planted in her (his) soul (Proverbs 3:13-18).

Chapter 30: Growing in Faith

Lord, I know that there have been and will be events in the life of (name of adult child) that will try his (her) faith. I pray that he (she) will come through each of these times with greater faith than before. May his (her) faith always continue to grow through whatever happens in life so that it becomes stronger and stronger with each passing year. Give him (her) faith to believe for all that You have for him (her). May his (her) success in life never be compromised by weakened faith in Your ability to do the impossible.

Praying Together with Other Parents

*A*fter experimenting with a number of ways to organize an intercessory prayer time for children, I found a format that works well. First of all, each prayer gathering has to be limited to praying for no more than twelve children at a time, because it takes twenty to thirty minutes per child to share concerns and requests and adequately pray for them. Even with only twelve children, that means six hours of praying. This is quite a sacrifice of time and commitment as a parent, not to mention how much it pushes the limits of patience for the children. That's why we only do it once or twice a year—usually on a Saturday or holiday.

The way we organize it is to start praying at 2:00 P.M., take a dinner break from 5:00 to 5:30 P.M. and then pray from 5:30 to 8:30 P.M. Sometimes everyone brings food to share; sometimes we order food to be delivered. We hire teenagers to keep the younger children entertained and cared for in a separate room while the adults pray in private.

We have found it doesn't work well to pray for all the children in a family one after the other, because often that family feels they're done at that point and might as well go home. It's also not good for people to drop in to be prayed for and then leave—or even worse, drop the child off to be prayed for and then come back and pick him (her) up. The only time we were happy to do that was in the case of a single parent who worked and couldn't arrange it otherwise. For the most part, this prayer time must be a commitment of *all* the parents to *all* the children for *all* the time it takes. Let people know in advance what's expected of them in this regard so they can decide whether they are able to make the commitment.

When we begin, we draw the names of each family to see in what order we will proceed. Then we pray in that order, one at a time, for the firstborn of every family. When we've finished with them, we pray for the second born, then the third born, and so on.

We always begin the prayer time without the child present so the parents can give their requests and concerns and we can pray for any sensitive issues which they don't want the child to hear. Then we invite the child into the room to share his (her) own specific requests. As we pray for those requests, we also pray for the child's health, safety, protection, guidance, development of gifts and talents, and possibly discreet mention of the previously stated concern of the parent.

For example, one parent expressed concern over the bad influence of certain friends in the child's life. When we prayed *without* the child, we interceded in great detail about the specific friends. When we prayed *with* the child, we prayed for the child to have discernment to seek out godly friends and resist ungodly associates. Discretion is the key here so that the child never feels betrayed or judged, but only loved.

The families we have prayed with over the years still talk about the powerful impact of our times together and the many answers to prayer that came about as a result. The children also enjoyed these prayer sessions because it made them feel cared for and special. There were even instances where parents came to have the group pray for an adult child living away from home, and they also later testified to the positive effect of those prayers.

Who knows how many lives have been—or can be—saved in one way or another just because praying parents join together? Don't be hesitant to organize a praying parent group in your area. The need is great. If you organize it, the people will come.

THE
POWER
OF A

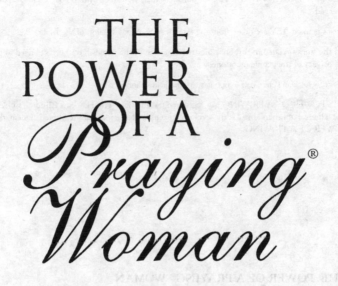

Praying®
Woman

STORMIE
OMARTIAN

HARVEST HOUSE PUBLISHERS

EUGENE, OREGON

All the stories related in this book are true, but most of the names have been changed to protect the privacy of the people mentioned.

Cover by Koechel Peterson & Associates, Minneapolis, Minnesota

THE POWER OF A PRAYING® WOMAN

Copyright © 2002 by Stormie Omartian
Published by Harvest House Publishers
Eugene, Oregon 97402
www.harvesthousepublishers.com

Library of Congress Cataloging-in-Publication Data

Omartian, Stormie.
    The power of a praying woman / Stormie Omartian.
        p.   cm.
    Includes bibliographical references.
    ISBN 0-7369-0855-2 (pbk.)
    ISBN 0-7369-0974-5 (Deluxe Edition)
    1. Christian women—Religious life.   2. Prayer—Christianity.   I. Title.
BV4527 .O435   2002
248.8' 43—dc21   2002006077

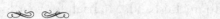

This book is dedicated to my sisters in Christ all over the world who long to deepen their walk with the Lord, move into everything God has for them, and become all He made them to be.

Acknowledgments

With special thanks:

To Susan Martinez, for your prayer support and hard work as my secretary, assistant, prayer partner, and friend.

To my husband, Michael, for your love, prayers, and good cooking.

To my children, for simply living.

To my faithful prayer partners.

To Pastor Jack Hayford, Pastor Rice Broocks, Pastor Tim Johnson, Pastor Ray McCollum, Pastor John Roher, Pastor Jim Laffoon, and Pastor Scott Bauer, for your life-saving prayers and life-changing words.

To my Harvest House family—Bob Hawkins Jr., Carolyn Mc-Cready, Terry Glaspey, Betty Fletcher, Julie McKinney, Teresa Evenson, LaRae Weikert, Kim Moore, and Peggy Wright—for all your encouragement and support.

To the thousands of women who have sent letters, e-mail, and faxes to me sharing your struggles, joys, longings, and the desires of your heart.

Contents

Let the beauty of the LORD our God be upon us,
and establish the work of our hands for us.
PSALM 90:17

The Power

It doesn't matter what age you are, what your marital status is, what the condition of your body and soul is, or how long you have or have not been a believer—if you are a woman, this book is for you. I've been a devoted follower of the Lord for over 30 years and I have not fallen away from Him in all that time, yet I need this book too. In fact, I wrote it for myself as much as I wrote it for you. That's because I'm like you. Many days I find life difficult rather than easy, complex rather than simple, potentially dangerous rather than safe, and exhausting rather than exhilarating. Often it's more like a strong, hot, dry wind than it is a soft, cool, refreshing breeze.

But I have come to know that God can smooth my path, calm the storms, keep me and all I care about safe, and even make my way simple when I ask Him to carry the complexities of life for me. But these things don't just happen. Not without prayer.

In the midst of our busy lives, too often we don't pray enough. Or we only pray about the most pressing issues and neglect to take the time to really get close to God, to know Him better, and to share with Him the deepest longings of our heart. In our pray-and-run existence, we shut off the very avenue by which He brings blessings into our lives. And we risk waking up one day with that empty, insecure feeling in the pit of our stomach frightening us with the thought that our foundation may be turning into sand and our protective armor may be becoming as fragile as an eggshell. This is what happened to me.

A few years ago, I had become so busy with working, taking care of teenagers, trying to be a good wife, running a home, writing books and traveling to promote them, being at all church meetings, helping people who needed it, and trying to make everyone happy, that I neglected the most important thing—my intimate walk with God. It's not that I stopped walking with Him. To the contrary, I couldn't make it through a day without Him. It's not that I stopped praying. Actually, I was praying more than ever about everyone else on the planet. But I didn't pray about my own walk with Him. It's not that I didn't read His Word. I read for hours as I did research in the Scriptures for different projects I was working on and the Bible study classes I was taking. But I didn't give God time to speak to me personally through it. I was busy doing good and neglected to do what was best. I became Martha instead of Mary without even realizing it (Luke 10:38-42).

I didn't take enough time for God and me alone, and as a result I became so depleted I couldn't go on. I felt like that eggshell, as if I could be crushed with very little outside pressure. I knew I needed more of God in my life, and nothing on earth was more important than that. There wasn't anything else that could satisfy the hunger I felt inside except more of His presence. And I came to realize how important it was for me to guard and protect my personal relationship with God in prayer.

The way to avoid the kind of thing I experienced is to pray about every aspect of our life in such a manner that it will keep us spiritually anchored and reminded of what God's promises are to us. It will keep us focused on who God is and who He made us to be. It will help us live God's way and not our own. It will lift our eyes from the temporal to the eternal and show us what is really important. It will give us the ability to distinguish the truth from a lie. It will strengthen our faith and encourage us to believe for the impossible. It will enable us to become the women of God we *long* to be and believe we *can* be. Who among us doesn't need that?

In my previous books on prayer, I have shared the ways husbands and wives can pray for one another, parents can pray for their children, and people can pray for their nation. In this book, I want to share how *you* can pray for YOU. I want to help you draw close to your heavenly Father, to feel His arms around you, to maintain a right heart before Him, to live in the confidence of knowing you are in the center of His will, to discover more fully who He made you to be, to find wholeness and completeness in Him, and to move into all He has for you. In other words, I want to show you how to effectively cover your life in prayer so that you can have more of God in your life.

Why Is It So Hard to Pray for Myself?

Do you find it is easier to pray for other people than it is to pray for yourself? I know I do. I can pray for my husband, my children, other family members, acquaintances, friends, and people I've never even met whom I hear about in the news far easier than I can pray for my own needs. For one thing, their needs are easy for me to identify. Mine are numerous, sometimes complicated, often difficult to determine, and certainly not easy to label. We women know what we *think* we need most of the time. We are able to recognize the obvious. But we are often too emotionally involved in the people around us and the day-to-day existence of our lives to be able to figure out how we should be praying for ourselves beyond the immediate and urgent. Sometimes we can be so overwhelmed by our circumstances that our prayer is simply a basic cry for help.

Do you ever have times when your life seems out of control? Do you ever feel pressured, as if your days are so busy that you fear you're missing out on a certain quality of life because of it? Do you worry that you are neglecting one or more areas of your life because you are trying to fill numerous roles and meet many expectations? I've experienced that too.

Have you ever felt as if your life is stuck in one place and you're going nowhere? Or worse yet, you are going backward? Have you had times when you've lost your vision for the future? Or have you never really had one to begin with? Have you wondered whether you can actually move into the full purpose and destiny God has for you? Have you experienced feelings of emptiness, frustration, or unfulfillment? I, too, have felt all those things.

Do you hunger for a greater sense of the Lord's presence in your life? Do you desire to know God in a deeper way? Do you want to serve Him better and more completely but don't feel you have the time, energy, or opportunity to do so? Do you need to spend more time with Him in prayer? Do you want your prayers to be accompanied by greater faith so that you can see greater answers to them? Do you need a more complete knowledge and understanding of God's Word? Do you ever just long to throw your arms wide open and embrace Jesus, white robes and all, and feel His embrace of you? So do I.

The good news is that this is the way God *wants* you to feel.

God wants you to long for *His* presence. He wants you to find your fulfillment in *Him* and nothing else. He wants you to walk closely with *Him*. He wants you to increase in faith and knowledge of *His* Word. He wants you to put all your hopes and dreams in *His* hands and look to *Him* to meet all of your needs. When you do, *He* will open the storehouse of blessing upon your life. That's because these things are *His* will for you.

But none of this happens without prayer.

Where Do I Go to Get My Needs Met?

Every woman has needs. But many of us are guilty of looking to other people to meet them—especially the men in our lives. Too often we expect *them* to meet the needs that only *God* can fill. And then we are disappointed when they can't. We expect too much from *them* when our expectations should be in *God*.

My friend Lisa Bevere expressed it best when she said that for centuries women have "wrestled and waged war with the sons of Adam in an attempt to get them to bless us and affirm our value. But this struggle has left us frustrated at best....In the end, it is all a senseless and exhausting process in which both parties lose. It is not the fault of the sons of Adam; they cannot give us the blessing we seek, and we have frightened them by giving them so much power over our souls. We must learn that the blessings we truly need come only from God."*

---

* Lisa Bevere, *Kissed the Girls and Made Them Cry*, (Nashville: Tommy Nelson, 2002), pp 189-90.

We will never be happy until we make God the source of our fulfillment and the answer to our longings. He is the *only* one who should have power over our souls.

We have to put our expectations in the Lord and not in other things or people. I know this is easier said than done. So let's start with the easy part. Let's say to God, "Lord, I look to You for everything I need in my life. Help me to put all my expectations in You." And whenever you are disappointed because your needs are not being met, talk to yourself and say, "My soul, wait silently for God alone, for my expectation is from Him" (Psalm 62:5). Then tell God about all your needs and everything that is in your heart. Don't worry, He won't be surprised or shocked. He already knows. He is just waiting to hear it from you.

More Than Just a Survivor

If you're like me, you don't want to live the kind of life where you are barely hanging on. You don't want to merely eke out an existence, find a way to cope with your misery, or just get by. You want to have the abundant life Jesus spoke of when He said, "I have come that they may have life, and that they may have it more abundantly" (John 10:10).

We don't want to be women who hear the truth but seldom act in faith to appropriate it for our lives. We don't want to be forever grappling with doubt, fear, insecurity, and uncertainty. We want to live life *on* purpose and *with* purpose. We find it boring to live like a baby, feeding only on milk. We want the solid food of God's truth so we can grow into a life that is exciting and productive.

None of us enjoys going around in circles, always passing through the same territory and coming back to the same problems, same frustrations, same mistakes, and same limitations. We don't want to become calloused, hard-hearted, bitter, unforgiving, anxious, impatient, hopeless, or un-teachable. We don't want to end up with a negative attitude that says, "My situation will never *be* any different because it hasn't *been* any different for a long time." We want to break out of any self-defeating cycle of repeated patterns and habits and be able to transcend ourselves, our limita-tions, and our circumstances. We want to be more than just a survivor.

We want to be an overcomer. We want to be a part of something greater than ourselves. We want to be connected to what God is doing on earth in a way that bears fruit for His kingdom. We want to have a sense of purpose in our lives. We want to abound in God's love and blessings. We want it all. All God has for us. But we can never achieve that quality of life outside the power of God. And then only as we pray.

How Do I Move in the Power of God?

We've all had times when we feel completely powerless in the face of our circumstances. We've proven to ourselves over and over that we don't have what it takes to attain any kind of permanent transformation in our lives. We know without a doubt that our best efforts to change ourselves or our circumstances in ways that are significant or lasting never work. We recognize our need for a power outside of and far greater than ourselves. But there is only one power in the world great enough to help us rise above ourselves and the difficult things we face. That is the power of God.

Without God's power, we can't transcend our limita-tions or get out of our rut. We can't stand strong in the face of all that opposes us. We are doomed to a life of spiritual mediocrity. Without the power of God's Holy Spirit working in us, we can't be liberated from everything that keeps us from moving into all God has for us.

We don't want to spend our lives waiting to be delivered from all that limits us and separates us from God's best. We want to be set free *now*. But that can't happen if we refuse to acknowledge the Holy Spirit's power. When we deny the Holy Spirit's attributes we become like those people the Bible speaks of who live "having a form of godliness but denying its power" (2 Timothy 3:5). We become professional Christians who talk "Christianese" with such a slick veneer of superficiality that it makes us untouchable and keeps us untouched. We become all show and no heart. All correctness and no love. All judgment and no mercy. All self-assurance and no humility. All talk and no tears. We live powerless and meaningless lives without any hope for real transformation. And without transformation, how can we ever rise above our limitations and be God's instrument to reach the world around us? And that is what life is all about.

God wants us to understand "what is the exceeding greatness of His power toward us who believe" (Ephesians 1:19). He wants us to know this power that raised Jesus "from the dead and seated Him at His right hand in the heavenly places, far above all principality and power and might and dominion, and every name that is named" (Ephesians 1:20-21). He wants us to understand that Jesus is not weak toward us, but mighty *in* us (2 Corinthians 13:3). He wants us to understand that "though He was crucified in weakness, yet He lives by the power of God," and even though we are also weak, we live by the power of God too (2 Corinthians 13:4). God wants us to see that "we have received, not the spirit of the world, but the Spirit who is from God, that we might know the things that have been freely given to us by God" (1 Corinthians 2:12).

I can't make you see or cause you to comprehend the power of God or the way the Holy Spirit wants to work in you. That is beyond my capabilities and authority in your life. But you don't need me to convince you because the Holy Spirit will do that Himself. Jesus said, "the Helper, the Holy Spirit, whom the Father will send in My name, He will teach you all things" (John 14:26). But you first have to acknowledge the Holy Spirit and invite Him to move in you freely.

We can only move in the power of God's Spirit if we have first received Jesus as Savior. You need to "know the love of Christ which passes knowledge; that you may be filled with all the fullness of God" (Ephesians 3:19). When you have Jesus as ruler of your life, you will come to know Him as the one "who is able to do exceedingly abundantly above all that we ask or think, according to the power that works in us" (Ephesians 3:20). Because of His Holy Spirit in us—or His *power* in us—He can do more in our lives than we can even think to ask for. How great is that?

Being filled with the Holy Spirit is not something that happens against our will. It is something we have to be open to, something we must desire, something for which we have to ask. "If you then, being evil, know how to give good gifts to your children, how much more will your heavenly Father give the Holy Spirit to those who ask Him!" (Luke 11:13). We have a choice about whether we will be filled with the Holy Spirit or not. We have to ask God to do that.

I am not going to get into the various doctrines of men about the Holy Spirit of God. There seem to be as many of these as there are denominations. All I am asking is that you recognize the Holy Spirit of God as the *power* of God, and that you ask God to fill you with His Holy Spirit so He can empower you to move into all He has for you. The Bible says, "be filled with the Spirit" (Ephesians 5:18). Life works better when we do what the Bible says.

The Power to Become All God Made You to Be

Today, more and more believing women are being given an open door to become all they were created to be. They are moving out in different areas of expertise and ministry and making an important difference in the lives of those whom God puts in their realm of influence. They are learning to rely on the power of God to prepare them and open the doors. They are also realizing that they are not just an afterthought in the order of God's creation, but they were created for a special purpose. They might not know exactly what that purpose is or all that it entails, but they know that it is to do good for others and glorify God.

An important reason more women are rising up to fulfill the destiny God has for them is because men are rising up to their place of spiritual authority and leadership. This is an answer to the prayers of countless women and something for which we must praise God. Women need this spiritual covering. When it's done right—with strength, humility, kindness, respect, and understanding—and not with abuse, arrogance, self-promotion, cruelty, harshness, or lovelessness, it becomes a place of safety for a woman. Being in right order in our lives is something to be desired.

The Bible says that "the woman ought to have a symbol of authority on her head" (1 Corinthians 11:10). This means spiritual authority, and it is very important. *Everyone* is supposed to be submitted to divinely appointed authority. It's part of God's order. God won't pour into our lives all He has for us until we are in right relationship with the proper authority figures whom He has placed in our lives. They are there for our protection and benefit. God's power is too precious and too powerful to be let loose in an unsubmitted soul. (This is something to *pray* about, not *worry* about, so we'll do that in chapter 9.)

God's Promises to You

So often we don't move into all God has for us because we don't understand what it *is* He has for us. We may know He has given many promises for our lives, but if we don't know *exactly* what these promises are, we can't get a clear perspective on our situation. God's "divine power has given to us all things that pertain to life and godliness, through the knowledge of Him who called us by glory and virtue, by which have been given to us exceedingly great and precious promises, that through these you may be partakers of the divine nature" (2 Peter 1:3-4).

We need to know these promises well enough to keep them perpetually in our minds and on our hearts. In fact, the *deeper* they are etched in our souls the better off we will be. That's because the enemy of our soul will try to steal them from us. He doesn't want us to know the truth about ourselves. So we must grab on to these promises with all our might. We must cling to them like life and refuse to let them go.

For this reason, at the end of each chapter in this book there is a section called "God's Promises to Me." In it I have listed important promises from God's Word that are applicable to that particular subject. I want us to declare these promises out loud in the face of all obstacles in order to erase any doubt about those priceless truths for our lives. As you read each one, determine what God's promise in that particular Scripture means specifically for you and your life.

In some instances, determine what promise is *implied* in that Scripture. Take for example the verse, "Watch and pray, lest you enter into temptation. The spirit indeed is willing, but the flesh is weak" (Matthew 26:41). The implied promise here is that if you pray and are watchful, you won't fall into temptation.

While most of God's promises are pleasant and positive, some are not because they are warnings to us. It's like saying to a child, "If you do *this*, there is this reward. But if you do *that*, I *promise* you there will be these unpleasant consequences." Because God keeps *all* of His promises, it's important to know them well.

Time to Move On

Although it may often feel like it, there is never a time when *nothing* is happening in your life. That's because whether you realize it or not, you are never standing still. You are either going forward or you're sliding back. You are either becoming *more* like Christ every day or you're becoming *less* like Him. There is no neutral position in the Lord. And that is the very reason I wrote this book. I want you and me to keep moving forward. I don't want us to wake up one morning and realize we never laid a good foundation in the things of God or we didn't protect the foundation we had with prayer. I want us to move forward by spending quality time with the Lover of our soul every day. I want us to become *passionate* about God. I want us to find out what we are supposed to be doing and then do it. This is not about getting things *from* God, although He has much He wants to give to us. It's about getting *into* God and allowing Him to get into *us*. It's about letting *Him* make us complete.

When we live this way, according to God's Word and by the power of His Holy Spirit, then we can trust that we are in the right place at the right time and that the Lord is working His perfect will in our lives. We can trust that He is moving us into the life of wholeness and blessing He has for us. Shall we get started?

— My Prayer to God —

Lord, You have said in Your Word that whoever believes in You will have rivers of living water flowing from their heart (John 7:38). I believe in You, and I long for Your living water to flow in and through me today and every day that I'm alive. I invite Your Holy Spirit to fill me afresh right now. Just as a spring is constantly being renewed with fresh water so that it stays pure, I ask You to renew me in that same way today.

Your Word says that "the Spirit also helps in our weaknesses. For we do not know what we should pray for as we ought, but the Spirit Himself makes intercession for us with groanings which cannot be uttered" (Romans 8:26). Lord, I realize I don't know how to pray as I need to, nor as often as I want to, but I invite You, Holy Spirit, to pray through me. Help me in my weakness. Teach me the things I don't know about You.

I am desperately aware of how much I need Your power to transform me and my circumstances. I don't want to live an ineffective life. I want to live in the dynamic power of Your Spirit. I don't want to be a spiritual underachiever. I want to be an overcomer. You paid a price for me so that I could be owned by You. Help me to live like it. You planned out a course for my life so that I could be defined by You. Help me to act like it. You made it possible for me to defeat my enemy. Help me not to forget it. You sent Your Holy Spirit so that I could live in power. Help me to fulfill that promise. You gave Your life for me because You loved me. Help me to do the same for You.

I put all my expectations in You, Lord. I repent of the times I have expected other people or other things to meet my needs when I should have been looking to You. I know that You are the only one who can complete me because You are everything I need. All that I have ever wanted in my life can be found in You. Help me to remember to live not in my own strength, but by the power of Your Spirit living in me. Forgive me for the times I have forgotten to do that. Enable me to grow in the things of Your kingdom so that I can become a whole, properly functioning, contributing, productive child of Yours who moves forward in Your purpose for my life.

❧ GOD'S PROMISES TO ME ❧

We have this treasure in earthen vessels,
that the excellence of the power may be of God and
not of us.

2 CORINTHIANS 4:7

The message of the cross is foolishness to those who
are perishing, but to us who are being saved it
is the power of God.

1 CORINTHIANS 1:18

My grace is sufficient for you, for My strength is
made perfect in weakness.
2 CORINTHIANS 12:9

God both raised up the Lord and will also raise us up
by His power.
1 CORINTHIANS 6:14

When the Helper comes, whom I shall send to you
from the Father, the Spirit of truth who proceeds
from the Father, He will testify of Me.
JOHN 15:26

CHAPTER ONE

Lord, Draw Me into a Closer Walk with You

$\mathcal{B}$efore I came to know the Lord, I was involved in all kinds of occult practices and Eastern and New Age religions. I searched for God in each one of them, hoping to find some meaning or purpose for my life. I was desperate to find a way out of the emotional pain, fear, and depression I had experienced on a daily basis since I was a child. I thought there surely must be a God, and if I could just be good enough to get close to Him, perhaps something of His greatness would rub off on me, and then I could feel better about myself and my life.

Of course I was never able to do that because the gods I chased after were distant, cold, and remote. And this depressed me all the more because I was raised by a mother who was distant, cold, and remote, not to mention abusive, frightening, and cruel. It was later determined that she was mentally ill, and I have since forgiven her for all that I suffered at her hand. Nevertheless, the memories of my childhood eventually snowballed into an avalanche of pain that became so unbearable that I ended up being suffocated by my own hopelessness and crushed into suicidal despair.

But it was here at the lowest point in my life, when I was 28 years old, that I learned who God really is and received Jesus as my Savior. This began a process of deliverance, healing, and restoration, the likes of which I had never dreamed possible.

From the time I received the Lord and began to feel His life working *in* me, I could see the common thread in all those *other* religions and practices I had dabbled in previously. This similarity was that the gods of each of those religions had no power to save or transform a human life. But the God of the *Bible* did. *He* is the one, true, living God. And when we find *Him* and receive *Him*, His Spirit comes to dwell *in* us. By the power of His spirit, He transforms us from the inside out and miraculously changes our circumstances and our lives.

I also learned that He is a God who can be found. A God who can be known. A God who wants to be close to us. That's why He is called Immanuel, which means "God *with* us." But He draws close to *us* as we draw close to *Him* (James 4:8).

If I could sit down and talk with you in person about your life, I would tell you that if you have received the Lord, the answer to what you need is within you. That's because the Holy Spirit of God is within you, and He will lead you in all things and teach you everything you need to know. He will transform you and your circumstances beyond your wildest dreams if you will give up trying to do it on your own and let *Him* do it *His* way and in *His* time.

This is not about striving to be good enough to get to God, for there is no way any of us can be. This is about letting all of the goodness of God be *in* you. It's about drawing closer to God and sensing Him drawing closer to you. This is about an intimate walk with God and the wholeness that will be worked in you because of it.

I Know What You Want

I traveled all over the United States speaking to women's groups during three of the last four years. Nearly everywhere I went in that period of time, I took a survey for a book I was writing called *The Power of a Praying® Husband.* I wanted to know how women most wanted to be prayed for. Their response was not surprising, but the fact that it was unanimous in every city and every state was amazing. The number one personal need of all women surveyed was that they would grow spiritually and have a deep, strong, vital, life-changing, faith-filled walk with God. I eventually stopped taking the survey because the results were always the same. I got the point!

I'm sure that you, like me and many women, want a deep, intimate, loving relationship with God. You wouldn't be reading this book if you didn't. You long for the closeness, the connection, the affirmation that who you are is good and desirable. But God is the only one who can give all that to you all of the time. Your deepest needs and longing will only be met in an intimate relationship with Him. No person will ever reach as deeply into you as God will. No one can ever know you as well or love you as much. That insatiable longing for more that you feel, the emptiness you want those closest to you to fill, is put there by God so that *He* can fill it.

God wants us to want Him. And when we realize that it's Him that we want, we become free. We are free to identify the longings, loneliness, and emptiness inside of us as our signal that we need to draw near to God with open arms and ask Him to fill us with more of Himself. But this deep and intimate relationship with God that we all desire and can't live without doesn't just happen. It must be sought after, prayed for, nurtured, and treasured. And we must *continually* seek after, pray for, nurture, and treasure it.

Five Good Ways to Tell if Your Walk with God Is Shallow

1. *If you follow the Lord for only what He can do for you,* your walk with Him is shallow. If you love Him enough to ask Him what *you* can do for *Him,* then your relationship is growing deep.

2. *If you only pray to God when things are tough or you need something,* then your walk with Him is shallow. If you find yourself praying to Him many times a day just because you love to be in His presence, then your relationship is growing deep.

3. *If you get mad at God or disappointed in Him when He doesn't do what you want,* then your walk with Him is shallow. If you can praise God no matter what is going on in your life, then your relationship with Him is growing deep.

4. *If you love God only because of what He does,* then your walk with Him is shallow. If you love and reverence Him for who He *is,* then your relationship with Him is growing deep.

5. *If you think you have to beg God or twist His arm to get Him to answer your prayers,* then your walk with Him is shallow. If you believe that God wants to answer the prayers you pray in line with His will, then your relationship with Him is growing deep.

Spending Time Alone with Him

We can never draw close to God and get to know Him well, or develop the kind of intimate relationship we want, unless we spend time alone with Him. It's in those private times that we are refreshed, strengthened, and rejuvenated. It's then we can see our lives from God's perspective and discover what is really important. That's where we understand who it is we belong to and believe in.

God has so much to speak into your life. But if you don't draw apart from the busyness of your day and spend time alone with Him in quietness and solitude, you will not hear it. Jesus Himself spent much time alone with God. If anyone could get away with not doing it, surely it would have been Him. How much more important must it be for us?

I know finding time alone to pray can be difficult. Especially when the enemy of your soul doesn't want you to do that. But if you will make it a priority by setting a specific time to pray daily, perhaps writing it in your calendar the way you would any other important date, and determine to keep that standing appointment with God, you'll see answers to your prayers like never before.

Remember, if you haven't been praying much, you can't expect things to change overnight. It takes a while to get the enormous ocean liner of your life turned around and headed in a different direction. It doesn't immediately reposition itself the moment you begin steering. In fact, you may hardly see any changes at first. It's the same way with prayer. Prayer can turn your life around, but it doesn't always happen the moment you utter your first words. It may take a time of continued prayer before you actually see the scenery change. This is normal, so don't give up. You will soon be heading full speed in a new direction. Far too often people give up just before their breakthrough into the realm of answered prayer. Remember, this trip is not a mini-vacation tour around the harbor, it's a lifelong voyage to meet your destiny. Giving up is not an option.

Naming Names

Do you ever have trouble remembering names? I know I do. Especially when I meet a large number of people at one time. I can remember faces and names separately, but I don't always put the right ones together. And that can get me into trouble. With God it's a different situation. He has only one face, but many, many names. But if we don't know all of His names, we may not understand all the aspects of His character.

God has literally hundreds of names. Sometimes, though, it seems we often have trouble just remembering a few of the basic ones. We may forget one just when we need to remember it. For example, we may think of God as our heavenly *Father*, but forget that He is also our *Husband* and *Friend*. Or we may remember Him as our *Comforter*, but forget that He is our *Deliverer*. We might think of Him as our *Protector*, but fail to remember Him as our *Healer*. Some people never think of God beyond being their Savior, which in itself is more than we deserve. But God wants to be even more than that to us. He wants us to know all the aspects of His character because the way we recognize God will affect the way we live our lives.

Each of God's names in the Bible represents a way He wants us to trust Him. Do you trust Him to be your *Strength* (Psalm 18:1)? Is He your *Peace* (Ephesians 2:14)? Is He the *Lifter of Your Head* when you are down (Psalm 3:3)? Is He your *Refiner* (Malachi 3:2-3)? Your *Wisdom* (1 Corinthians 1:24)? Your *Counselor* (Psalm 16:7)? Your *Resting Place* (Jeremiah 50:6)? Each of His names is sacred, and we must treat each one as such.

When I worked in the secular entertainment world in Los Angeles, I heard the word "Jesus" a hundred times a day, spoken as a curse word by people with no reverence, love, or understanding of Him. It wasn't until I received Jesus that I realized exactly how much of a curse word that name was when it was used profanely. Taking God's name in vain brings a curse on whoever uses it in that manner because it breaks one of the Ten Commandments. "You shall not take the name of the LORD your God in vain, for the LORD will not hold him guiltless who takes His name in vain" (Exodus 20:7). It also violates God's *greatest* commandment, which is "you shall love the LORD your God with all your heart, with all your soul, with all your mind, and with all your strength" (Mark 12:30). No one who loves God uses His name in vain.

However, this same word—"Jesus"—when spoken in love by one who reverences Him, has great power in it. Power to save, deliver, heal, provide, protect, and so much more. Using it profanely shuts off these very things from our lives. There is also great power in each one of God's names, and when spoken with faith, love, understanding, and reverence, it brings a blessing and increases your faith.

For example, God's name is always a safe place to run to any time you need help. "The name of the LORD is a strong tower; the righteous run to it and are safe" (Proverbs 18:10). If you are sick, run to your Healer. If you can't pay your bills, run to your Provider. If you are afraid, run to your Hiding Place. If you are going through a dark time, run to your Everlasting Light. By speaking His name with reverence and thanksgiving, you invite Him to be that to you. Often there is so much we don't have in our lives simply because we do not acknowledge God as the answer to that need. How can you be healed if you don't acknowledge God as the Healer?

In the following list of God's names, I have included only 30. But there are hundreds more in His Word. Though

He is one God, there are so many dimensions to Him that in order for us to comprehend them all, He has given Himself many names. It's the only way we, who are so *small*, can begin to understand Him, who is so *great*. I suggest that every time you come across another name for God in the Bible, underline it or jot it in the margin or add it to a list. It will remind you of who God wants to be to you. As you read the following list, invite God to be each one of these names to you in a new, real, and life-changing way.

Thirty Good Names to Call Your God

1. *Healer* (Psalm 103:3)
2. *Redeemer* (Isaiah 59:20)
3. *Deliverer* (Psalm 70:5)
4. *My Strength* (Psalm 43:2)
5. *Shelter* (Joel 3:16)
6. *Friend* (John 15:15)
7. *Advocate* (1 John 2:1)
8. *Restorer* (Psalm 23:3)
9. *Everlasting Father* (Isaiah 9:6)
10. *Love* (1 John 4:16)
11. *Mediator* (1 Timothy 2:5-6)
12. *Stronghold* (Nahum 1:7)
13. *Bread of Life* (John 6:35)
14. *Hiding Place* (Psalm 32:7)
15. *Everlasting Light* (Isaiah 60:20)
16. *Strong Tower* (Proverbs 18:10)
17. *Resting Place* (Jeremiah 50:6)
18. *Spirit of Truth* (John 16:13)
19. *Refuge from the Storm* (Isaiah 25:4)
20. *Eternal Life* (1 John 5:20)
21. *The Lord Who Provides* (Genesis 22:14)
22. *Lord of Peace* (2 Thessalonians 3:16)
23. *Living Water* (John 4:10)
24. *My Shield* (Psalm 144:2)
25. *Husband* (Isaiah 54:5)
26. *Helper* (Hebrews 13:6)
27. *Wonderful Counselor* (Isaiah 9:6)
28. *The Lord Who Heals* (Exodus 15:26)
29. *Hope* (Psalm 71:5)
30. *God of Comfort* (Romans 15:5)

If you will go through this list of names periodically and speak each of them out loud, thanking God for being that to you, you'll be amazed at how your faith will grow and how much closer to God you will feel.

My Prayer to God

Lord, I draw close to You today, grateful that You will draw close to me as You have promised in Your Word (James 4:8). I long to dwell in Your presence, and my desire is for a deeper and more intimate relationship with You. I want to know You in every way You can be known. Teach me what I need to learn in order to know You better. I don't want to be a person who is "always learning and never able to come to the knowledge of the truth" (2 Timothy 3:7). I want to know the truth about who You are, because I know that You are near to all who call upon You in truth (Psalm 145:18).

I am open to whatever You want to do in me. I don't want to limit You by neglecting to acknowledge You in every way possible. I declare this day that You are my Healer, my Deliverer, my Redeemer, and my Comforter. Today I especially need to know You as (put in a name of the Lord). I believe You will be that to me.

God, help me to set aside time each day to meet with You alone. Enable me to resist and eliminate all that would keep me from it. Teach me to pray the way You want me to. Help me to learn more about You. Lord, you have said, "If anyone thirsts, let him come to Me and drink" (John 7:37). I thirst for more of You because I am in a dry place without You. I come to You this day and drink deeply of Your Spirit.

I know You are everywhere, but I also know that there are deeper manifestations of Your presence that I long to experience. Draw me close so that I may dwell in Your presence like never before.

❧ GOD'S PROMISES TO ME ❧

Draw near to God and He will draw near to you.
JAMES 4:8

I will pray the Father, and He will give you another Helper, that He may abide with you forever—the Spirit of truth, whom the world cannot receive, because it neither sees Him nor knows Him; but you know Him, for He dwells with you and will be in you.
JOHN 14:16-17

It is your Father's good pleasure to give you the kingdom.
LUKE 12:32

Until now you have asked nothing in My name. Ask, and you will receive, that your joy may be full.
JOHN 16:24

Let us hold fast the confession of our hope without wavering, for He who promised is faithful.
HEBREWS 10:23

CHAPTER TWO

Lord, Cleanse Me and Make My Heart Right Before You

Before we go any further, let's get something straight. That is, you and I are not perfect. No one is perfect. None of us has arrived. None of us is incapable of sin. None of us is without problems. None of us have walked so long with the Lord that we know it all and therefore have nothing to learn. None of us is so complete that we don't need anything from God. None of us has it all together.

There! It's out in the open.

Please don't think I said this because I believe *you* need to know it. To the contrary, I believe you already *do* know it. I said it because I want you to know that we *all* know it. We know it about ourselves and we know it about each other. Therefore, we can be completely honest with ourselves about ourselves.

I don't want you to feel when reading this book that you have to live up to some impossibly high standard for your life. This book is not about living up to a standard. It's about letting *God* become your standard. It's not about trying to make something happen for yourself. It's recognizing that you *can't* make anything happen, but you *can* surrender your life to God and let *Him* make things happen. It's not about finding ways to avoid God's judgment and feeling like a failure if you don't do everything perfectly. It's about fully experiencing God's love and letting it perfect you. It's not about being somebody you are not. It's about becoming who you really are. But in order to see these things happen, you have to be completely honest with yourself and with God about who you are at the moment.

Women all over the world want to live fruitful lives. They want to dwell in God's grace while still obeying His laws. They want to be *unshakable* in God's truth yet *moved* by the suffering and needs of others. They want to know God in all the ways He can be known, and they want to be transformed by the power of His Spirit. But they are often hard on themselves when they don't see all these things happening on a daily basis. They are quick to observe all they are doing wrong and slow to appreciate all they are doing right.

For that reason, I want you to look upon this idea of cleansing your heart not as a judgment that your heart is dirty, but as God's call for you to get completely right before Him so He can bring all the blessings He has for you into your life. See it as God preparing you for the important work He has ahead for you to do.

In order to accomplish this, you have to examine your life closely. You have to be brave enough to say, "Lord, show me what is in my heart, soul, mind, spirit, and life that shouldn't be there. Teach me what I am not understanding. Convict me where I am missing the mark. Tear down my arrogance, pride, fear, and insecurities, and help me to see the truth about myself, my life, and my circumstances. Expose me to myself, Lord. I can take it. Enable me to correct the error of my ways. Help me to replace lies with truth and make changes that last."

It takes courage to pray a prayer like that. Perhaps more courage than many of us have at the moment. If you are hesitant to let the Lord expose your heart because of what He might reveal, then ask Him to give you the courage you need. In order to see positive changes happen in your life, you have to be open to the cleansing and stretching work of the Holy Spirit. You have to allow Him to expose your heart so you won't be deceived about yourself and your life. You have to invite Him to create a clean heart within you. Then be willing to do these two things:

1. *Confess* to God any sins of thought or action that He shows you.

2. *Repent* of the things you have just confessed.

True Confession

Don't think just because you are not a serial killer or have never robbed a bank that you don't have any sin to confess. Don't think because you have walked with the Lord for a number of years and go to church every Sunday morning and Wednesday night, and to all prayer meetings in between, that you have nothing for which you need to repent. Sin doesn't have to be glaring and obvious in order for it to be sin. For example, have you ever doubted that God can do what He promises in His Word? Doubt is a sin. Have you ever said anything about a person to someone else that isn't exactly flattering? Gossip is a sin. Have you ever avoided someone because you thought they might ask something of you that you didn't want to give? Selfishness is a sin. Have you ever had an unloving attitude toward another person? Whatever does not come from love is a sin.

Sin is hard to avoid 100 percent of the time. That's why confession is crucial. When we don't confess our sins, faults, or errors, they separate us from God. And we don't get our prayers answered. "Your iniquities have separated you from your God; and your sins have hidden His face from you, so that He will not hear" (Isaiah 59:2).

When we don't confess our sins, we end up trying to hide ourselves from God. Just like Adam and Eve in the garden, we feel we can't face Him. But the problem with attempting to hide from God is that it's impossible. The Bible says that everything we do will be made known. Even the things we said and thought in secret. "There is nothing covered that will not be revealed, nor hidden that will not be known. Therefore whatever you have spoken in the dark will be heard in the light, and what you have spoken in the ear in inner rooms will be proclaimed on the housetops" (Luke 12:2-3). "There is no creature hidden from His sight, but all things are naked and open to the eyes of Him to whom we must give account" (Hebrews 4:13).

What a frightening thought! If each of us will have to give an account, the quicker we get it straight with God the better. In fact, the sooner we deal with the sins we *can* see, the sooner God can reveal to us the ones we *can't*. And God only knows how much of that there is residing in each of us.

There is always a consequence for sin. King David described it best when he wrote of his own unconfessed sin: "When I kept silent, my bones grew old through my groaning all the day long. For day and night Your hand was heavy upon me; my vitality was turned into the drought of summer" (Psalm 32:3-4).

I remember having resentment toward my husband for words he said that hurt me deeply. As long as I held on to the hurt and resentment, it made me feel physically ill. I didn't want to confess it because I thought my feelings were justified and *he* was the one who was wrong. But I finally realized that all sin is sin, so I confessed my resentment to God as sin—and the moment I did, the feeling of sickness in my body left. "There is no soundness in my flesh because of Your anger, nor any health in my bones because of my sin. For my iniquities have gone over my head; like a heavy burden they are too heavy for me. My wounds are foul and festering because of my foolishness" (Psalm 38:3-5). Life is hard enough without us having to carry around old, dry, sick, weak bones.

Nothing is heavier than sin. We don't realize how heavy it is until the day we feel its crushing weight bringing death to our souls. We don't see how destructive it is until we smash into the wall that has gone up between us and God because of it. That's why it's best to confess every sin as soon as we are aware of it and get our hearts cleansed and right immediately. Confession gets sin out in the open before God. When you confess your sin, you're not informing God of something He doesn't know. He already knows. He wants to know that *you* know.

Confessing, however, is more than just apologizing. Anyone can do that. We all know people who are good apologizers. The reason they are so good at it is because they get so much practice. They have to say "I'm sorry" over and over again because they never change their ways. In fact, they sometimes say, "I'm sorry" without ever actually admitting to any fault. Those are the professional apologizers. And their confessions don't mean anything. But *true* confession means admitting in full detail what you have done and then fully *repenting* of it.

Full Repentance

It's one thing to recognize when you have done something that has violated God's laws; it's another to be saddened by it to such a degree that you are determined to never do it again. That's repentance. Repentance means to change your mind. To turn and walk the other way. Repentance means being so deeply sorry for what you have done that you will do whatever it takes to keep it from happening again. Confession means we *recognize* we have done wrong and *admit* our sin. Repentance means we are *sorry* about our sin to the point of grief, and we have *turned* and *walked away* from it.

Repenting of something doesn't necessarily mean we will never commit that sin again. It means we don't *intend* to ever commit it again. So if you find that you have to confess the same sin again after you have only recently confessed and repented of it, then do it. Don't let the enemy saddle you with guilt and ride on your back shouting words of failure in your ear. Confess and repent as many times as necessary to throw him off and see yourself win the battle over this problem. Don't entertain thoughts such as, *Surely God won't forgive me again for the same thing I just confessed to Him last week.* He forgives *every time* you confess sin before Him and fully repent of it. "Blessed is he whose transgression is forgiven, whose sin is covered" (Psalm 32:1). You can turn things around in your life when you turn to the Lord and repent.

Learn to confess and repent quickly so that the death process that is set in motion each time we violate God's rules is not given time to do it's full damage, "for the wages of sin is death" (Romans 6:23). Ask God every day to show you where your heart is not clean and right before Him. Don't let anything separate you from all God has for you.

My Prayer to God

Lord, I come humbly before You and ask You to cleanse my heart of every fault and renew a right spirit within me. Forgive me for thoughts I have had, words I have spoken, and things that I have done that are not glorifying to You or are in direct contradiction to Your commands. Specifically, I confess to You (name any thoughts, words, or actions that you know are not pleasing to God). I confess it as sin and I repent of it. I choose to walk away from this pattern of thought or action and live Your way. I know that You are "gracious and merciful, slow to anger and of great kindness" (Joel 2:13). Forgive me for ever taking that for granted.

Lord, I realize that You are a God who "knows the secrets of the heart" (Psalm 44:21). Reveal those to me if I am not seeing them. Show me any place in my life where I harbor sin in my thoughts, words, or actions that I have not recognized. Show me the truth about myself so that I can see it clearly. Examine my soul and expose my motives to reveal what I need to understand. I am willing to give up meaningless and unfruitful habits that are not Your best for my life. Enable me to make changes where I need to do so. Open my eyes to what I need to see so that I can confess all sin and repent of it. I want to cleanse my hands and purify my heart as You have commanded in Your Word (James 4:8).

I pray that You will "have mercy upon me, O God, according to Your lovingkindness; according to the multitude of Your tender mercies, blot out my transgressions. Wash me thoroughly from my iniquity, and cleanse me from my sin" (Psalm 51:1-2). Lord, "create in me a clean heart...and renew a steadfast spirit within me. Do not cast me away from Your presence, and do not take Your Holy Spirit from me" (Psalm 51:10-11). "Cleanse me from secret faults" (Psalm 19:12). "See if there is any wicked way in me, and lead me in the way everlasting" (Psalm 139:24). Make me clean and right before You. I want to receive Your forgiveness so that times of refreshing may come from Your presence (Acts 3:19).

❧ GOD'S PROMISES TO ME ❧

If we confess our sins, He is faithful and just to
forgive us our sins and to cleanse us from
all unrighteousness.
1 JOHN 1:9

Beloved, if our heart does not condemn us, we have
confidence toward God. And whatever we ask we
receive from Him, because we keep His
commandments and do those things that
are pleasing in His sight.
1 JOHN 3:21-22

I acknowledged my sin to You, and my iniquity I
have not hidden. I said, "I will confess my
transgressions to the LORD," and You forgave the
iniquity of my sin.
PSALM 32:5

Repent therefore and be converted, that your sins may be blotted out, so that times of refreshing may come from the presence of the Lord.

ACTS 3:19

He who covers his sins will not prosper, but whoever confesses and forsakes them will have mercy.

PROVERBS 28:13

CHAPTER THREE

Lord, Help Me to Be a Forgiving Person

My mother was abusive when I was growing up, but my father wasn't. When I became a Christian, forgiving my mother was the obvious thing to do. It wasn't until years later that God revealed my unforgiveness toward my dad. When a Christian counselor I was speaking with about the unrest and frustration in my soul asked me if I had any unforgiveness toward my dad, I said no. Why would I? *He* wasn't the abusive parent. But when the counselor told me to pray and ask God to show me the truth, a lifetime of rage, anger, hurt, unforgiveness, and tears flooded my entire being. Down deep I felt my dad never came to my rescue. He never rescued me from my mother's insanity. He never came and let me out of the closet she had locked me in for so much of my early childhood. I didn't realize how much I blamed him for allowing my mother, who he knew was severely mentally ill, to treat me with such cruelty and abuse. When I forgave him that day, I felt peace like I had never known before.

Often we don't recognize the unforgiveness that is in us. We *think* we are forgiving, but we really aren't. If we don't ask God to reveal our unforgiveness to us, we may never get free of the paralyzing grip it has on our lives. A big part of making sure our lives are clean and right before God has to do with forgiving other people. We can never move into all God has for us unless we do.

An Excellent Choice

I know "hate" is a very strong word, and we hate to use the word "hate" about anything. And we certainly hate the thought that we might actually have hate for another person. But that's what unforgiveness is—the root of hate. When we entertain unforgiving thoughts, they turn to hate inside of us. Jesus felt so strongly about this that He said, "Whoever hates his brother is a murderer, and you know that no murderer has eternal life abiding in him" (1 John 3:15). He also said, "Whenever you stand praying, if you have anything against anyone, forgive him, that your Father in heaven may also forgive you your trespasses" (Mark 11:25).

Now let's get this straight. When we don't forgive, we are considered murderers without any eternal hope who shouldn't expect God to forgive us until we have forgiven others. I'd say that if it's between *forgiving* and *not forgiving*, forgiving seems like the better choice.

When we choose not to forgive, we end up walking in the dark (1 John 2:9-11). Because we can't see clearly, we stumble around in confusion. This throws our judgment off and we make mistakes. We become weak, sick, and bitter. Other people notice all this because unforgiveness shows in the face, words, and actions of those who have it. They see it, even if they can't specifically identify what it is, and they don't feel comfortable around it. When we choose to forgive, not only do *we* benefit, but so do the people around us.

Family First

It's very easy to have unforgiveness toward family members because they are with us the most, know us the best, and can hurt us the deepest. But for those very same reasons, unforgiveness toward one of them will bring the greatest devastation to our lives. That's why forgiveness must start at home.

First of all, it is very important to make sure you have forgiven your parents. The Bible is crystal clear about this issue. The fifth of the Ten Commandments says, "Honor your father and your mother, that your days may be long upon the land which the LORD your God is giving you" (Exodus 20:12). If you don't honor them it will shorten your life. And you can't fully honor them if you haven't forgiven them.

When I made the decision to forgive my mother, I did it because I wanted to obey God and move into all He had for me. It must have worked because look how old I am. But forgiving her once did not mean that I never had to worry about it again. There were layers and layers of unforgiveness that had built up in me over the years, and I found I had to forgive her every time one of them surfaced. Actually, I had to forgive her every time I saw her because she only became worse as the years went on.

Just because we confess our unforgiveness toward someone one day doesn't mean we won't have unforgiveness in us the next. That's why forgiveness is a choice we must make *every* day. We *choose* to forgive whether we feel like it or not. It's a decision, not a feeling. If we wait for good feelings, we could end up waiting a lifetime. If we have any bitterness or unforgiveness, it's always our fault for not choosing to let it go. It's our responsibility to confess it to God and ask Him to help us forgive and move on with our lives.

We also need to ask God to show us if we have any other family members we need to forgive. We don't tend to think of ourselves as unforgiving people. Irritated maybe, but not unforgiving. But we have to remember that our standards are much lower than God's, and therefore we often don't see where we need to forgive. Ask God to reveal any unforgiveness you have toward a family member. You are going to be miserable until you get it resolved.

When You Can't Forgive

Forgiveness is never easy. But sometimes it feels down-right impossible in light of the devastating and horrendous pain we have suffered. If you have a hard time forgiving someone, ask God to help you. That's what I did regarding my mother, and by the time she died, I had absolutely no hard feelings toward her. If you can think of someone whom you find it hard to forgive, ask God to give you a heart of forgiveness for them. Pray for them in all the ways you can think of to pray. It's amazing how God softens our hearts when we pray for people. Our anger, resentment, and hurt turn into love.

Don't worry, however. When we forgive someone, it doesn't make them right or justify what they have done. It releases them into God's hands so *He* can deal with them. Forgiveness is actually the best revenge because it not only sets us free from the person we forgive, but it frees us to move into all God has for us. Our forgiving someone doesn't depend on them admitting guilt or apologizing. If it did, most of us would never be able to do it. We can forgive no matter what the other person does.

Sometimes incidents happen in our lives that are so devastating we can go for years without realizing the depth of the bitterness we have because of it. Sometimes we don't forgive *ourselves* for things we've done, and so we give ourselves a lifetime of punishment for whatever we did or did not do. Sometimes we blame God for things that have happened. Ask God to show you if any of these things are true about you. Don't let unforgiveness limit what God wants to do in your life.

Whatever It Takes

Four hundred and ninety times! That's how many times we have to forgive a person. Peter asked Jesus, "Lord, how often shall my brother sin against me, and I forgive him? Up to seven times?" Jesus said to him, "I do not say to you, up to seven times, but up to seventy times seven" (Matthew 18:21-22). You may be able to think of someone you have to forgive 490 times a *day*, but the point is that God wants you to forgive as many times as it takes. He wants you to be a forgiving person.

Jesus told the story of a man who was released from a large debt by his master. But he turned right around and made his own poor servant go to prison for not paying *him* a small debt. When the master heard about this he said, "I forgave you all that debt because you begged me. Should you not also have had compassion on your fellow servant, just as I had pity on you?" The master was so angry that he delivered that man to the torturers until he paid all that was due to him. Jesus said, "So My heavenly Father also will do to you if each of you, from his heart, does not forgive his brother his trespasses" (Matthew 18:32-35).

This is very serious. We who have received Jesus have been forgiven a *large* debt. We have no right to be unforgiving of others. God says, "Be kind to one another, tenderhearted, forgiving one another, just as God in Christ forgave you" (Ephesians 4:32). If we don't forgive, we will be imprisoned by our hatred and tortured by our bitterness.

Everything we do in life that has eternal value hinges on two things: loving God and loving others. It's far easier to love God than it is to love others, but God sees them as being the same. One of the most loving things we can do is forgive. It's hard to forgive those who have hurt, offended, or mistreated us. But God wants us to love even our enemies. And in the process of doing so, He perfects us (Matthew 5:48). It's always going to be easy to find things to be unforgiving about. We have to stop looking.

God wants you to move into all He has for you. But if you don't forgive, you get stuck where you are and shut off God's work in your life. Forgiveness opens your heart and mind and allows the Holy Spirit to work freely in you. It releases you to love God more and feel His love in greater measure. Life is worth nothing without that.

My Prayer to God

Lord, help me to be a forgiving person. Show me where I am not. Expose the recesses of my soul so I won't be locked up by unforgiveness and jeopardize my future. If I have any anger, bitterness, resentment, or unforgiveness that I am not recognizing, reveal it to me and I will confess it to You as sin. Specifically, I ask You to help me fully forgive (name anyone you feel you need to forgive). Make me to understand the depth of Your forgiveness toward me so that I won't hold back forgiveness from others. I realize that my forgiving someone doesn't make them right; it makes me free. I also realize that You are the only one who knows the whole story, and You will see justice done.

Help me to forgive myself for the times I have failed. And if I have blamed You for things that have happened in my life, show me so I can confess it before You. Enable me to love my enemies as You have commanded in Your Word. Teach me to bless those who curse me and persecute me (Matthew 5:44-45). Remind me to pray for those who hurt or offend me so that my heart will be soft toward them. I don't want to become hard and bitter because of unforgiveness. Make me a person who is quick to forgive.

Lord, show me if I have any unforgiveness toward my mother or father for anything they did or did not do. I don't want to shorten my life by not honoring them and breaking this great commandment. And where there is distance between me and any other family member because of unforgiveness, I pray You would break down that wall. Help me to forgive every time I need to do so. Where I can be an instrument of reconciliation between other family members who have broken or strained relationships, enable me to do that.

I don't want anything to come between You and me, Lord, and I don't want my prayers to be hindered because I have entertained sin in my heart. I choose this day to forgive everyone and everything, and walk free from the death that unforgiveness brings. If any person has unforgiveness toward me, I pray You would soften their heart to forgive me and show me what I can do to help resolve this issue between us. I know that I cannot be a light to others as long as I am walking in the darkness of unforgiveness. I choose to walk in the light as You are in the light and be cleansed from all sin (1 John 1:7).

∽ GOD'S PROMISES TO ME ∾

Judge not, and you shall not be judged. Condemn not, and you shall not be condemned. Forgive, and you will be forgiven.

LUKE 6:37

The discretion of a man makes him slow to anger, and his glory is to overlook a transgression.

PROVERBS 19:11

Love your enemies, bless those who curse you, do good to those who hate you, and pray for those who spitefully use you and persecute you, that you may be sons of your Father in heaven.

MATTHEW 5:44-45

He who hates his brother is in darkness and walks in darkness, and does not know where he is going, because the darkness has blinded his eyes.

1 JOHN 2:11

If you forgive men their trespasses, your heavenly Father will also forgive you. But if you do not forgive men their trespasses, neither will your Father forgive your trespasses.

MATTHEW 6:14-15

CHAPTER FOUR

Lord, Teach Me to Walk in Obedience to Your Ways

I remember when I was in high school and had to take a required swimming class one semester. I hated it because it was at 7:30 every morning and my hair was ruined for the rest of the day. (There weren't any portable hair dryers back then, if you can even imagine such primitive times.) We had to swim daily, rain or shine, and it could get quite cold on those foggy California winter mornings. The only way I could be excused from swimming was if I were dying, and even then I had to have a note from the doctor.

In spite of the misery of that experience, I loved swimming and I became fairly good at it. I learned that if I was positioned correctly and did all the right moves, I could go forward quickly in the water. It became a smooth maneuver that would get me speedily to the other side of the giant pool. And nothing would make me falter—not even turbulence from other swimmers on either side of me.

The same principle is true for us. If we want to successfully navigate the waters of our lives, we must position ourselves correctly and learn all the right moves. If we don't, when we come to turbulent situations we will not be able to navigate through them. We will end up flailing around and exhausting ourselves just trying to stay afloat. And we will never actually get anywhere.

But when we position ourselves under the headship of Christ and learn to do what He requires of us, there is a flow of the Holy Spirit that will carry us wherever we need to go.

All the Right Moves

The way we learn what God expects of us is by reading His Word. We can't begin to make the right moves if we don't know what they are. And we can study all we want in this holy manual of life and learn everything we are supposed to do, but at some point we still have to jump in the water. The proof of our sincerity is in the *doing*, not just the knowing. It's one thing to make a list of do's and don'ts, but it's quite another to have a heart for God's ways and a soul that longs to live them out. It's one thing to read about life, it's another to live it. Obedience is something you *do*; having a heart to obey is something you *pray* about.

God, Help Me Be Disciplined

I hear this plea from women all over the world. We know a lot about what we're *supposed* to be doing, but we often have a hard time *doing* it. We must pray that God will enable us to be disciplined enough to do what we need to do.

I am a fairly disciplined person for the most part. But I wasn't always that way. There was a time in my life when I was the exact opposite. I was plagued with depression. And, as many of you who have been depressed know, you can't think clearly or organize your life well when you are struggling to find a reason to live. You are unable to do the things that are good for you because you don't know if you're worth it. You don't move forward in your life because it takes all your energy just to survive each day.

When I started learning to pray about every aspect of my life, I asked God to help me be disciplined enough to be daily in His Word, to pray faithfully, and to take the steps of obedience I needed to take. I asked Him to deliver me from depression and anything else that kept me from all He had for me. I was surprised at how quickly God answered those prayers. I have become disciplined, organized, and obedient beyond what I believe are my natural capabilities. I am still learning new levels of obedience, however, even after 32 years of walking with God. My body is getting older, but as a result of obeying God in new ways, my spirit is being renewed with each passing year. And with each new step of obedience I take, I experience new blessings and new freedoms I have not known before and never thought possible.

Don't fall into the trap of thinking that once you are saved you don't have to put forth any effort. That's like getting married and never taking a shower again. You might be able to get away with it for a while, but it's risky business and your quality of life will definitely suffer. Learning obedience is a lifelong process. There are always new dimensions of it to conquer. Even if you have walked with the Lord for 40 years, you still need to ask God to show you any area where you are not being obedient. *We get into trouble when we think we know what to do and we stop asking God if we're doing it.* "We must give the more earnest heed to the things we have heard, lest we drift away" (Hebrews 2:1).

We can never get prideful about how perfectly we are obeying God because He is continually stretching us and asking us to move into new levels of growth. Nor can we go to the other extreme, saying, "This is just the kind of person

I am—undisciplined and unteachable." We have no excuse for not doing what we need to do when God says He will *enable* us to do it if we will just call upon Him for help. All we have to say is, "Lord, help me to be disciplined enough to obey You the way You want me to so I can become the person You created me to be." Without the perfecting, balancing, refining work of His Holy Spirit, the freedom you have in Christ will turn into a license to do anything you want.

Personal Obedience

In addition to the rules we all have to obey, there are specific things God asks each of us to do as individuals in order to move us into the purpose He has for our lives. These are different for each person. For example, eight years ago God instructed my husband and me to move from California to Tennessee. This was not something I wanted to do nor did the thought of doing that ever enter my mind. I was happy where I was and didn't want to leave. But because it was a clear directive from God, we packed up and obeyed. The reasons why we moved have become increasingly evident over the years, and I am so grateful we heard God's directive and followed it. But we probably wouldn't have heard if we hadn't actually said the words, "Lord, show us what we are supposed to be doing."

It's important that you keep asking God to show you what He wants *you* to do. If you don't ask, you won't know. It's that simple. For example, God may ask you to take a different job, stop a certain activity, join a certain church, or change the way you've always done something. Whatever He asks you to do, remember He does this for your greatest blessing. But you must understand that you may not hear Him speaking to you at all if you are not taking the other steps of obedience He expects all of us to take that are found in His word. "One who turns away his ear from hearing the law, even his prayer is an abomination" (Proverbs 28:9). It doesn't hurt to ask.

Doing Things You'd Rather Not

We all have to do things we don't want to do. In even the most wonderful of jobs, there are still aspects of it that we don't enjoy. But part of being successful in life means doing things we would rather not. When we do things we don't like simply because we know we need to do them, it builds character in us. It makes us disciplined. It forms us into a leader God can trust. And there is always a price to pay when we forsake the things we *need* to do in order to do only the things we *feel* like doing. We must be willing to make sacrifices for the blessings we want.

When you find it difficult to do what you *know* you need to, ask the Holy Spirit to help you. Of course, you still have to take the first step, no matter how daunting, intimidating, dreadful, uncomfortable, or distasteful. But when you do, the Holy Spirit will assist you the rest of the way. "I will put My Spirit within you and cause you to walk in My statutes, and you will keep My judgments and do them" (Ezekiel 36:27).

Ten Good Reasons to Obey God

There are countless reasons to obey God, but there is one primary reason: He said to. If there were no other reason, that would certainly be enough. However, there are many important benefits that you and I should be reminded of regularly, and below I've listed ten good ones.

1. *We get our prayers heard.* "If I regard iniquity in my heart, the Lord will not hear. But certainly God has heard

me; He has attended to the voice of my prayer" (Psalm 66:18-19).

2. *We enjoy a deeper sense of the Lord's presence.* "If anyone loves Me, he will keep My word; and My Father will love him, and We will come to him and make Our home with him" (John 14:23).

3. *We gain wisdom.* "He stores up sound wisdom for the upright; He is a shield to those who walk uprightly" (Proverbs 2:7).

4. *We have God's friendship.* "You are my friends if you do whatever I command you" (John 15:14).

5. *We can live safely.* "You shall observe My statutes and keep My judgments, and perform them; and you will dwell in the land in safety" (Leviticus 25:18).

6. *We are perfected.* "Whoever keeps His word, truly the love of God is perfected in Him. By this we know that we are in Him" (1 John 2:5).

7. *We are blessed.* "Behold, I set before you today a blessing and a curse: the blessing, if you obey the commandments of the LORD your God which I command you today" (Deuteronomy 11:26-27).

8. *We find happiness.* "Happy is he who keeps the law" (Proverbs 29:18).

9. *We have peace.* "Mark the blameless man, and observe the upright; for the future of that man is peace" (Psalm 37:36).

10. *We have a long life.* "My son, do not forget my law, but let your heart keep my commands; for length of days and long life and peace they will add to you" (Proverbs 3:1-2).

A Stepping-Stone to Destiny

God has great plans for you. He has important things He wants you to do. And He is preparing you for your destiny right now. But you have to take steps of obedience in order to get there. And you have to trust that He knows the way and won't hurt you in the process.

God's rules are for our benefit, not to make us miserable. When we live by them, life works. When we don't, life falls apart. When we obey, we have clarity. When we don't, we have confusion. And there is a definite connection between obedience and the love of God. Even though God loves us, we won't sense His love if we are walking in disobedience to His ways.

There is also a direct connection between obedience and getting your prayers answered (1 John 3:22). If you have been frustrated because you don't see answers to your prayers, ask God if it is because of disobedience. Say, "Lord, is there any area of my life where I am not obeying You?" Don't keep telling God what *you* want without asking Him what *He* wants.

You never know when you will step into the moment for which God has been preparing you. And it is not just one moment; it's many successive ones. It doesn't matter whether you are a single career woman or a married lady with nine children under the age of ten, it doesn't matter whether you are nineteen or ninety, God is preparing you daily for something great. He wants you to be willing to let Him purify you, fortify you, and grow you up in Him. But you have to play by the rules. "If anyone competes in athletics, he is not crowned unless he competes according to the rules" (2 Timothy 2:5). You can't swim into the mainstream of those moments successfully if you are not doing all the right moves now.

My Prayer to God

Lord, Your Word says that those of us who love Your law will have great peace and nothing will cause us to stumble (Psalm 119:165). I love Your law because I know it is good and it is there for my benefit. Enable me to live in obedience to each part of it so that I will not stumble and fall. Help me to obey You so that I can dwell in the confidence and peace of knowing I am living Your way.

My heart wants to obey You in *all* things, Lord. Show me where I am not doing that. If there are steps of obedience I need to take that I don't understand, I pray You would open my eyes to see the truth and help me to take those steps. I know I can't do all things right without Your help, so I ask that You would enable me to live in obedience to Your ways. "With my whole heart I have sought You; oh, let me not wander from Your commandments!" (Psalm 119:10).

Your Word says that "if we say we have no sin, we deceive ourselves, and the truth is not in us" (1 John 1:8). I don't want to deceive myself by not asking You where I am missing the mark You have set for my life. Reveal to me when I am *not* doing things I *should* be doing. Show me if I'm doing things I should not. Help me to hear Your specific instructions to me. Speak to me clearly through Your Word so I will know what's right and what's wrong. I don't want to grieve the Holy Spirit in anything I do (Ephesians 4:30). Help me to be ever learning about Your ways so I can live in the fullness of Your presence and move into all You have for me.

❧ GOD'S PROMISES TO ME ❧

Whatever we ask we receive from Him, because we
keep His commandments and do those things that
are pleasing in His sight.
1 JOHN 3:22

For the LORD God is a sun and shield; the LORD will
give grace and glory; no good thing will He withhold
from those who walk uprightly.
PSALM 84:11

He who keeps His commandments abides in Him,
and He in him. And by this we know that He abides
in us, by the Spirit whom He has given us.
1 JOHN 3:24

Blessed are those who hear the word of
God and keep it!
LUKE 11:28

He who has My commandments and keeps them, it
is he who loves Me. And he who loves Me will
be loved by My Father, and I will love him
and manifest Myself to him.
JOHN 14:21

CHAPTER FIVE

Lord, Strengthen Me to Stand Against the Enemy

When an unthinkable tragedy burst upon our nation on September 11 in New York City, many people asked, "Why did this happen?" In their unbearable grief and shock they wanted an answer. There are many answers to that question, but the main one is this: We have an enemy. I don't mean just we the people of New York or we the people of the United States. I mean we the people who stand for the things of God. There is an enemy who opposes all that God is and everything He does and anyone who believes in Him or tries to live His way.

We all have an enemy who is like a terrorist to our soul. If we don't realize this, it will be easy for him to manipulate us. Of course, he is not omniscient nor omnipresent—he can't be everywhere and know our every thought—but if we don't fully realize that he is a limited and defeated foe, then we will be harassed by him continually. One of the things Jesus accomplished when He died and rose again was to break the power of the enemy. When He defeated the enemy on the cross, He gave us authority over him. He said,

"I give you the authority...over all the power of the enemy, and nothing shall by any means hurt you" (Luke 10:19).

We are all involved in a spiritual battle with an enemy who will never let up. Even though it is people who do evil things to us, we have to keep in mind that it is our ultimate enemy, the devil, who is behind it. "For we do not wrestle against flesh and blood, but against principalities, against powers, against the rulers of the darkness of this age, against spiritual hosts of wickedness in the heavenly places" (Ephesians 6:12). Even when we are being attacked by a person, recognizing who our real enemy is will be the first step in standing strong against him.

Just as God has a plan for you, so does Satan. Satan's plan is to steal from you and destroy your life. "The thief does not come except to steal, and to kill, and to destroy" (John 10:10). He disguises himself so that he doesn't look threatening, and he lulls you into thinking that you are not in any danger (2 Corinthians 11:14). But he never takes a day off. He is constantly trying to see his plan for your life fulfilled. That's why you have to "be sober, be vigilant; because your adversary the devil walks about like a roaring lion, seeking whom he may devour" (1 Peter 5:8).

For the most part, we are able to recognize obvious attacks of the enemy. But the more subtle ones, when we are being seduced into accepting something into our lives that will ultimately get us offtrack or destroy us, are harder to recognize. For example, he will attempt to make you believe you deserve every bad thing that happens to you. But deserving is not the issue with God. We didn't deserve to have Jesus die for us. Yet He did. The point is not whether we deserve the things the devil throws our way. The point is Jesus died so we don't have to experience them. Ask God to help you discern the enemy's work in your life. Then "resist the devil and he will flee from you" (James 4:7).

Five Good Weapons Against Mass Destruction

God has given us many weapons to use against the enemy's plan for our destruction. Here are the top five:

1. *A powerful weapon against the enemy is God's Word.* This is *the most* powerful weapon. Jesus Himself used it against the devil when He was led into the wilderness by the Holy Spirit and Satan came to tempt Him (Matthew 4:1). One would think that if you were the Son of God you wouldn't have to go into the wilderness at all, let alone to be tempted by the devil. But "the tempter came to Him" the way he comes to all of us, and Jesus used the Word of God to refute him. He said, "Man shall not live by bread alone, but by every word that proceeds from the mouth of God" (Matthew 4:4). When the devil tries to destroy your life, refute him with God's Word. "A prudent man foresees evil and hides himself; the simple pass on and are punished" (Proverbs 27:12). The moment you identify evil working in your midst, hide yourself in the Word of God.

2. *A powerful weapon against the enemy is praise.* The devil hates it every time we worship God. That's because he can't tolerate people worshiping anyone else but him. He detests it so much he can't even be around it. When we praise and worship God, His presence dwells powerfully in our midst and the devil has to leave.

3. *A powerful weapon against the enemy is obedience.* If we are living in sin or walking in disobedience in any way, this leaves the door open in our lives for the devil to gain a point of entry and ultimately a foothold. Bad things happen to us that might be the enemy's work, but it could also be because our own sin has given him a place to erect a stronghold in

our life. Satan does not have jurisdiction over you, but disobedience to the laws of God opens the door and puts out a welcome mat for him. Confession and repentance will shut the door in his face.

4. *A powerful weapon against the enemy is faith.* Keep in mind that the enemy is always planting land mines out ahead of you. You have no idea where they are because they are not visible to the human eye. The way to avoid them is to walk closely with God and let Him guide your steps. That takes faith. "Resist him, steadfast in the faith, knowing that the same sufferings are experienced by your brotherhood in the world" (1 Peter 5:8-9). Walking in faith is a powerful way to avoid the enemy's trap.

5. *A powerful weapon against the enemy is prayer and fasting.* Prayer is a strong weapon against the enemy. Fasting makes it even more so. Often the hold of the enemy upon our lives can only be broken by prayer and fasting. It doesn't seem as though such a simple thing could do so much, but it does. And it might not seem as though anything is happening while you fast, but there are powerful things being broken in the spirit realm. Often just a simple 24-hour fast is enough to break the hold of the enemy upon our lives. Regular fasts will keep evil at bay and strongholds broken down. It's a way of saying, "I deny myself what I want most and put God first in my life." The enemy hates that because he knows it's a sure way of resisting and defeating him.

I'm a Good Person, so Why Is He Attacking Me?

Many people have asked this question, but the question answers itself. The enemy attacks you *because* you are a good person. The devil will always attack anyone who loves God and lives His way. In fact, this is the main criteria for his enmity against you. The only way you could get him to not do that is to become like him. You would have to stand for what he represents. As long as you have a heart for the things of God, you are his target.

Keep in mind that the greater your commitment is to the Lord, the more the devil will try to harass you. That's why if you are moving into a deeper level of commitment to God, or coming into a new time of deliverance and freedom, or entering into new ministry or work God is opening up for you, you can depend on your enemy trying to stop it. He will do all he can to wear you down with discouragement, sickness, confusion, guilt, strife, fear, depression, or defeat. He may try to threaten your mind, your emotions, your health, your work, your family, or your relationships. He will try to get you to give up. Even though he is not close to being as powerful as God, he attempts to make you think otherwise. He will try to gain a point of rule in your life through deception. He will try to blind you to the truth and get you to believe his lies. He will try to convince you he is winning the battle, but the truth is that he has already lost.

This is the deal. The devil has come to steal, kill, and destroy. Jesus has come to give you life abundantly. Hmm. Let's see. Death and destruction from Satan. Life and abundance from Jesus. Does that mean if you're not living a life of abundance then the devil must be robbing you? I think that's a good possibility, especially since this is his life goal. The only other possibility is that you have not truly aligned yourself with God and are not living His way. Ask God to show you the truth about your situation. Don't let the enemy of your soul talk you into accepting anything less than what God has for you.

My Prayer to God

Lord, I thank You for suffering and dying on the cross for me, and for rising again to defeat death and hell. My enemy is defeated because of what You have done. Thank You that You have given me all authority over him (Luke 10:19). By the power of Your Holy Spirit I can successfully resist the devil and he must flee from me (James 4:7). Show me when I am not recognizing the encroachment of the enemy in my life. Teach me to use that authority You have given me to see him defeated in every area.

Reveal to me any place in my life where I am walking in disobedience. If I have given the enemy a place in my protective armor through which he can secure a hook, show me so I can rectify it. Gird me with strong faith in You and in Your Word. Help me to fast and pray regularly in order to break any stronghold the enemy is trying to erect in my life.

Lord, I know that in the midst of the battle I don't have to be fainthearted. I don't have to be afraid in the face of the enemy (Deuteronomy 20:3). Thank You that even though the enemy tries to take me captive to do his will, You have given me the power to escape his snares completely (2 Timothy 2:26). Thank You that You have delivered me from him (Psalm 18:17) and You are my shield because I live Your way (Proverbs 2:7). Help me to "not be overcome by evil," but instead give me the strength to "overcome evil with good" (Romans 12:21). Hide me in the secret place of Your presence from the plots of evil men (Psalm 31:20). Thank You that I will never be brought down by the enemy as long as I stand strong in You.

❧ GOD'S PROMISES TO ME ❧

The Lord is faithful, who will establish you and
guard you from the evil one.
2 THESSALONIANS 3:3

Take up the whole armor of God, that you may be
able to withstand in the evil day, and having done
all, to stand. Stand therefore, having girded your
waist with truth, having put on the breastplate of
righteousness, and having shod your feet with the
preparation of the gospel of peace; above all, taking
the shield of faith with which you will be able to
quench all the fiery darts of the wicked one. And
take the helmet of salvation, and the sword of the
Spirit, which is the word of God; praying always with
all prayer and supplication in the Spirit, being
watchful to this end with all perseverance and
supplication for all the saints.
EPHESIANS 6:13-18

When the whirlwind passes by, the wicked is
no more, but the righteous has an
everlasting foundation.
PROVERBS 10:25

Be strong in the Lord and in the power of His might.
Put on the whole armor of God, that you may be
able to stand against the wiles of the devil.
EPHESIANS 6:10-11

CHAPTER SIX

Lord, Show Me How to Take Control of My Mind

$\mathcal{I}$ remember one particular Friday afternoon when my husband was out of town on a trip and my children were each spending the night at a friend's house. With everyone away it was a rare opportunity for me to have some quiet time and get a lot of writing done.

Much to my surprise, however, I felt tremendous loneliness and sadness after they left. I thought about everything that was wrong with my life, and it made me hopelessly depressed. It was so bad I couldn't think about anything else. These thoughts paralyzed me to such a degree that I wasn't able to call anyone, go anywhere, catch up on mail, or do any work around the house. And, of course, I didn't get any writing done. I just sat crying in my room with the Bible open on my lap.

"Lord, show me what's the matter with me and what I should do about it," I prayed. "I am going to fast until I hear from You or this thing breaks."

I fasted through Saturday and into the night. About 4:00 Sunday morning I awoke with deep anxiety in my soul. I got up and began reading my Bible. When my eyes fell upon the words in Isaiah about exchanging "the garment of praise for the spirit of heaviness" (Isaiah 61:3), I knew in that instant I was dealing with a spirit of heaviness. There was nothing wrong with me or my life, but the enemy was trying to get me to believe there was.

For the next 20 minutes I sang praises to God and spoke His Word out loud. I told the enemy to get away from me, and I thanked the Lord for giving me the authority to do that. Then, as clearly as I have ever felt anything, I sensed the dark, heavy blanket of spiritual oppression lift. It lifted so suddenly and completely that I realized I had been dealing with a direct and specific attack from the enemy.

As I look back, I believe it was because I was in the middle of writing *The Power of a Praying® Wife* and the enemy was trying to make me give up. But the opposite happened. In the days ahead I had new vision for my life and my future, and a renewed commitment to identifying and resisting the enemy's lies. I realized I should have caught his lies the minute they entered my mind instead of entertaining them as truth.

Take Control

A big part of standing against the enemy of our souls is taking control over our minds. As the Bible says, we must learn to bring every thought into captivity (2 Corinthians 10:5).

It was an astounding revelation to me as a new believer when I learned that I didn't have to entertain every thought that came into my head. I had a choice about whether to listen to them or not. Many serial killers talk about how they heard a voice in their head telling them to kill and they just followed orders. When people are not raised to discern the voices in their head, they don't recognize the voice of the devil. He is a clever deceiver who will come to each one of us and try to speak lies into our minds. We have to be ready for him.

The Lies We Believe

Do you ever have certain thoughts that play over and over in your mind like an old broken record? Have you ever had a thought come to your mind that produces a physical feeling in your body, such as a pain in your heart, a queasy sensation in the pit of your stomach, tightness in your throat, weakness in your arms and legs, tears in your eyes, a rash on your face and neck? Do "what if" thoughts ever plague your mind, such as "What if I jumped off the balcony?" or "What if I ran my car into that wall?" Have you ever had "if only" thoughts? Such as, "If only I hadn't done that." "If only I had been there." "If only I would have said something." Do you ever have self-punishing thoughts? "No one cares about me." "I'm such a failure." "I'm no good." "Nothing I do turns out right."

If you've had thoughts like these, please know that this is not God giving you revelation for your life. It is the enemy trying to gain control of your mind.

Life has much suffering, but too often we suffer unnecessarily because of lies we believe about ourselves and our circumstances. We accept as fact the words that are spoken to our souls by an enemy who wants us destroyed. We can become fearful, depressed, lonely, angry, doubtful, confused, insecure, hopeless, beaten down, worried, and full of self-pity, all because of lies we believe. But we can overcome each one of these lies with prayer, faith, and the truth of God's Word.

You must be aware, however, that one of the enemy's tactics is to try and steal God's Word from you. He will do that by getting you to question God's Word, just as he did with Eve in the Garden. "Did God really say that?" "Does God really mean that?" "Will God really mind if you do that?" "Does God really care about you?"

Then he will contradict God's Word. "God didn't say that." "God doesn't mind that." "God doesn't think you're worth much." "God's withholding good things from you."

When the thoughts that you think begin to question and contradict God's Word, you are being set up by your enemy. Remember, "there is a way that seems right to a man, but its end is the way of death" (Proverbs 14:12). Certain thoughts may appear to you to be accurate, but when you hold them up next to God's Word, the lie is exposed.

Deception is the enemy's ongoing plan of attack. Jesus said the devil "was a murderer from the beginning, and does not stand in the truth, because there is no truth in him. When he speaks a lie, he speaks from his own resources, for he is a liar and the father of it" (John 8:44). The *only* power the devil has is in getting people to believe his lies. If they don't believe his lies, he is powerless to get his work done.

Choose Your Thoughts Carefully

You have a choice about what you will accept into your mind and what you won't. You can choose to take every thought captive and "let this mind be in you which was also in Christ Jesus" (Philippians 2:5), or you can allow the devil to feed you lies and manipulate your life. Every sin begins as a thought in the mind. "For from within, out of the heart of men, proceed evil thoughts, adulteries, fornications, murders, thefts, covetousness, wickedness, deceit, lewdness, an evil eye, blasphemy, pride, foolishness" (Mark 7:21-22). If you don't take control of your mind, the devil will.

That's why you must be diligent to monitor what you allow into your mind. What TV shows, magazines, and books do you look at? What music, radio programs, or CDs do you listen to? Do they fill your mind with godly thoughts and feed your spirit so you feel enriched, clear-minded, peaceful, and blessed or do they deplete you and leave you feeling empty, confused, anxious, and fearful? "God is not the author of confusion but of peace" (1 Corinthians 14:33). When we fill our minds with God's Word and godly books and magazines written by people in whom God's Spirit resides, and we listen to music that praises and glorifies Him, we leave no room for the enemy's propaganda.

If you want to determine whether your thoughts are from the enemy or the Lord, ask yourself, "Are these thoughts I would *choose* to have?" If you answer no, then they are probably from your enemy. If, for example, you are sitting in church and you suddenly envision the choir naked, recognize where this is coming from. Rather than beat yourself up for having impure thoughts, tell the enemy to get off your brain because you will not allow your soul to be a dumping ground for his trash. Tell him you "have the mind of Christ" and you won't listen to anything that is inconsistent with that (1 Corinthians 2:16).

Refusing to entertain unrighteousness in your thought life is part of resisting the devil. How many people have we known who should have done that and didn't?

You don't have to live with confusion or mental oppression. You don't have to "walk as the rest of the Gentiles walk, in the futility of their mind, having their understanding darkened, being alienated from the life of God, because of the ignorance that is in them, because of the hardnening of their heart" (Ephesians 4:17-18). Instead you can have clarity and knowledge. Even though your enemy tries to convince you that your future is as hopeless as his, or that you are a failure with no purpose, value, gifts, or abilities, God says exactly the opposite. Believe God and don't listen to anything else.

My Prayer to God

Lord, help me to never exchange Your truth for a lie. Where I have accepted a lie as truth, reveal that to me. Help me to clearly discern when it is the enemy who is speaking. I don't want to think futile and foolish thoughts or give place to thoughts that are not glorifying to You (Romans 1:21). I don't want to walk according to my own thinking (Isaiah 65:2). I want to bring every thought captive and control my mind.

Your Word is "a discerner of the thoughts and intents of the heart" (Hebrews 4:12). As I read Your Word, may it reveal any wrong thinking in me. May Your Word be so etched in my mind that I will be able to identify a lie of the enemy the minute I hear it. Spirit of Truth, keep me undeceived. I know You have given me authority "over all the power of the enemy" (Luke 10:19), and so I command the enemy to get away from my mind. I refuse to listen to lies.

Thank You, Lord, that I "have the mind of Christ" (1 Corinthians 2:16). I want Your thoughts to be my thoughts. Show me where I have filled my mind with anything that is ungodly. Help me to resist doing that and instead fill my mind with thoughts, words, music, and images that are glorifying to You. Help me to think upon what is true, noble, just, pure, lovely, of good report, virtuous, and praiseworthy (Philippians 4:8). I lay claim to the "sound mind" that You have given me (2 Timothy 1:7).

❧ God's Promises to Me ❧

Do not be conformed to this world, but be
transformed by the renewing of your mind, that you
may prove what is that good and acceptable
and perfect will of God.
Romans 12:2

Though we walk in the flesh, we do not war
according to the flesh. For the weapons of our
warfare are not carnal but mighty in God for pulling
down strongholds, casting down arguments and every
high thing that exalts itself against the knowledge of
God, bringing every thought into captivity to
the obedience of Christ.
2 Corinthians 10:3-5

To be carnally minded is death, but to be spiritually
minded is life and peace.
Romans 8:6

Put off, concerning your former conduct, the old man
which grows corrupt according to the deceitful lusts,
and be renewed in the spirit of your mind, and...put
on the new man which was created according to
God, in true righteousness and holiness.
Ephesians 4:22-24

You will keep him in perfect peace, whose mind is
stayed on You, because he trusts in You.
Isaiah 26:3

CHAPTER SEVEN

Lord, Rule Me in Every Area of My Life

I know a young man who has a heart for God and is tremendously gifted to lead worship and teach the Word. But he can't bring himself to fully surrender his life to the Lord. He continues to live his own way, doing his own thing, and is constantly frustrated that nothing has worked out in his life—not only his personal life, but also his career and finances. I know if he would just say, "Whatever You want, Lord, I will do it" and truly live that out, God would use him powerfully and every part of his life would be blessed.

Why do some people never seem to grow in the Lord? Why is it they go from one calamity to the next, never able to get beyond survival mode? Why do they seldom, if ever, experience the joy of the Lord? Spritual breakthrough? A deeper of relationship with Him? The release to step out in the area of their gifting? Why can't they move forward into the purposes and destiny God has for them?

The answer, I believe, lies in the word "surrender." They have not fully surrendered everything to God. They have not truly made Jesus Lord over their lives.

Surrendering everything means being willing to say, "Lord, whatever You want me to do I'll do it. I say yes to anything You ask of me, even it means dying to myself and my desires. I will give up the things of the flesh that I want in order to have more of You in my life. I will go to church when I feel like staying home. I will fast when I feel like eating. I will pray when I would rather go to bed. I will read Your Word when I would rather watch TV. I will give when I would rather spend my money on myself. I will enter into praise and worship as my first reaction instead of my last resort. I will do whatever You say so that I can please You and move into all You have for me." This attitude of surrender means putting God first and submitting to His rulership. And it makes all the difference in our lives.

Jesus is Lord whether we declare it or not. That's because "God also has highly exalted Him and given Him the name which is above every name, that at the name of Jesus every knee should bow, of those in heaven, and of those on earth, and of those under the earth, and that every tongue should confess that Jesus Christ is Lord, to the glory of God the Father" (Philippians 2:9-11). But He is not only Lord over the universe, He is Lord over our individual lives as well. Whether we acknowledge that or not will determine the success and quality of our life. If we don't personally declare Jesus to be Lord over our lives, it shows we are not controlled by the Spirit. "No one can say that Jesus is Lord except by the Holy Spirit" (1 Corinthians 12:3). It reveals we are still controlled by the flesh.

Whatever You Say, Lord

Do you remember watching old western movies where the good guy (in the white shirt) catches the bad guy (in the black shirt) and points his gun at him and says, "Stick 'em up!" (It just doesn't sound as menacing to say, "Stick *them* up.")

The bad guy drops everything, raises his hands, and says, "I give up."

Well, this is the kind of surrender God wants. Only you are not the bad guy and God is not pointing a gun at you. He is pointing His finger. But not in an accusatory or embarrassing way. He is pointing to you in a loving way, just as He would if He had picked you for His team. He is saying, "You! I want you! Surrender to Me so I can give you all that I have for you."

If we would drop everything and say, "I give up, Lord. I surrender. Take everything. I will do whatever You say," our lives would be better in every way.

Why is it so hard for us to simply say, "Whatever You want, Lord. I'll do anything You ask"? It's because we want what we want and we're afraid of what God might ask of us. We think He might do something to hurt us. Also, it's not just a matter of *saying*, "Jesus is Lord." We must then *do* what He *says*. Jesus said, "Why do you call Me 'Lord, Lord,' and do not do the things which I say?" (Luke 6:46). We doubt that what God asks us to do will be for our greatest blessing. But that's wrong. God just wants us to be on the winning team.

If you feel you aren't experiencing any breakthrough in your life, check to see if you have truly surrendered yourself to the Lord. Have you given Jesus that place of Lordship? Have you let go of everything? If not, lift your hands and take that first step.

Jesus said, "Whoever does not bear his cross and come after Me cannot be My disciple" (Luke 14:27). You can't bear His cross unless you surrender your life to Him. A surrendered life, a life ruled entirely by God, is one that can be used powerfully for His kingdom purposes. God doesn't want just part of you. He wants it all. Pray that you will give God what He wants.

My Prayer to God

Lord, I bow before You this day and declare that You are Lord over every area of my life. I surrender myself and my life to You and invite You to rule in every part of my mind, soul, body, and spirit. I love You with all my heart, with all my soul, and with all my mind. I commit to trusting You with my whole being. I declare You to be Lord over every area of my life today and every day.

Enable me to deny myself in order to take up my cross daily and follow you (Luke 9:23). I want to be Your disciple just as You have said in Your Word (Luke 14:27). Help me to do what it takes. I want to lose my life in You so I can save it (Luke 9:24). Teach me what that means. Speak to me so that I may understand.

Help me to say yes to You immediately when You give me direction for my life. My desire is to please You and hold nothing back. I surrender my relationships, my finances, my work, my recreation, my decisions, my time, my body, my mind, my soul, my desires, and my dreams. I put them all in Your hands so they can be used for Your glory. I declare this day that "I have been crucified with Christ; it is no longer I who live, but Christ lives in me; and the life which I now live in the flesh I live by faith in the Son of God, who loved me and gave Himself for me" (Galatians 2:20). Rule me in every area of my life, Lord, and lead me into all that You have for me.

❧ GOD'S PROMISES TO ME ❧

If anyone desires to come after Me, let him deny
himself, and take up his cross daily, and follow Me.
For whoever desires to save his life will lose it, but
whoever loses his life for My sake will save it.
LUKE 9:23-24

If we live, we live to the Lord; and if we die, we
die to the Lord. Therefore, whether we
live or die, we are the Lord's.
ROMANS 14:8

As you have therefore received Christ Jesus the Lord,
so walk in Him, rooted and built up in Him and
established in the faith, as you have been taught,
abounding in it with thanksgiving.
COLOSSIANS 2:6-7

Trust in the LORD with all your heart, and lean not on
your own understanding; in all your ways acknowledge Him, and He shall direct your paths.
PROVERBS 3:5-6

Therefore humble yourselves under the mighty hand
of God, that He may exalt you in due time, casting
all your care upon Him, for He cares for you.
1 PETER 5:6-7

CHAPTER EIGHT

Lord, Take Me Deeper in Your Word

ome time ago I went into the hospital for emergency surgery. I stayed there about two weeks and then spent six weeks at home with a nurse. I had eight months of recovery after that. It was over a year before I was even close to being back to normal. (I'll give you more details about this in a later chapter.)

During that time in the hospital I was too sick and weak and in too much pain to read the Word. I was hooked up to a machine with tubes running in and out of my body, so I couldn't sit up or turn over. That meant holding a heavy Bible was out of the question. Because I needed round-the-clock care, my sister organized my husband, children, and close friends to spend specific times with me. Each person took a three-hour shift on different days, except for my daughter, who took a twelve-hour shift from 8:00 every night until 8:00 in the morning. This was extremely difficult for her because she was in college at the time and had to be up with me every couple hours at night and then go to school all day. Besides everything else these loving people did for me, I depended on them to read the Word of God to me.

When I was sent home with a nurse, I had to be isolated from all people except my immediate family members because of the risk of infection. During that time, no one was able to read the Bible to me because they were too busy. (I don't say that as a criticism; they each had to take care of me plus do the work I usually do in addition to their own full-time work.) It was a considerable strain for everyone.

So during that time I spent convalescing at home I listened to the Bible on tape. But it wasn't the same as reading it myself. I don't retain information as well when I hear it as I do when I read it. Also, on tape the speaker keeps talking without stopping. I found I would get caught up thinking about a verse I'd just heard and then not hear the next ten. Normally, when I read the Word myself, I go over each verse slowly and thoroughly, especially the ones speaking to me at that moment. I let it digest in my inner being, and I ask God to teach me new things that I haven't seen before.

Even after I began to recover and was able to sit up and read the Word myself, my mind was so foggy and my eyes so blurry from all the anesthetic and drugs I'd had to take every day that I had a hard time absorbing it. I knew the problem was in *me*, but the Bible wasn't speaking to me like it used to, and I felt helpless as to what to do about it. Reading the Word had always been life-giving for me, but now it became more of a duty. I read because I knew I needed to.

Another factor in all this was that I couldn't go to church for five months, so I wasn't being taught the Word from the pulpit or from a Bible study. I had not been without that type of teaching for longer than two weeks at a time since I had become a believer 31 years before. I listened to tapes of sermons, but my mind wandered, and I often fell asleep in the middle of them.

Because I didn't have regular feeding in the Word of God the way I usually had, I began to lose ground in my life. It became harder to make decisions because I didn't hear God's voice as clearly as I used to. It was difficult to write because I couldn't focus on what God wanted me to say. But most of all I felt empty inside. It wasn't until I thought to actually *pray* about the problem itself that I experienced breakthrough in this area. I prayed, "Lord, I need to have Your Word come alive to me again. Make that happen, Father. Clear my mind and soul. Teach me new things. Help me to go deeper into Your Word than ever before."

About a week after I started praying that prayer, God answered it. The Bible became fresh and exciting again. I found new revelation. New understanding. I decided if God answered that simple prayer, then why shouldn't we pray *every* time we read the Bible, "Lord, take me deeper into Your Word"? Our time in God's Word is one of the most important aspects of our lives, and it should be covered in prayer.

Daily Bread for Our Souls

God's Word is food for our souls. We can't live without it. It is written that "man shall not live by bread alone, but by every word that proceeds from the mouth of God" (Matthew 4:4). If we are not continually fed with God's Word, we will starve spiritually.

In those months when I was in the hospital and recovering, I was amazed at how much of the Word I lost from my memory. I realize that all the medicine and anesthetic I had in me contributed a lot to that, but I was shocked that I couldn't remember certain Scriptures I used to quote so easily. After all those years of reading the Bible, how could

I lose so much so quickly? Of course, there are some Scriptures that are engraved in my brain and soul that I probably could recite in my sleep, but I realized then how important it is for each of us to *guard* the Word of God that has been deposited in our souls. "Therefore we must give the more earnest heed to the things we have heard, lest we drift away" (Hebrews 2:1). We don't realize how quickly it can be stolen from us.

Be a Doer of the Word

It doesn't matter how long you walk with God; He always has new things for you to learn. It may be new dimensions of what you already know, or it may be something you have never seen before. Either way, it's not enough to just *learn* the truth; you must *act* on it. "Be doers of the word, and not hearers only, deceiving yourselves. For if anyone is a hearer of the word and not a doer, he is like a man observing his natural face in a mirror; for he observes himself, goes away, and immediately forgets what kind of man he was" (James 1:22-24). If we don't *do* what the Word says, we not only *forget* it but we also forget who we are in the process.

Whenever you read God's Word, it is essential to ask Him to help you practically apply it to your life. Take a step that indicates you believe what you read and are going to live like it. If you don't, what you know of the Word will be taken from you. It's possible to *hear* the Word, *read* the Word, and even *teach* the Word and still remain unchanged and unaffected. All Scripture will teach us, convict us, enrich us, heal us, warn us, and expose our hearts. But we have to act on it. That's why you have to ask God to speak to you every time you read His Word and show you what you should be doing in response to it.

Ten Good Reasons to Read God's Word

If you have trouble being in God's Word every day, here are just a few of the many reasons to read the Bible that should inspire you:

1. *To know where you are going.* You can't foresee the future or *exactly* where you are heading, but God's Word will guide you. "Direct my steps by Your word, and let no iniquity have dominion over me" (Psalm 119:133).

2. *To have wisdom.* Knowledge of God's Word is where wisdom begins to grow in you. "The law of the LORD is perfect, converting the soul; the testimony of the LORD is sure, making wise the simple" (Psalm 19:7).

3. *To find success.* When you live according to the teachings of the Bible, life works. "This Book of the Law shall not depart from your mouth, but you shall meditate in it day and night, that you may observe to do according to all that is written in it. For then you will make your way prosperous, and then you will have good success" (Joshua 1:8).

4. *To live in purity.* You must live a life of holiness and purity in order to enjoy more of the Lord's presence, but you can't be made pure without being cleansed through God's Word. "How can a young man cleanse his way? By taking heed according to Your word" (Psalm 119:9).

5. *To obey God.* If you don't understand what God's laws are, how can you obey them? "Teach me, O LORD, the way of Your statutes, and I shall keep it to the end. Give me understanding, and I shall keep Your law; indeed, I shall observe it with my whole heart. Make me walk in the path of Your commandments, for I delight in it" (Psalm 119:33-35).

6. *To have joy.* You cannot be free of anxiety and unrest without the Word of God in your heart. "The statutes of the LORD are right, rejoicing the heart; The commandment of the LORD is pure, enlightening the eyes" (Psalm 19:8).

7. *To grow in faith.* You can't grow in faith without reading and hearing the Word of God. "So then faith comes by hearing, and hearing by the word of God" (Romans 10:17).

8. *To find deliverance.* You won't know what you need to be free of unless you study God's Word to find out. "If you abide in My Word, you are My disciples indeed. And you shall know the truth, and the truth shall make you free" (John 8:31-32).

9. *To have peace.* God will give you a peace that the world can't give, but you must find it first in His Word. "Great peace have those who love Your law, and nothing causes them to stumble" (Psalm 119:165).

10. *To distinguish good from evil.* Everything has become so relative today, how can you know for sure what is right and wrong without God's Word? "Your Word I have hidden in my heart, that I might not sin against You!" (Psalm 119:11).

Going for the Gold

God has gold nuggets and diamonds everywhere in His Word, but we must dig them out. And, just like precious gems and metals when they are first pulled from the ground, the treasures of God's Word need to be polished and refined in us in order to have the brilliance they are capable of revealing. Every time you go over one of God's promises in your heart, it will become more refined and polished in you and shine more brightly in your soul.

One of the most priceless gems you will find in God's Word is His voice. That's because He speaks to us through His Word as we read it or hear it. In fact, we can't really learn to recognize God's voice to our soul if we are not hearing Him speak to us first in His Word. The more you hear it, the easier it is to recognize, and the less chance you will accept a counterfeit.

There were countless times in my early walk with the Lord when I was still suffering from depression and anxiety that I turned to his Word. All it took was reading the Bible for a few minutes, and I would feel calm and hopeful again. That's because the Word straightens out our mind and soul and helps us think clearly about things. It leads us away from self-destructive thoughts and enables us to enjoy a sense of well-being. It gives us hope and keeps us on course. It provides us a solid foundation upon which to build a life of wholeness. Ask God to meet you in His Word every day. He looks forward to that, and He wants you to also.

There is no way to draw closer to God, or have a clean and right heart before Him, or be a forgiving person, or walk in obedience to His ways, or take control of your mind, or stand against the enemy, or make Jesus Lord of your life unless you are in the Word of God every day. It's your compass. Your guide. You can't get where you need to go without it.

My Prayer to God

Lord, I thank You for Your Word. "Your Word is a lamp to my feet and a light to my path" (Psalm 119:105). It is food to my soul, and I can't live without it. Enable me to truly comprehend its deepest meaning. Give me greater understanding than I have ever had before, and reveal to me the hidden treasures buried there. I pray that I will have a heart that is teachable and open to what You want me to know. I desire Your instruction. Teach me so I may learn.

Help me to be diligent to put Your Word inside my soul faithfully every day. Show me where I'm wasting time that could be better spent reading Your Word. Give me the ability to memorize it. Etch it in my mind and heart. Make it become a part of me. Change me as I read it.

Lord, I don't want to be just a hearer of Your Word. Show me how to be a doer of Your Word as well. Enable me to respond the way I should and obey You. Show me when I am not doing what it says. Help me to apply my heart to Your instruction and my ears to Your Words of knowledge (Proverbs 23:12). May Your Word correct my attitude and remind me of what my purpose is on earth. May it cleanse my heart and give me hope that I can rise above my limitations. May it increase my faith and remind me of who You are and how much You love me. May it bring the security of knowing my life is in Your hands and You will supply all my needs.

Thank You, Lord, that when I look into Your Word I find You. Help me to know You better through it. Give me ears to recognize Your voice speaking to me every time I read it (Mark 4:23). I don't want to ever miss the way You are leading me. When I hear Your voice and follow You, my life is full. When I get off the path You have for me, my life is empty. Guide, perfect, and fill me with Your Word this day.

❧ GOD'S PROMISES TO ME ❧

The Word of God is living and powerful, and sharper than any two-edged sword, piercing even to the division of soul and spirit, and of joints and marrow, and is a discerner of the thoughts and intents of the heart.

HEBREWS 4:12

He who looks into the perfect law of liberty and
continues in it, and is not a forgetful hearer
but a doer of the work, this one will be
blessed in what he does.

JAMES 1:25

Blessed is the man who walks not in the counsel of
the ungodly, nor stands in the path of sinners, nor
sits in the seat of the scornful; but his delight is in
the law of the LORD, and in His law he meditates day
and night. He shall be like a tree planted by the
rivers of water, that brings forth its fruit in its season,
whose leaf also shall not wither; and whatever
he does shall prosper.

PSALM 1:1-3

Whoever keeps His word, truly the love of God is
perfected in him. By this we know that
we are in Him.

1 JOHN 2:5

He who heeds the word wisely will find good,
and whoever trusts in the LORD, happy is he.

PROVERBS 16:20

CHAPTER NINE

Lord, Instruct Me as I Put My Life in Right Order

Tabitha was a disciple of Christ. A *female* disciple! This means she was a believer who followed faithfully the teachings of Jesus. She also did many good works and charitable deeds which benefited others. As a result, she was dearly loved.

Some time after Jesus was crucified and had risen, Tabitha became ill and died. Several men went to find Peter, one of the original 12 disciples, and bring him back to where Tabitha's body was being prepared for burial. When Peter arrived at the house, he went to the upper room where she had been laid. He asked the women who were weeping over her to leave him alone in the room, and then he knelt down to pray.

When Peter finished praying, he turned toward the dead woman's body and said, "Tabitha, arise." Immediately she opened her eyes and sat up. Extending his hand to her, Peter helped her to her feet. When all the people saw that Tabitha had been brought back from the dead, many believed in the Lord (Acts 9:36-42).

There is nothing else known about Tabitha, but from this short account of her life it's clear that she was a woman who had her priorities in order. She loved the Lord. She loved others. She had a servant's heart. She lived her life in a way that pleased God and blessed people. All this information about her is found in that one word—"disciple."

When trouble came into Tabitha's life and she was struck down even to the point of death, God sent one of His faithful disciples to pray for her and raise her up again. Would this have happened if she were just a nominal believer, living on the distant edge of the life God wanted her to live? Would this have happened if she didn't love God? Didn't love others? Didn't have a servant's heart? Didn't give of herself? Didn't obey? I don't think so. Her life was in order and God blessed her because of it. And He gave her a second chance. That's what He wants to do for us if we will put Him first.

Top Priority

We can't live successfully without right priorities in our lives. Yet some of us try to do that every day. Correct priorities are not something we can figure out on our own. We have to be led by the Holy Spirit and have a clear knowledge of God's Word in order to understand what they should be.

Our two most important priorities come directly from the Word of God. Jesus told us about them saying, "'You shall love the LORD your God with all your heart, with all your soul, and with all your mind.' This is the first and great commandment. And the second is like it: 'You shall love your neighbor as yourself'" (Matthew 22:37-39). It can't get much clearer than that. If you maintain these two top priorities—love God and love others—they will guide you in setting all the other priorities in your life.

Your relationship with the Lord must always have top priority over everything else. The Lord said, "You shall have no other gods before Me" (Exodus 20:3), and He means it. God wants your *undivided* attention. When you seek Him first every day and ask Him to help you put your life in order, He will do that. I know from experience, and I'm sure you do too, that when we don't seek God first, our lives get out of control. As a result, our lives start ruling *us* instead of us being in charge of *them*.

God is a God of order. We can tell that by looking at the universe. None of it is random or accidental. He doesn't want our lives to be either. His will is that we "let all things be done decently and in order" (1 Corinthians 14:40). And when we pray to Him about it, He will help us do just that. He will show us how to align ourselves under proper authority so that we can come under the covering of His protection. This is crucial to our moving into all God has for us.

The Submission Issue

Submission is something you *decide* to do, not something someone *forces* you to do. The meaning of the word "submit" is "to submit yourself." It's a condition of the heart. Having a submitted heart means you are *willing* to submit yourself and come into proper alignment in accordance with God's will.

Our first priority in submission must always be to "submit to God" (James 4:7). This means you do not have to submit to the wishes of anyone who asks you to do something that is against God's commands. You can have a submitted heart and still be able to draw the line when what is being asked of you violates your conscience and the laws of God.

For example, if a person who is a designated authority over your life asks you to do something that is wrong, or if that person says or does something to you that is inappropriate and violates what is right in the sight of God, you must decline to be a party to it and declare it to be wrong. But you don't have to scream at the person saying, "You idiot! You fool! What is the matter with you? Get behind me, Satan!" Instead, give them a respectful explanation such as, "With all due respect, I believe that what you are asking me to do is a violation of the laws of God, and I could not with any good conscience do it, knowing it would bring God's judgment on us both." Or "What you just said and did to me is offensive in the eyes of God, and I must tell you that such inappropriate behavior will not serve either of us well."

The difference between having a submitted heart and one that is not is that one will garner blessings for you and the other will get you into trouble.

Jesus Himself was submitted to God. His priorities were definitely in order. God wants that "this mind be in you which was also in Christ Jesus, who, being in the form of God, did not consider it robbery to be equal with God, but made Himself of no reputation, taking the form of a bondservant, and coming in the likeness of men. And being found in appearance as a man, He humbled Himself and became obedient to the point of death, even the death of the cross" (Philippians 2:5-8). Now that's submission! It would seem that if anyone might not have to be in perfect submission it would be Jesus. Yet in order to accomplish God's purpose for His life, He was submitted to the will of the

Father, even to the point of unfathomable suffering and death. What a role model He is for all of us.

When Trust Is Violated

Many women have a problem with submission because their trust has been violated or they were hurt in the past when they submitted to someone. No one wants to be a doormat or the object of another person's abuse. God does not want that either. Nor is He asking you to be a mindless robot. That's why you must pray for wisdom about this issue. It is a highly sensitive one, and you need to discern what the Lord is telling you.

For those of you who have had a terrible experience with this issue, I want to encourage you. God is not asking you to be stupid, sacrifice your sanity for a principle, or suffer at the hand of an abuser. He will give you wisdom when you ask for it. If you find yourself going along with someone who violates the Word of God and His holy laws, not to mention your own conscience, that's not submission. That's just dumb. Don't let yourself go there.

I know of a woman who submitted to an abusive husband, and he ended up killing her. She wasn't spiritually discerning because she didn't put God first and seek Him as to what to do. She stayed in that violent relationship until it turned disastrous instead of doing what was necessary to find help. That is *not* submission, that's foolishness.

I know of another woman who refused to submit to her husband in any way, and she ended up losing her whole family and her home. Because she had been sexually violated by a leader in her church when she was a teenager, she would not consider trusting any man enough to submit to him.

There has to be a balance. And that balance can only be found by submitting to *God first*. Ask Him to help you discern exactly to whom you are to be submitted and in what way. Don't just submit blindly or ignorantly. Know what you are doing. When your heart's desire is to do what's right and be in right order, God will help you find that perfect balance.

It All Falls into Place

The Bible says we should submit to authority figures designated by God in our church, in our family, in our work, and in our government. To be in right order and have our lives work well, we need to be planted in a church home. It gives us a base of operation. We can't get as far as God wants us to go without it.

Each church has a unique distinction and purpose, and you will not be happy until you find the one God has for you. This doesn't mean you have to go to a different church every week until you find one that is perfect and makes you 100 percent happy. Those don't exist. Churches are, after all, made up of imperfect people like us. What it does mean is that you need to ask God to show you where your church family is.

When you are in the church you are supposed to be in, you will recognize the pastor's voice as an important spiritual authority in your life. Again, you need to have wisdom and the leading of the Lord. If the authority figures in your church get offtrack and there is immorality, financial corruption, unbiblical teaching, or sin, then you should not be subject to that kind of leadership. Ask God to lead you away from an unholy alignment.

We all need a pastor, a strong Christian leader, or a mentor speaking truth into our lives. God will help you discern who that is. Don't get me wrong, this is not a case for having a guru. The spiritual authority in your life is God's *messenger*, not someone to be worshiped instead of God. This is also not a gender issue. The Bible says, "there is neither male or female; for you are all one in Christ Jesus" (Galatians 3:28). This is about having someone in your life to speak truth to you in love and cover you in prayer.

Beyond your submission to God and your submission to other designated authorities in your life, you must be in right relationship to other people, "submitting to one another in the fear of God" (Ephesians 5:21). Submission to others takes a heart that loves others as ourselves. That's the key. When you love God first and others second, all the other priorities in your life will fall into place and you will be in right order. When you ask God to show you clearly what your priorities should be, He will.

My Prayer to God

Lord, I pray You would help me set my life in right order. I want to always put You first above all else in my life. Teach me how to love You with all my heart, mind, and soul. Show me when I am not doing that. I don't want to have any other gods but You in my life. Show me if I have lifted up my soul to an idol. My desire is to serve You and only You. Help me to live accordingly.

Give me a submissive heart. Help me to always submit to the governing authorities and the correct people in my family, work, and church. Show me who the proper spiritual authorities are to be in my life. Plant me in the church you want me to be in. Help me to move into proper alignment in every area of my life by willingly submitting myself to others where I need to do so. Show me clearly to whom I am to be submitted and how I am to do it. Give me discernment and wisdom about this. Show me any time I am not submitted to the right people in the right way.

I know that if my life is not in proper order I will not receive the blessings You have for me. But I also know that if I seek You first, all that I need will be added to me (Matthew 6:33). I seek You first this day and ask that You would enable me to put my life in perfect order. May I never come out from under the covering of spiritual protection You have placed in my life.

◆◎ GOD'S PROMISES TO ME ◎◆

Seek first the kingdom of God and His righteousness, and all these things shall be added to you.
MATTHEW 6:33

He who finds his life will lose it, and he who loses his life for My sake will find it.
MATTHEW 10:39

All of you be submissive to one another, and be clothed with humility, for "God resists the proud, but gives grace to the humble."
1 PETER 5:5

And this commandment we have from Him:
that he who loves God must love his brother also.
1 JOHN 4:21

Obey those who rule over you, and be submissive, for they watch out for your souls, as those who must give account. Let them do so with joy and not with grief, for that would be unprofitable for you.
HEBREWS 13:17

CHAPTER TEN

Lord, Prepare Me to Be a True Worshiper

When I used to work as a singer, dancer, and actress on television during the time when musical variety shows were at their peak, I would have to sing a song over and over all day long while I was rehearsing it with the choreography. Then I had to sing it over and over again in the evening as we prerecorded it for the show the next day. It had to be prerecorded because when I was dancing and singing at the same time, I could not be miked for sound. There were no portable headsets back then as there are now. I used to go home at night after the last session of the day and could hardly sleep because the music and lyrics of the songs we had been working on would still be playing over and over in my mind. I could not get them out of my head.

That is exactly what happens to us when we hear and sing praise and worship songs over and over. They continue to play in our mind, soul, and spirit even when we are not actually worshiping God. Even when we are sleeping.

I learned that principle years ago when I became a believer. Back then when I suffered with severe depression, there were countless times I would get up in the middle of the night to sing or speak praises to the Lord in order to get rid of it. I had gone to several doctors about it, but the medicine they gave me only seemed to cover up the problem. It was always still there when the medicine wore off. I'm not saying that people shouldn't take medicine if they are depressed. I'm saying it didn't solve the problem for *me*. I had suffered from depression from the time I was a young child and was locked in a closet by my mother. The hopelessness, futility, and sadness I felt about myself and my life made it hard to get through each day. I needed an infusion of the joy of the Lord, and that's what praising God did for me.

When I praised and worshiped God, it was like being hooked up to a spiritual IV. As long as I had my heart and eyes lifted to God in worship and praise, the joy of the Lord poured into my body, mind, soul, and spirit and crowded out the darkness and depression. It worked every time.

I started buying praise and worship songs on tape and later CDs. I played them in the car as I drove, in the bathroom when I was drying my hair, in the kitchen as I was cooking, through the house when I was doing housework, or at my desk when I was writing letters or going through the mail. Sometimes I would sing along to them, but other times I would just let the music play through my mind and spirit. It amazed me that confusion, oppression, fear, or anxiety couldn't exist in the heart of a worshiping child of God. Eventually, I got free of depression completely.

Nothing we do is more powerful or more life-changing than praising God. It is one of the means by which God transforms us. Every time we praise and worship Him, His presence comes to dwell in us and changes our hearts and allows the Holy Spirit to soften and mold them into whatever He wants them to be.

Because praise and worship is not something our flesh naturally *wants* to do, we have to *will* ourselves to do it. And because it's not the first thing we think of to do, we have to decide to do it no matter what our circumstances. We have to say, "I *will* praise the Lord." Of course, the more we get to know God, the easier praise becomes. When we get to the point where we can't keep from praising Him, then we are at the place we are supposed to be. If you ever find yourself unmotivated in this regard, try reading the following 20 reasons to worship God from Psalm 103. It works for me every time.

Twenty Good Reasons to Worship God

1. *He forgives my iniquities.*
2. *He heals all my diseases.*
3. *He redeems my life from destruction.*
4. *He crowns me with lovingkindness.*
5. *He satisfies my mouth with good things.*
6. *He executes righteousness and justice for the oppressed.*
7. *He makes His ways known.*
8. *He is merciful.*
9. *He is gracious.*
10. *He is slow to anger.*
11. *He will not strive with us.*
12. *He will not keep His anger forever.*
13. *He does not punish us according to our iniquities.*
14. *He shows great mercy to those who fear Him.*
15. *He removes our transgressions from us.*
16. *He has pity on us.*
17. *He remembers we are dust.*
18. *His mercy is everlasting.*
19. *He blesses our children and grandchildren who obey Him.*
20. *He rules over all and His throne is established.*

Worship His Way

We can claim to know and love God, but if we are not worshiping and praising Him every day, we are in the dark about who He really is. "Although they knew God, they did not glorify Him as God, nor were thankful, but became futile in their thoughts, and their foolish hearts were darkened" (Romans 1:21). We shut off so much in our lives when we don't give God the glory due Him. We don't want to be wandering around in the dark entertaining futility in our minds, all because we are not *true* worshipers of our awesome God.

Five Good Ways to Praise the Lord

God wants us to give our whole self to worshiping Him, and He wants us to do it *His* way.

1. *God wants us to sing our praises to Him.* "Praise the LORD! For it is good to sing praises to our God; for it is pleasant, and praise is beautiful" (Psalm 147:1). "Serve the LORD with gladness; come before His presence with singing" (Psalm 100:2).

2. *God wants us to lift our hands to Him.* "Lift up your hands in the sanctuary, and bless the LORD" (Psalm 134:2).

3. *God wants us to speak our praise to Him.* "Therefore by Him let us continually offer the sacrifice of praise to God, that is, the fruit of our lips, giving thanks to His name" (Hebrews 13:15).

4. *God wants us to praise Him with dancing and instruments.* "Let them praise His name with the dance; let them sing praises to Him with the timbrel and harp" (Psalm 149:3).

5. *God wants us to praise Him together with other believers.* "I will declare Your name to My brethren; in the midst of the assembly I will sing praise to You" (Hebrews 2:12).

Praising and worshiping God with other believers is one of the most powerful and significant things we can do in our lives. Corporate worship causes bondages to be broken, and it makes the way for wonderful changes in us that might never happen otherwise. A powerful dynamic occurs in the spirit realm when we worship God together that can't happen any other way.

No matter what your church background is or has been, ask God to make you into the true worshiper He wants you to be. Give your whole self to it. As long as you have breath you can "rejoice always, pray without ceasing, in everything give thanks; for this is the will of God in Christ Jesus for you" (1 Thessalonians 5:16-18). The songs of worship you sing over and over in your heart in the day will fill your soul in the night.

My Prayer to God

Lord, there is no source of greater joy for me than worshiping You. I come into Your presence with thanksgiving and bow before You this day. I exalt Your name for You are great and worthy to be praised. Thank You that "You have put gladness in my heart" (Psalm 4:7). All honor and majesty, strength and glory, holiness and righteousness are Yours, O Lord.

Thank You that You are "gracious and full of compassion, slow to anger and great in mercy" (Psalm 145:8). Thank You that You are "mighty in power" and Your "understanding is infinite" (Psalm 147:5). Thank You that You lift up the humble and cast the wicked down (Psalm 147:6). Thank You that You execute justice for the oppressed, You give food to the hungry, and You give freedom to the prisoners. Thank You that You open the eyes of the blind and raise up those who are bowed down (Psalm 146:7-8).

Thank You, Lord, that Your plans for my life are good, and You have a future for me that is full of hope. Thank You that You are always restoring my life to greater wholeness. I praise You and thank You that You are my Healer, my Deliverer, my Provider, my Redeemer, my Father, and my Comforter. Thank You for revealing Yourself to me through Your Word, through Your Son, Jesus, and through Your mighty works upon the earth and in my life. Thank You for Your love, peace, joy, faithfulness, grace, mercy, kindness, truth, and healing. Thank You that I can depend on You, for You and Your Word are unfailing. Thank You that You are the same yesterday, today, and tomorrow.

Lord, forgive me when I neglect to praise and worship You as You deserve. Teach me to worship You with my whole heart the way You want me to. Make me a *true* worshiper, Lord. May praise and worship of You be my first response to every circumstance.

I praise Your name this day, Lord, for You are good and Your mercy endures forever (Psalm 136:1). "Because Your lovingkindness is better than life, my lips shall praise You. Thus I will bless You while I live; I will lift up my hands in Your name" (Psalm 63:3-4). I will declare Your "glory among the nations" and Your "wonders among all peoples" (Psalm 96:3). I worship You in the splendor of Your holiness and give You the glory due Your name (Psalm 29:2).

✎ GOD'S PROMISES TO ME ✎

But the hour is coming, and now is, when the true
worshipers will worship the Father in spirit and truth;
for the Father is seeking such to worship Him.
God is Spirit, and those who worship Him
must worship in spirit and truth.
JOHN 4:23-24

Offer to God thanksgiving, and pay your vows to the
Most High. Call upon Me in the day of trouble; I will
deliver you, and you shall glorify Me.
PSALM 50:14-15

Let all those rejoice who put their trust in You; let
them ever shout for joy, because You defend them; let
those also who love Your name be joyful in You. For
You, O LORD, will bless the righteous; with favor You
will surround him as with a shield.
PSALM 5:11-12

Whoever offers praise glorifies Me; and to him who
orders his conduct aright I will show the
salvation of God.
PSALM 50:23

I will praise You with my whole heart; before the
gods I will sing praises to You. I will worship toward
Your holy temple, and praise Your name for Your
lovingkindness and Your truth; for You have magni-
fied Your word above all Your name. In the day when
I cried out, You answered me, and made me bold
with strength in my soul.
PSALM 138:1-3

CHAPTER ELEVEN

Lord, Bless Me in the Work I Do

I know what it's like to go to bed hungry. When I was a child, we were so poor there were many times when we had no food in the house and no way of getting any. That feeling of hunger was frightening, and the fear never left me, even after I grew up. In fact, this fear caused me to always work hard in order to ensure it would never happen again. It drove me to take every baby-sitting job I could get, for 50 cents an hour on weekends, instead of being with my friends when I was a young teenager. It's what made me work after school most days and into the night, plus all day Saturday and Sunday, when I was in high school and college. Even after I left college and was in the workforce, I held down *two* jobs instead of one for the same reason. Always in the back of my mind was the fear that there wouldn't be enough money for food, so I often labored beyond what my body and mind could take.

It wasn't until I came to know the Lord and began to understand the way He provides for His children that I finally got rid of the fear. It was such a relief to discover that I could trust *God* to take care of me. I no longer had to kill myself in desperation; I could look to Him for everything I needed.

I also became more discerning about the work I was doing. I no longer had to take any and every job I could get. Instead, I asked God what work *He* wanted me to do. I found that when I was led by the Lord in the work I did, and I committed all my work to Him for His glory, He blessed it. It was no longer drudgery. I prayed God would help me do it well, and as a result, my work soon became fruitful, successful, and fulfilling.

Everyone Has a Job to Do

It doesn't matter if you are a stay-at-home mom, a full-time student, a CEO of a giant corporation, a single woman who is self-supporting, a married woman running a home, a skilled career woman, a disabled person, a baby-sitter, a house sitter, a single working mom, or a volunteer at the rescue mission downtown—you have work to do. It doesn't matter if your work is recognized by the whole world or only God sees it. It doesn't matter if you are getting paid big bucks or receiving no financial compensation whatsoever. Your work is valuable. And you want it to be blessed by God.

Whatever work we do, we want to do it well and be successful. When our work is good, it gives us fulfillment. When we accomplish something worthwhile that makes life better for other people, our families, or ourselves, it gives us satisfaction. But when the work of our hands is not blessed, we are weighed down with frustration and unfulfillment.

The ideal woman described in the Bible is a hard worker (Proverbs 31). She buys and sells property (a real estate agent?). She plants a vineyard (a landscaper?). She makes clothing (a designer?). And she sells it (manager of a clothing store?). She is a woman of strength, energy, and vision who works hard into the night and knows that what she has to offer is good. God wants us to experience that kind of success and satisfaction. But it doesn't happen without prayer.

Prayer helps us to find the balance between being "greedy for gain," which depletes our life (Proverbs 1:19), and having "a slack hand," which makes us poor (Proverbs 10:4). Prayer helps us to not "overwork to be rich" (Proverbs 23:4-5) yet still be diligent in our work, which may ultimately bring us monetary rewards (Proverbs 10:4). Prayer helps us find the balance between laziness and obsession, between gaining the whole world and losing our own soul (Matthew 16:26).

The Bible says that "the laborer is worthy of his wages" (1 Timothy 5:18). This means you deserve to be paid or rewarded for your work. Sometimes the reward is in the actual doing of it itself. You don't get paid for maintaining a home, serving soup at the rescue mission, or teaching a child to tie his shoes, but your reward for seeing the result of your labor is priceless. "The labor of the righteous leads to life" (Proverbs 10:16).

If you have a paying job, don't hesitate to pray that you will be compensated fairly and generously. Pray for your employer to be blessed in his business so he in turn can afford to pay all employees well. Pray that your work is recognized and appreciated by others. Pray to receive promotions and advancement in line with God's will. Say, "Lord, I would like to have that promotion and that raise if it's Your will for my life." As you pray that way and commit your work to the Lord, He will bless it.

No matter what your paycheck reflects, your work is important to God, it's important to others, and it's important to you. You can't afford not to pray about it. Commit your work to the Lord and ask Him to bless it.

My Prayer to God

Lord, I pray You would show me what work I am supposed to be doing. If it is something other than what I am doing now, reveal it to me. If it is something I am to do in addition to what I am already doing, show me that too. Whatever it is You have called me to do, both now and in the future, I pray You will give me the strength and energy to get it done well. Enable me to do what I do successfully. May I find great fulfillment and satisfaction in every aspect of it, even the most difficult and unpleasant parts.

Thank You that in all labor there is profit of one kind or another (Proverbs 14:23). I pray that the rewards of my work will be great. May I always be compensated fairly and richly out of the storehouse of Your abundance. Bless the people I work for and with. May I always be a blessing and a help to each one of them. As I come in contact with others in my work, I pray that Your love and peace will flow through me and speak loudly of Your goodness. Enable me to touch them for Your kingdom.

Lord, I thank You for the abilities You have given me. Where I am lacking in skill help me to grow and improve so that I do my work well. Teach me to excel so that the result of what I do will be pleasing to others. Open doors of opportunity to use my skills and close doors that I am not to go through. Give me wisdom and direction about that.

I commit my work to You, Lord, knowing You will establish it (Proverbs 16:3). May it always be that I love the work I do and be able to do the work I love. According to Your Word I pray that I will not lag in diligence in my work, but remain fervent in spirit, serving You in everything I do (Romans 12:11). Establish the work of my hands so that what I do will find favor with others and be a blessing for many. May it always be glorifying to You.

❧ GOD'S PROMISES TO ME ❧

Blessed is every one who fears the LORD, who walks in His ways. When you eat the labor of your hands, you shall be happy, and it shall be well with you.
PSALM 128:1-2

The blessing of the LORD makes one rich, and He adds no sorrow with it.
PROVERBS 10:22

Let the beauty of the LORD our God be upon us, and establish the work of our hands for us; yes, establish the work of our hands.
PSALM 90:17

Do you see a man who excels in his work? He will stand before kings; he will not stand before unknown men.
PROVERBS 22:29

Every man should eat and drink and enjoy the good of all his labor; it is the gift of God.
ECCLESIASTES 3:13

CHAPTER TWELVE

Lord, Plant Me so I Will Bear the Fruit of Your Spirit

*M*y dad was a farmer for most of his life. He knew how to plant and grow healthy crops. The main thing I learned from him was how to grow a garden of vegetables and fruit. We didn't have the fancy tools people have today—just a shovel and a hoe. We didn't even have running water or indoor plumbing, let alone a sprinkler system outside. We had to wait for the irrigation water to come through our land and then channel it to where the crops were by digging little furrows for the water to travel on either side of the rows of seed. That way it would water the roots without washing the seedlings or young plants away.

After we planted the seeds and watered them, we nurtured, fed, and tended the soil around the seeds so they could grow without hindrance. We also tried to protect the young plants from elements such as hail, wind, and frost. We made sure that when the fruit or vegetables were being formed they didn't disconnect from the vine and that the vine didn't disconnect from the roots. If we were careful and diligent, we produced a good crop. And it always made my father proud.

All of us are planting something in our lives every single day, whether we realize it or not. And we are also reaping whatever we have planted in the past. The quality of our lives right now is the result of what we planted and harvested some time before. We reap the good and the bad for years after we have sown. That's why it is so important to plant and nurture the right seeds now.

Jesus said that He is the vine and you and I are the branches. If we abide in Him we will bear fruit (John 15:5). "Abide" means to remain, to stay, to dwell. In other words, if we dwell with Him and He dwells with us, we will bear the fruit of His Spirit (Galatians 5:22-23). That's what we want.

It is said that we begin to resemble the person with whom we live and with whom we are most closely associated. When we share our lives with Jesus, His likeness is stamped on our spirit and soul. When we plug into Him, the fruit of His Spirit is manifested in us.

Nine Good Ways to Produce a Great Crop

1. *Plant seeds of love.* Ask God to plant His love in you in such a profound and powerful way that you are able to fully experience it. Ask also that His love will flow through you to others. Jesus said, "If you keep My commandments, you will abide in My love, just as I have kept My Father's commandments and abide in His love" (John 15:10). Ask God to help you obey all of His laws so that nothing will keep the fullness of His love from blossoming in You.

2. *Plant seeds of joy.* Joy has nothing to do with your circumstances. You can have joy in spite of difficult and painful problems, because joy comes through a close, intimate relationship with the Lord. You can't have joy if you

feel separated from God or don't trust His promises to you. Jesus said, "These things I have spoken to you, that My joy may remain in you, and that your joy may be full" (John 15:11). When you live in the joy of the Lord, you have expectations that God is going to do something great in your life. Pray for the joy of the Lord to be so planted *in* you and manifested *through* you that the crop you reap will spread like wildfire and overtake the fields around you.

3. *Plant seeds of peace.* Pray that the presence of the Lord planted in your life will provide peace that is beyond comprehension. Pray that this peace will grow strong and prevail no matter what your circumstances are. "The peace of God, which surpasses all understanding, will guard your hearts and minds through Christ Jesus" (Philippians 4:7). We can only have true peace if we live in right relationship to God. Pray that God will help you to know His peace in such a powerful way that it brings peace to those around you.

4. *Plant seeds of patience.* Why do you think it's important to God that patience be growing in us? It's because God's timing is not our timing. He is always doing more than we see or know, so we have to trust Him on how long He takes to bring things to pass. God perfects and refines us before He brings us into all He has for us, and that takes time. "Do not become sluggish, but imitate those who through faith and patience inherit the promises" (Hebrews 6:12). "Let patience have its perfect work, that you may be perfect and complete, lacking nothing" (James 1:4). "By your patience possess your souls" (Luke 21:19). Another word for patience is longsuffering. And that says it all. When you suffer for a long time, it means you put up with more than you want to. Pray for God's patience to so be established in your soul that nothing you have to put up with will ever uproot it.

5. *Plant seeds of kindness.* You have a choice in what you plant in a garden. You take the seeds you want and put them in the soil, and God makes them grow. Kindness is something you have to deliberately plant. Or, to put it another way, kindness is something you choose to put on, like a garment. "Therefore, as the elect of God, holy and beloved, put on tender mercies, kindness, humility, meekness, long-suffering" (Colossians 3:12). The ultimate act of kindness was when Jesus gave His life for us. Pray that His brand of kindness will grow in you so that you can lay down your life for others with acts of kindness too.

6. *Plant seeds of goodness.* When the goodness of God is sown in your soul, it leads you to produce good deeds. "A good man out of the good treasure of his heart brings forth good things, and an evil man out of the evil treasure brings forth evil things" (Matthew 12:35). "Every good tree bears good fruit, but a bad tree bears bad fruit. A good tree cannot bear bad fruit, nor can a bad tree bear good fruit" (Matthew 7:17-18). Ask God to help you abide in Him so that His goodness will grow in you. As it grows in your heart, good things will automatically come forth from your life.

7. *Plant seeds of faithfulness.* When we are solid, steadfast, dependable, reliable, loyal, and trustworthy and do what is right no matter what, we exhibit faithfulness. "He who is faithful in what is least is faithful also in much; and he who is unjust in what is least is unjust also in much" (Luke 16:10). Pray that His faithfulness will continually grow strong in you every day that you are alive. Pray that your faithfulness will strengthen everyone you touch and inspire others to greater faithfulness too.

8. *Plant seeds of gentleness.* When we are brash and arrogant, it makes people feel bad about us and bad about themselves. Gentleness is a humble meekness that is calm,

soothing, peaceful, and easy to be around. The Bible says, "a servant of the Lord must not quarrel but be gentle to all" (2 Timothy 2:24). "The wisdom that is from above is first pure, then peaceable, gentle, willing to yield, full of mercy and good fruits, without partiality and without hypocrisy" (James 3:17). Being considerate of the feelings and needs of others by exhibiting gentleness shows you are responding to the Spirit of God and what has been planted in you has taken root. Pray that you can be as gentle and meek as Jesus was (2 Corinthians 10:1).

9. *Plant seeds of self-control.* Self-control is not fragile like a strawberry plant; it's big and solid like an apple tree. Only God can plant something of that magnitude in you and make it bear fruit. Having no self-control means you do whatever pleases you no matter what the consequences are. Pray that you will not be powerless against the forces that tug on your soul. "Add to your faith virtue, to virtue knowledge, to knowledge self-control, to self-control perseverance, to perseverance godliness" (2 Peter 1:5-6). Ask God to plant self-control in you that will grow up like a tree of strength. Ask Him to help you to rein in your passions, desires, and emotions and make them subject to His Spirit. He will give you the self-discipline you need.

If you've not been bearing the fruit of the Spirit in your life the way you'd like, ask God to help you plant good seeds and pull up any weeds that may have grown up around your soul. Feed the soil of your heart with the food of God's Word and ask the Holy Spirit to water it afresh every day. As long as you abide faithfully in the true vine, I guarantee you'll produce a crop of spiritual fruit that will make your heavenly Father proud.

My Prayer to God

Lord, search my heart and try me and see if there is any wickedness in me. Replace all that is wrong in my character with the goodness in Yours. Plant the fruit of Your Spirit in me and cause it to flourish. Help me to abide in You, Jesus, so that I will bear fruit in my life. I invite You, Holy Spirit, to fill me afresh with Your *love* today so that it will flow out of me and into the lives of others.

You said in Your Word to "let the peace of Christ rule in your hearts" (Colossians 3:15). I pray that Your *peace* would rule my heart and mind to such a degree that people would sense it when they are around me. Help me to "pursue the things which make for peace and the things by which one may edify another" (Romans 14:19).

Give me the *joy* that knowing You produces. Make me *patient* with others so that I reflect Your character to them. Help me to be *kind* whenever there is opportunity for it, and may Your *goodness* flow through me so that I will do good to everyone. Make me to be a *faithful* person so that I can be trusted in all things. Help me to have the "meekness and gentleness of Christ" so that I will reflect Your *gentle* spirit (2 Corinthians 10:1). Enable me to be *self-controlled* in my thoughts, words, and habits.

Where I need to be pruned in order to bear more fruit, I submit myself to You. I know that without You I can do nothing. You are the vine and I am the branch. I must abide in You in order to bear fruit. Help me to do that. Thank You for Your promise that if I abide in You and Your Word abides in me, I can ask what I desire and it will be done for me (John 15:7). Thank You for Your promise that says if I ask I will receive (John 16:24). May I be like a tree planted by the rivers of Your living water so that I will bring forth fruit in season that won't wither (Psalm 1:3). In Jesus' name, I ask that the fruit of Your Spirit will grow in me and be recognized clearly by all who see me so that it glorifies You.

∞ GOD'S PROMISES TO ME ∞

The fruit of the Spirit is love, joy, peace, long-suffering, kindness, goodness, faithfulness, gentleness, self-control. Against such there is no law.
GALATIANS 5:22-23

I am the true vine, and My Father is the vinedresser. Every branch in Me that does not bear fruit He takes away; and every branch that bears fruit He prunes, that it may bear more fruit. You are already clean because of the word which I have spoken to you. Abide in Me, and I in you. As the branch cannot bear fruit of itself, unless it abides in the vine, neither can you, unless you abide in Me. I am the vine, you are the branches. He who abides in Me, and I in him, bears much fruit; for without Me you can do nothing. If anyone does not abide in Me, he is cast out as a branch and is withered; and they gather them and throw them into the fire, and they are burned. If you abide in Me, and My words abide in you, you will ask what you desire, and it shall be done for you. By this My Father is glorified, that you bear much fruit; so you will be My disciples.
JOHN 15:1-8

CHAPTER THIRTEEN

Lord, Preserve Me in Purity and Holiness

Don't let the title of this chapter intimidate you. Being holy is not being perfect. It's letting *Him* who is holy be *in* you. We can't be holy on our own, but we can make choices that allow holiness and purity to be manifested in our lives. We can separate ourselves from that which dilutes God's holiness in us and die to our lusts. And we are able to do this because "those who are Christ's have crucified the flesh with its passions and desires" (Galatians 5:24). We are not slaves to our flesh. We are able to live pure lives consecrated to the Lord.

You may have heard people say, "I can't tell you exactly what pornography is, but I know it when I see it." Well, the opposite is true for holiness and purity. You may not be able to describe exactly what holiness is, but you know it when you *don't* see it. Here are seven descriptions of what holiness is and how to know when you don't see it in yourself.

Seven Good Ways to Live in Holiness

1. *Holiness means separating yourself from the world.* This doesn't mean you head for the hills, isolate yourself, and

never speak to another nonbeliever. It means your heart detaches from the world's value system. You, instead, value the things God values above all else. The consequences for not doing so are serious. "Do you not know that friendship with the world is enmity with God? Whoever therefore wants to be a friend of the world makes himself an enemy of God" (James 4:4). Who wants to be God's enemy?

I know it's hard to be separate from the world when you live in it. But if that is the desire of your heart, you can ask God to help you do it. Of course, you have to make choices to turn off certain TV programs, not go to certain movies, not read certain magazines, and not frequent certain places. "Do not love the world or the things in the world. If anyone loves the world, the love of the Father is not in him. For all that is in the world—the lust of the flesh, the lust of the eyes, and the pride of life—is not of the Father but is of the world" (1 John 2:15-16). Ask God to help you separate yourself from the things of the world, and learn to love *Him* more than you love *it*.

2. *Holiness means purifying yourself.* Purifying yourself does not mean putting on a white robe to cover up all that is not holy about you. It means asking God, who is holy, to purify your heart. Unholiness happens there first. Purifying ourselves means taking stock of our lives, thoughts, actions, associations, and business dealings, and cleansing ourselves from anything that contaminates us. It is something we *actively* do. It means deciding to be morally and ethically pure. "Everyone who has this hope in Him purifies himself, just as He is pure" (1 John 3:3).

When God said, "Be holy" (Leviticus 19:2), the commands He gave following that had to do with not stealing, not lying, not committing fraud, not slandering people, not trying to get revenge, and not falling into idolatry. It means that we are to take specific steps to see that we do not live an impure lifestyle. We are to deliberately turn away from anything that glorifies immorality and other unholiness. "As He who called you is holy, you also be holy in all your conduct, because it is written, 'Be holy, for I am holy'" (1 Peter 1:15-16). Pray that you will be able to thoroughly search out and examine your ways, and turn to the Lord (Lamentations 3:40).

3. *Holiness means living in the Spirit and not in the flesh.* Our fleshly thoughts will disqualify us as much as our actions. Are we jealous of anyone? Do we have strife? Is there unresolved division in our lives? Do we willfully allow sin a place? If so, then we are living in the flesh. And it will destroy us. "For those who live according to the flesh set their minds on the things of the flesh, but those who live according to the Spirit, the things of the Spirit. For to be carnally minded is death, but to be spiritually minded is life and peace. Because the carnal mind is enmity against God; for it is not subject to the law of God, nor indeed can be. So then, those who are in the flesh cannot please God" (Romans 8:5-8).

When you look honestly at the fruit of your life, you can see by what you are reaping whether you have sown to the flesh or to the Spirit. "Do not be deceived, God is not mocked; for whatever a man sows, that he will also reap. For he who sows to his flesh will of the flesh reap corruption, but he who sows to the Spirit will of the Spirit reap everlasting life" (Galatians 6:7-8). Pray that God will help you live in the Spirit and not the flesh.

4. *Holiness means staying clear of sexual immorality.* The greatest lie our society has blindly accepted is that sexual sin is okay. It must grieve the Holy Spirit to see how women sell themselves short of all God has for them because they have

bought into this lie. For example, a self-deceived generation believes that oral sex with someone they aren't married to is not actually sex at all, so therefore they can indulge their flesh and not reap any consequences. "There is a generation that is pure in its own eyes, yet is not washed from its filthiness" (Proverbs 30:12). While they may be safe from conceiving a baby, they will conceive death in their souls and then wonder why after they are married the passion in their marriage dies. Holiness means not falling prey to fashion or trends of thought or deed. "For this is the will of God, your sanctification: that you should abstain from sexual immorality; that each of you should know how to possess his own vessel in sanctification and honor, not in passion of lust, like the Gentiles who do not know God" (1 Thessalonians 4:3-5). Ask God to keep you sexually pure in your mind, soul, and body.

5. *Holiness means being sanctified by Jesus.* Once we have received Jesus, we can't continue to live our old sinful lifestyle. Now that we have Him living in us and the Holy Spirit filling us and transforming us, we have no excuse. "We have been sanctified through the offering of the body of Jesus Christ once for all" (Hebrews 10:10). "For by one offering He has perfected forever those who are being sanctified" (Hebrews 10:14). This doesn't mean we don't have to be concerned about sin anymore and can do whatever we want because He took care of it. It means we must *continue* to dwell with Him and ask God to help us live in all He bought for us on the cross.

6. *Holiness means walking close to God.* When we do not pursue a close walk with God and a lifestyle of purity and peace, we are unable to see the Lord with any kind of clarity. "Pursue peace with all people, and holiness, without which no one will see the Lord" (Hebrews 12:14). Esteeming the

holiness of God and living in purity is the only way we are able to be close to Him. "Who may ascend into the hill of the LORD? Or who may stand in His holy place? He who has clean hands and a pure heart, who has not lifted up his soul to an idol, nor sworn deceitfully" (Psalm 24:3-4). "By those who come near Me I must be regarded as holy; and before all the people I must be glorified" (Leviticus 10:3). There is nothing more important than being close to God.

There comes a time in all of our lives when we are *desperate* to know that God is close and that He hears our prayers and will answer. We won't have time to *get* right with God; we will have to *be* right with God. "The LORD has set apart for Himself him who is godly; the LORD will hear when I call to Him" (Psalm 4:3). Now is the time to start living righteous, pure, and holy lives if we want to see our prayers answered in the future.

7. *Holiness means letting God keep you.* Holiness is not something you slip in and out of like a nightgown. Holiness is God's will for our lives, and something God has planned for us from the beginning. "Just as He chose us in Him before the foundation of the world, that we should be holy and without blame before Him in love, having predestined us to adoption as sons by Jesus Christ to Himself, according to the good pleasure of His will" (Ephesians 1:4-5). God has made a way for us to live in holiness. And He is able to *keep* us holy. When our heart wants to live in purity and do the right thing, God will keep us from falling into sin.

When Abraham told King Abimelech that Sarah was his sister instead of telling him that she was his wife, Abimelech took her into his own house. But in a dream God told Abimelech that he would soon be a dead man because he had taken another man's wife. Abimelech said, "In the integrity of my heart and innocence of my hands I have done this" (Genesis 20:5).

God replied to Abimelech, "Yes, I know that you did this in the integrity of your heart. For I also withheld you from sinning against Me; therefore I did not let you touch her" (Genesis 20:6).

When we live right, God will *keep* us from sin.

It is only by the grace of God that we can live in holiness, even after we have chosen to do so. That's because God enables us to do what He asks us to do. But we still need to *ask* Him to do it. God wants to know that His holiness is important enough to us to seek after it. People are drawn to holiness because it is attractive, even though they may resist it in their own lives. Ask God to enhance your beauty with the beauty of His holiness.

My Prayer to God

Lord, You have said in Your Word that You did not call me to uncleanness, but in holiness (1 Thessalonians 4:7). You chose me to be holy and blameless before You. I know that I have been washed clean and made holy by the blood of Jesus (1 Corinthians 6:11). You have clothed me in Your righteousness and enabled me to put on the new man "in true righteousness and holiness" (Ephesians 4:24). Continue to purify me by the power of Your Spirit. Help me to "cling to what is good" (Romans 12:9) and keep myself pure (1 Timothy 5:22).

Lord, help me to separate myself from anything that is not holy. I don't want to waste my life on things that have no value. Give me discernment to recognize that which is worthless and remove myself from it. Help me not to give myself to impure things, but rather to those things that fulfill Your plans for my life. Enable me to do what it takes to get everything rooted out of my life that is not Your best for me, so I can live the way You want me to live. Show me how to tear down any idols in my life and eliminate any sources of unholy thoughts, such as TV, movies, books, videos, and magazines, that do not glorify You. Help me to examine my ways so that I can return to Your ways wherever I have strayed. Enable me to take any steps necessary in order to be pure before You.

Lord, I want to be holy as You are holy. Make me a partaker of Your holiness (Hebrews 12:10), and may my spirit, soul, and body be kept blameless (1 Thessalonians 5:23). I know that You have called me to purity and holiness and You have said that "He who calls you is faithful, who will also do it" (1 Thessalonians 5:24). Thank You that You will keep me pure and holy so I will be fully prepared for all You have for me.

❧ GOD'S PROMISES TO ME ❧

He chose us in Him before the foundation of the world, that we should be holy and without blame before Him in love.
EPHESIANS 1:4

Blessed are the pure in heart, for they shall see God.
MATTHEW 5:8

In a great house there are not only vessels of gold and silver, but also of wood and clay, some for honor and some for dishonor. Therefore if anyone cleanses

himself from the latter, he will be a vessel for honor,
sanctified and useful for the Master,
prepared for every good work.
2 TIMOTHY 2:20-21

Therefore, having these promises, beloved, let us
cleanse ourselves from all filthiness of the flesh and
spirit, perfecting holiness in the fear of God.
2 CORINTHIANS 7:1

A highway shall be there, and a road, and it shall be
called the Highway of Holiness. The unclean shall
not pass over it, but it shall be for others. Whoever
walks the road, although a fool, shall not go astray.
No lion shall be there, nor shall any ravenous
beast go up on it; it shall not be found there. But the
redeemed shall walk there. And the ransomed of the
LORD shall return, and come to Zion with singing,
with everlasting joy on their heads. They shall
obtain joy and gladness, and sorrow and
sighing shall flee away.
ISAIAH 35:8-10

CHAPTER FOURTEEN

Lord, Move Me into the Purpose for Which I Was Created

When my children were growing up, I frequently prayed they would have a sense of who God made them to be and what their purpose was. I had observed so many young people floundering around and wasting their lives because they had no idea they were called to something great in the Lord. I had done the same thing when I was young, and I ended up in serious trouble. I certainly wanted more than that for my children. As a result of those prayers, I have never seen my children without a sense of purpose. Now that they are in their 20s, they continue to move in their gifts and their paths are becoming more and more clear. They don't know the exact details of their future, but they each know that they have one and that it is good.

When I wrote *The Power of a Praying Parent* and shared my many years of experiences in praying for children, I received a large volume of mail from people telling me how they wished they'd had someone praying for them like that when they were growing up. They now feared they had wasted too many years trying to figure out what they were supposed to be doing and missed the purpose God had for their lives. I encouraged them with this good news. "No matter how far off the path you have gotten from the plans and purposes God has for you, when you surrender your life to the Lord and declare your utter dependence upon Him, He carves a path from where you are to where you are supposed to be, and He sets you on it. It may take you longer than it would have taken had you been on the right path from the beginning, but if you keep walking closely with God, He will get you where you are supposed to be."

Don't ever think it's too late for you. The Bible says, "The gifts and the calling of God are irrevocable" (Romans 11:29). That means the gifts and abilities He gives to you He doesn't take back. They won't be recalled, repealed, or annulled. You will always have your gifts. However, this is not true of the anointing. The anointing is the presence and touch of God upon your gifts that gives them supernatural power to penetrate darkness and bring life and light. This spiritual touch of the Holy Spirit can be lost through sin without repentance. We've all seen people who have fallen into immorality, yet they kept on using their gifts without recognizing that the anointing was gone. They had been so deceived and their sin had so blinded them that they didn't even realize what it was they had lost.

Everyone Has a Purpose

Each one of us has a purpose in the Lord. But many of us don't realize that. And when we don't have an accurate understanding of our identity, we either strive to be like someone else or something we're not. We compare ourselves to others and feel as though we always fall short.

When we don't become who *we* think we're *supposed* to be, it makes us critical of ourselves and our lives. It causes us to be insecure, oversensitive, judgmental, frustrated, and unfulfilled. We become self-absorbed, constantly having to think about ourselves and what we *should* be. It forces us to try too hard to make life happen the way we think it is supposed to. In the extreme, it makes us tell lies about ourselves and become dishonest about who we really are. When you are around people who don't have any idea of what they are called to do, you sense their unrest, unfulfillment, anxiety, and lack of peace.

God doesn't want that for you. He wants you to have a clear vision for your life. He wants to reveal to you what your gifts and talents are and show you how to best develop them and use them for His glory.

Know Who You Are and Where You Are Going

Predestination means your destination has already been determined. The Bible says we are predestined according to God's purposes and will (Ephesians 1:11). That means God knows where you are supposed to be going. And He knows how to get you there. But even though you have a purpose and a destiny, you can't get to it without being connected to the one who gave it to you in the first place. When you don't stay connected to the one who planned your destiny, then in one moment of weakness, such as passion or anger, you can sell it out. We see people on the news all the time who do that. When you clearly understand that God has a high purpose for your life, you won't throw it away with a foolish decision. You won't allow insecurity to ruin your life.

It doesn't seem fair that insecurity is sin. That's like hitting someone when they are down. But insecurity is a lack of faith. And a lack of faith is sin, because it signifies a lack of trust in God. When we are insecure about who we are and what our purpose is, it means we don't trust God with our lives. We don't believe that what He says about us in His word is true. Insecurity causes us to focus on ourselves and what *we* want, instead of focusing on Him and what *He* wants.

We all want to accomplish something significant with our lives. And we all have the potential to do something great. That's because we are the Lord's and His Spirit dwells in us. Because of His greatness *in* us, He can accomplish great things *through* us. We just have to remember not to confuse success in the eyes of men as being the same as success in the eyes of God. Men and women of the world glory in their accomplishments. Children of God glory in the Lord. "Let not the wise man glory in his wisdom, let not the mighty man glory in his might, nor let the rich man glory in his riches; but let him who glories glory in this, that he understands and knows Me" (Jeremiah 9:23-24). When you know you are the Lord's and you trust where He is taking you, you feel very secure.

Surrender Your Dreams

I have found that we can never move into all God has for us and become all He created us to be without surrendering our dreams to Him. Jesus said, "Whoever desires to save his life will lose it, but whoever loses his life for My sake will find it" (Matthew 16:25). That means if we want to have a life that is secure in the Lord, we have to let go of *our* plans and say, "Not my will, but *Yours* be done, Lord." This is hard to do, because letting go of our dreams is the last thing we want to do. But we have to ask Him to take away the dreams in our heart that are not of Him and bring to pass the ones that are.

If you have a dream that is not of God, when you surrender it to Him He will take away your desire for it and give you what *He* has for you. This can be very painful, especially if it is a dream you've been clinging to for a long time. But you don't want to spend your life chasing after a dream that God will not bless. You will be constantly frustrated if you do, and it will never be realized. You want to be living the dreams God puts in your heart.

Even if the dreams you have in your heart are from God, you will still have to surrender them. That's because God wants you clinging to *Him* and not to your dreams. He doesn't want you trying to make them happen. He wants you to trust *Him*, and *He'll* make them happen.

Finding Your Purpose

We all need to have a sense of why we are here. We all need to know we were created for a purpose. We will never find fulfillment and happiness until we are doing the thing for which we were created. But God won't move us into the big things He has called us to unless we have been proven faithful in the small things He has given us. So if you are doing what you deem to be small things right now, rejoice! God's getting you ready for big things ahead.

Don't think for a moment that if you haven't moved into the purposes God has for you by now that it's too late. It is *never* too late. I did everything late. I didn't come to the Lord until I was 28. I got married late, had children late, and didn't even start writing professionally until I was over 40. My whole ministry happened when I was in my 40s and most of it in my 50s. Trust me, if you are still breathing, God has a purpose for you. He has something for you to do *now*.

If you are not sure what God wants you do, start as an intercessor. We are all called to pray for others. Start by serving in your church. We are all called to submit ourselves to a body of believers and help others. When we are faithful in these things, He moves us into others.

Keep in mind that God "has saved us and called us with a holy calling, not according to our works, but according to His own purpose and grace which was given to us in Christ Jesus before time began" (2 Timothy 1:9). "Having then gifts differing according to the grace that is given to us, let us use them" (Romans 12:6). For "each one has his own gift from God, one in this manner and another in that" (1 Corinthians 7:7). So then, "as God has distributed to each one, as the Lord has called each one, so let him walk" (1 Corinthians 7:17).

I pray that God will "give to you the spirit of wisdom and revelation in the knowledge of Him, the eyes of your understanding being enlightened; that you may know what is the hope of His calling" (Ephesians 1:17-18). "May He grant you according to your heart's desire, and fulfill all your purpose" (Psalm 20:4).

May you never forget, dear sister, that God has an important purpose for your life and that it is good.

— My Prayer to God —

Lord, I thank You that You have called me with a holy calling, not according to my works, but according to Your purpose and grace which was given to me in Christ Jesus (2 Timothy 1:9). I know that Your plan for me existed before I knew You, and You will bring it to pass. Help me to "walk worthy of the calling with which [I was] called" (Ephesians 4:1). I know there is an appointed plan for me, and I have a destiny that will now be fulfilled.

Help me to live my life with a sense of purpose and understanding of the calling You have given me. I lay down all pride, selfishness, and anything else that would keep me from moving into all You have for me. I don't want to miss out on Your full purpose for my life because I did not walk the way You wanted me to. I repent of every day I haven't fully lived for You. Help me to live the way You want me to from now on.

Lord, help me to understand the call You have on my life. Take away any discouragement I may feel and replace it with joyful anticipation of what You are going to do through me. Use me as Your instrument to make a positive difference in the lives of those whom You put in my path. Help me to rest in the confidence of knowing that Your timing is perfect. I know that whatever You have called me to do, You will enable me to do it.

I pray that nothing will draw me away from fulfilling the plan You have for me. May I never stray from what You have called me to be and do. Give me a vision for my life and a strong sense of purpose. I put my identity in You and my destiny in Your hands. Show me if what I am doing now is what I am supposed to be doing. I want what You are building in my life to last for eternity. I don't want to waste time going after things that are not what You have for me. Help me to be content where I am, knowing You won't leave me there forever.

Lord, I know that "all things work together for good" to those who love You and are called according to Your purpose (Romans 8:28). I don't want to presume that I know what that purpose is. Nor do I want to spend a lifetime trying to figure out what I am supposed to be doing and miss the mark.

So I pray that You would show me clearly what the gifts and talents are that You have placed in me. Lead me in the way I should go as I grow in them. Enable me to use them according to Your will and for Your glory.

⊱ GOD'S PROMISES TO ME ⊰

Walk worthy of the calling with which you were called, with all lowliness and gentleness, with longsuffering, bearing with one another in love, endeavoring to keep the unity of the Spirit in the bond of peace.
EPHESIANS 4:1-3

Be even more diligent to make your call and election sure, for if you do these things you will never stumble.
2 PETER 1:10

You are a chosen generation, a royal priesthood, a holy nation, His own special people, that you may proclaim the praises of Him who called you out of darkness into His marvelous light.
1 PETER 2:9

In Him also we have obtained an inheritance, being predestined according to the purpose of Him who works all things according to the counsel of His will, that we who first trusted in Christ should be to the praise of His glory.
EPHESIANS 1:11-12

Whom He predestined, these He also called; whom He called, these He also justified; and whom He justified, these He also glorified.
ROMANS 8:30

CHAPTER FIFTEEN

Lord, Guide Me in All My Relationships

I once heard a radio interview with some gang members in Los Angeles. At the time crime was extremely high in that city due to a terrifying wave of random drive-by shootings and murders perpetrated by gang members. These boys—some barely teenagers and some in their early 20s—said the main reason they joined their gang was to have a sense of belonging. In a chilling statement a number of them admitted they would do whatever it took to ensure they were accepted and esteemed by the group. Even commit murder.

Some of the boys revealed that the test of whether they could even be accepted into the gang was to go out and kill someone. There was no other reason for the murder other than to complete the initiation requirement and prove that they would do anything for the group. Some confessed how much they hated doing it and wished there had been another alternative. But they were desperate to belong to a family, so they went ahead with it. This was a frightening revelation to all of us who lived there, because it meant no place was safe.

Around that same time, a friend of ours was out in front of his own home in broad daylight and was approached by two such young boys. They were walking down the street, which was in a very nice and quiet residential neighborhood, when one of the boys pulled out a gun, shot our friend point-blank and fled. There was no robbery or attempt to commit any other crime. Our friend must have had angels watching over him, because he lived through it. Most people involved in such incidents didn't. But the damage to his body greatly affected his ability to do the work he was an expert in doing, and it took him years to recover.

These young boys in the interview had no sense of purpose for their lives outside of belonging to a gang. Most of them were raised without fathers and in some cases the mother was absent too. I'm sure that if each of them would have had a strong sense of family, and love and acceptance from other people, they would not have chosen this destructive lifestyle. This illustrates how desperately people need people. When young people are deprived of good, godly relationships, they will seek those that aren't. That's how gangs are formed.

We *all* desperately need a sense of family, of relationship, of belonging. If you don't realize that about yourself, it's probably because you have always had it. God created us to be in families. We have a natural hunger to be a part of something that gives us a sense of acceptance, affirmation, and being needed and appreciated. But even if we have never received that from our own biological families, there is good news. God sets us in *spiritual* families. In many ways these can be just as important.

The Importance of Having a Spiritual Family

God is our Father. We are God's kids. That means we who are believers in Jesus are all brothers and sisters. There are too many of us to all live in the same house, so God puts us in separate houses. We call them churches. Our relationships within these church families are crucial to our well-being. How we relate to the other people there will greatly affect the quality of our life in the Lord. We can never reach our full destiny apart from the people God puts in our lives. I don't mean they will necessarily help us do what we do, but our relationships with them will contribute to our success.

It's important to be yoked with people who walk closely with God. Accountability results from having close relationships with strong believers who are themselves accountable to other strong believers. It's important to be accountable because we are all capable of being deceived. We all have blind spots. We need people who will help us see the truth about ourselves and our lives. And we need to have the kind of relationships that don't break down when truth is spoken in love.

This doesn't mean that you will never have a problem in any of your church relationships or that if you do it's a sign that you are in the wrong place. *All* relationships have things that need to be worked out. Getting beyond those problems are what make relationships rich. But we have to learn to protect our relationships with our spiritual family in prayer.

Your enemy doesn't want you to be in a spiritual family or have godly relationships. That's because he knows how beneficial they are for you. He knows that without a spiritual family you won't grow properly. He knows if you are not joined and committed to a spiritual family, you will end up living in rebellion in some way whether you mean to or not. He knows you will never be all God created you to be if you are not connected to a spiritual family. That's why he will try to break apart your relationships. And that's why you should cover them in prayer.

More Than Just Friends

So much is made of the importance of the right kind of friends in the Bible that we can't treat this part of our lives lightly. "The righteous should choose his friends carefully, for the way of the wicked leads them astray" (Proverbs 12:26). If it's true that we become like the friends we spend time with, then we must select our friends wisely. The main quality to look for in a close friend is not how attractive, talented, wealthy, smart, influential, clever, or popular they are. It's how much they love and fear God. The person who will do what it takes to live in the perfect will of God is the kind of friend who imparts something of the goodness of the Lord to you every time you are with them.

God doesn't want us to be unequally yoked with unbelievers, but that doesn't mean we should have nothing to do with anyone who doesn't know the Lord. Far from it. We are God's tool to reach others for His kingdom. But our closest relationships, the ones that influence us the most, need to be with people who love and fear God. If you don't have close friends who are believers, pray for godly and desirable friends to come into your life.

Seven Good Signs of a Desirable Friend

1. *A desirable friend tells you the truth in love.* "Faithful are the wounds of a friend, but the kisses of an enemy are deceitful" (Proverbs 27:6).

2. *A desirable friend gives you sound advice.* "Ointment and perfume delight the heart, and the sweetness of a man's friend gives delight by hearty counsel" (Proverbs 27:9).

3. *A desirable friend refines you.* "As iron sharpens iron, so a man sharpens the countenance of his friend" (Proverbs 27:17).

4. *A desirable friend helps you grow in wisdom.* "He who walks with wise men will be wise, but the companion of fools will be destroyed" (Proverbs 13:20).

5. *A desirable friend stays close to you.* "A man who has friends must himself be friendly, but there is a friend who sticks closer than a brother" (Proverbs 18:24).

6. *A desirable friend loves you and stands by you.* "A friend loves at all times, and a brother is born for adversity" (Proverbs 17:17).

7. *A desirable friend is a help in time of trouble.* "Two are better than one, because they have a good reward for their labor. For if they fall, one will lift up his companion. But woe to him who is alone when he falls, for he has no one to help him up" (Ecclesiastes 4:9-10).

If you have friends with these qualities, protect those friendships with prayer. If you have friends who have less than desirable qualities, you need to pray about those as well.

Seven Signs of an *Undesirable* Friend

1. *An undesirable friend is immoral and has no regard for others.* "I have written to you not to keep company with anyone named a brother, who is sexually immoral, or covetous, or an idolater, or a reviler, or a drunkard, or an extortioner—not even to eat with such a person" (1 Corinthians 5:11).

2. *An undesirable friend is changeable and unstable.* "Do not associate with those given to change; for their calamity will rise suddenly, and who knows the ruin those two can bring?" (Proverbs 24:21-22).

3. *An undesirable friend is frequently angry.* "Make no friendship with an angry man, and with a furious man do not go, lest you learn his ways and set a snare for your soul" (Proverbs 22:24-25).

4. *An undesirable friend gives ungodly counsel.* "Blessed is the man who walks not in the counsel of the ungodly, nor stands in the path of sinners, nor sits in the seat of the scornful" (Psalm 1:1).

5. *An undesirable friend is a lawless unbeliever.* "Do not be unequally yoked together with unbelievers. For what fellowship has righteousness with lawlessness? And what communion has light with darkness? And what accord has Christ with Belial? Or what part has a believer with an unbeliever?" (2 Corinthians 6:14-15).

6. *An undesirable friend is a fool.* "He who walks with wise men will be wise, but the companion of fools will be destroyed" (Proverbs 13:20).

7. *An undesirable friend is irreverent toward God and His laws.* "I am a companion of all who fear You, and of those who keep Your precepts" (Psalm 119:63).

If you have friends with such characteristics as these, ask God to send you new friends while you pray for the old ones to be transformed.

Pray for Your Relationships

Severe injuries to relationships can often be fatal. Even if they aren't completely destroyed, relational injuries can take years to heal. It's easier to *protect* them in prayer than it is to *fix* them. The way we learned to cope, survive, or interact in our relationships when we were growing up will be carried with us into adulthood and affect every one of our important or close relationships now. And it could be exactly how the devil will try to destroy them. Ask God to make you a good friend to others and give you a pure and loving heart in all your relationships. Pray especially for the people you live with. The Bible says that "every...house divided against itself will not stand" (Matthew 12:25). You can't have peace if you are living in discord with anyone in your home.

Don't leave your relationships to chance. Pray for godly people to come into your life with whom you can connect. Don't *force* relationships to happen, *pray* for them to happen. Then when they do, nurture them with prayer. This doesn't mean you have to have large numbers of friends. There is great strength in small numbers when the people involved are strong in the Lord. The quality of your relationships is more important than the quantity.

Throughout your whole life relationships will be crucial to your well-being. It is not emotionally or spiritually healthy to be isolated. Right relationships will enrich and balance you and give you a healthy perspective. Godly people will help you walk in the right direction, and the good in them will rub off on you. The quality of your relationships will determine the quality of your life. And this is something worth praying about.

My Prayer to God

Lord, I lift up every one of my relationships to You and ask You to bless them. I pray that each one would be glorifying to You. Help me to choose my friends wisely so I won't be led astray. Give me discernment and strength to separate myself from anyone who is not a good influence. I release all my relationships to You and pray that Your will be done in each one of them.

With my most difficult relationships, I ask that Your peace would reign in them. Specifically I lift up to You my relationship with (name a difficult friend). I know two can't walk together unless they are agreed (Amos 3:3), so help us to find a place of agreement, unity, and like-mindedness. Where either of us needs to change, I pray that You would change us. Break down any "wall of separation" (Ephesians 2:13-15) or misunderstanding. I release this person into Your hands and ask that You would make our relationship what You want it to be so that it will glorify You.

I pray for my relationship with each of my family members. Specifically, I pray for my relationship with (name the family member with whom you are most concerned). I pray You would bring healing, reconciliation, and restoration where it is needed. Bless our relationship and make it strong.

I pray for any relationships I have with people who don't know You, Lord. Give me words to say that will turn their hearts toward You. Help me to be Your light to them. Specifically I pray for (name an unbeliever or someone who has walked away from God). Soften this person's heart to open her (his) eyes to receive You and follow You faithfully.

I pray for godly friends, role models, and mentors to come into my life. Send people who will speak the truth in love. I pray especially that there will be women in my life who are trustworthy, kind, loving, and faithful. Most of all I pray that they be women of strong faith who will add to my life and I to theirs. May we mutually raise the standards to which we aspire. May forgiveness and love flow freely between us. Make me to be Your light in all my relationships.

ᵒᵇ GOD'S PROMISES TO ME ᵇᵒ

You are no longer strangers and foreigners, but fellow citizens with the saints and members of the household of God, having been built on the foundation of the apostles and prophets, Jesus Christ Himself being the chief cornerstone, in whom the whole building, being joined together, grows into a holy temple in the Lord, in whom you also are being built together for a dwelling place of God in the Spirit.
EPHESIANS 2:19-22

God sets the solitary in families; He brings out those who are bound into prosperity; but the rebellious dwell in a dry land.
PSALM 68:6

Let all bitterness, wrath, anger, clamor, and evil speaking be put away from you, with all malice. And be kind to one another, tenderhearted, forgiving one another, just as God in Christ forgave you.
EPHESIANS 4:31-32

We should no longer be children, tossed to and fro and carried about with every wind of doctrine, by the trickery of men, in the cunning craftiness of deceitful plotting, but, speaking the truth in love, may grow up in all things into Him who is the head—Christ—from whom the whole body, joined and knit together by what every joint supplies,

according to the effective working by which every
part does its share, causes growth of the body for
the edifying of itself in love.

EPHESIANS 4:14-16

CHAPTER SIXTEEN

Lord, Keep Me in the Center of Your Will

When my children and I walked through the rubble of our house in Northridge, California, not long after the Northridge earthquake of 1993 had destroyed it, we all wept. We knew that if we'd been in the house at the time, we might not have lived through that earthquake. We all loved that great house and had hated to leave it when we moved just months before. A lot of prayer and inner struggle went into the decision to relocate to another state, but we were certain it was God's leading. We had not even sold the house before we moved because we felt we were to leave right away. Had we not sought the will of God for our lives and followed it, even with reluctance, we would have been there when the earthquake happened.

God's will is a place of safety. I'm not saying that anyone who was in California during the earthquake was out of the will of God. But, I believe that *we* would have been. And I believe that the reason the house had not sold is that anyone who was in it at the time would have been seriously injured or killed. When we walk in the will of God, we find safety. When we live outside of God's will, we forfeit His protection.

We all want to be in the center of God's will. That's why we shouldn't pursue a career, a move to another place, or any major life change without the knowledge that it is the will of God. We must regularly ask God to show us what His will is and lead us in it. We must ask Him to speak to our heart so He can tell us. "Your ears shall hear a word behind you, saying, 'This is the way, walk in it,' whenever you turn to the right hand or whenever you turn to the left" (Isaiah 30:21). My family and I will always be grateful that we listened to God and followed His leading.

Four Good Things That Are True About God's Will

1. *Following God's will does not mean we will never have trouble*. Trouble is a part of life. Having fulfillment and peace in the midst of trouble is what living in God's will is all about. There is great confidence in knowing that you are walking in the will of God and doing what He wants you to do. When you are sure of that, you can better deal with what life brings you. So don't think that trouble in your life means you are out of God's will. God uses the trouble you have to perfect you. There is a big difference between being out of God's will and being pruned or tested by God. Both are uncomfortable, but one leads to life and one doesn't. In one you will have peace, no matter how uncomfortable it gets. In the other, you won't.

2. *Following God's will is not easy*. The life of Jesus confirms that following God's will is not always fun, enjoyable, pleasant, and easy. Jesus was doing God's will when He went to the cross. He said, "For I have come down from heaven, not to do My own will, but the will of Him who sent Me" (John 6:38). If anyone could have said, "I don't want to

follow God's will today," I think it would have been Him. But He did it perfectly. And now He will enable us to do it too.

3. *Following God's will can make you very uncomfortable.* In fact, if you don't ever feel stretched or uncomfortable in your walk with the Lord, then I would question whether you are actually *in* the will of God. It has been my personal experience that stretched and uncomfortable is a way of life when walking in the will of God.

4. *Following God's will doesn't happen automatically.* That's because God gave us a choice as to whether we subject our will to Him or not. We make that decision every day. Will we *seek* His will? Will we *ask* Him for wisdom? Will we *do* what He says? "Do not be unwise, but understand what the will of the Lord is" (Ephesians 5:17). God's will is the way we choose to live each day of our lives.

God doesn't want you to live your life for the lusts of the flesh, "but for the will of God" (1 Peter 4:2). He wants to "make you complete in every good work to do His will, working in you what is well pleasing in His sight" (Hebrews 13:21). "For it is God who works in you both to will and to do for His good pleasure" (Philippians 2:13). I pray that in everything you do "you may stand perfect and complete in all the will of God" (Colossians 4:12).

The best place to start seeking God's will for your life is "in everything give thanks; for this is the will of God in Christ Jesus for you" (1 Thessalonians 5:18). Thank Him for keeping you in the center of His will. Then ask Him to guide your every step. It feels so good to be confident you are on the right path and doing what God *wants* that I know you will do whatever it takes to experience it.

My Prayer to God

Lord, I pray You will fill me with the "knowledge of [Your] will in all wisdom and spiritual understanding" (Colossians 1:9). Help me to walk in a worthy manner, fully pleasing to You, being fruitful in every good work and increasing in the knowledge of Your ways. Guide my every step. Lead me "in Your righteousness" and "make Your way straight before my face" (Psalm 5:8). As I draw close and walk in intimate relationship with You each day, I pray You will get me where I need to go.

Even as Jesus said, "Not My will, but Yours, be done" (Luke 22:42), so I say to You, not *my* will but *Your* will be done in my life. "I delight to do Your will, O my God" (Psalm 40:8). You are more important to me than anything. Your will is more important to me than my desires. I want to live as Your servant, doing Your will from my heart (Ephesians 6:6).

Lord, align my heart with Yours. Help me to hear Your voice saying, "This is the way, walk in it." If I am doing anything outside of Your will, show me. Speak to me from Your Word so that I will have understanding. Show me any area of my life where I am not right on target. If there is something I should be doing, reveal it to me so that I can correct my course. I want to do only what You want me to do.

Lord, I know we are not to direct our own steps (Jeremiah 10:23). So I pray *You* would direct my steps. Only You know the way I should go. I don't want to get off the path You want me to walk on and end up in the wrong place. I want to move into all You have for me and become all You made me to be by walking in Your perfect will for my life now.

❧ GOD'S PROMISES TO ME ❧

Not everyone who says to Me, "Lord, Lord," shall
enter the kingdom of heaven, but he who does
the will of My Father in heaven.
MATTHEW 7:21

You have need of endurance, so that after you have
done the will of God,
you may receive the promise.
HEBREWS 10:36

For it is better, if it is the will of God,
to suffer for doing good than for doing evil.
1 PETER 3:17

Therefore let those who suffer according to the will
of God commit their souls to Him in doing good, as
to a faithful Creator.
1 PETER 4:19

The world is passing away, and the lust of it;
but he who does the will of God abides forever.
1 JOHN 2:17

Lord, Protect Me and All I Care About

Recently I had the privilege of staying in a highrise condominium right on the beach. This particular unit was on the top floor, and one entire side of it—which included the bedroom, living room, and dining area—was all glass and overlooked the ocean. The view was breathtaking.

The first morning I awakened there, I opened up the curtains and crawled back into bed to gaze out over the ocean and jot down some thoughts on a notepad. Because the condo was so high, I couldn't see anything but ocean and sky from where I was sitting. In order to have seen the sand of the beach, I would have had to go into the living room and walk out on the balcony to look over the edge.

I was deep in thought, lost in the blue of the sky and ocean, when suddenly a large airplane flew by my window at eye level. It was over the water but it seemed very close. The sudden appearance of something so loud and enormous nearly caused my heart to stop. I felt a surge of panic and fright so severe that it sent a sharp pain throughout my chest. I was terrified by what I saw and shocked at my reaction.

I don't know when I have ever responded so violently to something that was not really a threat. But it was so unexpected, and I had never dreamed of seeing a plane at eye level. I felt utterly vulnerable. I realized at that very moment the only thing standing between me and instant death was the hand of God and a pilot who was a decent human being.

Before September 11, a plane coming in my window was not a thought that would have ever entered my mind. But actually that possibility was always there, whether I realized it or not. I began to wonder about how many other potentially dangerous things are around us every day. Things we don't see until the plans of evil explode them in our lives. Dangers we can't even imagine until they come crashing in upon us, changing us forever.

Personally, I believe our heavenly Father looks out for us and protects us from danger far more than we realize. But it's not something we can take for granted. It's something we must pray about often.

Part of being protected by God has to do with obeying Him and living in His will. When we don't do either of those things, we come out from under the umbrella of His covering. We don't hear His voice telling us which way to go. How many times would people have been spared from something disastrous if they had only asked God to show them what to do and then obeyed Him? Or if they had only just been listening?

I remember traveling one time in my four-wheel-drive vehicle a few days after a freezing snowstorm. Slowly approaching a red light at a busy intersection, I put my foot on the brake but nothing happened. I had hit a patch of black ice that was completely invisible. The intersection consisted of narrow two-lane highways crossing one another, with deep water-drainage ditches on either side. There were cars going both ways across the intersection in front of me, and I realized my car was entirely out of control and I couldn't stop.

"Jesus, help me," I prayed. I tried my best to maintain control over the car and keep it from flipping over into one of the ditches on either side of me. In an effort to do that, however, I spun out in the center of the intersection. Cars dodged all around me as they tried to maintain control as well. One green car was headed directly toward me, and I don't even know how I missed hitting it, except to say that I was praying fervently at the time and the hand of God must have intervened. It was miraculous that nothing happened to me or anyone else. Before I had left home that day, I prayed specifically that God would keep me safe. There is no doubt in my mind that He answered that prayer.

In those precarious moments, when your future is hanging in the balance, you want the confidence of knowing you have been communicating with your heavenly Father all along and He has His eye on you. These are the times, such as what I experienced, when you need a prayer answered instantly. But in order to be sure that happens, you must be praying every day. God is a place of safety you can run to, but it helps if you are running to Him on a daily basis so that you are in familiar territory. The Bible says, "In the fear of the LORD there is strong confidence, and His children will have a place of refuge. The fear of the LORD is a fountain of life, to turn one away from the snares of death" (Proverbs 14:26-27). When we have our eyes on *God*, He keeps an eye on *us*.

My Prayer to God

Lord, I pray for Your hand of protection to be upon me. Keep me safe from any accidents, diseases, or evil influences. Protect me wherever I go. Keep me safe in planes, cars, or any other means of transportation. I trust in Your Word, which assures me that You are my rock, my fortress, my deliverer, my shield, my stronghold, and my strength in whom I trust.

Lord, I want to dwell in Your secret place and abide in Your shadow (Psalm 91:1). Keep me under the umbrella of Your protection. Help me never to stray from the center of Your will or off the path You have for me. Enable me to always hear Your voice guiding me. Send Your angels to keep charge over me and keep me in all my ways. May they bear me up, so that I will not even stumble (Psalm 91:12). You, Lord, are my refuge and strength and "a very present help in trouble." Therefore I will not fear, "even though the earth be removed and though the mountains be carried to the midst of the sea" (Psalm 46:1-2).

Thank You, Lord, that no weapon formed against me will prosper (Isaiah 54:17). Thank You that You will not leave me in the hands of wicked people who would try to destroy me (Psalm 37:32-33). "Hide me under the shadow of Your wings, from the wicked who oppress me, from my deadly enemies who surround me" (Psalm 17:8). Protect me from the plans of evil people. Keep me from sudden danger. "Be merciful to me, O God, be merciful to me! For my soul trusts in You; and in the shadow of Your wings I will make my refuge" (Psalm 57:1). Thank You that "I will both lie down in peace, and sleep; for You alone, O LORD, make me dwell in safety" (Psalm 4:8). Thank You for Your promises of protection. I lay claim to them this day.

❧ GOD'S PROMISES TO ME ❧

Because you have made the LORD, who is my refuge,
even the Most High, your dwelling place,
no evil shall befall you, nor shall any
plague come near your dwelling.
PSALM 91:9-10

No weapon formed against you shall prosper.
ISAIAH 54:17

When you pass through the waters, I will be with
you; and through the rivers, they shall not overflow
you. When you walk through the fire,
you shall not be burned, nor shall
the flame scorch you.
ISAIAH 43:2

He shall cover you with His feathers, and under His
wings you shall take refuge; His truth shall be your
shield and buckler. You shall not be afraid of the
terror by night, nor of the arrow that flies by day, nor
of the pestilence that walks in darkness, nor of the
destruction that lays waste at noonday.
A thousand may fall at your side, and ten thousand
at your right hand; but it shall not come near you.
PSALM 91:4-7

He shall give His angels charge over you, to keep you
in all your ways.
PSALM 91:11

CHAPTER EIGHTEEN

Lord, Give Me Wisdom to Make Right Decisions

As I was sitting out on the balcony of that same high-rise beachfront condominium I described in the previous chapter, I had a rare perspective of the water below. I could clearly see where there were very shallow places and where the ocean floor suddenly fell off, making the water very deep. I watched as people would swim a ways out and then find themselves in a place so shallow they were forced to stand up. The water at those places was barely knee level. It was fascinating to watch the swimmers walk around on the sandy plateau and then suddenly fall over the edge into deep water.

I realized that if I could have been connected to each of those swimmers by perhaps a waterproof cell phone or walkie-talkie, I could have told them when they were near the edge. But they had no connection with me. They didn't know to call. So I couldn't tell them what I saw from my perspective.

I think that's the way it is with God. He sees all because He is above all. If we were to connect with Him on a regular basis and say, "Lord, guide me so I won't fall," He could lead us away from the edge. But so often we don't make that connection with God. We don't call. We don't seek His guidance. We don't ask Him for wisdom. We don't consider His perspective. And too often we fall in over our heads because of it.

Lot, Abraham's nephew in the Bible, ended up being captured by the enemy because he chose to live in land that *he* thought was good (Genesis 13:10-11), but it was among wicked people (Genesis 13:13). He chose what *he* thought was best rather than what was *God's* best. How many times do people walk out from under God's umbrella of protection and away from *His* best, all because they have chosen what *they* think is best for their lives? They don't ask for *His* wisdom and *His* direction.

Haven't we all done that at one time or another? And just because we have walked with the Lord for some time doesn't make us immune to this problem. We may think we know God's will for a situation today because of what His will was the last time we asked. But what worked last year might not be the same thing He would direct us to do now. We always need to ask God for wisdom and guidance.

The things of God can only be discerned in the spirit. But the natural man doesn't get this. He can't. "The natural man does not receive the things of the Spirit of God, for they are foolishness to him; nor can he know them, because they are spiritually discerned" (1 Corinthians 2:14). Have you ever observed someone with no wisdom clearly doing the wrong thing or making a foolish decision? The consequences are crystal clear to you, but *they* don't see it at all. It's always easier to see a lack of wisdom in others than it is to see it in ourselves. That's why we must pray daily for wisdom.

Wisdom means having clear understanding and insight. It means knowing how to apply the truth in every situation. It's discerning what is right and wrong. It's having good judgment. It's being able to sense when you are getting too close to the edge. It's making the right choice or decision. And only God knows what that is. "When He, the Spirit of truth, has come, He will guide you into all truth; for He will not speak on His own authority, but whatever He hears He will speak; and He will tell you things to come" (John 16:13). We have no idea how many times simple wisdom has saved our lives or kept us out of harm's way or how many times it will do so in the future. That's why we can't live without it and need to ask God for it. We have to pray, "Lord give me wisdom in all I do. Help me to walk in wisdom every day."

Ten Good Ways to Walk in Wisdom

1. *Be in the Word of God.* "My son, if you receive my words, and treasure my commands within you, so that you incline your ear to wisdom, and apply your heart to understanding...then you will understand the fear of the LORD, and find the knowledge of God" (Proverbs 2:1-2,5).

2. *Pray for wisdom.* "If any of you lacks wisdom, let him ask of God, who gives to all liberally and without reproach, and it will be given to him" (James 1:5).

3. *Acknowledge the Lord in everything.* "In all your ways acknowledge Him, and He shall direct your paths" (Proverbs 3:6).

4. *Walk in reverence of God.* "The fear of the LORD is the beginning of wisdom" (Proverbs 9:10).

5. *Listen to wise people.* "Incline your ear and hear the words of the wise, and apply your heart to my knowledge" (Proverbs 22:17).

6. *Value wisdom above all.* "Get wisdom! Get understanding! Do not forget, nor turn away from the words of my mouth. Do not forsake her, and she will preserve you; love her, and she will keep you" (Proverbs 4:5-6).

7. *Walk in obedience.* He stores up sound wisdom for the upright; He is a shield to those who walk uprightly" (Proverbs 2:7).

8. *Be humble.* "When pride comes, then comes shame; but with the humble is wisdom" (Proverbs 11:2).

9. *Love your neighbor.* "He who is devoid of wisdom despises his neighbor, but a man of understanding holds his peace" (Proverbs 11:12).

10. *Seek the wisdom of God, not the wisdom of the world.* "But of Him you are in Christ Jesus, who became for us wisdom from God—and righteousness and sanctification and redemption" (1 Corinthians 1:30). "Has not God made foolish the wisdom of this world? For since, in the wisdom of God, the world through wisdom did not know God, it pleased God through the foolishness of the message preached to save those who believe" (1 Corinthians 1:20-21).

Ten Good Reasons to Ask for Wisdom

1. *To enjoy longevity, wealth, and honor.* "Length of days is in her right hand, in her left hand riches and honor" (Proverbs 3:16).

2. *To have a good life.* "Her ways are ways of pleasantness, and all her paths are peace" (Proverbs 3:17).

3. *To enjoy vitality and happiness.* "She is a tree of life to those who take hold of her, and happy are all who retain her" (Proverbs 3:18).

4. *To secure protection.* "Then you will walk safely in your way, and your foot will not stumble" (Proverbs 3:23).

5. *To experience refreshing rest.* "When you lie down, you will not be afraid; yes, you will lie down and your sleep will be sweet" (Proverbs 3:24).

6. *To gain confidence.* "For the LORD will be your confidence, and will keep your foot from being caught" (Proverbs 3:26).

7. *To know security.* "Do not forsake her, and she will preserve you; love her, and she will keep you...when you walk, your steps will not be hindered, and when you run, you will not stumble" (Proverbs 4:6,12).

8. *To be promoted.* "Exalt her, and she will promote you; she will bring you honor, when you embrace her" (Proverbs 4:8).

9. *To be protected.* "When wisdom enters your heart, and knowledge is pleasant to your soul, discretion will preserve you; understanding will keep you, to deliver you from the way of evil, from the man who speaks perverse things" (Proverbs 2:10-12).

10. *To gain understanding.* "A wise man will hear and increase learning, and a man of understanding will attain wise counsel" (Proverbs 1:5).

Seek the Counsel of God

It's important to always seek out God's counsel before you seek anyone else's. I don't mean that you can't take advice from your unbelieving doctor or lawyer. I'm saying that *before* you go to them, ask God *who* you are to go to and then ask Him to give that person wisdom and knowledge to impart to you. Ask God to show you if you are receiving any advice or guidance from a source that is not of the Lord. Ask Him to lead you away from any ungodly counsel and onto the path of the righteous and wise.

Just out of curiosity, I went down to the beach and out in the water to one of those shallow plateaus I had been observing. I walked around on top of it to see exactly how much of the depth of the water could be determined from that close perspective. Because I had the advantage of knowing there was a steep drop-off on one side, I confidently walked toward the edge. Suddenly the whole edge collapsed and I fell in just as I'd seen other swimmers do. With my pride dripping wet, I made my way back to shore. I realized that even when you *think* you know something, you still can't get too cocky. We will always need to ask God for His wisdom and counsel about *everything*, because He is the only one who knows the *whole* truth.

My Prayer to God

Lord, I pray You would give me Your wisdom and understanding in all things. I know wisdom is better than gold and understanding better than silver (Proverbs 16:16), so make me rich in wisdom and wealthy in understanding. Thank You that You give "wisdom to the wise and knowledge to those who have understanding" (Daniel 2:21). Increase my wisdom and knowledge so I can see Your truth in every situation. Give me discernment for each decision I must make.

Lord, help me to always seek godly counsel and not look to the world and ungodly people for answers. Thank You, Lord, that You will give me the counsel and instruction I need, even as I sleep. Thank You that "You will show me the path of life" (Psalm 16:7-11).

I delight in Your law and in Your Word. Help me to mediate on it day and night, to ponder it, to speak it, to memorize it, to get it into my soul and my heart. Lord, I know that whoever "trusts in his own heart is a fool, but whoever walks wisely will be delivered" (Proverbs 28:26). I don't want to trust my own heart. I want to trust Your Word and Your instruction so that I will walk wisely and never do ignorant or stupid things. Make me to be a wise person.

You said in Your Word that You store up sound wisdom for the upright (Proverbs 2:7). Help me to walk uprightly, righteously, and obediently to Your commands. May I never be wise in my own eyes, but may I always fear You. Keep me far from evil so that I can claim the health and strength Your Word promises (Proverbs 3:7-8). Give me the wisdom, knowledge, understanding, direction, and discernment I need to keep me away from the plans of evil so that I will walk safely and not stumble (Proverbs 2:10-13). Lord, I know that in You "are hidden all the treasures of wisdom and knowledge" (Colossians 2:3). Help me to discover those treasures.

❧ GOD'S PROMISES TO ME ❧

The fear of the LORD is the beginning of wisdom, and
the knowledge of the Holy One is understanding.
For by me your days will be multiplied, and
years of life will be added to you.
PROVERBS 9:10-11

The mouth of the righteous speaks wisdom,
and his tongue talks of justice.
The law of his God is in his heart;
none of his steps shall slide.
PSALM 37:30-31

Through wisdom a house is built, and by
understanding it is established; by knowledge the
rooms are filled with all precious and pleasant riches.
PROVERBS 24:3-4

Call to Me, and I will answer you, and show
you great and mighty things,
which you do not know.
JEREMIAH 33:3

If you cry out for discernment, and lift up your voice
for understanding, if you seek her as silver,
and search for her as for hidden treasures; then you
will understand the fear of the LORD, and find the
knowledge of God. For the LORD gives wisdom; from
His mouth come knowledge and understanding.
PROVERBS 2:3-6

CHAPTER NINETEEN

Lord, Deliver Me from Every Evil Work

I know God as my Deliverer. He has set me free from many things, including alcohol, drugs, fear, depression, anxiety, and unforgiveness, to mention just a few. I have seen the Lord set me free in an instant, and I have also been through a process of deliverance that took years. Sometimes I had to fast and pray to get free, sometimes it took other strong believers praying for me, and sometimes it happened just by being in the Lord's presence. Regardless of *how* it happened, what matters most is that it *did*.

We all need deliverance at one time or another. That's because no matter how spiritual we are, we're still made of flesh. And no matter how perfectly we live, we still have an enemy who is trying to erect strongholds of evil in our lives. God wants us free from everything that binds, holds, or separates us from Him.

Jesus taught us to pray, "Deliver us from the evil one" (Matthew 6:13). He would not have instructed us in that manner if we didn't need to do it. But so often we don't pray that way, acting as if He never said it at all. So often we live our lives as if we don't realize Jesus paid an enormous price so we could be free. Jesus "gave Himself for our sins, that He might deliver us from this present evil age, according to the will of our God and Father" (Galatians 1:4). He wants to *continue* to set us free in the future.

God Wants You Free

Do you ever have trouble with finances to the point where it seems you will never get ahead? Are you constantly sick with one thing after another or with one reccurring illness that never gets diagnosed or cured? Do you feel that the things you do are never acknowledged as having worth? Are you hopelessly drawn to things that are not good for you, such as alcohol, food, drugs, ungodly relationships, or gambling? Are you drawn toward immorality? Do you find it impossible to rise above your resentment toward someone no matter how hard you try? Do you have continual strife in an important relationship?

Do you always feel distant from God no matter what you do? Does it seem as though your prayers are never being heard or answered? Do you feel discouraged and sad more than you feel the joy of the Lord? Do you find yourself coming back time and again to the same old problem, the same old habits of action and thought, the same old unhealthy situation? Do you always feel bad about yourself? If you said yes to any of these questions, I have good news for you. God wants to set you free. He wants you to remember that He is the Deliverer (Romans 11:26) and He promises to "deliver those who are drawn toward death" (Proverbs 24:11).

Do you realize that any one of these inclinations or symptoms could be the enemy's weapon formed against you? So often we go along with the devil's plans for our lives, not knowing we don't have to put up with it. We think it's just fate or bad luck when it's really the enemy. But Jesus came to set us free from all the things that bind us. He came to lift us above the enemy who wants to destroy us. God hears the groaning of those who are held captive (Psalm 102:19-20). If you cry out to Him, He will set you free. And "if the Son makes you free, you shall be free indeed" (John 8:36). No matter how strong the thing is you're struggling with, God's power to deliver you is stronger.

God wants you free not only because He loves you and has compassion upon you, but because He wants you to be able to "serve Him without fear, in holiness and righteousness before Him," all the days of your life (Luke 1:74-75). Of course, we are responsible to *walk away* from evil. The Bible says, "The highway of the upright is to depart from evil; he who keeps his way preserves his soul" (Proverbs 16:17). Sometimes *we* are responsible for the things that happen in our lives. But sometimes there are plans of the enemy erected against us that we must be delivered from.

How to Find Freedom

Deliverance is found by praying for it yourself (Psalm 72:12), by having someone else who is a strong believer pray with you for it (Psalm 34:17), by reading the truth of God's Word with great understanding and clarity (John 8:32), or by spending time in the Lord's presence. The most effective and powerful way to spend time in the Lord's presence is in praise and worship. Every time you worship God, something happens in the spirit realm to break the power of evil. That's because He inhabits your praises, and this means you are in His presence. "Now the Lord is the Spirit; and where the Spirit of the Lord is, there is liberty" (2 Corinthians 3:17).

The Bible says, "The angel of the LORD encamps all around those who fear Him, and delivers them" (Psalm 34:7). Whenever the enemy tries to tell you that you will never get free, drown him out with praise. Thank God that He is the Deliverer and you are being delivered even as you praise Him. And once you have been set free, tell others about it. "Let the redeemed of the LORD say so, whom He has redeemed from the hand of the enemy" (Psalm 107:2).

If you ever seem to be sliding back into the very thing you've already been set free of, don't even waste time getting discouraged. Often what seems like the same old thing coming back again may be a new layer surfacing that needs to come off. You're not going backwards—you are going deeper. Those deep layers of bondage can hurt far worse than the earlier ones. Trust that your times are in His hands, and He will deliver you in His timing (Psalm 31:14-15).

Remember that deliverance comes from the Lord, and it is an ongoing process. It is God who has "delivered us from so great a death, and does deliver us; in whom we trust that He will still deliver us" (2 Corinthians 1:10). God does a complete work, and He will see it through to the end. So don't give up because it's taking longer than you hoped. Be confident that "He who has begun a good work in you will complete it until the day of Jesus Christ" (Philippians 1:6).

He will not rest until your righteousness goes forth as brightness and your salvation as a lamp that burns (Isaiah 62:1). Deliverance won't change you into someone else. It will release you to be who you really are—an intelligent, secure, loving, talented, kindhearted, witty, attractive, wonderful woman of God.

My Prayer to God

Lord, thank You that You have promised to "deliver me from every evil work and preserve me" for Your heavenly kingdom (2 Timothy 4:18). I know that "we do not wrestle against flesh and blood, but against principalities, against powers, against the rulers of the darkness of this age, against spiritual hosts of wickedness in the heavenly places" (Ephesians 6:12). Thank You that You have put all these enemies under Your feet (Ephesians 1:22), and "there is nothing covered that will not be revealed, and hidden that will not be known" (Matthew 10:26).

Lord, I know that I can't see all the ways the enemy wants to erect strongholds in my life. I depend on You to reveal them to me. Thank You that You came to "proclaim liberty to the captives and recovery of sight to the blind, to set at liberty those who are oppressed" (Luke 4:18). Without You I am held captive by my desires, I am blind to the truth, and I am oppressed. But with You comes freedom from all that. "My times are in Your hand; deliver me from the hand of my enemies, and from those who persecute me" (Psalm 31:15).

I know that my deliverance comes from You. Thank You that You "drew me out of many waters" and "delivered me from my strong enemy" (Psalm 18:16-17). Help me to stand fast in the liberty by which Christ has made me free, and help me not to become tangled in any yoke of bondage (Galatians 5:1).

I call upon You, Lord, and ask that You would deliver me from anything that binds me or separates me from You. I specifically ask to be delivered from (name a specific area where you want to be set free). Where I have opened the door for the enemy with my own desires, I repent of that. Where I am walking in disobedience, show me so I can turn and live in obedience to Your ways. Give me wisdom to walk the right way and strength to rise above the things that would pull me down (Proverbs 28:26).

I know that though I walk in the flesh, I do not war according to the flesh because "the weapons of our warfare are not carnal but mighty in God for pulling down strongholds" (2 Corinthians 10:3-4). In Jesus' name, I pray that every stronghold erected around me by the enemy will be brought down to nothing. Make darkness light before me and the crooked places straight (Isaiah 42:16). I know that You who have begun a good work in me will complete it (Philippians 1:6). Give me patience to not give up and the strength to stand strong in Your Word.

❧ GOD'S PROMISES TO ME ❧

The righteous cry out, and the LORD hears, and delivers them out of all their troubles.
PSALM 34:17

Call upon Me in the day of trouble; I will deliver you, and you shall glorify Me.
PSALM 50:15

I will give you the keys of the kingdom of heaven,
and whatever you bind on earth will be bound in
heaven, and whatever you loose on earth
will be loosed in heaven.
MATTHEW 16:19

He who trusts in his own heart is a fool, but
whoever walks wisely will be delivered.
PROVERBS 28:26

Because he has set his love upon Me, therefore I will
deliver him; I will set him on high, because
he has known My name.
PSALM 91:14

CHAPTER TWENTY

Lord, Set Me Free from Negative Emotions

I used to think that living with anxiety, depression, fear, and hopelessness was a way of life. *This is just the way I am*, I thought. But when I came to know the Lord and started living God's way, I began to see that *all* things are possible to anyone who believes and obeys God. It's even possible to live without negative emotions. God will take them off of us like a thick wet blanket if we ask Him to. But we have to pray.

Have you ever felt as though God has forsaken you? Well, if you have, you're not alone. In fact, you are in very good company. Not only do millions of other people feel that way right now, but Jesus felt that way at one time too. At the lowest point in His life, Jesus said, "My God, my God, why have You forsaken Me?" (Matthew 27:46). We all have difficult times. Times when we feel all alone and abandoned. But the truth is we aren't. God is with us to help us when we call upon Him. In the midst of these times, we don't have to be controlled by our negative emotions. We can resist them by praying and knowing the truth of what God's Word says about them.

Seven Good Ways to Get Free of Negative Emotions

1. *Refuse to be anxious*. No matter what problems we have in our life, Jesus has overcome them. "In the world you will have tribulation; but be of good cheer, I have overcome the world" (John 16:33). We can find freedom from anxiety just by spending time with Him. "In the multitude of my anxieties within me, Your comforts delight my soul" (Psalm 94:19).

When you are anxious, it means you aren't trusting God to take care of you. But He will prove His faithfulness if you run to Him. "Do not seek what you should eat or what you should drink, nor have an anxious mind. For all these things the nations of the world seek after, and your Father knows that you need these things. But seek the kingdom of God, and all these things shall be added to you" (Luke 12:29-31). God says we don't need to be anxious about *anything*; we just need to pray about *everything*.

2. *Refuse to be ruled by anger*. When we frequently give place to anger it shuts off all God has for us the way pressure on a hose shuts off the water flow. I've seen it happen count-less times with people. Just when God is moving in their lives in a powerful way, they give in to anger and completely shut Him off. When we give anger a home in our souls, we open the door to sin and the devil. " 'Be angry, and do not sin': do not let the sun go down on your wrath, nor give place to the devil" (Ephesians 4:26-27).

An angry person upsets everyone around them, and they make serious mistakes as a result. "An angry man stirs up strife, and a furious man abounds in transgression" (Proverbs 29:22). How many angry men abuse their wives, or even kill them, and destroy their lives forever because of it? How many angry women destroy their relationships and their families and sacrifice the destiny God has for them?

Only foolish people are quick to get angry. People with wisdom don't want to pay the price. "Do not hasten in your spirit to be angry, for anger rests in the bosom of fools" (Ecclesiastes 7:9). Ask God to keep you free from anger so you can remain in the flow of all God has for you.

3. *Refuse to be dissatisfied.* It's easy to focus on the negative and look for everything that's wrong with your life. But when we have constant unrest because we are never at peace, it not only makes *us* miserable—it makes everyone around us miserable too. There is nothing wrong with wanting things to be different when they need to be, but when that attitude becomes a way of life, we sacrifice our peace. Whenever you feel discouraged by your circumstances, remember that the apostle Paul said "I have learned in whatever state I am, to be content: I know how to be abased, and I know how to abound. Everywhere and in all things I have learned both to be full and to be hungry, both to abound and to suffer need. I can do all things through Christ who strengthens me" (Philippians 4:11-13).

God promises you rest. "There remains therefore a rest for the people of God" (Hebrews 4:9). It's possible to find contentment, rest, peace, and joy in any situation. Tell God you are making that your goal and you need Him to help you.

4. *Refuse to be envious.* When you set your eyes on someone else and what *they* have instead of on the Lord and what *He* has, a covetous spirit is about to make your life miserable. "For where envy and self-seeking exist, confusion and every evil thing are there. But the wisdom that is from above is first pure, then peaceable, gentle, willing to yield, full of mercy and good fruits, without partiality and without hypocrisy" (James 3:16-17). Don't allow yourself to entertain thoughts such as, "If only I had *her* hair...*her* face...*her* body...*her* clothes...*her* talent...*her* gifts...*her* husband...*her*

kids...*her* wealth...*her* luck...*her* blessings." Turn your thoughts toward Jesus instead. Think about *His* beauty, *His* wealth, *His* talents, *His* nature, *His* provision, *His* help, and *His* power. Thank Him for the rich inheritance you have in Him, and tell Him you can't wait to experience it all.

Covetousness started when Cain wanted what Abel had, and he killed him for it. But he suffered the rest of his life as a result. "Where there are envy, strife, and divisions among you, are you not carnal and behaving like mere men?" (1 Corinthians 3:3). We don't want to suffer for the rest of our lives because of covetousness. The price we pay for envy is way too high. "A sound heart is life to the body, but envy is rottenness to the bones" (Proverbs 14:30). Ask for God's love to be manifested in you and through you at all times. "Love suffers long and is kind; love does not envy" (1 Corinthians 13:4).

5. *Refuse to be depressed.* Of all the negative emotions, I believe depression is the one we most readily accept as part of our lives. So many of us live with depression and accept it without even realizing it. It feels natural to us because it is so familiar. But God doesn't want us to accept this as a way of life.

Many people of the Bible understood what depression feels like. "I am weary with my groaning; all night I make my bed swim; I drench my couch with my tears. My eye wastes away because of grief; it grows old because of all my enemies" (Psalm 6:6-7). "Reproach has broken my heart, and I am full of heaviness; I looked for someone to take pity, but there was none; and for comforters, but I found none" (Psalm 69:20). "My soul melts from heaviness; strengthen me according to Your word" (Psalm 119:28). Does any of this sound familiar? The good news is that God doesn't want us to live with these feelings. He wants us to have the joy of the Lord rise in us and chase away spirits of heaviness. "Depart from me, all you workers of iniquity; for the LORD has heard the voice of my weeping. The LORD has heard my supplication; the LORD will receive my prayer" (Psalm 6:8-9). God wants us to cry out to Him so He can lift us out of depression.

6. *Refuse to be bitter.* Bitterness burns away your body and soul the way acid eats skin. When a root of bitterness takes hold of your life, it consumes you and cuts off the blessings of God. "For I see that you are poisoned by bitterness and bound by iniquity" (Acts 8:23). When we constantly have thoughts such as, "How long shall I take counsel in my soul, having sorrow in my heart daily? How long will my enemy be exalted over me?" (Psalm 13:2), then we have bitterness growing in us like a cancer. But we can identify those thoughts and refuse to give place to them. We can ask God to help us resist them. "Looking diligently lest anyone fall short of the grace of God; lest any root of bitterness springing up cause trouble, and by this many become defiled" (Hebrews 12:15).

Pray for God to set you free from any bitterness. Ask Him to give you a spirit of thankfulness, praise, and worship. Ask the Holy Spirit to crowd out anything in your heart that is not of Him.

7. *Refuse to be hopeless.* Hopelessness is a slow killer that will eventually affect the health of your body and soul. But when you deliberately choose to put your hope in the Lord, He will meet all your needs and take all hopelessness away. Just as we can choose what attitude we will have every day, we can choose to put our hope in God. We can guard our soul. "Thorns and snares are in the way of the perverse; He who guards his soul will be far from them" (Proverbs 22:5). Hopelessness is death to our souls. Refuse to live with it. No

matter how bad things appear to get in your life, you *always* have hope in the Lord. Ask God to give you hope for your future and an attitude of gratefulness every day of your life.

Negative emotions reveal doubt. If we thoroughly trust God, what do we have to be anxious about? Why would we be angry, dissatisfied, envious, depressed, bitter, or hopeless? Yet we all are susceptible to experiencing these kinds of emotions at some time in our life. So don't feel bad about having them, but don't live with them either. Refuse to allow the ugliness of negative emotions to mar the beauty of the life God has for you.

My Prayer to God

Lord, help me to live in Your joy and peace. Give me strength and understanding to resist anxiety, anger, unrest, envy, depression, bitterness, hopelessness, loneliness, fear, and guilt. Rescue me when "my spirit is overwhelmed within me; my heart within me is distressed" (Psalm 143:4). I refuse to let my life be brought down by negative emotions such as these. I know You have a better quality of life for me than that. When I am tempted to give in to them, show me Your truth.

You have said in Your Word that by our patience we can possess our souls (Luke 21:19). Give me patience so that I can do that. Help me to keep my "heart with all diligence," for I know that "out of it spring the issues of life" (Proverbs 4:23). Help me to not be insecure and self-focused so that I miss opportunities to focus on You and extend Your love. May I be sensitive to the needs, trials, and weaknesses of others and not oversensitive to myself.

What You accomplished on the cross is my source of greatest joy. Help me to concentrate on that.

"The enemy has persecuted my soul; he has crushed my life to the ground; he has made me dwell in darkness, like those who have long been dead. Therefore my spirit is overwhelmed within me; my heart within me is distressed. I remember the days of old; I meditate on all Your works; I muse on the work of Your hands. I spread out my hands to You; my soul longs for You like a thirsty land. Answer me speedily, O LORD; my spirit fails! Do not hide Your face from me, lest I be like those who go down into the pit. Cause me to hear Your lovingkindness in the morning, for in You do I trust; cause me to know the way in which I should walk, for I lift up my soul to You" (Psalm 143:3-8). Thank You, Lord, that in my distress I can call on You. And when I cry out to You, Lord, You hear my voice and answer (Psalm 18:6). May the joy of knowing You fill my heart with happiness and peace.

❧ GOD'S PROMISES TO ME ❧

Be anxious for nothing, but in everything by prayer and supplication, with thanksgiving, let your requests be made known to God; and the peace of God, which surpasses all understanding, will guard your hearts and minds through Christ Jesus.
PHILIPPIANS 4:6-7

Then they cried out to the LORD in their trouble, and He saved them out of their distresses. He brought them out of darkness and the shadow of death, and broke their chains in pieces.
PSALM 107:13-14

Come to Me, all you who labor and are heavy laden,
and I will give you rest. Take My yoke upon you and
learn from Me, for I am gentle and lowly in heart,
and you will find rest for your souls. For My yoke is
easy and My burden is light.

MATTHEW 11:28-30

The righteous cry out, and the LORD hears, and
delivers them out of all their troubles. The LORD is
near to those who have a broken heart,
and saves such as have a contrite spirit.

PSALM 34:17-18

Those who wait on the LORD shall renew their
strength; they shall mount up with wings like eagles,
they shall run and not be weary, they
shall walk and not faint.

ISAIAH 40:31

CHAPTER TWENTY-ONE

Lord, Comfort Me in Times of Trouble

E very time I take off in an airplane on a gray, dreary, rainy day, I'm always amazed at how we can fly right up through the dark wet clouds, so thick that we can't see one thing out the window, and then suddenly rise above it all and have the ability to see for miles. Up there the sky is sunny, clear, and blue. I keep forgetting that no matter how bad the weather gets, it's possible to rise above the storm to a place where everything is fine.

Our spiritual and emotional lives are much the same. When the dark clouds of trial, struggle, grief, or suffering roll in and settle on us so thick that we can barely see ahead of us, it's easy to forget there is a place of calm, light, clarity, and peace we can rise to. If we take God's hand in those difficult times, He will lift us up above our circumstances to the place of comfort, warmth, and safety He has for us.

One of my favorite names for the Holy Spirit is the Comforter (John 14:26 ASV). Just as we don't have to beg the sun for light, we don't have to beg the Holy Spirit for comfort either. He *is* comfort. We simply have to separate ourselves from anything that separates us from Him. We have to pray that when we go through difficult times, He will give us a greater sense of His comfort in it.

Tough times happen to everyone at one time or another. Pain and loss are a part of life. There are many different reasons why these things occur, but God is always there to bring good out of it when we invite Him to. If we understand the different possibilities for our suffering, it will help us overcome our pain and see our faith grow in the midst of it.

Four Good Reasons for Difficult Times

1. *Sometimes difficult things happen to us so that the glory and power of God can be revealed in and through us.* When Jesus passed by a man who was born blind, His disciples asked Him if the man's blindness was because he had sinned or because his parents had sinned. Jesus replied, "Neither this man nor his parents sinned, but that the works of God should be revealed in him" (John 9:3). We may not be able to understand why certain things are happening at the time, and we may never know why we have to go through them until we go to be with the Lord, but when we turn to God in the midst of difficult situations, God's glory will be seen in them and on you.

2. *God uses difficult times to purify us.* The Bible says, "Since Christ suffered for us in the flesh, arm yourselves also with the same mind, for he who has suffered in the flesh has ceased from sin" (1 Peter 4:1). This means our suffering during difficult times will burn sin and selfishness out of our lives. God allows suffering to happen so that we will learn to live for Him and not for ourselves. So that we will pursue His will and not our own. It's not pleasant at the time, but God's desire is "that we may be partakers of His holiness" (Hebrews 12:10). He wants us to let go of the things we lust after and cling to what is most important in life—Him.

3. *Sometimes our misery is caused by God disciplining us.*
"No chastening seems to be joyful for the present, but
painful; nevertheless, afterward it yields the peaceable fruit
of righteousness to those who have been trained by it" (Hebrews 12:11). The fruit that this godly disciplining and
pruning produces in us is worth the trouble we have to go
through to get it, and we have to be careful not to resist it
or hate it. "Do not despise the chastening of the LORD, nor
be discouraged when you are rebuked by Him; for whom the
LORD loves He chastens, and scourges every son whom He
receives" (Hebrews 12:5-6).

4. *Sometimes we are caught in the midst of the enemy's
work.* It's the enemy's delight to make you miserable and try
to destroy your life. Often the reason for the anguish,
sorrow, sadness, grief, or pain you feel is entirely his doing
and no fault of your own or anyone else's. Your comfort is in
knowing that as you praise God in the midst of it, He will
defeat the enemy and bring good out of it that you can't
even fathom. He wants you to walk with Him in faith as He
leads you through it, and He will teach you to trust Him in
the midst of it.

None of us wants to hear about how good pain and suffering are for us. When we're in the midst of trouble,
tragedy, loss, devastation, or disappointment, we hurt ter-
ribly and find it impossible to think beyond the pain. But
the Holy Spirit is there to help us. In other translations of
the Bible, He is called the Helper. Jesus said, "I will pray the
Father, and He will give you another Helper, that He may
abide with you forever—the Spirit of truth" (John 14:16-
17). When we turn to the Holy Spirit for help and comfort,
He will not only give us aid, but He will give us a richer portion of His presence than we have ever had before. We will

be blessed when we mourn, because it will be the Comforter who comforts us (Matthew 5:4).

When my friend died of breast cancer a number of years ago, I was devastated with grief. We had been best friends since high school, and I didn't know how I could survive the loss. The day after the funeral was the worst pain of all. Reality set in and I couldn't stop crying. Plus, along with my six- and ten-year-old children, I now had her eight-year-old son to care for too. I asked God to lift me out of my grief so I could function well enough to help him cope with his loss. God answered that prayer every day as I turned to Him for strength and comfort.

Every time you rise above the pain in your life and find the goodness, clarity, peace, and light of the Lord there, your faith will increase. God will meet you in the midst of your pain and not only perfect you, but increase your compassion for the sufferings of others. As you continue to live in the presence of the Lord, His glory will be revealed in you.

My Prayer to God

Lord, help me to remember that no matter how dark my situation may become, You are the light of my life and can never be put out. No matter what dark clouds settle on my life, You will lift me above the storm and into the comfort of Your presence. Only You can take whatever loss I experience and fill that empty place with good. Only You can take the burden of my grief and pain and dry my tears. "Hear me when I call, O God of my righteousness! You have relieved me in my distress; have mercy on me, and hear my prayer" (Psalm 4:1).

In times of grief, suffering, or trial, I pray for an added sense of Your presence. I want to grow stronger in these times and not weaker. I want to increase in faith and not be overcome with doubt. I want to have hope in the midst of it and not surrender to hopelessness. I want to stand strong in Your truth and not be swept away by my emotions.

Thank You that I do not have to be afraid of bad news because my heart is steadfast, trusting in You (Psalm 112:7). Thank You that "You have delivered my soul from death, my eyes from tears, and my feet from falling" (Psalm 116:8). Thank You that I walk before You with hope in my heart and life in my body. Thank You that "I shall not die, but live, and declare the works of the LORD" (Psalm 118:17). Even when "my soul melts from heaviness," I pray that You would "strengthen me according to Your word" (Psalm 119:28).

Help me to remember to give thanks to You in all things, knowing that You reign in the midst of them. Remind me that You have redeemed me and I am Yours and nothing is more important than that. I know when I pass through the waters You will be with me and the river will not overflow me. When I walk through the fire I will not be burned, nor will the flame touch me (Isaiah 43:1-2). That's because You are a good God and have sent Your Holy Spirit to comfort and help me. I pray that You, O God of hope, will fill me with all joy and peace and faith so that I will "abound in hope by the power of the Holy Spirit" (Romans 15:13). Thank You that You have sent Your Holy Spirit to be my Comforter and Helper. Remind me of that in the midst of difficult times.

❧ GOD'S PROMISES TO ME ❧

Beloved, do not think it strange concerning the fiery
trial which is to try you, as though some strange
thing happened to you; but rejoice to the extent that
you partake of Christ's sufferings, that when His glory
is revealed, you may also be glad with exceeding joy.
1 PETER 4:12-13

May the God of all grace, who called us to His
eternal glory by Christ Jesus, after you have suffered a
while, perfect, establish, strengthen, and settle you.
1 PETER 5:10

Wait on the LORD; be of good courage, and He shall
strengthen your heart; wait, I say, on the LORD!
PSALM 27:14

Blessed are the poor in spirit, for theirs
is the kingdom of heaven.
Blessed are those who mourn,
for they shall be comforted.
MATTHEW 5:3-4

The LORD shall preserve your going out and
your coming in from this time forth,
and even forevermore.
PSALM 121:8

CHAPTER TWENTY-TWO

Lord, Enable Me to Resist the Temptation to Sin

Why would a young man with everything going for him want to risk losing it all? One particular man I know of had good looks, musical talent, courage, wealth, prominence, authority, a wife, and God's favor. In addition to all this, he had single-handedly defeated one of the worst enemy threats to his nation's military. Yet he fell into temptation and succumbed to it with sin on top of sin.

King David obviously had too much time on his hands *and* he wasn't where he was supposed to be. He was out on the roof of his palace watching the woman next door take a bath instead of going to war with his men the way other kings did. His biggest mistake was not that he fell into temptation, for that can happen to anyone, but that he didn't turn away from it and run to God in repentance immediately. He stayed and stared. He thought and schemed. He let his lust rule him instead of his God. As a result, he became a murderer and an adulterer and ended up paying for it for the rest of his life—even to the point of witnessing the death of his own son.

Temptation happened to Jesus, too. But He did the right thing and David did not. David went with the lust of his flesh and Jesus didn't. Jesus stood strong in the Word of God and David forgot about it.

I have lived long enough, and I'm sure you have too, to have seen far too many people—men and women both—sacrifice their lives by giving in to temptation. There are many kinds of temptation, just as there are many kinds of sin. The one that seems to trip people up most often is sexual temptation. I have seen talented people succumb to sexual temptation and forfeit the promising life God had for them. They fell like meteors and burned themselves out when they could have been a shining star today. Even though they have been redeemed and restored, I have never seen them regain the anointing and glory of God that was once upon them.

When people fall into adultery, the life they *would* have had is forever sacrificed. Of course, when they repent they can receive forgiveness and be restored, but they have lost what *would* have been had this sin never happened. David was forgiven and restored, but he lost the thing he loved most—his son—and his reign was marred from that point on with one disaster after another, including the destruction of many of his beloved family members. God still loved him, but his sin still had consequences. People don't realize how much they lose when they give in to sexual temptation. Their light never shines as brightly as it would have if they had not given in to the lust of their flesh.

From the volumes of mail I receive I know that improper attraction to a person of the opposite sex is the biggest temptation for many men and women. Often it is not acted upon, but it is still entertained in the mind. And sins of the mind have serious consequences too. Sexual sin begins with thoughts such as, "This is the person of my dreams, never mind that he (she) is married and I am married." "This must be right or I wouldn't feel so good doing it." "I deserve to have what I want." "No one will ever know." "This must be fate."

Don't let the devil rob you of all God has for you by tempting you with impure thoughts. It's okay to appreciate a man's talents, godliness, brilliance, or appearance, but unless you are married to him, remember that he is your brother in the Lord. If you ever find yourself with any kind of unholy attraction, confess it immediately before God and ask Him to set you free from it. Then tell Satan that you recognize his plan to destroy you and separate you from all God has for you, and you are not going to allow him to do it. Fast and pray if you have to in order to break down that stronghold. Don't let up until it's gone. "Watch and pray, lest you enter into temptation. The spirit indeed is willing, but the flesh is weak" (Matthew 26:41). The more you have been given, the more you will be approached by the enemy who will try to take it away from you. Be ready for him with a full knowledge of the Word of God.

Six Good Things to Remember About Temptation

1. *Who:* Temptation can happen to anyone. No matter how spiritual and solid you think you are, you can fall into temptation. The people I have seen who fell the hardest were those who were prideful about what good Christians they were. They bragged about their spiritual strength and godliness, and yet they fell the hardest and without repentance. We can't let spiritual pride be our downfall.

2. *What:* You can be tempted by anything. The most common temptation today is sexual because the opportunity for it is everywhere. But there are other kinds of lust as

well. Money tempts us. Power tempts us. Desire tempts us. "Each one is tempted when he is drawn away by his own desires and enticed. Then, when desire has conceived, it gives birth to sin; and sin, when it is full-grown, brings forth death. Do not be deceived, my beloved brethren" (James 1:14-16). The enemy will tempt you in the way you are most susceptible. Whatever your flesh lusts after, ask God to give you the strength to resist it. Guard your vulnerable areas with prayer.

3. *When:* Temptation can happen any time and often when you least expect it and are most susceptible. When it does happen, the danger is in thinking you can handle it alone. It's best to take it to God and confess it immediately, and then find someone trustworthy to pray with you about it. Don't think it will just pass. The risk is too great. Treat it as a serious threat no matter when it happens.

4. *Where:* Temptation can happen anywhere. In church, at work, at home, on a bus or plane. It will happen in the place you least expect it. Wherever it is, separate yourself from it immediately. If chocolate tempts you, don't hang out in the candy store. The smell of it will drive you crazy and weaken your resistance. If a certain man tempts you, don't be around him. Or if you must, don't be alone with him. Separate yourself from the temptation and ask God to kill that lust in you.

5. *Why:* The reason the enemy tempts you is because he knows of the great things God wants to do in your life, and he thinks you are dumb enough to give it all up for a few moments of pleasure. He knows that not only do *you* stand to lose from it, but other people will be hurt by your sin as well. So he has the potential for multiple victories. When you see his trap, tell him you are not going to allow him to destroy your life or anyone else's.

6. *How:* You have to remember that no matter how you are being tempted, it is a set-up by the enemy intended to bring you down. He will find your weakness, need, or insecurity and tempt you with whatever you are most easily tempted. This is the best reason to get rid of all insecurities and become whole people. It eliminates one of the ways the enemy has access to our lives.

The best time to pray about temptation is *before* you fall into it. After the lure presents itself, resisting temptation becomes much more difficult. The model prayer Jesus taught us to pray as a matter of course is a good place to start. "Do not lead us into temptation, but deliver us from the evil one" (Matthew 6:13). We can also do as Jesus did and rebuke the enemy with God's Word. We can "stand fast therefore in the liberty by which Christ has made us free, and do not be entangled again with a yoke of bondage" (Galatians 5:1). We can call on the name of the Lord "for in that He Himself has suffered, being tempted, He is able to aid those who are tempted" (Hebrews 2:18).

Don't ever think you are immune to temptation. The older you get, the more you are a target. Many people fail when they get older because they think they can get away with it. You don't want to be the kind of person who believes for a while and in time of temptation falls away (Luke 8:13). Jesus instructed His disciples to "rise and pray, lest you enter into temptation." You must do the same.

Jesus' temptation happened just before the greatest breakthrough in His life and ministry. It will happen before the greatest breakthrough in yours too. Be ready for it. And remember that no matter how great the temptation is you face, "He who is in you is greater than he who is in the world" (1 John 4:4). You have the power to overcome it.

My Prayer to God

Lord, help me to be strong in my mind and spirit so I don't fall into any traps of the enemy. Do not allow me to be led into temptation, but deliver me from the evil one and his plans for my downfall. The area I am most concerned about is (name any area where you might be tempted). In the name of Jesus, I break any hold temptation has on me. Keep me strong and able to resist anything that would tempt me away from all You have for me.

I pray I will have no secret thoughts where I entertain ungodly desires to do or say something I shouldn't. I pray that I will have no secret life where I do things I would be ashamed to have others see. I don't want to have fellowship with unfruitful works of darkness. Help me, instead, to expose them (Ephesians 5:11). Make straight paths for my feet (Hebrews 12:13). Don't allow the enemy to sneak up on my blind side and take me by surprise.

I know You are "not the author of confusion but of peace" (1 Corinthians 14:33). Help me not to fall into any confusion about this. Help me to hide Your Word in my heart so I will see clearly and not sin against You in any way (Psalm 119:11). By the power of Your Spirit in me, I will not allow sin to reign in me or draw me to obey its lusts (Romans 6:12).

Thank You, Lord, that You are near to all who call upon You, and You will fulfill the desire of those who fear You. Thank You that You hear my cries and will save me from any weakness that could lead me away from all You have for me (Psalm 145:18-19). Thank You that You know "how to deliver the godly out of temptations" (2 Peter 2:9). Thank You that You will deliver me out of all temptation and keep it far from me.

⪦ GOD'S PROMISES TO ME ⪧

Blessed is the man who endures temptation;
for when he has been approved, he will receive
the crown of life which the Lord has
promised to those who love Him.
JAMES 1:12

No temptation has overtaken you except such as is
common to man; but God is faithful, who will not
allow you to be tempted beyond what you are able,
but with the temptation will also make the way
of escape, that you may be able to bear it.
1 CORINTHIANS 10:13

Let us lay aside every weight, and the sin which so
easily ensnares us, and let us run with endurance the
race that is set before us, looking unto Jesus, the
author and finisher of our faith, who for the joy that
was set before Him endured the cross, despising the
shame, and has sat down at the right hand
of the throne of God.
HEBREWS 12:1-2

My brethren, count it all joy when you fall into
various trials, knowing that the testing of your
faith produces patience. But let patience have its
perfect work, that you may be perfect and
complete, lacking nothing.
JAMES 1:2-4

Therefore let him who thinks he stands
take heed lest he fall.
1 CORINTHIANS 10:12

CHAPTER TWENTY-THREE

Lord, Heal Me and Help Me Care for My Body

almost died two years ago. I had been extremely sick in my abdominal area for months, and I was in and out of different emergency rooms and hospitals, seeing different doctors and specialists, but none of these people could find anything wrong with me. All the tests came back proving I was as healthy as I could possibly be. No one could figure out why I was so miserable.

In the middle of the most awful night I have ever experienced in my life, I felt something explode in my body so violently that I knew I would die if I didn't get help. My husband rushed me to the hospital at 3:30 in the morning because I didn't have time to wait for an ambulance. But then I laid in the emergency room for hours begging someone to help me and telling people I was going to die if somebody didn't do something soon. I was given all the same tests they had given me many times before, and still no one could find anything wrong with me.

My husband prayed for me continually, and when my sister, Susan, and my close friend, Roz, arrived at the hospital, they prayed for me too. They called other people to pray that someone would figure out what was wrong and do something. I couldn't pray anything for myself except, "Help me, Jesus."

At one point I said to God, "Is this my time to die?" But I did not sense God saying that it was. In fact, I felt Him say there were things He still had for me to do.

It wasn't until eight hours after I was brought in to the hospital that a specialist called a surgeon in who was brave enough to say, "I can't tell what's wrong with you by any of the tests, but I believe your appendix has ruptured. I am going to take you into surgery immediately, and if I'm wrong I'll find out what the problem is."

As it turned out, he was right. After the surgery the doctor said, "In another hour you would have gone into a toxic-shock coma, and I could not have saved your life." I knew God had answered our prayers for healing and this surgeon was an important part of that answer.

For the next two weeks, I was hooked up to tubes and a machine and endured pain that made childbirth seem pleasant. Even constant morphine couldn't take it all away. When the doctor came to check on me one morning, I asked him why this had happened.

"Did I do something wrong?" I asked. "Did I take too many vitamins? Did I take too few? Did I take the wrong ones? Did I not exercise enough? Or too much? I have always tried to take good care of myself. Could I have done something differently to avoid this?"

"You couldn't have done anything to prevent this," he replied. "It's probably genetic and runs in your family."

He was right again. There were many people in my family who had experienced this same problem, only at a much younger age than I. In fact, I thought nothing like this would happen to me because I had passed the age when it occurred in other family members. I realized that no matter how hard we try to do the right thing, we can't always prevent bad things from happening in our body. We should do the best we can to take care of ourselves, but we will still always need God to be our Healer.

Two Separate Issues

Healing and body care are two different things. When you ask God to heal you, this is something *He* does. Taking care of your body is something *you* do. Both are vitally important.

God knows we are a fallen race and can't do everything perfectly. That's why He sent Jesus to be our Healer. But He also calls us to be good stewards over everything He gives us, including our body. He wants us to live in balance and temperance and to take care not to abuse our body in any way. He wants us to glorify Him in the care of our bodies because we are the temple of His Holy Spirit.

Many of us tend to think, "Everything I have is the Lord's, except for my eating and exercise habits. Those are mine." Or we think, "My life is the Lord's, but my body belongs to me, and I can do with it whatever feels good." But when we are the Lord's, our body has to be surrendered to Him just like everything else. Caring for our body is not something we can do successfully independent of God.

The motivation for what we do in the area of body care is very important. It will effect how successful we are. If we eat right and exercise merely to look great in our clothes, it won't be enough to sustain us as we get older. But if we eat right and engage in proper exercise for the purpose of being a more vital, healthy, energetic, and useful servant of the Lord, this has eternal consequences and you are more likely to stick with it.

I've actually heard people say, "I don't worry about taking care of my body because the Lord can just heal me when I get sick." This kind of presumptuous thinking is dangerous and can get us into trouble. Satan's plan for our lives is to do the very thing that will hurt us the most. We help him along by that kind of attitude. We sabotage our lives by not doing what's best for bodies and our health. Ask God to help you resist what is bad for you and to be disciplined enough to do what's right. God loves and values you. He created you. You are where His Holy Spirit dwells. He wants you to love and value yourself enough to take good care of your body.

In Touch with the Healer

In spite of all our best efforts, however, we can still get sick. We can do everything we know to do and still become seriously ill. That's because through no fault of our own we inherit predispositions or weaknesses from our ancestors. We can be exposed to things we aren't even aware of at the time that cause horrific diseases. We can have accidents. God knew all this, and so He sent Jesus as our Healer. His healing touch is God's mercy to us.

In the Bible, people who simply *touched* Jesus were healed. "Wherever He entered, into villages, cities, or in the country, they laid the sick in the marketplaces, and begged Him that they might just touch the hem of His garment. And as many as touched Him were made well" (Mark 6:56). We, too, must touch Him to find healing. The way we touch Him is to spend time in His presence. Ask God to heal you, and then trust Him to do it *His* way and in *His* time. Partner with God in the care of your body, knowing that, although you are the caregiver, He is the Healer.

My Prayer to God

Lord, I thank You that You are the Healer. I look to You for my healing whenever I am injured or sick. I pray that You would strengthen and heal me today. Specifically I pray for (name any area where you need the Lord to heal you). Heal me "that it might be fulfilled which was spoken by Isaiah the prophet, saying: 'He Himself took our infirmities and bore our sicknesses'" (Matthew 8:17). You suffered, died, and were buried for me so that I might have healing, forgiveness, and eternal life. By Your stripes I am healed (1 Peter 2:24). I know that in Your presence is where I will find healing. In Your presence I can reach out and touch You and in turn be touched by You.

Only You know what is best for me and what is not, so I ask that You would reveal that to me. Take away all confusing and conflicting information, and instruct me in what to eat and what to avoid. I can't do this without You, Lord, for only You know the way You created me. Give me a solid ability to be disciplined about what I eat and drink and how I exercise. Enable me to discipline my body and bring it into subjection (1 Corinthians 9:27).

Lord, You have said in Your Word, "My people are destroyed for lack of knowledge" (Hosea 4:6). I don't want to be destroyed because I lacked knowledge of the right thing to do. Teach me and help me learn. Lead me to people who can help or advise me. Enable me to follow their suggestions and directions. When I am sick and need to see a doctor, show me which doctor to see and give that doctor wisdom as to how to treat me.

The area I struggle with most in caring for my body is (name the area that presents the greatest challenge to you). Be Lord over this part of my life so that I can bring it into alignment with Your will. Help me to find freedom and deliverance in this area where it is needed.

Lord, I want everything I do to be glorifying to You. Help me to be a good steward of the body You have given me. I confess the times I have sat in judgment upon it, criticizing it in my mind for not being perfect. I repent of that and ask Your forgiveness. I know that my body is the temple of Your Holy Spirit, who dwells in me. Help me to fully understand this truth so that I will keep my temple clean and healthy. Help me not to mistreat my body in any way. Teach me how to properly care for my health.

❧ GOD'S PROMISES TO ME ❧

Is anyone among you sick? Let him call for the
elders of the church, and let them pray over him,
anointing him with oil in the name of the Lord.
And the prayer of the faith will save the sick,
and the Lord will raise him up. And if he has
committed sins, he will be forgiven. Confess your
trespasses to one another, and pray for one another,
that you may be healed. The effective, fervent
prayer of a righteous man avails much.

JAMES 5:14-16

Heal me, O LORD, and I shall be healed;
save me, and I shall be saved,
for You are my praise.
JEREMIAH 17:14

"I will restore health to you and heal you of your
wounds," says the LORD.
JEREMIAH 30:17

Therefore, whether you eat or drink,
or whatever you do, do all to the glory of God.
1 CORINTHIANS 10:31

For we know that if our earthly house, this tent, is
destroyed, we have a building from God, a house not
made with hands, eternal in the heavens.
2 CORINTHIANS 5:1

CHAPTER TWENTY-FOUR

Lord, Free Me from Ungodly Fear

For years I couldn't take a shower without being afraid. That's because all the frightening images from the film *Psycho* kept coming back to terrify me. I had seen that film when I was young, and my shower experiences were ruined from that point on. It wasn't until I received the Lord and someone prayed for me to be delivered from fear that I was actually able to close my eyes in the shower and enjoy the water.

There were many other things I was afraid of too, such as dying, starving, failing, flying, accidents, needles, knives, getting lost, being abandoned, getting sick, being injured, the dark, the unknown, people's opinions, and being rejected. But God healed me from every one of these fears. Some I prayed about specifically. Some just went away as I learned to walk with the Lord and spend time in His love and His presence.

God does not want us to live in fear. Fear does not come from Him. It's the world that teaches us to fear. The things we see in movies, videos, newspapers, and books make us afraid. The things we hear people say and see them do causes us to have fear. The enemy can make us afraid of everything, including our future. It wears us down worrying that something we fear is going to happen. But we don't have to be tormented by fear.

Ungodly Fear

There are two kinds of fear: godly and ungodly. We must pray that we live in godly fear, which is good, and not give place to ungodly fear, which is torment. One of the most common types of ungodly fear is the fear of man, or a fear of rejection. It's a trap we can fall into without ever realizing it. In order to protect ourselves from it, we have to care more about what God says than what anyone else says. We must look to Him for approval and acceptance and not to people. If God does not have first place in our hearts, we are constantly fearing man. "The fear of man brings a snare, but whoever trusts in the LORD shall be safe" (Proverbs 29:25).

There are so many things to be afraid of in this world. Sometimes all it takes is one news report to fill us with fear. Our imaginations alone can frighten us. But God wants to set us free from all fear for all time.

Four Good Ways to Get Rid of Ungodly Fear

1. *Get rid of ungodly fear by praying.* The Bible says that when we are afraid it's because we have not been made perfect in love. "There is no fear in love; but perfect love casts out fear, because fear involves torment. But he who fears has not been made perfect in love" (1 John 4:18). The only love that is perfect is the love of God. The way you get perfected in His love is to draw close to Him and let Him fill you with His love. When you do, He will deliver you from all fear.

2. *Get rid of ungodly fear by controlling what you receive into your mind.* The things of the world often make us afraid.

What kind of input are you receiving from the world? Is any of it causing fear in you? How could you change that? Do you go to scary movies or watch frightening television shows? Read the Word instead. If watching the news scares you, either don't watch it or use it as a time to pray for the people and situations you hear about in it. Do whatever you can to stay close to God (for instance, you could play worship music or sing praise songs). Fear disappears in the presence of the Lord.

3. *Get rid of ungodly fear by being in the Word of God.* Many times in my life when I was afraid, I found that all fear left me just from reading the Bible. Knowing what God's Word says about our fear and the promises He has given us can make all the difference. And in the face of fear, speaking the Word out loud is a powerful weapon against it. You don't even have to be reading or speaking Scriptures specifically about fear. Reading anywhere in the Bible can take away fear, because the Spirit of the Lord can be found on every page.

4. *Get rid of ungodly fear by living in the fear of the Lord.* The more you get to know the Lord and understand who He is, the more you will reverence Him and fear His displeasure. This is called the fear of the Lord, and it makes you want to obey Him. It's what draws you closer to God and increases your longing for more of Him. It makes you forget all the things that cause you fear, because they pale in comparison to His awesome power. When you have the fear of the Lord, you fear what your life would be like without Him.

Godly Fear

Noah is a good example of godly fear. The reason he spent all that time preparing the ark for the coming flood was because he had the fear of the Lord. "By faith Noah, being divinely warned of things not yet seen, moved with godly fear, prepared an ark for the saving of his household, by which he condemned the world and became heir of the righteousness which is according to faith" (Hebrews 11:7). People laughed and made fun of him while he was building the ark, but he believed God, and he cared more about what God said than what man said. And it ended up saving his life. The best thing you can do is to "fear God and keep His commandments, for this is man's all" (Ecclesiastes 12:13). It will save your life too.

Seven Good Things That Come from Fearing God

1. *The blessing of God's provision.* "Oh, fear the LORD, you His saints! There is no want to those who fear Him" (Psalm 34:9).

2. *The blessing of God's protection.* "The fear of the Lord leads to life, and he who has it will abide in satisfaction; he will not be visited with evil" (Proverbs 19:23).

3. *The blessing of God's mercy.* "For as the heavens are high above the earth, so great is His mercy toward those who fear Him" (Psalm 103:11).

4. *The blessing of God's goodness.* "Oh, how great is Your goodness, which You have laid up for those who fear You, which You have prepared for those who trust in You in the presence of the sons of men!" (Psalm 31:19).

5. *The blessing of God's abundance.* "By humility and the fear of the LORD are riches and honor and life" (Proverbs 22:4).

6. *The blessing of God's response.* "He will fulfill the desire of those who fear Him; He also will hear their cry and save them" (Psalm 145:19).

7. *The blessing of God's freedom.* "By the fear of the LORD one departs from evil" (Proverbs 16:6).

God has secrets. It's not that He doesn't want you to know these things, it's that He wants you to get close to Him and find out. "The secret of the LORD is with those who fear Him, and He will show them His covenant" (Psalm 25:14). God wants you to walk with Him and talk with Him and have the kind of relationship with Him where He shares Himself with you and tells you things you didn't know before and wouldn't know unless He revealed them to you. When you get close enough and quiet enough, He will whisper a secret to your heart and it will change your life. In that moment, all your fear will be gone. Ask God to speak to you today.

My Prayer to God

Lord, You are my light and my salvation. You are the strength of my life. Of whom, then, shall I be afraid? Even though an entire army may surround me and go to war against me, my heart will not fear (Psalm 27:1-3). I will be strong and of good courage, for I know that You are with me wherever I go (Joshua 1:9). Free me from all ungodly fear, for I know that fear is never of You.

Guard my heart and mind from the spirit of fear. What I am afraid of today is (name anything that causes you to have fear). Take that fear and replace it with Your perfect love. If I have any thoughts in my mind that are fueled by fear, reveal them to me. If I have gotten my mind off of You and on my circumstances, help me to reverse that process so that my mind is off my circumstances and on You. Show me where I allow fear to take root and help me to put a stop to it. Take away any fear of rejection and all fear of man from within me and replace it with the fear of the Lord.

Your Word says that You will put fear in the hearts of Your people and You will not turn away from doing them good (Jeremiah 32:40). I pray that You would do that for me. I know that You have not given me a spirit of fear, so I reject that and instead claim the power, love, and sound mind You have for me. "Oh, how great is Your goodness, which You have laid up for those who fear You" (Psalm 31:19). Because I have received a kingdom which cannot be shaken, may I have grace by which to serve You acceptably with reverence and godly fear all the days of my life (Hebrews 12:28).

Thank You that "the fear of the LORD leads to life, and he who has it will abide in satisfaction; he will not be visited with evil" (Proverbs 19:23). Help me to grow in fear and reverence of You so that I may please You and escape the plans of evil for my life. Thank You that those who fear You will never lack any good thing.

❧ GOD'S PROMISES TO ME ❧

God has not given us a spirit of fear, but of power and of love and of a sound mind.
2 TIMOTHY 1:7

There is no fear in love; but perfect love casts out fear, because fear involves torment. But he who fears has not been made perfect in love.
1 JOHN 4:18

Teach me Your way, O LORD; I will walk in Your
truth; unite my heart to fear Your name.
PSALM 86:11

Then they will call on me, but I will not answer;
they will seek me diligently, but they will not find
me. Because they hated knowledge and did not
choose the fear of the LORD.
PROVERBS 1:28,29

Yes, if you cry out for discernment, and lift up your
voice for understanding, if you seek her as silver, and
search for her as for hidden treasures; then you
will understand the fear of the LORD, and find
the knowledge of God.
PROVERBS 2:3-5

CHAPTER TWENTY-FIVE

Lord, Use Me to Touch the Lives of Others

*D*uring the months when I was writing *The Power of a Praying Wife*, I felt led by the Holy Spirit to pray something I had never prayed before. I have always asked God to help me write every book, but this time in addition to that I felt led by the Spirit to pray that this would be a breakthrough book in terms of how many people it would reach. I had written three books previously and had never thought to pray that way. I shared what I was feeling with my prayer group, and they were in complete agreement. Together we prayed that God would take this book to the ends of the earth and see that it was translated into many other languages. I could hardly believe I was asking God for something so grand, but I felt with all my heart this was exactly the way God wanted us to pray. We prayed that prayer every week until long after the book was published.

Over the next several years, publishers from different countries around the world wrote to ask for permission to translate the book in their nation's language and publish it. Soon copies of my book arrived at my door that were translated into French, German, Portuguese, Nigerian, Indian,

Dutch, Hungarian, Korean, Spanish, Japanese, Indonesian, and Afrikaans. Each time my heart leaped with joy that God had answered my prayer so powerfully.

One day I received a box of my books that had been translated into Chinese, and I broke down and cried. It was something I never dreamed possible. I could picture all these precious Chinese women, whom I would never meet, reading this book and learning to pray for their families. There was no way I could physically travel all over the world to reach this many people in all these different countries, and I knew I would never get to China. But the message God had given me would. These people will never know me, but they will know God better.

What a powerful answer to prayer. The members of my prayer group and I have spoken many times about the first day we prayed that prayer and what God has done in response to it. Since then, with each book I have written I have prayed, "God, use me to touch the lives of others around the world with Your love, mercy, hope, and truth." You can pray that prayer too, and God will use your abilities and talents to touch others powerfully. When your heart is to give to others from what God has given to you, He will enable you to do that.

Giving to God and to other people is such a vitally important part of our life on this earth that we can never achieve all we want to see happen in our lives if we're not doing that. It's a major factor in realizing the complete purposes of God for us. We can never be truly whole and fulfilled or find any lasting peace unless we are giving to others. We release the flow of God's blessings *to* us by letting them flow *through* us. Giving to God and to others creates a vacuum into which God pours more blessings. If we stop up that flow, we stop up our lives. We must pray that God will show us how give and enable us to do it.

The Gift of Prayer

Many people have written to me and told me how my books have helped save their marriages, their children, or their lives. They asked what they could do for me in return. I always respond by saying, "The greatest thing you can do for me is to pray for me. Pray for my protection, my health, my family, and my marriage. Pray for me to have a clear mind and be able to write books that will draw people to the Lord so He can transform their lives." There is no greater gift I can receive than someone's prayers. I believe the prayers of thousands of people saved my life when I was in the hospital. If you were one of them, I am eternally grateful. I felt your prayers, and they are the reason I am alive today.

Prayer is the greatest gift we can give to anyone. Of course, if someone needs food, clothes, and a place to live, those needs must be met. But in giving that way, we can't neglect to pray for them as well. Material things are temporary, but our prayers for another person can affect them for a lifetime.

We can never move into all God has for us until we first move into intercessory prayer. This is one part of our calling that we have in common, because we are *all* called to intercede for others. God wants us to love others enough to lay down our lives for them in prayer.

On September 11, intercessors began immediately to pray for the people involved in the tragedies in New York City, Pennsylvania, and Washington, D.C. Then from all over the United States people drove to New York City because they wanted to help. They stood in line to give blood.

They gave money to bereaved families. Everyone did what they could, but it all started with prayer. "Let us not love in word or in tongue, but in deed and in truth" (1 John 3:18). If you love God, you will love people and it will motivate you to do whatever you can to help them. Prayer is a good place to start.

God wants us to give to others. He says if we don't help others in need, we don't really love Him. "But whoever has this world's goods, and sees his brother in need, and shuts up his heart from him, how does the love of God abide in him?" (1 John 3:17). "Let no one seek his own, but each one the other's well-being" (1 Corinthians 10:24). "He who has a generous eye will be blessed, for he gives of his bread to the poor" (Proverbs 22:9). The greatest blessings will come to you when you ask God to use you to touch the lives of others.

My Prayer to God

Lord, help me to serve You the way You want me to. Reveal to me any area of my life where I should be giving to someone right now. Open my eyes to see the need. Give me a generous heart to give to the poor. Help me to be a good steward of the blessings You have given me by sharing what I have with others. Show me whom You want me to extend my hand to at this time. Fill me with Your love for all people, and help me to communicate it in a way that can be clearly perceived. Use me to touch the lives of others with the hope that is in me.

Help me to give to You the way I should. I don't want to rob You of anything that is due You. Lord, I know that where my treasure is, there my heart will be also (Matthew 6:21). May my greatest treasure always be in serving You.

Lord, show me what You want me to do today to be a blessing to others around me. Specifically, show me how I can serve my family, my friends, my church, and the people whom You put in my life. I don't want to get so wrapped up in my own life that I don't see the opportunity for ministering Your life to others. Show me what You want me to do and enable me to do it. Give me all I need to minister life, hope, help, and healing to others. Make me to be one of Your faithful intercessors, and teach me how to pray in power. Help me to make a big difference in the world because You are working through me to touch the lives of others for Your glory.

❧ GOD'S PROMISES TO ME ❧

As each one has received a gift, minister it to one another, as good stewards of the manifold grace of God. If anyone speaks, let him speak as the oracles of God. If anyone ministers, let him do it as with the ability which God supplies, that in all things God may be glorified through Jesus Christ, to whom belongs the glory and the dominion forever and ever.

1 PETER 4:10-11

By this we know love, because He laid down His life for us. And we also ought to lay down our lives for the brethren.

1 JOHN 3:16

And let us not grow weary while doing good, for in due season we shall reap if we do not lose heart.

GALATIANS 6:9

Those who are wise shall shine like the brightness
of the firmament, and those who turn many to
righteousness like the stars forever and ever.
DANIEL 12:3

Most assuredly, I say to you, he who believes in Me,
the works that I do he will do also; and greater works
than these he will do, because I go to My Father.
And whatever you ask in My name, that I will do,
that the Father may be glorified in the Son. If you
ask anything in My name, I will do it.
JOHN 14:12-14

CHAPTER TWENTY-SIX

Lord, Train Me to Speak Only Words That Bring Life

When I was 14, I introduced a neighbor boy to one of my girlfriends as "Fat Mike." All the other kids called him "Fat Mike" to distinguish him from the other Mikes who weren't. The moment I did that, however, I saw a hurt look in his eyes, and I realized that this was not a name *he* called himself. I felt very bad about that because I never intended to hurt him. In fact, I thought Mike was good-looking, and I didn't find his being on the heavy side as unattractive. But he obviously did. I just thought this was a funny nickname that he was okay with. He obviously wasn't. I was too ignorant at the time to realize no one feels good about a name like that. And I was also too embarrassed and immature to apologize. I hoped that by pretending the entire incident didn't happen that he would forget about it and everything would be fine.

I moved away not long after that and never saw him again. I didn't think much about that incident until about 15 years later, after I became a believer. Wanting to be completely right with God and mend the past, I asked the Lord to bring to my mind anything I needed to be forgiven of so

I could confess it to Him. My mind was flooded with many memories of things I had done wrong, and one of them was my introduction of Mike. I felt terrible about my unintentionally cruel and thoughtless words and the damage they must have done. I couldn't believe that after all the times I had been hurt in my life by the callous comments of others, I had done the same thing to someone else. I asked God to forgive me for being so unloving and stupid.

If I could have found Mike and apologized to him in person, I would have. But I couldn't, so I tried to make it up to him by praying that God would bless his life in every way. I prayed that somehow the words I said would be retracted from his memory or at least lose their sting and he would be healed of any pain my comment must have caused him. I prayed he would be able to forgive me. I prayed I could forgive myself.

One of areas that can cause the greatest trouble in our lives is located on the face between the chin and the nose. With our mouth we can say things we shouldn't and end up hurting others and paying the consequences. I was paying the consequences for words I had said 15 years ago. We can't take our words back once we speak them. All we can do is apologize and hope to be forgiven by the offended party. The best way to make sure that what comes out of our mouth is good is to put thoughts in our heart that are good. "Out of the abundance of the heart the mouth speaks" (Matthew 12:34). If we fill our heart with God's truth and God's love, that's what will come out.

Have you ever been around someone who complains all the time or speaks negatively about themselves and others? Isn't it exhausting? Have you been with the kind of person who you never knew what horrible thing might come out of their mouth? You can hardly wait to get away from them.

The Bible says we are to "do all things without complaining and disputing" (Philippians 2:14). If we complain, it reflects our lack of faith in God. It proves that we don't believe God is in charge and can take care of us. It suggests that we don't trust God will answer prayer. It shows we are not praying. Being around people with such an obvious lack of faith is depleting.

Imagine if every time we opened our mouths we spoke words that were laced with healing, edification, encouragement, comfort, wisdom, love, and truth. That's possible to do if we ask God to help us. It's dangerous to speak whatever comes into your mind—unless what comes into your mind is good. If you have your mind fixed on good things, then the words of your mouth will reflect that.

Eight Good Things to Think About Daily
(From Philippians 4:8)

1. *Whatever things are true.* If you think about what is honest, genuine, authentic, sincere, faithful, accurate, and truthful, then you won't be saying anything false, incorrect, erroneous, deceitful, or untrue.

2. *Whatever things are noble.* If you think about what is admirable, high quality, excellent, magnanimous, superior, or honorable, then you won't be saying anything that is base, petty, mean, dishonorable, or low-minded.

3. *Whatever things are just.* If you think about what is fair, reasonable, equitable, proper, lawful, right, correct, deserved, upright, honorable, and seemly, then you won't be saying anything that is unjustified, biased, unreasonable, unlawful, or unfair.

4. *Whatever things are pure.* If you think about what is clean, clear, spotless, chaste, unsullied, undefiled, or untainted with evil, then you won't be saying anything that is

inferior, tainted, adulterated, defiled, polluted, corrupted, tarnished, or unholy.

5. *Whatever things are lovely.* If you think about what is pleasing, agreeable, charming, satisfying, or splendid, then you won't be saying anything that is unpleasant, offensive, disagreeable, revolting, unlovely, ominous, or ugly.

6. *Whatever things are of good report.* If you think about what is admirable, winsome, worthwhile, recommended, positive, or worthy of repeating, then you won't be saying anything that is negative, discouraging, undesirable, or full of bad news, gossip, and rumor.

7. *Whatever things are virtuous.* If you think about what is moral, ethical, upright, excellent, good, impressive, or conforming to high moral standards, then you won't be saying anything that is depraved, unethical, licentious, bad, self-indulgent, dissipated, evil, or immoral.

8. *Whatever things are praiseworthy.* If you think about what is laudable, admirable, commendable, valuable, acclaimed, applauded, glorified, exalted, honored, or approved of, then you won't be saying anything that is critical, condemning, deprecating, disapproving, disparaging, denouncing, belittling, or depressing.

When a Wise Woman Speaks

When a wise woman speaks, she gives a reason for the hope that is within her. The most important words we can speak are ones that explain our faith to anyone who asks or who will listen. We must be able to give a reason for the hope we have within us (1 Peter 3:15). We have to pray that God will help us become bold enough to clearly explain our faith in God. We have to ask God to help us tell others why we call Jesus our Messiah, why we can't live without the Holy Spirit, and why we choose to live God's way. And we must be able to do this in a manner that is loving and humble, otherwise we will alienate those whom God wants to draw to Himself. If the love of God and the testimony of His goodness are not in our heart, then they will not come out of our mouth. And what we say will not draw people to the Lord. It may, in fact, do the exact opposite.

When a wise woman speaks, she knows that timing is important. When things need to be said that are difficult for the hearer to receive, timing is everything. Certain words cannot be uttered with any success if the person listening is not open and ready to hear them. It's important to discern that, and the only way to know for certain when to speak and what to say is to pray about it in advance. The Bible says that we are not to be too hasty to speak (Proverbs 29:20). A wise woman knows she shouldn't share every single thought that comes into her head. "A fool vents all his feelings, but a wise man holds them back" (Proverbs 29:11). You may have good things to say, but people aren't always ready to hear them. Only God knows for sure when someone is ready. Ask Him to show you.

When a wise woman speaks, she tells the truth. When we don't speak the truth, we hurt others as well as ourselves. "Therefore, putting away lying, 'Let each one of you speak the truth with his neighbor,' for we are members of one another" (Ephesians 4:25). But we can't run around speaking the truth without wisdom, sensitivity, and a sense of the Lord's timing. People don't want to hear every bit of truth about themselves every moment. It's too much for them. Sometimes it's better to say nothing and pray for God to show you when a person is ready to hear the truth.

When a wise woman speaks, she doesn't talk too much. We have to be careful that we don't spend more time talking than is necessary. "A fool's voice is known by his many words" (Ecclesiastes 5:3). I always told my prayer group that we shouldn't spend more time talking about our requests than we do praying for them. And we can't just spill words out of our mouth without giving thought to what we are saying. We will give account of every idle word in the day of judgment (Matthew 12:36). This is a very scary thought. We must ask God to make us wise in the amount of talking we do.

When a wise woman speaks, her words are gracious. We can't speak words that are mean, insensitive, harsh, coarse, rude, deceitful, offensive, or arrogant without reaping the consequences. With our words we will either build lives or we will tear them down. "Those things which proceed out of the mouth come from the heart, and they defile a man" (Matthew 15:18). "The words of a wise man's mouth are gracious, but the lips of a fool shall swallow him up" (Ecclesiastes 10:12). Ask God to create in you a clean heart so filled with His Spirit, His love, and His truth that it will overflow love, truth, and healing in your speech. Ask Him to help you find words that speak life to those around you.

My Prayer to God

Lord, help me be a person who speaks words that build up and not tear down. Help me to speak life into the situations and people around me, and not death. Fill my heart afresh each day with Your Holy Spirit so that Your love and goodness overflow from my heart and my mouth. Help me to speak only about things that are true, noble, just, pure, lovely, of good report, virtuous, and praiseworthy. "Let the words of my mouth and the meditation of my heart be acceptable in Your sight, O LORD, my strength and my Redeemer" (Psalm 19:14). Keep my mouth from speaking any evil or anything that is not true. Holy Spirit of truth, guide me in all truth. Help me to "speak as the oracles of God" and with the ability You supply so that You may be glorified (1 Peter 4:11). May every word I speak reflect Your purity and love.

Your Word says that "the preparations of the heart belong to man, but the answer of the tongue is from the LORD" (Proverbs 16:1). I will prepare my heart by being in your Word every day and obeying Your laws. I will prepare my heart by worshiping You and giving thanks in all things. Fill my heart with love, peace, and joy so that it will flow from my mouth. Convict me when I complain or speak negatively. Help me not to speak too quickly or too much. Help me not to speak words that miscommunicate. I pray You would give me the words to say every time I speak. Show me when to speak and when not to. And when I do speak, give me words to say that will bring life and edification.

Help me to be a woman who speaks wisely, graciously, and clearly and never foolishly, rudely, or insensitively. Give me words that speak of the hope that is within me so I can explain my faith in a persuasive and compelling way. May the words I speak bring others into a fuller knowledge of You.

❧ GOD'S PROMISES TO ME ❧

He who would love life and see good days,
let him refrain his tongue from evil, and his
lips from speaking deceit.
1 PETER 3:10

The heart of the wise teaches his mouth,
and adds learning to his lips.
PROVERBS 16:23

Sanctify the Lord God in your hearts, and always be
ready to give a defense to everyone who asks you a
reason for the hope that is in you, with meekness and
fear; having a good conscience, that when they
defame you as evildoers, those who revile your good
conduct in Christ may be ashamed. For it is better,
if it is the will of God, to suffer for doing
good than for doing evil.
1 PETER 3:15-17

Pleasant words are like a honeycomb, sweetness to
the soul and health to the bones.
PROVERBS 16:24

Righteous lips are the delight of kings, and they love
him who speaks what is right.
PROVERBS 16:13

CHAPTER TWENTY-SEVEN

Lord, Transform Me into a Woman of Mountain-Moving Faith

On my tenth birthday, I received a necklace that consisted of a small glass ball hanging from a delicate gold chain. Inside the ball was the tiniest mustard seed. I thought at the time, *Why in the world did they bother putting a seed in there that was so small it could hardly be seen.* Obviously, I didn't get the point.

It wasn't until some time later that I learned the significance of that little seed. Jesus said, "If you have faith as a mustard seed, you will say to this mountain, 'Move from here to there', and it will move; and nothing will be impossible for you" (Matthew 17:20). I've since thought a lot about how tiny that seed was. If that's all the faith it takes to move mountains, then surely I can come up with enough to move the obstacles in my life.

God takes the tiniest bit of faith we have and makes it grow into something big when we act on it. The Bible says that "God has dealt to each one a measure of faith" (Romans 12:3). We already have some faith to start with.

When we step out in that faith, God *increases* our faith. In other words, acting in faith begets more faith.

Whether you realize it or not, you are living by faith everyday. Each time you go to a doctor, you trust he will do the right thing. When you buy medicine from the pharmacist, you believe he will fill your prescription correctly. When you go to a restaurant, you have faith they will not poison you. (Some restaurants require more faith than others.) How much easier and more certain is it to trust God?

We have no idea what great things God wants to do through us if we would just step out in faith when He asks us to. That's why He lets us go through some difficult times. Times when we feel weak and vulnerable. He allows certain things to happen so that we will turn to Him and give Him our full attention. It's in those times, when we are forced to pray in greater faith, that our faith grows stronger.

Jesus said, "According to your faith let it be to you" (Matthew 9:29). This could be a frightening thought, depending on the kind of faith you have. But there are things we can do to increase our faith, such as read the Word of God. Faith comes by simply hearing it (Romans 10:17). When you take the promises and truths in His Word and declare them out loud, you'll sense your faith increasing.

Praying increases our faith as well because it's how we reach out and touch God. At one point a woman reached out to the Lord believing that if she just "touched the hem of His garment" she could be healed. Jesus told her that her faith had made her well, and she was healed at that very time (Matthew 9:20-22). Every time we reach out and touch Him in prayer, our lives are healed in some way and our faith is increased.

Every day it becomes more and more crucial that we have faith. There will be times in each of our lives when we will need the kind of faith that makes the difference between success or failure, winning or losing, life or death. That's why asking for more faith must be an ongoing prayer. No matter how much faith you have, God can increase it.

Even when your faith seems small, you can still speak in faith to the mountains in your life and tell them to move, and God will do the impossible. You can pray for the crippled parts of your life to be healed and God will restore them. You can ask God to increase your faith and give you boldness to act on it, and He will do it.

What promise of God would you like to claim in faith as your own right now? What prayer would you like to boldly pray in faith and see answered? What would you like to see accomplished in your life, or in the life of someone you know, that would take a prayer of great faith? Ask God to take that seed you have and grow it into a giant tree of faith so you can see these things come to pass.

My Prayer to God

Lord, increase my faith. Teach me how to "walk by faith, not by sight" (2 Corinthians 5:7). Give me strength to stand strong on Your promises and believe Your every word. I don't want to be like the people who did not profit from hearing the Word because it wasn't mixed with faith (Hebrews 4:2). I know that "faith comes by hearing, and hearing by the word of God" (Romans 10:17). Make my faith increase every time I hear or read Your Word. Help me to believe for Your promises to be fulfilled in me. I pray that the genuineness of my faith, which is more precious than gold that perishes even when it is tested by fire, will be glorifying to You, Lord (1 Peter 1:7).

I know "faith is the substance of things hoped for, the evidence of things not seen" (Hebrews 11:1). I know I have been "saved through faith," and it is a gift from You (Ephesians 2:8). Increase my faith so that I can pray in power. Give me faith to believe for healing every time I pray for the sick. I don't want to see a need and then not have faith strong enough to pray and believe for the situation to change.

Help me to take the "shield of faith" to "quench all the fiery darts of the wicked one" (Ephesians 6:16). Help me "to ask in faith, with no doubting." For I know that "he who doubts is like a wave of the sea driven and tossed by the wind." I know that a doubter is double-minded and unstable and will not receive anything from You (James 1:6-8). I know that "whatever is not from faith is sin" (Romans 14:23). I confess any doubt I have as sin before You, and I ask You to forgive me. I don't want to hinder what You want to do in me and through me because of doubt. Increase my faith daily so that I can move mountains in Your name.

❧ GOD'S PROMISES TO ME ❧

Without faith it is impossible to please Him, for he who comes to God must believe that He is, and that He is a rewarder of those who diligently seek Him.

HEBREWS 11:6

All things are possible to him who believes.
MARK 9:23

If you have faith as a mustard seed, you will say to
this mountain, "Move from here to there," and it will
move; and nothing will be impossible for you.
MATTHEW 17:20

Having been justified by faith, we have peace with
God through our Lord Jesus Christ.
ROMANS 5:1

In this you greatly rejoice, though now for a little
while, if need be, you have been grieved by various
trials, that the genuineness of your faith,
being much more precious than gold that perishes,
though it is tested by fire, may be found to praise,
honor, and glory at the revelation of Jesus Christ.
1 PETER 1:6-7

CHAPTER TWENTY-EIGHT

Lord, Change Me into the Likeness of Christ

I recently heard a pastor speak about his experience as a missionary starting a church in a remote part of the world. He told how when he and his wife first arrived at the little village where they were going to plant this new church, they were shocked at how little the native people of that region wore in the way of clothing. It was a hot and humid land, so the men and women only wore strips of cloth that covered the area between their waist and mid-thigh. The women were completely topless. The first thing the pastor and his wife did was to instruct the ladies that they needed to be covered on top. In order to help them do that, the pastor sent for T-shirts to be delivered to the village.

When the shirts arrived, one was given to each woman. They were very excited to receive them and eagerly took them home, promising to wear them when they came back. The next day when everyone gathered together again, the pastor and his wife were even more shocked than before. Each woman had taken her shirt and cut two large round holes out of the front of it so that when they put the shirts on, their breasts stuck through the holes.

I laughed when I heard that story and wondered how many times God gives us something to cover us or to make us right with Him, and we cut out the part that we don't want so that our flesh can still stick through.

No wonder we aren't able change ourselves. We don't even understand what we're supposed to be changed to or why. Only God can open our eyes to see these things. That's why we have to pray the "Change me, Lord" prayer. I know it's one of the most frightening and difficult prayers to pray. We'd so much rather pray, "Change *him*, Lord" or "Change *her*, Lord." Plus if we give the Lord *carte blanche* to do whatever He wants in us, God only knows what He might do.

But there is a way we can pray that will change us, and it's not frightening. That is to pray, "Make me more like Christ." Who doesn't want to exhibit the character of Jesus? Who doesn't want to be more like Him in every way?

Seven Good Ways to Be More Like Christ

1. *Jesus was loving.* Not only was Jesus loving, but His love was beyond comprehension. We will never have to bear the sin of the world unto death the way He did, but He wants us to lay down our lives for people in other ways. "By this we know love, because He laid down His life for us. And we also ought to lay down our lives for the brethren" (1 John 3:16). His love can work miracles in your life and in the lives of people you touch. The love of God in you will grow and reproduce as you share it. "A new commandment I give to you, that you love one another; as I have loved you, that you also love one another" (John 13:34). Pray for God's love to be revealed in you as you reach out to the world around you.

2. *Jesus was humble.* Jesus was Lord of the universe, yet "He humbled Himself and became obedient to the point of death, even the death of the cross" (Philippians 2:8). Even a fraction of His humility will get us a long way in this world, because it's such a rare commodity. And we need it because there is a steep price to pay for having pride. "Everyone proud in heart is an abomination to the LORD; though they join forces, none will go unpunished" (Proverbs 16:5). "Pride goes before destruction, and a haughty spirit before a fall" (Proverbs 16:18). Nothing will speak louder to people around you than your own humility, because it will be a refreshing departure from the norm. Pray for God to give you a humble heart.

3. *Jesus was faithful.* Jesus never wavered in His conviction and knowledge of who He was and why He was on earth. "I am the way, the truth, and the life. No one comes to the Father except through Me" (John 14:6). Even when He was tempted by Satan, He never faltered. We need to know with that same certainty who *He* really is, so we can know who *we* really are. Then we won't waver. Ask God to strengthen your inner being and make you as faithful as He is.

4. *Jesus was giving.* Jesus gave of Himself to disciple a few men so that many lives would be touched. He gave of His power so that many would be healed, delivered, and made whole. "If I then, your Lord and Teacher, have washed your feet, you also ought to wash one another's feet. For I have given you an example, that you should do as I have done to you" (John 13:14-15). His ultimate gift was His life. "Christ also suffered for us, leaving us an example, that you should follow His steps" (1 Peter 2:21). When we don't feel we have anything to give, God supplies it all. "God is able to make all grace abound toward you, that you, always having

all sufficiency in all things, may have an abundance for every good work" (2 Corinthians 9:8). Pray that God will fill you with His good gifts to give to those He brings into your life.

5. *Jesus was separate*. Jesus was *in* the world, but He was not a *part of* the world. He came to *touch* the world, but He never became *like* the world. He was separate from the world, yet He changed the world around Him. We must pray that we can find that balance too. We can't stay so separate that we have no touch with the outside world. Nor can we be looking, living, talking, and acting so much like the world that people don't see anything different about us. Jesus never lost sight of where He was going. He always kept eternity in His perspective. We must do the same. Pray that you will always remember who you are, what you are called to do, and where you are going to spend eternity.

6. *Jesus was obedient*. One of the most amazing things about Jesus was that even though He was Lord, He still did not do anything on His own. He prayed and did not act until He had instructions from God. We must live that way too. "He who says he abides in Him ought himself also to walk just as He walked" (1 John 2:6). Jesus was obedient to the point of death. Can there be any greater level of obedience? He did what He had to do because He knew the great things that would come out of it. We have to do the same, "looking unto Jesus, the author and finisher of our faith, who for the joy that was set before Him endured the cross, despising the shame, and has sat down at the right hand of the throne of God. For consider Him who endured such hostility from sinners against Himself, lest you become weary and discouraged in your souls" (Hebrews 12:2-3). Ask God to help you die to yourself so that you can live for Him.

7. *Jesus was light.* People are drawn to light. We want them to be drawn to the light of the Lord in us. Jesus said, "I am the light of the world. He who follows Me shall not walk in darkness, but have the light of life" (John 8:12). We don't want to walk in the dark. We want to be in the light as He is in the light. Ask God to make you more like Christ so that everyplace you go people will stop you and say, "Tell me what you know." "What is this special thing you have?" "What must I do to get what you've got?" And you will be able to give them the reason for the light within you.

──── *My Prayer to God* ────

Lord, I want to be changed, and I pray those changes will begin today. I know I can't change myself in any way that is significant or lasting, but by the transforming power of Your Holy Spirit all things are possible. Grant me, according to the riches of Your glory, to be strengthened with might through Your Spirit in my inner being (Ephesians 3:16). Transform me into Your likeness. I know that You will supply all that I need according to Your riches in Christ Jesus (Philippians 4:19).

Help me to become separate from the world without becoming isolated from it or turning my back on it. Show me when I am not humble and help me to resist pride of any kind. Let my humility be a testimony of Your Spirit in me. May Your love manifested in me be a witness of Your greatness. Teach me to love others the way You do.

Soften my heart where it has become hard. Make me fresh where I have become stale. Lead me and instruct me where I have become unteachable. Make me to be faithful, giving, and obedient the way Jesus was. Where I am resistant to change, help me to trust Your work in my life. May Your light so shine in me that I become a light to all who know me. May it be not I who lives, but You who lives in me (Galatians 2:20). Make me to be so much like Christ that when people see me they will want to know You better.

❧ GOD'S PROMISES TO ME ❧

I have been crucified with Christ; it is no longer I who live, but Christ lives in me; and the life which I now live in the flesh I live by faith in the Son of God, who loved me and gave Himself for me.
GALATIANS 2:20

The Spirit Himself bears witness with our spirit that we are children of God, and if children, then heirs—heirs of God and joint heirs with Christ, if indeed we suffer with Him, that we may also be glorified together.
ROMANS 8:16-17

Come out from among them and be separate, says the Lord. Do not touch what is unclean, and I will receive you. I will be a Father to you, and you shall be my sons and daughters, says the LORD Almighty.
2 CORINTHIANS 6:17-18

My grace is sufficient for you, for My strength is made perfect in weakness. Therefore most gladly I will rather boast in my infirmities, that the power of Christ may rest upon me.
2 CORINTHIANS 12:9

I can do all things through Christ who strengthens me.
PHILIPPIANS 4:13

CHAPTER TWENTY-NINE

Lord, Lift Me out of My Past

Imagine that you are running in a race, and you're trying to reach the goal and ultimately win the prize. But as hard as you try you can never get to the finish line because there is a heavy weight tied around one of your legs. You struggle to pull it along, but it slows you down and causes you to be so weary and exhausted that you are tempted to give up altogether. It doesn't occur to you that this is something you don't have to carry. It has been so much a part of you for so long that you never imagined life without it. Yet you can't finish the race and secure the prize God has for you until you become free of it.

This scenario is true for so many of us. We are trying to run the race of life, but we are having trouble getting up to speed. That's because we've been carrying excess baggage from the past around with us without even realizing it. In fact, we've carried it around with us for so long we think it's part of us. Some days are so hard we feel like giving up and getting out of the race. But I have good news. God wants to take that burden from you so you will never have to carry it again.

Whether it's something that happened as long ago as your early childhood or as recently as yesterday, the past can keep you from moving into all God has for you. That's why He wants to set you free from it. And not only that, He wants to redeem and restore what has been lost or destroyed in your past and make it count for something important in your life now. The truth is, you can never move into the future God has for you if you are continually stuck in the past. When you received Jesus you became a new creation. He made *all* things new in your life, and He wants you to live like it.

God says to forget the former things, but that's not easy to do. How do we forget what happened to us? Do we need to have amnesia? Or a frontal lobotomy? Must we live in denial? Do we have to pretend that the past did not happen? Should we have part of our brain liposuctioned? The answer is no to all of the above. We just have to pray that God will set us free from the past so we can live successfully in the present.

One of the great mysteries of the Lord is how He can take the horrible, the tragic, the painful, the devastating, the embarrassing, and the ruinous experiences and memories of our lives and not only heal them, but use them for good. It's not that He will make you unable to recall them, but He will heal you so thoroughly from their effects that you no longer think about them with any pain. He will give you a new life you enjoy so much you don't want to travel back in your mind to the old one. You will still have the memory, but you no longer have the pain. Instead, you will have praise in your heart for the way God has restored you to wholeness. And you will want to share your experience with others so that they can know this kind of deliverance, restoration, and healing is there for them too.

Intended for Good

The reason God doesn't want to wipe your past completely out of your memory is because He wants to use that part of your life for the work He has called you to do. He can take the worst thing about your past and make it to be your greatest blessing in the future. He will weave it into the foundation of your ministry to the world, and out of it you will bring the life of the Lord to other people.

That's why God wants you to learn from the past and witness firsthand how He can redeem it, but He doesn't want you living there. He wants you to read your past like a history book, but not like a prophecy for your future. He wants you to forget those things that are behind you and reach forward to those things which are ahead (Philippians 3:13).

Many people never get to the future God has for them because they are perpetually stuck in the past. A good example of this are people who have experienced rejection in their past and still fear being rejected now. They expect to be rejected, so they read rejection into other people's words and actions. This causes them to always be hurt, afraid, angry, or bitter, and it makes them oversensitive to other people's comments. In other words, their *fear* of rejection *causes* the very rejection they feared. It becomes an endless cycle.

Whatever weight from the past you are carrying will be observed by others, even if they don't know what it is. The bad things that happened to us, or the good things that *didn't* happen to us, will be part of what we wear daily and people will see the total look even if they can't recall the specific details. But God will deliver you from your past and use it for His glory if you ask Him to.

Don't Look Back

Once you step out of the past it's important you don't keep looking over your shoulder to see if it's following you. That's what Lot's wife did, and it paralyzed her. It will paralyze you too. And it will definitely slow you down in the race. Good runners look forward and keep focused on the goal.

Even if you have never had one bad thing happen to you in your life, or you have been completely delivered from every negative memory you ever had, you still need to pray to be free of your past. That's because even the good things of your past can keep you from allowing God to do a new thing now. If we get locked into what we did before, we may miss what God wants to do now. God is always wanting to take you to a new place in your life, and you will keep Him from doing that if you are hanging on to the way things have always been done. He will never allow us to rest on past success. If we rely on the way things have always been done, we aren't relying on Him. And that's the whole point.

I guarantee that no matter how old you are, God has something new He wants to do in your life. Ask Him to show you what that is. Tell Him you intend to stay in the race and you don't want to carry any baggage from the past around with you. Tell Him you want to run in such a way so that you will obtain the prize (1 Corinthians 9:24).

My Prayer to God

Lord, I pray that You would set me free from my past. Wherever I have made the past my home I pray that You would deliver me, heal me, and redeem me from it. I choose to make my home with You. Help me to let go of anything I have held onto of my past that has kept me from moving into all You have for me. Enable me to put off all former ways of thinking and feeling and remembering (Ephesians 4:22-24). Give me the mind of Christ so I will be able to understand when I am being controlled by memories of past events.

I don't want to tie myself to the past by neglecting to forgive any person or event associated with it. Help me to forgive what needs to be forgiven. Specifically, I pray that You would deliver me from the effects of (name any painful or bad memory you have). I release my past to You and everyone associated with it so You can restore what has been lost. Everything that was done to me or I have done which causes me pain, I surrender to You. May it no longer torment me or affect what I do today. Make me glad according to the days in which I have been afflicted and the years I have seen evil (Psalm 90:15). Thank You that You make all things new and You are making me new in every way (Revelation 21:5).

Help me to keep my eyes looking straight ahead and not back on the former days and old ways of doing things. I know You want to do something new in my life today. Help me to concentrate on where I am to go now and not where I have been. Release me from the past so I can move out of it and into the future You have for me.

❧ GOD'S PROMISES TO ME ❧

If anyone is in Christ, He is a new creation;
old things have passed away; behold all
things have become new.
2 CORINTHIANS 5:17

Do not remember the former things, nor consider the
things of old. Behold, I will do a new thing,
now it shall spring forth; shall you not know it?
I will even make a road in the wilderness
and rivers in the desert.
ISAIAH 43:18-19

Brethren, I do not count myself to have appre-
hended; but one thing I do, forgetting those
things which are behind and reaching forward to
those things which are ahead, I press toward
the goal for the prize of the upward call
of God in Christ Jesus.
PHILIPPIANS 3:13-14

Let your eyes look straight ahead, and your eyelids
look right before you. Ponder the path of your feet,
and let all your ways be established.
Do not turn to the right or the left;
remove your foot from evil.
PROVERBS 4:25-27

God will wipe away every tear from their eyes;
there shall be no more death,
nor sorrow, nor crying. There shall be no more pain,
for the former things have passed away.
REVELATION 21:4

CHAPTER THIRTY

Lord, Lead Me into the Future You Have for Me

I'm writing this chapter as a letter to you personally, my dear sister in Christ, so that if you become anxious about your future, or you need encouragement about what is ahead, you can read it and hopefully hear God speak to your heart. For this is really His message to all of us.

Dear_____(please fill in your name),

I am writing this because I want to remind you of the great future God has for you. I know this because He said so. He says you have not seen, nor heard, nor have even imagined anything as great as what He has prepared for you (1 Corinthians 2:9). You have no idea how great your future is. He says that what He has for you is so great that if you truly understood it, you would feel "that the sufferings of this present time are not worthy to be compared with the glory which shall be revealed" in you (Romans 8:18). That means whatever you envision for your life right now is already too small.

Although God promises you a future full of hope and blessing, it's not going to happen automatically. There are some things *you* have to do. One of them is pray about it (Jeremiah 29:11-13). Another is obey God. But don't worry, God will help you with both of those if you ask Him. The Holy Spirit is God's guarantee to you that He will help you do what you need to do and bring to pass everything He promised (Ephesians 1:13-14). Just know that every time you pray and obey, you are investing in your future.

Although we live in a world where everything in our lives can change in an instant, and we can't be certain what tomorrow will bring, God is unchanging. You may already have lost your false sense of security, and this is good because God wants you to know that your only *real* security is found in Him. Although you may not know the specific details about what is ahead, you can trust that God knows. And He will get you safely where you need to go. In fact, the way to get to the future God has for you is to walk with Him today.

Remember, my precious sister in the Lord, that walking with God doesn't mean there won't be obstacles. Satan will see to it that there are. While God has a plan for your future that is good, the devil has one too and it's not good. But the devil's plan for your life cannot succeed as long as you are walking with God, living in obedience to His ways, worshiping only Him, standing strong in His Word, and praying without ceasing. God's plan for your life won't happen without a struggle, however, so don't give up when times get tough. Just keep on doing what's right and resist the temptation to quit. Ask God to give you the strength and endurance you need to do what you have to do.

Don't judge your future by what you read in the newspapers or the words someone spoke over you one time. Your future is in God's hands. The only thing that is important is what *He* says about it. He doesn't want you to be concerned about your future anyway. He wants you to be concerned with *Him,* because *He* is your future.

Remember that you are God's daughter and He loves you. As you *walk* with Him, you will become more like Him every day (1 John 3:1-3). As you *look* to Him, you will be "transformed into the same image from glory to glory, just as by the Spirit of the Lord" (2 Corinthians 3:18). As you *live* with Him, He will take you from strength to strength. So even though your "outward man is perishing, yet the inward man is being renewed day by day" (2 Corinthians 4:16).

Don't become discouraged if things don't happen as fast as you would like them to. They never do. God wants you to learn patience. Our perspective is temporal. His is eternal. So don't be concerned if you are not seeing all that you want in response to your prayers. You will. If you draw close to God and do what He asks you to do, if you worship Him in spirit and in truth, if you love others and give of yourself to them, if you speak God's Word in faith and pray, you will see God's blessings poured out on your life.

I believe that we are denied certain things for a time because God wants us to fervently pray and intercede for them. That's because He wants to do something great in response to our prayers, something that can *only* be birthed in prayer. Do you remember how Hannah prayed long and fervently for a child (1 Samuel 1:1-28)? When God finally answered her prayer, it wasn't just any child who was born. Samuel was one of the world's greatest prophets and most influential judges in Israel's history. If she had not prayed so fervently, that might not have happened. There may be things that won't happen in your life unless you are praying that long and fervently too.

If you start being consumed by the details of life, and it feels as if your future won't ever be any different than it is at this moment, please know the truth is quite the opposite. It's at these very times, when you feel as though you're not getting anywhere, or you're missing the future God has for you, that God is actually *preparing* you for your future. And when the time is right, He has been known to do a very quick work. While it's good to set goals, don't look so far ahead that you become overwhelmed. Look to the Lord instead. Remember that "the Lord is near to all who call upon Him, to all who call upon Him in truth. He will fulfill the desire of those who fear Him; He also will hear their cry and save them" (Psalm 145:18-19).

One day you will be with God in heaven. And He will wipe away every tear from your eyes and "there shall be no more death, nor sorrow, nor crying. There shall be no more pain, for the former things have passed away" (Revelation 21:4). You want to be able to reach the end of your life and say, "I have fought the good fight, I have finished the race, I have kept the faith. Finally, there is laid up for me the crown of righteousness, which the Lord, the righteous Judge, will give to me on that Day, and not to me only but also to all who have loved His appearing" (2 Timothy 4:7-8). Jesus said, "Let not your heart be troubled; you believe in God, believe also in Me. In My Father's house are many mansions; if it were not so, I would have told you. I go to prepare a place for you. And if I go and prepare a place for you, I will come again and receive you to Myself; that where I am, there you may be also" (John 14:1-3). He promises that because you love Him, your eternal future in heaven with Him is secure.

In the meantime I know that you want to do something significant for the Lord and move into new areas of service for Him. God is looking for women who will be committed to living His way and stepping into the purposes He has for their lives. He wants a woman who is willing to sacrifice herself for His kingdom, who is willing to say, "Not my will, but Yours be done." You are one of those women. I pray that you will be equipped and ready when God says, "Now is the time," and the doors of opportunity open. Just keep doing what's right and when you least expect it, you will get a call from God giving you your assignment.

Remember, God "is able to do exceedingly abundantly above all that we ask or think, according to the power that works in us" (Ephesians 3:20). He has more for you than you can imagine. And now may "the God of hope fill you with all joy and peace in believing, that you may abound in hope by the power of the Holy Spirit" (Romans 15:13). Stay focused on God, and He will keep you in perfect peace as He moves you into the future He has for you.

Your sister in Christ,

Stormie Omartian

My Prayer to God

Lord, I put my future in Your hands and ask that You would give me total peace about it. I don't want to be trying to secure my future with my own plans. I want to be in the center of *Your* plans, knowing that You have given me everything I need for what is ahead. I pray You would give me strength to endure without giving up. You have said that "he who endures to the end will be saved" (Matthew 10:22). Help me to run the race in a way that I shall finish strong and receive the prize You have for me (1 Corinthians 9:24). Help me to be always watchful in my prayers, because I don't know when the end of my life will be (1 Peter 4:7).

I know Your thoughts toward me are of peace, to give me a future and a hope (Jeremiah 29:11). I know that You have saved me and called me with a holy calling, not according to my works, but according to Your own purpose and grace (2 Timothy 1:9). Thank You, Holy Spirit, that You are always with me and will guide me on the path so that I won't lose my way.

Move me into powerful ministry that will impact the lives of others for Your kingdom and Your glory. I humble myself under Your mighty hand, O God, knowing that You will lift me up in due time. I cast all my care upon You, knowing that You care for me and will not let me fall (1 Peter 5:6-7). I reach out for Your hand today so I can walk with You into the future You have for me.

⊱ GOD'S PROMISES TO ME ⊰

I know the thoughts I think toward you, says the
LORD, thoughts of peace and not of evil, to give you
a future and a hope. Then you will call on Me and go
and pray to Me, and I will listen to you.
And you will seek Me and find Me, when you search
for me with all your heart.

JEREMIAH 29:11-13

Those who are planted in the house of the LORD
shall flourish in the courts of our God. They shall
still bear fruit in old age; they shall be fresh and
flourishing, to declare that the LORD is upright.

PSALM 92:13-15 .

I am persuaded that neither death nor life, nor angels
nor principalities nor powers, nor things present nor
things to come, nor height nor depth,
nor any other created thing, shall be able to
separate us from the love of God which is
in Christ Jesus our Lord.

ROMANS 8:38-39

But the path of the just is like the shining sun,
that shines ever brighter unto the perfect day.

PROVERBS 4:18

Arise, shine; for your light has come! And the glory
of the LORD is risen upon you. For behold, the
darkness shall cover the earth, and deep darkness the
people; but the LORD will arise over you, and His
glory will be seen upon you.

ISAIAH 60:1-2

Other Titles
by Stormie Omartian

The Power of a Praying® Woman Bible

The Power of a Praying® Parent

The Power of a Praying® Parent

The Power of a Praying® Parent Prayer
and Study Guide

The Power of a Praying® Parent Book of
Prayers

The Power of a Praying® Wife

The Power of a Praying® Wife

The Power of a Praying® Wife Prayer
and Study Guide

The Power of a Praying® Wife Book
of Prayers

Just Enough Light

Just Enough Light for the Step I'm On

Just Enough Light for the Step I'm
On—A Devotional
Prayer Journey

Just Enough Light for the Step I'm On
Book of Prayers

The Power of a Praying® Husband

The Power of a Praying® Husband

The Power of a Praying® Husband
Prayer & Study Guide

The Power of a Praying® Husband Book
of Prayers

The Power of a Praying® Woman

The Power of a Praying® Woman

The Power of a Praying® Woman Prayer
and Study Guide

The Power of a Praying® Woman Book
of Prayers

The Prayer That Changes Everything®

The Prayer That Changes Everything®

The Prayer That Changes Everything®
Prayer and Praise Journey

The Prayer That Changes Everything®
Book of Prayers

Other Items

Greater Health God's Way

The Power of Praying®

The Power of Praying® Gift Collection

The Power of Praying®—Graduate
Edition

The Power of a Praying® Family—
Family Gift Edition

The Power of a Praying® Kid

The Power of a Praying® Teen

Stormie

The Power of Praying® Together

For This Child I Prayed

A Book of Prayer